In Search of Humanity and Deity

In Search of Humanity and Deity

A Celebration of
John Macquarrie's Theology

Edited by
Robert Morgan

scm press

British Library Cataloguing in Publication data

A catalogue record for this book is available
from the British Library

0 334 04049 3/978 0 334 04049 1

First published in 2006 by SCM Press
9–17 St Alban's Place,
London N1 0NX

www.scm-canterburypress.co.uk

SCM Press is a division of
SCM-Canterbury Press Ltd

Typeset by Regent Typesetting, London
Printed and bound in Great Britain by
CPD (Wales) Ltd, Ebbw Vale

Contents

Part I   LIFE AND WORK

CONTENTS

Part II PHILOSOPHY AND SYMBOLIC THEOLOGY

Contributors

John Bowden was Managing Director of SCM Press, 1966–2000

Michael W. Brierley has been Chaplain and Research Assistant to the Bishop of Oxford since 2001

Niall Coll is Senior Lecturer in Religious Studies at St Mary's University College, Belfast

Avery Dulles S.J. is Laurence J. McGinley Professor at Fordham University, New York

Philip Endean S.J. is a Tutor in Theology at Campion Hall, Oxford, and is Editor of *The Way*

David Fergusson has been Professor of Divinity at New College, Edinburgh since 2000

Paul Fiddes has been Principal of Regent's Park College, Oxford, since 1989 and is Professor of Systematic Theology in the University of Oxford

Peter Groves has been Chaplain and Fellow of Brasenose College, Oxford, since 2002 and Priest-in-charge of St Mary Magdalen's, Oxford, since 2005

Daniel W. Hardy was Van Mildert Canon-Professor at the University of Durham (1986–90) and Director of the Centre for Theological Enquiry at Princeton (1990–95)

Guanghu He is Professor of Religious Studies, Renmin University of China, Beijing

Robert Jeffery was Dean of Worcester (1987–96) and Sub-Dean of Christ Church, Oxford (1996–2003)

Alistair Kee is Professor of Religious Studies Emeritus at the School of Divinity, University of Edinburgh

David R. Law is Reader in Christian Thought at the University of Manchester

Eugene Thomas Long is Distinguished Professor of Philosophy Emeritus at the University of South Carolina

Morwenna Ludlow is A. G. Leventis Lecturer in Patristics and Research Fellow of Wolfson College, in the University of Oxford

Robert Morgan is a Fellow of Linacre College, Oxford, and Priest-in-charge at Sandford-on-Thames

Georgina Morley taught doctrine at the North-Eastern Ordination course until 2005 and is a priest in the Diocese of York

Christopher Morse is Dietrich Bonhoeffer Professor of Theology and Ethics at Union Theological Seminary, New York

George Newlands has been Professor of Divinity at the University of Glasgow since 1986

George Pattison has been Lady Margaret Professor of Divinity at Oxford since 2004

Stephen Platten has been Bishop of Wakefield since 2003 and Chairman of SCM Press since 2001

Ronald H. Stone was Witherspoon Professor of Christian Ethics, Pittsburgh Theological Seminary, 1969–2003

Geoffrey Wainwright was Roosevelt Professor of Systematic Theology at Union Theological Seminary, New York, 1979–1983, and has been Robert Earl Cushman Professor of Christian Theology at Duke University, North Carolina, since 1983.

Keith Ward was Regius Professor of Divinity at Oxford, 1991–2003

John Webster was Lady Margaret Professor of Divinity at Oxford 1996–2003 and is now Professor of Systematic Theology at Aberdeen

Paul Wignall is Director of Ministry and Mission Resources for the Diocese of Truro

Rowan Williams was Lady Margaret Professor of Divinity at Oxford, 1986–92 and has been Archbishop of Canterbury since 2002

Abbreviations of Main Books by John Macquarrie

Christology	*Christology Revisited* (1998)
Deity	*In Search of Deity* (1984)
Dictionary	*A Dictionary of Christian Ethics* (1967)
Ethics	*Three Issues in Ethics* (1970)
Existentialism	*Existentialism* (1972)
Existentialist	*An Existentialist Theology* (1955 cited from 1965 reprint)
God-Talk	*God-Talk: An Examination of the Language and Logic of Theology* (1967)
Heidegger	*Heidegger and Christianity* (1994)
Hope	*Christian Hope* (1978)
Humanity	*In Search of Humanity* (1982)
Humility	*The Humility of God* (1978)
Jesus Christ	*Jesus Christ in Modern Thought* (1990)
Mary	*Mary for All Christians* (1991)
Mediators	*The Mediators between Human and Divine* (1995)
Peace	*The Concept of Peace* (1973)
People	*The Faith of the People of God: A Lay Theology* (1972)
Principles	*Principles of Christian Theology* (1966, cited from 1977^2 = 2003 impression)
Sacraments	*A Guide to the Sacraments* (1997)
Scope	*The Scope of Demythologizing* (1960)
Secularity	*God and Secularity* (1968)

Spirituality	*Paths in Spirituality* (1972, 1992² cited from first edition unless stated)
Stubborn	*Stubborn Theological Questions* (2003)
Studies	*Studies in Christian Existentialism* (1965)
Theologian	*On Being a Theologian* (1999)
Theology	*Theology, Church and Ministry* (1986)
Thinking	*Thinking about God* (1975)
Twentieth-Century	*Twentieth-Century Religious Thought* (1963 cited from 2001⁵)
Two Worlds	*Two Worlds are Ours: An Introduction to Christian Mysticism* (2004)
Unity	*Christian Unity and Christian Diversity* (1975)

Foreword

ROWAN WILLIAMS

THE ARCHBISHOP OF CANTERBURY

The late Eric Mascall once wrote a verse tribute to Austin and Katherine Farrer, in affectionate parody of W.H. Auden: 'Great are the Farrers; they have conquered three kingdoms.' The Farrers had won distinction in philosophical theology, biblical scholarship – and detective fiction. And though (so far as I know) neither Ian nor Jenny Macquarrie has yet ventured into detective fiction, there will be a good many who could echo Mascall in acknowledging that Ian too has conquered a good few realms.

There is the translator of Heidegger and exponent of European existentialism to an often rather sluggish insular audience. The Heidegger work alone should win for Ian a place among the culture-heroes of the century; but he went on to conquer a territory where many if not most English-speaking theologians have been very nervous about travelling. Scots, however, have not on the whole shared this nervousness, and Ian's constructive and systematic labours were to shape the studies of many generations. His *Principles of Christian Theology* continues to stand the test of time, and the many substantial works, especially on Christology, that have followed will secure his place in a second pantheon. But he has also won a well-deserved reputation as a guide to Christian spirituality; the little book, *Paths in Spirituality*, which I remember encountering as a graduate student, was the first of several brief but luminous contributions, and I willingly acknowledge my debt to it.

Ian has always been a theologian of the Church – not in a narrow or sectarian way, but out of the conviction that the language of theology is answerable to more than just the academy at the end of the day. His own example of patient intellectual work inseparably combined with personal devotion and humility has been a beacon for many. It is a privilege to be able to commend this collection of tributes to a much-loved servant of God, God's Church and God's truth.

Introduction

ROBERT MORGAN

On 10 November 2005 the SCM Press celebrated the golden jubilee of one of its most distinguished authors. It was 50 years since the publication of *An Existentialist Theology*, the first volume and the first of this author's five contributions in the Library of Philosophy and Theology. The series was one of Ronald Gregor Smith's best initiatives as editor of the Press and provided a suitable cabinet for the 'early Macquarrie'.

As well as signifying 50 years, gold can suggest golden eggs being laid at regular intervals, helping to keep the Press serving its ecumenical and open readership with solid food to build up a robust faith in a changing world. Celebration of a life-time's achievement was appropriate, and the chairman Stephen Platten invited John (to most of us Ian) and Jenny Macquarrie with several of their local friends and SCM staff to a college dinner near their home in Oxford, where a suitably golden symbol was presented. It was liquid and (less viscous than Tate & Lyle) would flow as easily as the Macquarrie pen. Unlike the pen, however, it would leave no marks on the page. A more permanent pointer to the real memorial, the *oeuvre* itself, was wanted. This collection of essays greeting and sharing memories of the man and engaging with some of his work honours the man and his works. His long connection with the SCM Press (resisting the blandishments of wealthier publishers) is marked, in particular by the essay of John Bowden who was Editor and Managing Director for most of the fifty-odd years under review, and with whom for many the press is most intimately associated.

As a whole our collection of essays stands somewhere between *Being and Truth*, the handsome *Festschrift* edited by Alistair Kee and Eugene Long in 1986 to mark Ian's retirement, and *On Being a Theologian*, the largely autobiographical recollection edited by John Morgan, President of Graduate Theological Foundation in the United States, to mark his eightieth birthday on 27 June 1999. The more biographical essays in Part I on Macquarrie's Life and Thought inevitably overlap with the autobiographical material contained in *On Being a Theologian*, but they look from different angles and say things that autobiographical modesty omitted. Overlap with the *Festschrift* is limited to the welcome participation of its esteemed editors. Eugene Long had been co-supervised by Macquarrie in Glasgow and in 1985 published his excellent book on his teacher's philosophical theology. Alistair Kee, another former student, taught Religious Studies in Glasgow and later in Edinburgh. Their volume concentrated on those areas rather than doctrine or spirituality. Robert Scharlemann and Bowman Clark discussed Macquarrie's own thought, but as is normal in a *Festschrift* most contributors continued the work of their teacher rather than elucidating it.

The books listed in the bibliography provide more detailed discussions, but we hope that the variety of this collection will be an appropriate tribute to a friend, colleague, and teacher of the Church who is not only valued, but loved. Unlike the *Festschrift*, which without his knowledge excluded Macquarrie's Oxford colleagues and so may have given the impression of a distinguished but isolated figure, this collection began as a local celebration, but it has grown thanks to contributions from former colleagues and students in North America and other parts of Britain. Without aiming to be an Oxford Companion to John Macquarrie, discussing the whole of his work, or even a Cambridge Companion picking out its most salient topics, it aims to celebrate this remarkably productive theological life by combining some memories of the Christian man with respectful (even when dissenting) discussion of a part of what he has written.

No theologian would want to gloss over criticisms and disagreements, and while Macquarrie himself is a more eirenic thinker and personality than most, his religion and theology have occasionally stirred more polemical writers. His unhappy memories of reading Calvin and Barth as a student reveal his own temperament and preferences. Mid-century Protestant theology in Europe was largely divided between the camp followers of Barth and those of Bultmann who maintained their teachers' disagreements but sometimes without their teachers' mutual respect. This classroom rhetoric which once enlivened student interest in the subject is now a fading oral tradition, but for a very different theological style from Macquarrie's one may revisit T. F. Torrance's penetrating review of Heidegger's *Being and Time* in *The Journal of Theological Studies* (1964), or his friend D. M. MacKinnon's mostly negative review of *Studies in Christian Existentialism* (1965) in the same journal (1967). Torrance praised the translation, but disapproved of Heidegger's 'would-be followers' or 'religious disciples' Bultmann and Macquarrie making use of such a non-Christian philosopher. George Pattison's essay in this volume may be seen as a reply.

The main interest of MacKinnon's remarks (which he admitted were perhaps unfair) lies in what they tell us of their author's own passions and perplexities. Macquarrie made no reply, but a little later his essay on Schleiermacher (1969) reprinted in *Thinking about God* (1975) contained an answer, whether or not intended.

Reflecting on Hegel's criticism of Schleiermacher's subjectivism, and the suggestion that philosophy was being asked to supply edification rather than seek truth, he quoted a passage from MacKinnon's *Borderlands of Theology* (1968), p. 31, which could again have been aimed at himself. MacKinnon there criticizes 'much that calls itself radical theology' on the ground that it does not face (and may even deliberately eliminate) questions of truth and falsity, contenting itself with dwelling on the experience of the Christian, 'suggesting that, in the end, even as the proper study of mankind is man, so Christian man finds his appropriate study in himself'. Macquarrie comments on this Barthian criticism of Enlightenment theology as follows:

> Although for my own part I favour the anthropological approach to theology, here criticized by MacKinnon, I agree with this particular criticism, and indeed I have always resisted those forms of experiential, existential and pragmatic theology which have tried to by-pass the ontological questions and which really end up by reducing theology to anthropology and Christology to Jesusology. (*Thinking*, p. 161)

In the same way he expressed agreement with Torrance's criticism of the subjectivism of some recent theology (*Spirituality*, p. 56). He did not, however, share MacKinnon's obsession with *substance*. He later quoted with approval and at length the latter's 1972 article in *Christ, Faith and History* on 'Substance in Christology' in order to insist on 'getting involved in ontology'. But he did not agree with him that 'substance' language would be necessary *'if one can find other and more up-to-date expressions in which one can express the problems formerly discussed in the language of "substance" and the like'* (italics his) (*Jesus Christ*, p. 8).

In 1970 Macquarrie returned to Britain and later made a point of establishing friendly personal contact with these older Scottish critics. He saw no place for personal animosity in theological disagreement. It would be hard to find more contrasting philosophical and theological styles between two Scottish catholic Anglicans, but whereas the prophetic fire of MacKinnon could on occasion become unbalanced, Macquarrie's equable character would always expect to find some truth in opposing positions.

Several of the contributors to this volume are admirers of both men.

George Newlands, who draws out the Scottish background, is now divinity professor at Glasgow but, like his famous predecessors Ian Henderson and Ronald Gregor Smith, was himself a product of the less regional theological faculty of Edinburgh. It is therefore a bonus that he has been able to draw on local knowledge and also that Alistair Kee and Eugene Long have both included some personal reminiscences from their student days in Glasgow. We may also learn from Kee's essay that not all Macquarrie's students share his ecumenical spirit and that the catholic–protestant divide still yields the old fruit on trees planted in Scottish Calvinism. It would be a churlish editor who erased a contributor's best jokes, but Kee's story of our subject's possible war crimes must be apocryphal as he first read Heidegger in 1950.

A foreword by the Archbishop of Canterbury symbolizes the strongly ecclesial and apologetic orientation of Macquarrie's work in all its aspects – philosophical as well as theological – and in his reflections on ethics and spirituality as well as historical and systematic theology. Rowan Williams succeeded Macquarrie in the Lady Margaret chair at Christ Church and his association with this project at a time when the Anglican communion could learn more from these two of its most eirenic theologians completes our trio of Macquarrie's Oxford successors. When Dr Williams became bishop of Monmouth in 1992 he was himself succeeded by John Webster, then by George Pattison. All three are very different kinds of theologian from each other and from their illustrious predecessor, but it is fitting that the most obvious heir to his mantle as the leading *systematic* theologian of the Church of England should write our main discussion of *Principles of Christian Theology*, and that the present occupant of the chair should write on translating Heidegger, and that the only occupant of the chair in 500 years to become Archbishop of Canterbury should have the first word which could also be the last word about 'a much loved servant of God, God's Church, and God's truth' (p. xiii).

With the modifications made necessary by subsequent developments in New Testament scholarship and a few criticisms of his own, the theologian with whom (on a modest scale) Macquarrie can best be compared is surely Schleiermacher. But the twentieth-century thinkers from whom he has learned most, and helped others to learn much, are clearly Bultmann, Heidegger, and Rahner. These giants call for separate treatments in this collection, the first from both a Reformed theologian and an Anglican male, the last from both a Jesuit theologian and an Anglican woman. They all reinforce the more biographical essays on the three institutions, cities, and countries where Ian and Jenny have together spent their pastoral, teaching and writing ministries.

4

George Newlands' essay on the Glasgow years is therefore followed by David Fergusson's account of the interpretation of Bultmann and also by David Law's defence of existentialist theology. Although Macquarrie was perhaps the first British theologian to publish on Rahner (in 1963), his increasing admiration for him and their meeting in Oxford shortly before Rahner's death in 1984, link them especially at that final stage of his career. One of their shared debts was to Heidegger, about whom Macquarrie wrote short books in 1968 and 1994, in addition to the translation (with Edward Robinson) of *Being and Time* (1927, ET 1962) and another translation (1971), and other articles (1967 and 1993). Before the Oxford and Rahner essays, therefore, George Pattison on the almost impossible task of translating Heidegger follows those on Bultmann and existentialist theology in this collection.

Pattison considers Heidegger's own reflections on translating, and suggests that the Christian version of factical authenticity, faith, may give theology a possible vantage point for understanding – and therefore being able to translate – *Being and Time*. But it does so only by contesting Heidegger's own apparent view that the modern world is without any direct access to the ground of Being. A Christian translator of Heidegger such as Macquarrie will therefore have to be also a critical commentator, arguing with the text as he translates it.

The next stage of Macquarrie's 'pilgrimage in theology' (as he called it in 1980) were the wonderfully productive years at Union Seminary, New York (1962–70). It was here that in addition to publishing the first edition of *Twentieth-Century Religious Thought* (1963), *Studies in Christian Existentialism* (1965), *Principles of Christian Theology* (1966), *God-Talk* (1967), and some smaller books and articles, he wrote most of his work on ethics. This field does not have a separate essay here but the account of those years is by Ron Stone, a distinguished social ethicist and one-time assistant of Reinhold Niebuhr at Union, who elucidates this part of the Macquarrie corpus.

The same structure of biography being reinforced by accounts of major work from that period, dictated that this essay be followed by two discussions (from a Roman Catholic and a liberal evangelical Anglican) of *Principles of Christian Theology* (1966). This is clearly the centre-piece, so far as writing is concerned, of those precious years with a young family. It would be too easy to call such a truly ecumenical work as *Principles*, an 'Anglican' systematic theology, but it is almost the only proper systematic theology (as opposed to commentaries on the creed or Articles and introductory textbooks) to have been written since the Reformation by an Anglican, admittedly by one who in 1966 had been only recently adopted and ordained priest.

The Macquarries' farewell to New York included a symposium on his work held at the Trinity Institute in New York City on 14 May 1970. Professor Avery Dulles S.J., now Avery Cardinal Dulles S.J., claimed in an unpublished lecture that 'his presence here in the past decade has notably increased the vitality of theology on this side of the Atlantic'. He gave an appreciative and critical account of Macquarrie's writings up to that time and looked forward with 'high expectations with regard to the books which are still to come from his pen'. Dulles' perceptive criticisms of *Principles* from a 'moderately conservative' Roman Catholic standpoint are still worth discussing over 35 years later, and it is a pleasure to record the Cardinal's permission and good wishes and continuing admiration for his Anglican contemporary.

It is instructive to compare these criticisms with John Webster's reflections on the same classic. Webster (b. 1955) represents a generation of English students who were taught by a new breed of (then) young theologians such as Dan Hardy, Stephen Sykes, Paul Fiddes, George Newlands, Andrew Louth, and the late Colin Gunton, who saw that systematic theology was essential even for Anglicans, and who had learned much from the later Barth. Webster's gentle probings here reflect the sea-change in Celtic and English theology that resulted from this engagement with Barth, a development visible also in the work of Rowan Williams, Richard Roberts, and David Ford, for example. The later Macquarrie's own appreciative references to Barth reflect an advance on his student days when some British critics saw little further than Barth's alleged 'biblicism' and his repudiation of natural theology. That Macquarrie was slower to appreciate Barth than MacKinnon or Torrance, and quicker to appreciate Bultmann, illuminates the reservations about his theology once felt in Edinburgh and Cambridge.

The same ecumenical principle of matching a Roman Catholic with an Anglican accounts for the sketch of Macquarrie's Oxford years (to date – may there be more!) being followed by a Jesuit and an Anglican colleague from the Oxford Faculty writing about his relationship to Karl Rahner: Philip Endean S.J. from Campion Hall, and Morwenna Ludlow of Wolfson College. All Macquarrie's work has had a strong ecumenical dimension, and the relationship between Anglicanism and Roman Catholicism has naturally been central to this. The publication of a German translation of *God-Talk* by a Roman Catholic press in 1974 made him one of relatively few Anglicans to have received an Imprimatur. Not that he asked for it.

The ecumenical aspect of Macquarrie's work is perhaps better honoured by the participation of Roman Catholics in this volume than by analysis of his writings directly concerned with ecumenism, such as

Christian Unity and Christian Diversity (1975), or *Mary for all Christians* (1991). His dialogue with Fr Eamonn Conway (1998) is readily available in *On Being a Theologian*. Macquarrie was a student and admirer, and later friend and colleague, of Ian Henderson, whose *Power without Glory* (1967) remains the most bilious attack on Anglicanism to have emanated from that 'land of double darkness whose name is *Scotia* and her teacher *nox*'. One would therefore expect his ecumenism to be critical and open-eyed. He was in fact unimpressed by 'pan-protestantism' which ignored the largest Christian denomination, or was limited by national boundaries, or interested primarily in ecclesiastical mergers. And yet his broad and generous spirit could be called *anima naturaliter oecumenica.*

The major part of most theologians' ecumenical activity occurs through their teaching. The ecumenical character of the Oxford faculty is elaborated on below, p. 95, and most of Macquarrie's doctoral students were non-Anglicans. But many who heard his lectures became Anglican clergy and it is appropriate that one of these, Stephen Platten, now chairman of the SCM Press, should provide an overview of his writings and some account of his Oxford lecturing, together with the interesting suggestion that his later trilogy brings his expository gifts to bear on his own earlier creative work.

To represent Macquarrie's contribution to the wider Anglican communion and the wider still Christian and barely Christian world, Robert Jeffery, a key staff member at the 1968 Lambeth Conference, writes about Macquarrie's contributions as a consultant in both 1968 and 1978, and Professor He Guanghu, the leading translator and expositor of Macquarrian theology in Asia, informs us of its Chinese reception. His essay provides a reminder that Christian theology is very small beer in China, but also shows the growing influence of Macquarrie's very remarkable achievement, especially through the various editions of *Twentieth-Century Religious Thought* (1963–2001). Japanese translations of Macquarrie are not discussed in this book, so Professor He's input can represent these also. German, Dutch, Italian, and Spanish translations receive only bibliographical mention below, but their existence also speaks of his wider outreach.

Macquarrie's preparatory paper on 'The Nature of Theological Language' for the 1968 Lambeth Conference will have been helpful for those participants who realized there is a problem here, but were unable to read the then recently published *God-Talk* (1967). Ten years later, Macquarrie's status as the leading systematic theologian of the Anglican communion was reflected in his being asked to produce a preparatory paper on 'The Bishop and Theologians', and more importantly in his opening address on the vexed question of 'The Ordination of Women to the Priesthood', both reprinted in *Theology, Church and Ministry* (1986). In view of the painful history of several late twentieth-century churches on this issue, and the compromises thought necessary by the Church of England, that essay is particularly worth re-reading. As one would expect, it is marked by loyalty to the tradition, openness to what the Spirit may be saying to the churches, generosity in judging differing views, balance in consideration of the arguments, and a strong concern to work for consensus. Also worthy of note at a time when some more militant Anglo-catholics are preparing again to man the ramparts over women bishops is the fact that this ecclesiologically conservative Anglo-catholic could be quite relaxed about the issue itself, however unhappy he was about the lawless way in which his own American church had proceeded. He had 'for many years accepted that there are no decisive theological objections to the ordination of women' (*Theology*, p. 189), and adds what one would expect any catholic theologian to say, that 'the consecration of women bishops . . . is surely implicit in the ordination of women priests . . .' (p. 193). He did 'not think that the ordination of women priests in a church is a sufficient ground for people to leave that church and set up a schismatic body, and I very much regret that some have already done so' (p. 194). On the other hand this horror of schism and sense of ecumenical responsibility incline him to caution, as some notes he wrote recently for his local vicar confirm (see below, p. 103).

Few systematic theologians have been so consistently open to learning from other religious traditions, long before this became fashionable. As a BD student he had attended lectures on Buddhism and Islam, but like his younger Anglican Glaswegian contemporary, Ninian Smart, who was sent by the army to learn Chinese and then posted to Sri Lanka, his horizons were expanded by military service in alien cultures. In both cases their interest in mysticism encouraged that exploration, and their philosophical work on 'the borderlands of theology' contributed to their religious quests. Two of Macquarrie's latest books epitomize this. The title *The Mediators* (1995) again recalls Schleiermacher, and *Two Worlds are Ours* (2004) similarly introduces a choir of mystics who are evidently important for him personally. Some 30 years before *Mediators*, an article on 'Christianity and Other Faiths' (1966) spoke (as Schleiermacher could) of 'faiths' rather than 'religions' in order to rescue the word from Christian imperialism.

That argument has meanwhile been comprehensively won, and it is now more important to see how clearly Macquarrie rejects the religious relativism of someone like John Hick while speaking warmly of Hick personally, and with strong agreement about Hick's 'promoting relations of respect among the great religions of the world' and himself insisting 'that the Christian doctrine of incarnation should be understood and taught in such a way that it does not stand in the way of such a *rapprochement* or suggest that there can be no genuine knowledge of God apart from the revelation in Jesus Christ' (*Stubborn*, p. 93 [1993]). As always there is balance in Macquarrie's theology as he seeks to be open to whatever is true in the non-Christian religions, while also expressing his firm commitment to Christian faith as the avenue by which God has become a reality for him.

Conceived during the Golden Jubilee of the Macquarrie-SCM relationship and therefore published a few months after the event, this celebration coincides with the ruby anniversary of *Principles of Christian Theology* (1966). Forty years has biblical resonances, and some would consider the period a theological wilderness in Europe following the exodus of Barth, Bultmann, Bonhoeffer and Tillich. But that would be a very Protestant (as well as white and male) perspective. The patient work of such significant theologians as de Lubac, Congar, von Balthasar, and Chenu fed into the Second Vatican Council with the towering figure of Karl Rahner, and in this period even English-speaking Christianity had its manna and quails as well as its wanderings and plagues. Among the first 100,000 copies of *Principles* to be sold, a surprising number are to be found on the shelves (if not on the desk) of English students and clergy – shelves unburdened by the weight of a *Church Dogmatics*. Here was a textbook of Christian doctrine which a church unaccustomed to systematic theology could read and re-read. It is repeatedly referred to in the essays that follow. But it is two major books from the 1980s that have provided the title of this collection, and the main focus of the eight essays in Part II.

In Search of Humanity (1982) was originally conceived as Gifford lectures but preceded the actual Gifford lectures at St Andrews, *In Search of Deity* (1984) and that order reflects Macquarrie's 'anthropological approach to theology'. God, and even the sense of God, no doubt precede all our theologizing, and that priority is reflected in the structure of most systematic theologies, including Part Two (Symbolic Theology) of *Principles*, where 'Creation' follows 'The Triune God', and 'Man' is sandwiched between 'Nature' and 'The Holy Angels' in that chapter. But in Part One (Philosophical Theology), where anthropology is most substantively treated, 'Human Existence' precedes 'Revelation'. That general shape of Macquarrie's theology is followed in the second half of this collection too. The first two parts of *Principles* can be combined for this purpose because philosophy and theology are intertwined in Macquarrie's theological anthropology and his doctrine of God.

Essays on his Christology follow. Macquarrie's two books and several articles on Christology give this a central place in his later writing, unlike soteriology and pneumatology which naturally receive a chapter each in *Principles*, but are rarely accorded separate treatment. The tradition must be discussed but Macquarrie's own understanding of both Spirit and salvation are implicit in his understanding of God and the human, and so too in his treatment of any topic. Perhaps surprisingly in view of Macquarrie's 'high' ecclesiology and deep interest in this topic 'The Church' in *Principles* is assigned to Part Three (Applied Theology). We have followed that structure by calling Part III here 'Applied Theology' and including there the essays on ecclesiology, ministry, Eucharist, spirituality, and Mary.

But Part II is central to this collection, as our title implies, and we honour Macquarrie's (and Rahner's) 'anthropological approach to theology' by giving pride of place to Eugene Long's reflections on the self and other in Macquarrie's philosophical and theological anthropology. Long discusses in particular Macquarrie's analysis of the individual and the social (egoity and sociality) poles of persons, and his analysis of human suffering. He argues that Macquarrie's understanding of the tension between egoity and sociality offers a better account of persons than some contemporary views that tend to emphasize either the individual or the social. He also argues that although Macquarrie's analysis of suffering shares much in common with contemporary continental philosophers of religion who speak of the end of theodicy and the importance of the moral and the practical, he avoids some of the problems associated with the tendency to divorce the moral from the ontological.

Beginning with anthropology is widely held (outside the Barthian tradition) to offer the best chance of making talk of God intelligible in the modern world. But for Schleiermacher and Bultmann, Rahner, Ebeling, and Macquarrie, talk of God and talk of the human necessarily involve each other, and Georgina Morley's essay shows that theological anthropology opens out into talk of God. Both Long and Morley naturally concentrate on *In Search of Humanity* (1982) which is fuller and more recent than the chapter on human existence, and the short section on 'man' (sic) in *Principles*.

The last sentence of *Humanity* (p. 261) claims that 'the search for humanity merges into the search for deity and would call for another book'. That hypothetical was actualized within two years and we follow that order with three essays on God.

Paul Fiddes focuses on Macquarrie's often-repeated affirmation that God (or holy Being) is 'incomparable'. For Macquarrie this is a theological concept that arises as reflection upon spiritual experience and the practice of prayer, and is also to be understood in the context of

Heidegger's designation of Being as the incomparable *transcendens*. Fiddes explores the way that divine incomparability is central for several aspects of Macquarrie's doctrine of God, greeting Macquarrie's insight that God is 'three movements of Being in one event' as of fundamental importance for a trinitarian theology today. However, he suggests that the symbol of personal relations in God is just as capable of expressing our knowledge of the incomparable as is the language of God as Being: the image of 'movements of relation' can, like talk of Being, express both transcendence and immanence, both the unveiling and the hiddenness of God. In appreciative dialogue with Macquarrie, he suggests that a more complementary use of the symbols of personalness and of Being will enable us to think about the meaning of participation in God, and will issue in a theology that can be sustained against the test of prayer and spirituality.

Although Macquarrie came to avoid the term panentheism on account of its sounding too close to pantheism for comfort, Michael Brierley justifiably takes the term up and recognizes that there are varieties of panentheism, not all so close to traditional theism as Macquarrie's. His essay highlights 'the revolution in the idea of God' (*Thinking*, p. 109) to which Macquarrie's revision of classical theism has made such a major contribution that it may justly be considered his central achievement. By contextualizing it in the broader modern discussion of panentheism Brierley is himself quietly contributing to the revolution. In 1975 Macquarrie thought that 'its application to particular Christian doctrines is something that has still to be fully worked out'. *Principles* was only a start and the remaining essays in this collection touch on it directly or indirectly.

The doctrine of the Trinity does not play the part in Macquarrie's systematic theology that it does in Barth's, but he is able to write about it more positively than Bultmann would have done, and to give it a place in the structure of his presentation that Schleiermacher (for clearly stated reasons) could not. This gives *Principles* a more orthodox appearance than some have been willing to concede. Keith Ward's essay complements the profoundly trinitarian reflections of Paul Fiddes with the kind of contribution made by English philosophy of religion. Such clear thinking is not to be under-valued, especially when (as here) it is informed by a knowledge of the Christian tradition. These two very different essays reflect different aspects of Macquarrie's own thinking.

Christology is more heavily contested territory, especially in Britain (as the overblown controversy in 1977 about *The Myth of God Incarnate* shows), and while agreeing about Macquarrie's modernity the two essays on this last major phase of his writing disagree on whether he has maintained (as he intends) sufficient continuity with the tradition, or upheld its 'governing intention'.

His insistence on the Chalcedonian definition of Jesus as 'truly God, truly [a] human being', combined with sitting lightly to the Greek metaphysical terms in which it was then articulated, yet defending 'nature' from Schleiermacher's criticism, represent a 'middle way' between classical Christology and a radical liberal Protestantism which abandons the doctrine of the divinity of Christ. From the Irish Roman Catholic perspective of Fr Niall Coll, a former doctoral student of Gerald O'Collins S.J. in Rome, this is not traditional enough. In *Christ in Eternity and Time* (2001) he criticized Macquarrie's minimalist account of Jesus' preexistence, and his contribution to this volume remains quite critical.

A far more positive view of Macquarrie's 'Schleiermacherian Christology' is taken in the essay that follows. This argument over Christology concerns the identity of Christianity more directly than even the philosophical theologians' debate about classical theism. Whether or not Christians continue to confess Jesus as 'My Lord and my God' may come to be seen as a parting of the ways in modern Christianity. It is the achievement of Macquarrie and some other twentieth-century theologians, including Schillebeeckx and Walter Cardinal Kasper, to have integrated modern scientific and historical knowledge into their Christologies without surrendering the fundamental christological dogma.

Macquarrie's mediating solution implies a proposal about both the scope and the limits of historical Jesus research in Christology. Whether (in the words of the so-called Athanasian Creed) it 'do keep whole and undefiled' (as it intends to) 'the Catholick Faith', remains subject to debate, and Philip Endean's gently distancing of Macquarrie from Rahner is a further contribution to that. The balance between tradition and modernity is a central issue for any modern theology and there is nothing particularly Anglican about Macquarrie's 'middle way'. The Elizabethan settlement was not about Christology. But it was about theology and worship as well as polity, and Christology has roots in worship as well as in philosophy and history. Macquarrie's Christology both draws on his new natural theology and doctrine of God, and also makes room for a traditional Eucharistic theology and practice. Can the centre hold?

In the 35 years between *An Existentialist Theology* and *Jesus Christ in Modern Thought* Macquarrie (like many others) seems to have become less critical of Bultmann's account of the resurrection, without, however, becoming as radical as Schillebeeckx. Christopher Morse's remarkable essay on eschatology looks back to the 1960s discussions of the eschatological significance of the resurrection ignited by Pannenberg and Moltmann, and behind that to the Barth–Bultmann exchanges of the 1950s. His return to these debates through a post-modern anti-theological French discussion of St Paul shows how far styles of theologizing have changed in the past thirty years, or even in the past ten years.

The five essays which follow in Part III are concerned with ecclesiology, corresponding broadly to Part Three in *Principles*. Macquarrie calls this section Applied Theology, and explains that its general theme 'is the working out of faith in the world' (p. 382), and that it 'will provide the theological principles' for the more detailed divisions of 'practical theology' (pastoral, ascetical, homiletics etc.), liturgics, and ethics or moral theology (p. 40). Ecclesiology is said to be no less theological, but (arguably) less central than the main themes of doctrine considered in Part Two, and surely it is less central than the more fundamental matters expounded in Part One. This section does, however, relate to a very large part of Macquarrie's writing, and could not be ignored.

Dan Hardy draws on his experience as moderator of theological education for the Church of England as well as many years of teaching and reflection to set Macquarrie's understanding of the Church in its Anglo-American institutional context, where ecclesiology is usually demoted to practical theology. He shows how Macquarrie corrected existential theology from his own practical theological standpoint. Some later Roman Catholic interpreters of Bultmann have also found this theology more open to Catholic ecclesiological concerns than was congenial to some of his fellow-Lutherans. Hardy's brief criticisms of what he finds rather abstract about Macquarrie's approach invite careful pondering.

At a more practical level, Paul Wignall explores the implications of Macquarrie's view of a lay theology as 'by the people, for the people, of the people'. More than 30 years on from *The Faith of the People of God* (1972) lay leadership and leadership shared with those in ordained ministry are becoming common. Many different voices are heard with equal authority, and shared (diverse) ministry and shared (diverse) reading of Scripture raise questions about an ideology of power which has lain beneath much ecclesiology in the past. Wignall suggests that the radical, dissenting and republican traditions of English thought may play a significant role in future Anglican ecclesiology.

Moving from ministry to the sacraments, Peter Groves associates Macquarrie's eucharistic theology with early Tractarian discussions and relates this to the question of Benediction. Ecclesiology is related to practice and for Macquarrie the Eucharist is central. Sacramental theology has been a major component of Anglican theology and it is appropriate that this contribution comes from the incumbent at St Mary Magdalene's, a parish church with the Martyr's Memorial on its doorstep, and a few yards away from where the main framer of the Prayer Book was burned. Here too the conversation continues.

Many who would not agree with Macquarrie's eucharistic theology would be more positive about his other writings on worship and spirituality. Geoffrey Wainwright, whose *Doxology* (1980) attempted to write a systematic theology from the perspective of worship, focuses on perhaps the most popular of Macquarrie's smaller books, *Paths in Spirituality* (1972, 1992²) and draws on *Principles* to suggest how 'doctrine' may help in the regulation of 'subjectivity and objectivity', in worship, and in the relation between worship and theology, and in theology. Macquarrie does not think ecclesiology central, and welcomes diversity of practice, but it is highly controversial (*Principles*, p. 378), and criteria are necessary. Whether the Anglican recipe for Christian unity will succeed in holding even its own communion together is a question which the ecumenical Methodist Wainwright poses, ominously.

Finally, the collection ends with a topic that Macquarrie acknowledges is theologically peripheral: Mary. But it is devotionally very important to many, including Macquarrie himself, and devotional practices need theological assessment (*Principles*, pp. 392–9). Dr Kee sees his essay as a response to *Mary for all Christians* (1991), and it is perhaps right to end a book of this nature with some sharp dissent lest the eirenic character of our author mislead any into thinking that theology itself is bland. Growth in agreement is a desirable fruit of Church life, and ecumenical discussion (unlike the stale old *Kontroverstheologie*) can contribute to that if there is a willingness to listen to opposing views. But to make progress it would need first to clarify such hermeneutical issues as how to read the New Testament, and even see what a chapter such as Galatians 3 actually says and does not say. Dr Kee is, however, correct to insist that 'there are powerful forces at work within Christianity', not all of them in accord with the gospel, or even with what he calls 'the catholic tradition of Jesus, Peter and Paul'.

Expressions of disagreement are sometimes the very stuff of theology, and there will be places in this book, including this Introduction, where (as on p. 23) one can imagine Ian smiling gently and saying, 'No, I don't think so.'

Part I

Life and Work

1 John Macquarrie in Scotland

GEORGE NEWLANDS

John Macquarrie, known to his friends and family as Ian, was born in 1919 and brought up in Renfrew and then in Paisley, on the west coast of Scotland. The west often tends to be much more self-contained and 'Scottish' than the east coast, and it comes as no surprise that Professor Macquarrie, reflecting recently on 'Being a theologian' laid stress on his roots in Renfrew. The west coast tended and still tends to be more un-selfconsciously religious than the east, and Macquarrie naturally grew up in a Presbyterian Sunday-school context in the Church of Scotland. But already at the beginning of his reflections in *On Being a Theologian* he sets down the marker of the Celtic tradition – back to Eriugena – as a kind of balance to the image of Presbyterian Renfrew. He notes that for Celtic Christians, 'God was not a distant power in the heavens, but a presence that surrounded them. . . . The Celtic Christian lived every day in the communion of saints. They even accompanied him when he went out in his fishing boat' (pp. 8–9).

How far this thought is a theological rather than a historical reflection of early influences, will be for future research students comparing Macquarrie's with Augustine's *Confessions* to evaluate. He notes the residual Celtic influence on others from the west, notably John Baillie, theologian of the sense of the presence of God.

'Like Baillie too I thought of the mystery in terms of immanence rather than transcendence' (*Theology*, p. 1).

From a successful academic progress through high school in Renfrew and at Paisley Grammar School (1934–36) he proceeded to Glasgow University at the age of 17. He had already learned German as a teenager by listening to the BBC language course and buying the books. (Lord Reith's BBC has not received sufficient credit for its educational initiatives which led to the appearance of Heidegger in English.) He says that his life 'seems to have been largely a series of fortunate accidents, for I had no ambitious plans about a career or where I would eventually end up' (*Theologian*, p. 12). Unlike the famous Scottish preacher James S.

Stewart he appears not to have spent his childhood playing at being a minister in his pulpit! In 1940 he graduated with a first-class honours degree in Mental Philosophy, studying with the distinguished Scottish Hegelian philosopher A.C. Campbell of *Selfhood and Godhead* fame. 'The one who really bowled me over was F.H. Bradley, whose *Principles of Logic* we had to study in considerable detail' (*Theology*, p. 2). The following three years were spent (on the usual Scottish pattern) studying theology (BD) and so qualifying for the Presbyterian ministry. Looking back at 80 he says he was 'not enthused by theology' after philosophy, and despite getting high marks and gaining various awards he was not enticed by the offer of a scholarship to do research at Westminster College, Cambridge (*Theology*, p. 3). The war made practical matters more urgent and the exemption of ordinands from military service was not comfortable. He had already had pastoral experience as a seminarian at Dumbarton Parish Church, and as an assistant in charge of a new housing area in Paisley, so after graduating with a BD in 1943 he volunteered for a chaplaincy in the Royal Army Chaplain's Department.

He admitted in 1980 ('Pilgrimage in Theology') that 'dogmatic theology I had come to regard as little more than systematic superstition' in contrast to his interest in biblical criticism and church history (*Theology*, p. 2). When this essay was reprinted in *Theology, Church and Ministry* (1986) he added that 'theories of incarnation and atonement seemed to me a waste of time. If *The Myth of God Incarnate* had come out at that time, I should have swallowed it whole' (p. 2). Fortunately he read Rudolf Otto, *The Idea of the Holy*, which made a strong appeal, and Dr Gossip was fascinating on Buddhism, if not on his own subject of pastoral theology.

In 1945 he became responsible for co-ordinating religious services for German prisoners of war in Egypt, with the aid of a group of German pastors in captivity. His knowledge of German developed. Then 1948 saw him inducted into the parish of St Ninian's, Brechin, on the east coast of Scotland, and in 1949 he married Jenny Welsh, also from Renfrew, to whom he had been unofficially engaged for eight years – an experience he compared (a little inexactly) with that of Jacob and Rachel.

The Professor of Divinity in Glasgow, John Riddell, visited them and suggested a part-time PhD, supervised by Ian Henderson. Macquarrie later commented that Henderson's 'mind was both profound and acutely critical, and my theological pilgrimage owes more than I can express to his guidance and stimulation' (*Theology*, p. 3). The PhD became his first book, *An Existentialist Theology* (1955). Macquarrie's continuing interest in and interpretation of Rudolf Bultmann are the subject of a separate contribution from David Fergusson, and need no discussion here. But

Glasgow was to be a continuing source of Bultmann studies, from Ian Henderson to Ronald Gregor Smith and Iain Nicol, in contrast to the Barthian emphasis in Edinburgh. (In philosophy Glasgow had a traditional interest in Hegel, from the Cairds to Campbell, and Edinburgh in Kant, from Pringle-Pattison to Nowell-Smith. The contrast was not entirely complete, however, since Henderson and Smith were Edinburgh graduates, pupils of John Baillie, and both had studied with Barth.) The external examiner for PhD was to be Donald Baillie, and Bultmann wrote a *Gutachten* in commendation, which on the publisher's suggestion was translated and included as a Foreword to the 1960 printing of *An Existentialist Theology,* and is reprinted in *On Being a Theologian,* pp. 17–18. Bultmann writes of Macquarrie's 'outstanding power of exposition' and calls him 'a thinker of high rank'. He claims to 'have seldom found so unprejudiced and penetrating an understanding of my intentions and my work as in this book'. He 'cannot agree with the author's criticism at all points', but 'must concede that the criticism is not only fair and perceptive, but also touches upon points that are really problematic and must be cleared up in future discussion'. Bultmann also praises Macquarrie's 'essentially correct understanding of Heidegger, as well as a rare capacity for unfolding simply and clearly this philosopher's ideas, which are often hard to understand . . .' (p. 18). Apart from the master's wry humour in the echo of 2 Peter 3.16, this shows how Macquarrie's first great theological inspiration put a finger on his critical admirer's strengths right at the beginning of a wonderful career of theological writing.

Bultmann proved to be a surer guide to faith than Bradley had been. 'The idealist identifies the essence of Christianity with a high philosophy of the universe, but for Bultmann Christianity is a religion with saving power' (*Theology,* p. 4). But there were better guides to come. Tillich's *Systematic Theology* (1953–) 'attracted me, though I think that most of what is of value in its philosophical structure has been better said by Heidegger. But more important than Tillich was my discovery of Rahner, who at that time was untranslated and virtually unknown in Britain' (*Theology,* p. 4). Within days of his arrival in New York the John Knox who shortly afterwards became an Anglican became a very significant influence with his combination of a Bultmannian New Testament scholarship with a 'very high view of the church' – which Knox and soon Macquarrie saw as part of the Christ event. J. A. T. Robinson's panentheism in *Exploration into God* (1967) he felt very close to his own position, 'but the reader can readily believe that "death of God" and "religionless Christianity" were movements which I felt had to be resisted at all costs' (*Theology,* p. 6). There is only one reference to Ronald Gregor Smith in the 1999 reflections (*Theologian,* pp. 37–8), but both students and Macquarrie himself testify to his harmonious relation-ship with both Smith and Henderson, even after these two colleagues had famously fallen out.

Meanwhile Macquarrie was appointed to a lectureship in systematic theology ('I no longer called it "systematic superstition!",' *Theology*, p. 4) in Glasgow, where the family lived for nine years (1953–62). Here he started on the translation of *Being and Time*, gave the 1962 Hastie Lectures on the philosophy of religion which were to become *God-Talk* (1967), and wrote most of *Twentieth-Century Religious Thought* (1963) at the suggestion of Harper and Row, New York, to which he agreed on condition that SCM Press publish the British edition.

The early 1960s brought decisive change. In 1962 the Macquarries moved to New York, where John had been offered the Chair of System-atic Theology at Union Theological Seminary. (There had been an earlier proposal of a Chair in Philosophical Theology in 1956, suggested to Union by John Baillie, as so often at that time the hidden hand in Scottish and American theological appointments.)

With this geographical move came the ecclesiological move, to the Episcopal Church and ordination in 1965 to the priesthood. 'I should add, however, that in becoming an Anglican I did not feel that I was renouncing my past. Rather, I was taking it with me into something broader, richer, more fulfilling, more catholic' (*Theology*, p. 5). This is now material for other chapters. I recall, however, that when I was inter-viewed for the Chair of Divinity in Glasgow in 1985, John was one of the external assessors. He asked what I would do about churchmanship, since I was ordained in both the Reformed and the Anglican traditions. I said that I hoped to retain equally strong links with both. He replied that he regarded his Presbyterian years as a ministry completed.

Others have written here of John Macquarrie's later work in America and in Oxford. I confine myself here to noting the stress on the centrality of Christology – 'if *The Myth of God Incarnate* did anything for me, it was to persuade me finally that we cannot speak of God apart from Jesus Christ' (*Theologian*, p. 72). This is interesting, especially in view of the strong critique of John's work often made – I think mistakenly – by his fellow Scot Donald MacKinnon, though MacKinnon was talking about Macquarrie's early work and reflecting his own Barthian sympathies in the mid-century divide between followers of Barth and those of Bultmann. Prominent too was the stress on the need for dialogue with Rome – per-haps in part an antidote to West Coast Protestantism and perhaps too an indication of the strong affinity he felt for the work of Karl Rahner. Like Rahner Macquarrie was concerned for theological anthropology, and, like Rahner too, he stressed the importance of the religious dimension, in contrast to the secular theology which his colleague Gregor Smith developed in Glasgow, as professor until his early death in 1968.

The Macquarries chose to retire to Oxford rather than come back to Scotland, though they retain strong links with family and friends there. John graduated DLitt. in Glasgow in 1964, received an honorary DD in 1969 (he now had the degrees MA, BD, PhD, DLitt, DD from Glasgow!) and gave Gifford Lectures, *In Search of Deity* in St Andrews in 1983–4. Invited in 1976 to consider a Scottish Episcopal bishopric based in Oban, he characteristically thought that others were better qualified than he – as Donald MacKinnon's bishop he would have given a new resonance to Barth's phrase *senkrecht von oben*.

Macquarrie was and is a cosmopolitan theologian, who draws inspiration from wells in many places. At the same time it is pleasant to note his continuing interest in fellow Scots. There is a perceptive essay on John MacLeod Campbell, of whom it was famously said that he cast the first stone that cracked the ice of a rigid Calvinism. Macquarrie comments, '"Light" is one of the most frequently recurring words in Campbell's writing, but whether he deals adequately with darkness and death is open to question' (*Thinking*, p. 177). And of his old mentor Ian Henderson he writes, 'He has left an example of integrity, tolerance and courage, that should be inspiring for theologians of the future, both in Scotland and beyond' (*Thinking*, p. 212). One might think that there is quite a lot of ice still to be cracked – but that would be another story.

*

Some of Professor Macquarrie's Glasgow students, now themselves retired, have added the following contributions:

Iain Nicol, (lately Professor of Theology and Principal in Knox College, and Director of the Toronto School of Theology) writes:

It's probably common knowledge that John wanted to study theology at the Episcopal College in Edinburgh. Out of respect for his father, an elder in the Church of Scotland, he decided not to do so. It was not until he was at Union NY that he became Episcopalian. Probably from a fairly early age John was not too keen on Calvin, Calvinism or probably on Reformed theology in general. Entering John and Jenny's place at Christ Church one was confronted with a prominently placed photograph of John being received by the Pope. I suppose this was intended to annoy the stauncher Protestants.

Ronnie Gregor Smith and **Ian Henderson** taught the more glamorous subjects. John covered a number of areas including psychology of religion – not the most exciting subject until John came to Freud and Jung whom he treated with his usual lucidity. He also lectured in comparative religion, philosophy of religion (mainly on language, the basis for his *God-Talk*). I think he also gave some lectures on Christology. In a five-week summer term he also covered some of the main themes in the Westminster Confession of Faith – not his favourite document as you can well imagine. Still, he managed to bring it alive with some subtle Heideggerean and Bultmannian asides. Some of these areas may not have been of direct interest to John but he never conveyed any such impression to students. One could be confident that he worked hard on all of them, was always thoroughly prepared, presented his material with his customary lucidity. (I think this clarity of exposition and expression is a primary characteristic of all his work.)

I also had the impression that as far as possible John sought to avoid controversy and to give everyone one's due place in the sun. Nevertheless, I do think that he got into a *Streit* or two with his co-translator of *Sein und Zeit*. At lunch one day at Trinity College – I gather after what appeared to have been a rather exasperating session of translation work with Robinson – he remarked that should anyone become involved in the work of translation one should DO IT ONESELF. DIY. Otherwise I think the word 'eirenic' fitly describes John's life and work. (And my thanks to Jenny and John for their generous and warm hospitality.)

Ainslie McIntyre, who taught New Testament at the University of Glasgow, writes:

With Ronald Gregor Smith and Ian Henderson at loggerheads he was the only systematic theology man we really understood, and he covered everything from comparative religion to the Westminster Confession. He was peripatetic on the dais, slightly hunched and always with a bow tie. He had a habit of fixing his eye on students noted for previous careers or particular interests, and seeking their confirmation of some point he was making: for example, once he made a point relating to the behaviour of animals, and said 'Is that not so, Mr X?' to the Member of the Royal College of Veterinary Surgeons on the benches.

He was of course a noted Scoto-catholic in liturgical if not theological terms, prior to becoming a pisky in New York and confirming this in Oxford. His sole charge in the Kirk was in Brechin, and I recall him telling me that it was a union of City Road Church and Bank Street Church, adding wryly 'But they had the good grace not to call it "City Road & Bank Street"!' (I think they called it St Ninian's).

He acted as a locum in Govan Old, where I occasionally worshipped on summer evenings to savour its liturgical atmosphere, and I would go back to his house in Scotstoun for tea and a fag (those were heady days!) and meet his wife, and his cat Plato. I recall once Mrs Macquarrie asking him, when he admitted that he inclined his head at the name of Jesus in the Creed, whether he also crossed himself at the life everlasting; he replied, with coy deliberation, 'Well, no . . . but it would come quite naturally to me to do so!'

Douglas Templeton (who taught New Testament in Edinburgh after his PhD on Bultmann and Collingwood under Gregor Smith at Glasgow) writes:

In the period 1959–62, Dr John Macquarrie, Lecturer in Trinity College, Glasgow (as he then was), colleague in the Department of Systematic Theology of Ronald Gregor Smith and Ian Henderson, was known to some as: 'Honest John', and to others as: 'The Existentialist without *Angst*', a phrase from Gregor Smith.

It was clear to all that for him (as well as to some notable contemporaries and predecessors) *fides* was *fides quaerens intellectum*, or it was nothing. He spoke always with remarkable lucidity, sanity and what can only be called 'sweet reasonableness', all of these with pertinacity of judgement. Indeed, it was once observed that 'When Dr Macquarrie deals with a theological problem, he solves it'.

In the resounding tones of the Scots vernacular, he spoke boldly of 'the perpe'yull vurgini'i of the Vurgin Mairi' and of the betrayal among the Irish of 'an uneeconommic interest in relijon'. His later translation to Oxford effected no change at all in either his accent or his headgear (a beret, or tammy).

Any interest in religion, economic or not, is as often as not discoloured by fanaticism and what Plato called 'the eristic'. But Dr Macquarrie never uttered an unkind word, even when confronted by Calvinistic stupidity. Once when such a view was, in a cautious question, uttered by a devout elder of the Presbyterian sort, he replied in the mildest tones: 'No, I don't think so.'

It is clear that he was able to devour texts with the voracity of a woodworm in a forest of furniture. Professor Henderson once suggested to him that theological students would be the better for a course in logical positivism and linguistic empiricism. In the twinkling of an eye, such a course was produced – which, no doubt, proved to be one of the elements of what became *Twentieth-Century Religious Thought*.

He knew his texts and was not set back on his haunches by a challenge. Once when another theologian, Ian Ramsey, was, in debate, assaulted by Athanasius, the Cappadocians (all of them), Karl Barth, Hilary of

Poitiers and (finally) Leibniz, he replied to the questioner: 'But does not Leibniz go on to say...? And Ramsey then said it. Dr Macquarrie was, in this period, a man of the same kind.

Doubtless he remained and remains so.

Finlay Squires (who studied and lectured at Glasgow before moving to Aberdeen where he became Principal Lecturer in Religious Education) comments:

As one who talked repeatedly about 'being poised on the edge of an abyss', John's own personal lifestyle seemed, on the contrary, to be remarkably free of *Angst*. Not for John the perils of 'non-being'!

2 John Macquarrie as Interpreter of Bultmann

DAVID FERGUSSON

One of the earliest expositions of Rudolf Bultmann's theology in the English-speaking world, Macquarrie's *An Existentialist Theology*, remains a valuable introduction to his thought. It bears all the hallmarks of Macquarrie's subsequent writings: lucid exposition; sound scholarship; judicious comment and interpretation *in optimem partem*. Appearing in 1955, it registered for an English-speaking public the ferment aroused in European theology by Bultmann's demythologizing project. This was a programme that proposed the existential interpretation of a vast array of mythological thought patterns; these were found to be embedded in the New Testament but were deemed incredible to the modern mind.[1]

The study of Bultmann, and in particular his relationship to Heidegger, was one for which Macquarrie was unusually well equipped. A graduate in philosophy and theology, Macquarrie later worked with German prisoners of war, including many clergy, thus becoming thoroughly proficient *auf deutsch* prior to his doctoral studies. While ministering in the Church of Scotland at St Ninian's, Brechin from 1948, he was able simultaneously to undertake doctoral studies under the supervision of Ian Henderson who held the Chair of Systematic Theology in Glasgow from 1948 until his death in 1969. Having been a pupil of Brunner in Zürich and of Barth in Basel, Henderson himself was immersed in German-language theology. His brief study of the demythologizing controversy preceded Macquarrie's own more substantial contribution to the interpretation of Bultmann.[2] Initially presented as his PhD thesis to the University of Glasgow in 1954, *An Existentialist Theology* appeared the following year.[3]

With his capacity to study the primary sources prior to their appearance in English translation, Macquarrie succeeded not only in developing the main lines of criticism within Bultmannian theology but also in rendering Heidegger more accessible to a wider theological public. One remarkable spin-off from this project was the translation in 1962 with Edward Robinson of Heidegger's *Sein und Zeit (Being and Time)*. A time-consuming project, it defied those sceptics who claimed that Heidegger was untranslatable. Although a new and somewhat easier translation by Joan Stambaugh appeared in 1996, the Macquarrie-Robinson work continues to be recommended in many quarters as a more literal rendering of the original. Indeed some German theological students studying in Scotland have sometimes informed me that they could understand Heidegger better after reading this translation![4]

For Macquarrie, the attraction of Bultmann's appropriation of Heidegger is twofold. In reacting against the theological culture of early twentieth-century liberalism, Bultmann is able to rehabilitate biblical (especially Pauline) themes of sin, crisis, judgement and divine grace. At the same time, the borrowing from Heidegger provides theology with a contemporary account of human existence, expressing the self-understanding of much modern culture. This engagement with contemporary philosophy and society is regarded as vital for the communication of Christian faith in each age and generation.

Heidegger's analysis of human being and its possibilities of authentic and inauthentic existence are carefully expounded by Macquarrie. Treating *Sein* (Being) *und Zeit* (Time) primarily in existentialist terms,[5] he discusses *inter alia* the notions of understanding, care, anxiety, fallenness and being-towards-death. The self-involving nature of this analysis of human existence has a dual theological advantage; it erases any sense of the Christian faith as a religious philosophy or system of belief that can be grasped merely by intellectual assent. Here Bradleian idealism, which Macquarrie had studied extensively while a philosophy student in Glasgow, is a recurring target of his criticism. At the same time, Heideggerian existentialism provides an alternative conceptuality to the Barthianism that Macquarrie also deplored. Here his criticisms are more oblique yet unmistakable. Echoing the earlier criticism that one finds in Henderson's *Can Two Walk Together?*, they may be directed at trends in his native Scotland as much as the European continent.[6]

> Barth was right in rescuing the kerygmatic character of theology which was in danger of being lost, and in causing the Church again to hear the Word of God over against the voice of human speculation. But the danger in such a kerygmatic theology is that it may lose touch with man's actual situation. It is in danger of lapsing into a complacent orthodoxy which is curiously irrelevant to the modern mind. It should be said in fairness that this criticism applies more to the disciples of Barth than to their master himself. (*Existentialist*, p. 234)

In Macquarrie's exposition, the analysis of Heidegger precedes the discussion of Bultmann. What emerges is an existentialist account of the nature of human existence and its two fundamental possibilities. The theological dialectic of sin and faith is then mapped on to this account, providing two ways of living before God. Arguably this fails to take sufficient note of Bultmann's enduring indebtedness to the theology of his teacher Wilhelm Herrmann for the setting of his work, but it has the advantage of showing how thoroughly Bultmann's New Testament theology, especially the exposition of Paul and John, is expressed in Heideggerian terms. Macquarrie is impressed, both here and in his subsequent theological writings, by Heidegger's criticism of the role of the subject in Western philosophy since Descartes. Already situated within the natural and social world, the human being has no need to ask for proof of her existence. Paraphrasing Descartes, Heidegger claims, 'I think something, therefore I am in the world.'[7] We are cast on a world, as beings in a condition marked by anxiety, freedom, captivity, openness and death. This philosophical analysis resonates with biblical themes transposed into an existential key. The fundamental possibilities of authentic and inauthentic existence match up with the life before faith and life under faith. In particular, the Pauline category of σῶμα can be rendered so as to accommodate much of this Heideggerian description.[8] But the critical point of departure from Heidegger, for both Bultmann and Macquarrie, concerns the manner in which authentic human existence is realized (*Existentialist*, p. 148–53). Whereas for the philosopher this is achieved through our own resolution, for the theologian it is given only by divine grace. Thus the prior action of God is necessary for faith and the subsequent life that this enables. For Bultmann, the divine action is concentrated upon, one might even say reduced to, the single event of the cross. As it is proclaimed in the kerygma of the Church, it is taken up into the life of faith. Its verbal expression is not in mythological or dogmatic categories but in the self-involving concepts of existential faith. Yet while sympathetic to the Bultmannian project, Macquarrie already registers several criticisms which remain among the most problematic. Four of these are worthy of further comment as they shed light on Macquarrie's later theological commitments, while remaining among the standard objections to Bultmann's theology.

First, the sharp distinction between *Historie* and *Geschichte* cannot be pressed as far as Bultmann maintains. While there is some conceptual difference between the detached study of phenomena in the ancient world (*Historie*) and the vital existential significance of the past for today (*Geschichte*), these cannot be entirely divorced. This is a particular problem given Bultmann's exclusive concentration on the event of the crucifixion. Macquarrie rightly argues that we need to ask more about the identity of the one crucified, for example what he said and did (*Existentialist*, pp. 177–80). Without this, the significance of his crucifixion is opaque to human understanding. Here Macquarrie's own position is much closer to those pupils of Bultmann who initiated the 'new quest' of the historical Jesus. Like Käsemann, Ebeling and Bornkamm, Macquarrie argues that we need to connect an account of the meaning of the death of Jesus with the historical description of his ministry as found in the synoptic tradition. This is more for the sake of intelligibility than for seeking to demonstrate the salvific worth of his death. The link between the Jesus of history and the Christ of faith is a stronger one than that maintained by Bultmann, whose dialectical, cross-centred theology was judged too thin by even his most sympathetic disciples.

In his later christological writing, Macquarrie continues to argue for a 'minimum of factual history' (*Jesus Christ*, p. 358). Maintaining his view that Bultmann's historical minimalism is insufficient for a proper appreciation of Christian faith, Macquarrie claims that the historical study of the gospel traditions serves an important theological function. The difference from Bultmann is not so much one of historical disagreement since Bultmann had argued himself that we had access to reliable information about what Jesus said and did.[9] Instead, on theological grounds, Macquarrie objects to Bultmann's resolution of the faith-history problem. To appreciate the New Testament claim that 'God was in Christ', we require access to important aspects of Jesus' life. An account of how faith in Jesus emerged in the ancient world is required to explicate that same faith in today's terms. According to Macquarrie, the different perspectives of the gospel writers can reasonably be interpreted as converging on genuine reminiscences of the historical Jesus. The argument at this point is essentially similar to D. M. Baillie's earlier criticism of Bultmann, although the appeal is no longer to the historical work of C. H. Dodd but to the more recent findings of E. P. Sanders. (*Jesus Christ*, pp. 52–3).

Macquarrie's much greater sympathy with the 'right-wing pupils' of Bultmann emerges in his second book, the 1960 study of the demythologizing controversy. Criticizing the 'left-wing' represented by Buri and Jaspers, Macquarrie argues for the irreducible priority of divine grace and revelation in the presentation of the Christian faith.[10] This cannot be reduced to the terms of a general religious consciousness or existential description. The crucifixion as an act of God is not the final vestige of myth requiring elimination. The divine action at the centre of the kerygma should be retained, even if this demands an orthodox adjustment of Bultmann's original project. Here Macquarrie laments Bultmann's excessive preoccupation with the mindset of the modern person. Rightly pointing out that secularists also have their myths and world-views, he argues that these need to be challenged rather than meekly accepted. In an exchange of letters with Bultmann, Macquarrie drew attention to the large number of people who continued to flock to places like Lourdes in search of a miracle. Bultmann replied that these were not modern people! (*Scope*, p. 236).

Second, the attempt to strip all vestiges of myth from the Christian faith must inevitably falter since our God-talk cannot avoid the use of myth, symbol and analogy to describe the transcendent in creaturely terms. Bultmann's rendering of 'myth' is found to be equivocal. The broader definition regards as mythological any attempt to speak of 'other-worldly' realities in terms of this world. The narrower account confines 'myth' to those aspects of the first-century world-view that are clearly outmoded (demonology, the three-storey universe, a geocentric cosmos etc.) While sympathetic to the elimination of myth in this latter sense, Macquarrie senses the problems of demythologizing when pursued more radically in accordance with the former sense. The effect of such a procedure will be to eradicate all talk of God, thus reducing theology to anthropology. By interpreting myth in existential terms, there is a serious danger that the kerygma will comprise only human self-description. A glaring weakness in his position, this was addressed by Bultmann in lectures later published as *Jesus Christ and Mythology*.[11] Here he argued for a theory of analogy to make sense of the language of divine action and encounter. Yet, as Macquarrie was to show, this proved a rather lame response since it was never made clear how such an account of analogy could be squared with the radical demythologizing programme (*God-Talk*, pp. 40–1). If myth, broadly defined as any attempt to speak about the other-worldly in terms of this world, is to be entirely eliminated then it is difficult to see what scope remains for advancing a doctrine of analogy.

Macquarrie's own resolution of the problem was heavily indebted to the later ontological work of Heidegger. By identifying God with Being, Macquarrie maintained the classical distinction between God and particular beings. The divine is not to be assimilated to a general class of beings since it is to be thought of as the self-existent source and ground of every genus and species of being. We know this through the way in which Being discloses itself as gracious, immanent and yet radically other. The conceptuality here is strongly Heideggerian with Being described as 'the *incomparable* that *lets-be* and is *present-and-manifest*' (*Principles*, p. 105). The dependence and derivation of all that is, especially self-conscious beings, upon God as Being enables us to speak analogically, if not literally, of Being. This provides Macquarrie with an account of religious language and a theological epistemology that he finds lacking in Bultmann. But considered more broadly, it amounts not merely to an adjustment to Bultmann's theology but to a signficantly different orientation. No longer do we find the dialectical exclusivity of Bultmann's thought in which the action of God is restricted to the cross of Christ. For Macquarrie, the presence and knowledge of God are understood in a wider and more diffuse manner, thus enabling a positive correlation of Christian revelation with other faith traditions and religious experience more generally understood. We might conclude from this that it was the existentialist rather than the dialectical setting of Bultmann's work that proved to be its enduring attraction for Macquarrie. His commitment to a much greater degree of correlationism between theology and philosophy sets him apart even from Bultmann.

Third, the criticism levelled by Macquarrie under the term 'the mighty acts' merits some attention (*Existentialist*, pp. 181–92). The reference to the acts of God plural rather than singular indicates Macquarrie's unease with the narrowing of divine action in Bultmann to the event of the crucifixion. We have already seen this in his criticism of Bultmann's handling of the faith-history problem. In insisting upon the theological relevance of the life of Jesus, Macquarrie is able to offer a more temporally extended and narrative account of divine revelation. The life of Jesus must have had a 'numinous character' (*Existentialist*, p. 185) for his followers, thus enabling them to interpret his death in the manner they did. Neither incarnation nor resurrection is to be treated as a separate event subsequent to the crucifixion. These two are discrete moments in the revelatory process. For Macquarrie, the Pauline account of the resurrection, particularly the appearances, assumes a greater measure of independence than is conceded by Bultmann. While not reducible to historically verifiable circumstances or amenable to apologetic proof, the resurrection is nevertheless to be described as a separate and subsequent event to the crucifixion.

Although this line of argument is not extended to include a criticism of Bultmann's somewhat Marcionite evaluation of the Hebrew Bible, Macquarrie here signals another significant departure that adumbrates his later work on several key Christian doctrines. What we are offered is neither a reduction of Christian doctrines nor a functional reading of their significance. Their catholic vitality is maintained, albeit in treatments that remain sensitive to historical criticism and recent dogmatic reformulation. One finds this in his treatment *inter alia* of the incarnation, the Trinity, the human person, the Church, the sacraments and even Mariology. Seen in this light, his criticism of the *Myth of God Incarnate* (1977) can be viewed as symptomatic of a commitment to retain and rework traditional dogmatic themes. While it might seem surprising that a leading expositor of Bultmann should line up against those who sought to interpret the doctrine of the incarnation mythologically, we can already see in Macquarrie's earliest work the rationale for this. The classical doctrines of the Church can be reworked and reinterpreted, but without them it is doubtful if the belief structure of the Christian faith is sufficiently strong to sustain its life and practice. '[O]ne has to ask whether such a reduced Christianity would move us either to acceptance or rejection. No doubt it would survive as literature, but hardly as a living religious faith.'[12] In committing himself to existentialist themes, Macquarrie remains alive to the importance of belief in sustaining faith and practice. To remain distinctive, faith needs its own cognitive apparatus; our intellectual commitments cannot be divorced from our practical commitments. This insight has informed Macquarrie's life-long interest in the constructive study of Christian doctrine.

Finally, we can discern in *An Existentialist Theology* some dissatisfaction with Bultmann's doctrine of the Church. While the importance of ecclesiology is recognized, Bultmann's account of the self remains too individualistic. In criticizing an inadequate account of the nature of Christian community, Macquarrie signals his own concern for a stronger doctrine of the Church. The need to consider organically and organizationally how the Church becomes a distinctive body in the world is not properly registered in existentialist thought. Greater attention to structure, sacramental life, and worship needs to be accorded. For Bultmann, the actions of proclamation and ethical witness are rightly prominent but others are largely absent. Macquarrie states:

> But like Heidegger, (Bultmann) has nothing positive to contribute to the understanding of Christian κοινωνία. Neither of them has gone beyond the fringes of the problem, and one feels that for both of them it is individual existence that is really interesting. This is perhaps one of the weakest points both in existentialist philosophy itself and in any theology which attacks its problems from the existential approach. However admirable its treatment of individual Christian experience, it fails to make the transition to the Christian community. (*Existentialist*, p. 224)

Macquarrie's later writings reveal a keen interest in ecclesiology, sacramental thought, and the devotional life.[13] Perhaps this is not surprising given his own personal journey from Presbyterianism to Anglicanism. Yet, like his other criticisms of Bultmann, we can already see in *An Existentialist Theology* seeds that were to flower in subsequent output. Committed to a careful yet wide-ranging study of central Christian themes, John Macquarrie, it appears, has followed over many years a steady theological trajectory already discernible in that early critical engagement with Bultmann that commenced during his parish ministry in Brechin.

Notes

1 The original 1941 demythologizing essay was presented by Bultmann as a paper at two conferences of the Confessing Church. Though seemingly reductionist, Bultmann's concern was to argue for a strong reading of the New Testament kerygma without recourse to a narrow dogmatism. Cf. Rudolf Bultmann, *New Testament and Mythology and Other Basic Writings*, ed. S.M. Ogden, Philadelphia: Fortress Press, 1984 and London: SCM Press, 1985, pp. 1–43. An earlier translation with responses was published in *Kerygma and Myth*, Vol.1, ed. H.W. Bartsch, London: SPCK, 1953, 1972², pp. 1–44.

2 *Myth in the New Testament* London: SCM Press, 1952. One can find earlier mention of Bultmann in Scottish theology, particularly with reference to his account of the significance of the historical Jesus in Donald Baillie's *God Was in Christ* (London: Faber & Faber, 1948, 1955²), pp. 37 ff. Bultmann was awarded a DD degree by St Andrews University in 1935. Cf. Bernd Jaspert (ed.), *Karl Barth–Rudolf Bultmann Letter; 1922/1966*, Edinburgh: T&T Clark, 1982, pp. 80 ff. Yet Macquarrie's 1955 study was the first monograph in English to offer a full-length study of Bultmann's theology. Quotations are from the 1960 (=1965) reprint which contains a foreword by Bultmann.

3 Macquarrie had already taken up a lectureship in systematic theology in Glasgow in 1953.

4 Macquarrie himself suggests that he and Robinson might have revised their earlier translation had Robinson not been tragically killed in a road accident. (*Theologian*, p. 21).

5 Macquarrie notes that Heidegger regards himself primarily as an ontologist rather than as an existentialist. The analysis of human existence is intended to facilitate investigation of the deeper question of being. Yet, according to Macquarrie, the cryptic nature of Heidegger's later work requires the interpreter to focus more steadily on his early existentialist discussion (*Existentialist*, p. 30). Nevertheless, Macquarrie's subsequent writings would reveal a keener interest in the later Heidegger as he sought a more adequate doctrine of God than that discerned in Bultmann.

6 Ian Henderson had written: '[T]here are those described, generally by their opponents as Barthians, who seem to consider that their intellectual duty is to think the thoughts of Dr Barth, instead of thinking for themselves.' *Can Two Walk Together?* London: Nisbet, 1948, p. 22.

7 Cited by Macquarrie, *Existentialist*, p. 38.

8 For the discussion of somatic existence see *Existentialist*, pp. 41–7.

9 Cf. *Jesus and the Word*, London: Nicholson & Watson, 1935.

10 *The Scope of Demythologizing*, London: SCM Press, 1960; pp. 129ff.

11 Rudolf Bultmann, *Jesus Christ and Mythology*, New York: Scribner's, 1958.

12 John Macquarrie, 'Christianity without Incarnation? Some Critical Comments', in Michael Green (ed.), *The Truth of God Incarnate*, London: Hodder & Stoughton, 1977, p. 144; *Stubborn*, p. 82.

13 For example, he argues for several christologically-determined constants of ministry together with the sacramental character of ordination in *Theology*, pp.155–78.

3 The Abiding Significance of Existentialist Theology

DAVID R. LAW

In *An Existentialist Theology* (1955) Macquarrie writes of Bultmann's existentialist approach to theology that, 'we may proceed to the examination of his thought in the knowledge that here we have a serious, legitimate and possibly valuable contribution to the problems of a genuinely Christian theology' (*Existentialist*, p. 25). While few theologians today would question the seriousness of Bultmann's theological endeavours, many would be less confident than Macquarrie of the 'legitimate and possibly valuable contribution' of existentialist approaches to theology. Existentialism has fallen out of fashion, and is generally no longer regarded as a significant way of doing theology. In this paper I wish to examine Macquarrie's defence of existentialist theology and to consider whether existentialism may not still have a valuable contribution to make to theological thinking.

Assessment of existentialist approaches to theology is hampered by the difficulty of pinning down the meaning of the term 'existentialism'. The term used in Germany prior to World War Two was *Existenzphilosophie*, a term that Fritz Heinemann claims to have coined in 1929 to describe a philosophy that sought to combine rationalism and vitalism.[1] Jaspers, however, claims to have already been using the term in his lectures in the mid-1920s,[2] and states that his *Psychologie der Weltanschauungen* 'appears, in historical retrospect, as the earliest writing in the later so-called modern Existentialism'.[3] Nevertheless, he is prepared to concede that 'Heinemann carried the day as far as public usage is concerned'.[4] Although Jaspers was prepared to describe his thought as *Existenzphilosophie*, despite his concern that the term was becoming merely a slogan,[5] his preferred term for his philosophy is *Existenzerhellung*, 'illumination' or 'elucidation of existence'. *Existenzphilosophie*, however, has continued to be the term favoured in Germany.[6]

In France, on the other hand, *existentialisme* became the dominant term, pushing into the background such terms as *philosophie existentielle* and *philosophie de l'existence*. The term *existentialisme* seems to have been coined by Gabriel Marcel towards the end of World War Two to describe the philosophies of Sartre and de Beauvoir.[7] The term soon came to be applied to Heidegger and Jaspers, despite their rejection of the term. For Heidegger, Sartre's existentialism has nothing in common with *Being and Time*,[8] while for Jaspers Sartrean existentialism 'has sprung from an alien frame of mind'[9] and is an absolutization and distortion of *Existenz-erhellung*.[10] The English-speaking world has generally followed French usage, however, and has accepted 'existentialism' as a generic term for philosophies that place human existence at their centre.

The problem of defining the term 'existentialism' and its cognates is complicated still further by lack of agreement on who should be included among the ranks of the 'existentialists'. Some commentators have included under the heading of existentialism virtually everyone who has ever commented on human existence, and cite novelists and playwrights such as Ibsen, Kafka, Rilke, Camus, and others as 'existentialists'.[11] Another complicating factor in pinning down the meaning of 'existentialism' is the fact it became fashionable to describe oneself as an 'existentialist', regardless of whether the individual employing the term had any notion of the philosophy of existence.[12] In his lecture on existentialism Sartre complained with some justification that, 'the word is now so loosely applied to so many things that it no longer means anything at all'.[13]

If the term 'existentialism' is to be useful, it clearly needs to be de-limited in some way. Warnock and Cooper have attempted to limit the term by restricting its use to philosophy.[14] This allows them to exclude from consideration the authors of non-philosophical 'existentialist' works such as novels and plays, and to treat existentialism as a type of philosophy which can be compared with other types of philosophy. The key difference between the philosophical and non-philosophical existentialist is that although the latter shares the same interests as his or her philosophical counterpart, he or she does not share a *method*. This method is provided by Husserl's phenomenology.

Macquarrie's definition of existentialism is broader than that of Warnock and Cooper. In *An Existentialist Theology* he writes that 'existentialism is not a philosophy but a type of philosophy, and a type so flexible that it can appear in such widely differing forms as the atheism of Sartre, the Catholicism of Marcel, the Protestantism of Kierkegaard, the Judaism of Buber, and the Orthodoxy of Berdyaev' (*Existentialist*, p. 16). In contrast to Warnock and Cooper, Macquarrie is also prepared to number Camus among the 'existentialists'. In general, Macquarrie prefers to view existentialism as a *type* or *style* of philosophizing rather than as a fully fledged, coherent, systematic philosophy. In *Studies in Christian Existentialism* he describes existentialism as 'the type of philosophy which concerns itself with human existence and which tries to understand this existence out of the concrete experience which, as existents, we all have' (*Studies*, pp. 115–16). He offers a similar definition in *Existentialism*, where he describes existentialism 'not as a "philosophy" but rather as a "style of philosophizing"' (*Existentialism*, p. 14).

A further problem in grasping the meaning of 'existentialism' is the variety of terms used by 'existentialists' to denote 'existence'. Heidegger, for example, employs the terms *Vorhandenheit, Existenz, existenziell* and *existenzial*, to designate different modes or possibilities of existence. Each of these words could be translated into English as 'existence' or 'existential', terms which have also been employed to classify the entire philosophy of Heidegger, Jaspers and others.

Particularly troublesome are the terms *existenziell* and *existenzial*, and their relation to the term 'existentialist'.[15] *Existenziell*, or 'existentiell' as Macquarrie translates the term, denotes the concrete mode of existence that the individual has chosen for him or herself. It refers to the possibilities actualized by each human being in his or her life through the decision and choices that the individual has made. There are two noteworthy points here. First, the 'existentiell' mode of existence chosen by each human being is a manifestation of an understanding of human existence. That is, through the choices made by an individual human being – whether consciously or unconsciously – a particular understanding of human existence is brought to concrete expression. Second, the 'existentiell' understanding remains only at the 'ontic' level of the concrete entity.

The term 'existential', on the other hand, denotes the deeper, underlying structures in human being which make possible the actualization of a concrete mode of existence at the existentiell level. Thus whereas 'existentiell' is 'ontic', 'existential' is 'ontological'. Heidegger (and his translators) employ the term 'existential' as both a noun (plural: 'Existentialia') and an adjective.[16] As a noun it designates what we might term the categories of the ontological structure of human being.[17] When used in this way, 'Existential' denotes, in Macquarrie's words, 'one of the broad fundamental possibilities of *Dasein's* being, in analogy to the term category which denotes one of the basic formal characters of an object' (*Existentialist*, p. 34). Heidegger employs the noun 'existentiality' to describe the ontological structure of human being as a whole, or as Macquarrie puts it, 'The systematic description of all the fundamental possible ways of being of *Dasein* is called the existentiality (*Existenzialität*) of existence' (*Existentialist*, p. 34).

As an adjective 'existential' refers to phenomena that are related to, dependent upon, or evoke an Existential. An 'existential crisis', for example, is a crisis that reveals something about the deeper, ontological structure of human being and which can be described in terms of such Existentialia as possibility, care, anxiety, despair, guilt, and so on, which comprise this ontological structure.

The relation between the 'existentiell' and the 'existential' is that the former provides the basis for analysing the latter. That is, it is by examining the concrete modes of existence adopted by human beings that light can be shed on the Existentialia that make these existentiell modes of existence possible. Macquarrie comments that, 'in the terminology employed by some existentialist writers, *existential* philosophy has an *existentiell* root, where the adjective *existential* is understood as referring to the universal structures of existence while *existentiell* refers to the concrete situation of the individual existent' (*Existentialism*, p. 77; Macquarrie's emphases). Thus Roquentin's revulsion at the everyday objects he encounters in Sartre's *Nausea* can be read as an existentiell expression of the Existential *anxiety*. The examination of the Existentialia underlying existentiell modes of existence is the task of what Heidegger calls 'existential analytic'.

The problem is that not all 'existentialist' writers or commentators on existentialism have followed the technical use of the term 'existential' suggested by Heidegger. In much writing on existentialism the terms 'existentiell' and 'existential' are conflated. A further problem is that the term 'existential' has come to be used as a broad umbrella term to denote anything that pertains to human existence. In this looser usage of the term, 'existential philosophy' would simply denote philosophy that was concerned with human existence in some way, rather than specifically referring to the ontological approach developed by Heidegger in *Being and Time*.[18]

To avoid confusion we shall employ the term 'existentialist' as an umbrella term covering both the existentiell and the existential, and the term 'existentialism' as a generic term denoting modes of thinking that are concerned with the concrete existence of the human being, despite existentialist thinkers' dislike of the term. We shall designate as 'existentialist' types of philosophizing and theologizing that take as their starting-point the qualitative existence or *Existenz* which uniquely belongs or potentially belongs to human beings. Terms such as *Vorhandenheit*, *Existenz*, *existenzial*, and *existenziell* we shall use only in the technical sense in which they are employed by philosophers and theologians of existence.

Our evaluation of existentialist theology is dependent not only on our understanding of existentialism but also on our notion of theology and the task of the theologian. Bound up with the criticism of existentialist theology is the question of the *subject matter* of theology and the proper concerns of theology. An argument that has been advanced against the very notion of an existentialist theology is the claim that theology should be concerned first and foremost with God and only secondarily with human beings. Macquarrie cites Leopold Malevez as a representative of this view, who rejects Bultmann's existentialist approach on the grounds that, 'The Bible is not primarily a treatise on anthropology; its whole aim is the knowledge of God and the contemplation of God.'[19] Macquarrie deals with this type of objection in two ways. First, he argues that the indubitable truth of the claim that

> man can be properly understood only in the light of God . . . by no means rules out the possibility of taking man as the starting point for an interpretation of the Christian faith. If man is, as Christianity asserts, a creature of God and dependent on him, then this should show itself in a study of man. It should be possible to see man as fragmentary and incomplete in himself, so that we are pointed to God; and if we can see man in this way, then we can go on to a fuller understanding of him in his relation to God. (*Studies*, pp. 4–5)

Second, Macquarrie argues that there is an implicit 'existentialism' present in the New Testament. He points out that, 'the Christian knowledge of God is not a knowledge of him as he is in himself – for this would presumably be unattainable – but a knowledge of him as he relates himself to us'. This means that the New Testament's 'message about God is always oriented to human existence, and in so far as it presents us with an understanding of this existence – even if it asks us to look beyond the confines of what is *merely* human for such an understanding – we can properly speak of something like an "existentialism" in the New Testament' (*Studies*, p. 117).

'Existentialist theology', then, is the attempt to read the Bible and Christian doctrine as statements about human existence. It attends to the understanding of human existence and the existential possibilities for human flourishing manifested in the Christian world-view. Its classic representatives are Bultmann, Tillich, Buri, Marcel and in the English-speaking world, Macquarrie. Although it was an influential form of theology between *c.* 1930 and 1970, it is now regarded by many theologians as a spent force.[20] Reports of the death of existentialist theology are premature, however, and it is my contention that existentialist theology can still provide a useful tool in the theologian's toolbox for addressing theological questions today. It is my further contention that Macquarrie's Christian existentialism provides a particularly clear exposition of existentialist theology. Our first task, however, is to evaluate the criticisms that have been levelled against existentialist theology and consider whether they constitute a refutation of existentialist theology as a viable theological approach.

The Critique of Existentialist Theology

A widespread view is that existentialism is 'merely' a culturally conditioned response to the catastrophes of the twentieth century. For the Roman Catholic commentator Rintelen,

> the influence of the existentialist movement can be understood only as the aftermath of the two world wars, as an analysis of the basic mood engendered by these catastrophic events. If material possessions are lost in an instant, if friends and relatives are killed every day, the only thing left is oneself, one's own existence.[21]

For Marxist commentators existentialism is the result of the crisis of capitalism, and existentialist concepts such as anxiety and despair are not characteristics of the human self as such, but are merely expressions of bourgeois decadence.[22]

Such assessments, however, are guilty of a simplification of the origins of existentialism. First, it is not only two world wars that form the background to existentialism, but above all the modern experience of alienation. This alienation is not merely a twentieth-century phenomenon, but was already felt in the nineteenth century, as the thought of Hegel, Feuerbach, Marx and Kierkegaard indicates.

Second, even if we accept that existentialism has been coloured by the age in which the various existentialists were writing – and what philosophy or theology is not? – the significance of existentialism is not dependent upon the age in which it came into existence. It is true that many writers, including those sympathetic to existentialism, have made a connection between post-war depression and the rise of existentialism, but this depression is not the *cause* of existentialism, for existentialism is concerned first and foremost with the challenge of becoming a self, and this is a task that is common to all ages, regardless of how peaceful or war-torn they may be.

It is because existentialism is concerned with the problem of becoming a self that existentialist philosophers themselves see existentialism as having a long history. Jaspers claims that existentialist philosophy is 'really only a form of the one, primordial philosophy',[23] while Macquarrie cites commentators such as Mounier, Copleston, and Brock, who have detected existentialist elements or affinities with existentialism in the thought of philosophers and theologians going back to the pre-Christian era (*Existentialist*, p. 16).[24] This prompts Macquarrie to claim that existentialism is not a modern invention, but 'appears rather to be one of the basic types of thought that has appeared from time to time in the history of philosophy'. It is a type of thought that 'stresses the difference between the individual being of man (*Existenz*) and the being of objects in nature (*Vorhandenheit*) that lends itself to generalization and classification, and it asserts the importance of the former as against the latter' (*Existentialist*, p. 17). The identification of 'existentialist' elements in literature pre-dating the classic existentialists should alert us to the possibility that existentialism is not *merely* the product of the nineteenth and twentieth centuries.

More serious than these criticisms of the culturally conditioned character of existentialism are those criticisms that attack the central ideas of existentialism.

Subjectivism

Existentialism has frequently been accused of being 'subjectivist', by which is meant, in Cooper's words, the view that 'so-called external things are really contents of the mind or constructs of the imagination'.[25] This is far removed from the genuinely existentialist notion of subjectivity. Even Kierkegaard, who is often cited as a defender of a subjective notion of the truth, does not subscribe to the view that truth is anything that the human being chooses it to be. On the contrary, the crucial point Kierkegaard and his pseudonyms wish to drive home is that it is not enough just to *know* the truth; it is also necessary for the human being to *appropriate* the truth and *actualize* it in his or her own existence.

The charge of subjectivism is even more inappropriate with regard to the twentieth-century existentialists, who made use of impulses drawn from Husserl's phenomenology to articulate their understanding of human being. The critique of existentialism as a form of subjective idealism, Cooper points out, 'contradicts the main tenet of existentialist phenomenology, that no sense can be made of mind except as engaged, through embodied activity, in a world which cannot, therefore, be contained "inside" it'.[26]

Cartesian dualism

Closely connected with the criticism of existentialism as subjectivist is the charge that existentialism is guilty of Cartesian dualism. Robert Solomon makes this point in his *Continental Philosophy since 1750*, where he claims that existentialism is the 'culmination' of what he calls 'transcendental pretence.' This 'transcendental pretence', Solomon writes, 'has two central components: first, the remarkable inner richness and expanse of the self, ultimately encompassing everything; and secondly, the consequent right to project from the subjective structures of one's own mind, and ascertain the nature of humanity as such.'[27] Existentialism, particularly in its French form, is the culmination of this transcendental pretence because it is 'undeniably Cartesian, and its emphasis on individual subjectivity in many ways represents both the full fruition and the degeneration of Rousseau's original celebration of the self and its domain'.[28] 'Sartre, Camus, and Merleau-Ponty', Solomon claims, 'all adopt the metaphysical dualism of consciousness and the world.'[29]

Although there may be elements in Sartre's thought that lend themselves to a Cartesian reading, in general the accusation that existentialism is dualistic is puzzling, since several of the existentialists are on record as having rejected dualistic notions of the self. Heidegger criticizes the concept of a pure ego or subject on the grounds that the human being is not a pure, thinking substance, but is always engaged in the world and is therefore never without an object of thought.[30] Marcel condemns certain kinds of Cartesianism and all forms of Fichteanism as 'the most serious errors of which any metaphysic has been guilty,' and rejects Descartes' 'cogito ergo sum' as leading to 'pure subjectivism'.[31] We can thus agree with Cooper's assessment that the claim that existentialism is guilty of Cartesianism is 'the reverse of the truth, for one of the most salient aspects of existentialism, Gallic versions included, is the onslaught on Cartesian notions of self or subject, and on the dualisms which they inspire'.[32]

The charge of dualism has also been levelled against existentialism by some postmodernist thinkers, who claim that existentialism is based on a failure to recognize that the 'self' is an interweaving of a variety of factors over which the subject has no control. Saussure's semiotic theories have revealed how language determines our thinking and speaking, while Freud and his successors have shown how our conscious selves are determined by unconscious drives, instincts, and desires. The existentialist notion of the autonomous self standing over against a meaningless universe upon which the self imposes its own meaning is thus an illusion.

The postmodernist critique of existentialism, however, is based on a notion of a decentred subject which is itself problematic and controversial. Postmodernist criticisms can in any case be accounted for by an existentialist conception of the self. Existentialist thinkers emphasize that the human self consists of a relation of dipolar opposites, which it is the task of each human being to synthesize into a coherent whole. For Kierkegaard, 'A human being is a synthesis of the infinite and the finite, of the temporal and the eternal, of freedom and necessity, in short, a synthesis,'[33] while Macquarrie understands the human self to comprise the polarities of possibility–facticity; rationality–irrationality; responsibility–impotence; anxiety–hope; individual–society (*Principles*, pp. 62–8). The most fundamental of these is the possibility–facticity polarity, under which the other polarities can be subsumed. From the existentialist perspective, the factors identified by Saussure and Freud merely provide a fuller understanding of the elements that comprise the facticity of the self. This does not absolve the individual, however, of the task of synthesizing his or her facticity into a coherent whole with the other elements that comprise the self. In short, the postmodernist critique may add depth to the existentialist analysis of the finite and conditioned character of human existence, but it does not cancel out the existentialist challenge to strive to become a self in the limited, finite context in which each human being lives.

Irrationalism

Existentialism has been rejected as an irrationalist and anti-scientific philosophy. The Kierkegaardian notions of paradox and the leap of faith have frequently been cited as evidence for the irrationalist nature of existentialism, while Lukács claims that the existentialist emphasis on the boundaries of reason and the dependence of twentieth-century existentialists on phenomenology is further evidence of the irrationalism of existentialism.

Before we can evaluate whether existentialism is indeed irrationalist we need to get clear on what we mean by the term 'irrationalism'. There are several types of irrationalism of which existentialism is not guilty. Cooper points out that '… the Existentialist is not an irrationalist in the sense of supporting his claims by appeal to mystical insight, "gut" feeling, or other non-rational founts of knowledge'.[34] Nor, Cooper adds, does existentialism 'in the manner of a Rimbaud or a D. H. Lawrence, exhort us to cultivate wild or "vital" lives in conscious rejection of the exercise of reason'.[35] A mere glance at a few works by existentialists should be enough to dispel such notions. There is logic and argument present in the writings of the existentialists, even those of Kierkegaard and Nietzsche, who are arguably the least systematic of those who have been labelled existentialist.

Existentialism is 'irrationalist' only in the sense that it opposes the dominance of what existentialists regard as an impoverished notion of reason, namely the view that reality can be grasped only by 'objective', 'scientific' means, anything else being regarded as 'irrationalist'. Underlying this view of reason is an unreflective commitment to the subject–object dichotomy, according to which the thinking self is understood to stand over against the world. This ignores precisely what is so significant about existentialism, namely its exploration of how the human being is already engaged in the world before any such subject–object encounter can take place.

The fact that existentialism, at least in its twentieth-century forms, has made use of phenomenology is not in itself 'proof' of the irrationalism of existentialism. Phenomenology is a method, and consequently does not itself constitute scientific knowledge, but rather is a way of acquiring knowledge. This state of affairs, however, is no different from that faced by the scientific method. The scientific method is not itself an item of scientific knowledge, for it is not the result of scientific research, but is rather the means by which scientific results are obtained.

The allegedly anti-scientific character of existentialism stems from its critique of what it regards as an impoverished notion of reason. The popular view is that only scientific knowledge constitutes genuine knowledge, and that other kinds of knowledge are only matters of opinion or feeling. Macquarrie urges us to resist these exclusivist claims made for science, for they constitute an impoverishment of our understanding. Human existence cannot be dealt with adequately on a rigorously scientific basis. One of the distinctive features of human being, which does not lend itself to scientific analysis, is what Heidegger calls *Erschlossenheit* or 'disclosure'. That is, unlike other things in the world the human being possesses the capacity to be 'disclosed' or become open to himself in his being. Heidegger sees this capacity for self-disclosure to belong to the fundamental structure of human existence. What is disclosed in human existence, or to put it another way, what is illuminated by the structure of human existence as disclosure or openness to itself, is 'being-in-the-world'. For Macquarrie, this understanding of human existence as disclosure means that 'the phenomenological analysis of the experiences of the self as being-in-the-world should be able to yield knowledge which is more fundamental, certain and indubitable than any scientific understanding of nature' (*Existentialist*, p. 59).

In short, existentialism is critical not of reason as such but only of particular conceptions of reason and of the attempt to claim hegemony for the limited notion of reason as exclusively scientific. This does not mean that existentialism is irrationalist, however, but merely that it emphasizes that the human being does not live by (scientific) reason alone.

Nihilism and pessimism

It has often been claimed that existentialism is a deeply pessimistic and nihilistic doctrine. The East German Marxist commentator Manfred Buhr, for example, states that, 'According to its character existentialism is from first to last a profoundly pessimistic and nihilistic doctrine,'[36] while Bonhoeffer condemns the use of existentialism in theology as a last ditch attempt in 'a world come of age' to find a hiding place for God in the inner depths of the human self. Existentialism and its twin, psychotherapy, Bonhoeffer argues, are particularly pernicious forms of 'religion', for they seek to rescue God by cultivating a sense of despair and guilt in human beings.[37] For Bonhoeffer,

> Regarded theologically, the error is twofold. First, it is thought that a man can be addressed as a sinner only after his weaknesses and meannesses have been spied out. Secondly, it is thought that a man's essential nature consists of his inmost and most intimate background; that is defined as his 'inner life', and it is precisely in those secret human places that God is now said to have his domain![38]

Existentialist theologians, however, are not cultivating an awareness of sin and despair for the sheer sake of it, but are drawing our attention to what they believe to be a fundamental feature of the human condition, namely the radical alienation that blights human existence. This is not just an existentialist view; it is a fundamentally Christian view. Existentialist theologians do not intend to leave human beings imprisoned in their despair and alienation, however, but point them towards the possibility of overcoming these threats to human flourishing. This possibility, however, does not lie within the human being's capacity. As Macquarrie points out,

> Christian theology does not remain at the point of despair. It must bring us to this point, to make clear its conviction that *there is no human solution to the human problem* . . . Already the analysis of the situation points to another possibility, though only as a possibility. This is the possibility of *grace* – a power from beyond man which can heal his estrangement and enable him to live as the being which he is, the being in whom are conjoined the polarities of finitude and responsibility. (*Studies*, p. 8)

Existentialist theologians are not confronting human beings with their sin out of some peculiar form of sadism, as Bonhoeffer would apparently have us believe, but are providing an analysis of the human situation in order to open up to human beings awareness of their need for grace.

Underlying criticisms of existentialism as nihilistic and pessimistic is a caricature of the existentialist notions of anxiety, despair, and death. The existentialists make clear that anxiety is not fear of any specific object in the world or even of the world as such. Anxiety is rather the sense that the self that one has chosen for oneself is inadequate in some way. It is a sense that one's mode of existence does not and cannot lead to human flourishing or, in existentialist terminology, authenticity. Anxiety is thus both negative and positive. It is negative because it threatens one's present mode of existence; it is positive because it holds open the possibility of a new and more fulfilling mode of existence. Cooper's comment is helpful here:

> Existential *Angst* is . . . a sense of freedom, of a capacity to strike out on one's own in the formation of a scheme of beliefs and values. If *Angst* has special significance in modern times, this is not because life has become too 'dishevelled' or 'wide and wild', but because it has become too *comfortable*. Beliefs and values are too easily and readily received from what Kierkegaard called the 'Public', Nietzsche the 'herd', and Heidegger the 'they'. This *Angst* is not something to be 'treated'; on the contrary, we need to be called to it, and away from a state of 'tranquillization' induced through bad faith.[39]

Similar considerations apply to the existentialist notion of despair. Kierkegaard's concept of despair is not a call to wallow in self-pity, nor is it a form of depression. Kierkegaard warns that it is possible to fall in love with one's melancholy and cultivate it in a similar way to the way some people cultivate their talents. Despair in this sense is merely an aesthetic category, the negative counterpart of the pursuit of pleasure. The Kierkegaardian concept of despair, however, is a description of the self that is constructed upon and is therefore dependent upon an external condition. In other words, the self is constructed on something outside itself over which it has no control, and it is therefore based on insecure foundations.

Finally, the existentialist concern with death does not stem from a morbid fascination with mortality, but out of the challenge facing human beings of living meaningful lives in the face of death.

Existentialism is atheistic

A major reason for theologians' rejection of existentialism has been the view that existentialism is an atheistic philosophy and therefore incompatible with Christianity. Atheistic existentialism, however, is only one possible form of existentialism, and it is a mistake to identify it with existentialism as such. Among those who have been labelled 'existential-ist' we find a plethora of different theological positions, ranging from the atheism of Sartre and Camus to the Christian existentialism of Marcel, Bultmann, Tillich, Buri, and Macquarrie. The view that existentialism is inherently atheistic seems to be the result of existentialism's having become identified – particularly in the English-speaking world – with French rather than German existentialist philosophy. The French form of existentialism is primarily atheistic, and this may be the reason why existentialism has been regarded as incompatible with theology by some commentators. Macquarrie regards the identification of existentialism with Sartre as 'perhaps unfortunate, since Sartre represents existential-ism at its most negative and egocentric pitch, and this is the impression of the movement that has gained currency, so that it is often dismissed without serious consideration as merely a symptom of twentieth-century decadence' (*Twentieth-Century*, p. 358).

A further argument against the rejection of existentialism on the grounds that it is atheistic is that atheistic existentialism may itself be a flawed form of existentialist philosophy. This is Macquarrie's view, for he suggests that the absence of God from Heidegger's philosophy reflects a deficiency in Heidegger's philosophy. Heidegger has, we might say, not followed through his existential analytic to its necessary conclusion, but breaks off too early. If he had pursued his line of thinking to the end, he would have discovered that human beings do not possess the resources for achieving authenticity. This would have compelled him to introduce such theological terms as sin, grace, and redemption. In short, according to Macquarrie, 'the existential analytic should become religious for its completion' (*Existentialist*, p. 63).

We should also not forget that existentialism began life as a Christian mode of thought, a fact that should make us wary of condemning exis-tentialism as intrinsically incompatible with theology. Kierkegaard de-veloped his proto-existentialism as a means of highlighting the necessity of not merely thinking but *living* the truth. The existentialist notions of subjectivity, becoming a self, and authenticity are arguably a philosophi-cal expression of an incarnational understanding of truth, namely that truth was and is embodied in Christ, and that we too have the truth only in so far as we embody it and express it in our lives.

Existentialism is action without an object

Lukács claims that existentialism is a reactionary doctrine which sup-ports the status quo by relegating action from the political sphere to the inwardness of the bourgeois individual, thereby enabling the individual to 'act' without actually changing anything. It is certainly not the intention of the existentialists to propound such a notion of 'inactive action', as Heidegger's notion of being-in-the-world indicates. An essential feature of being-in-the-world is what Heidegger calls *Besorgen*. Because the human being is engaged with the world, his attitude towards the world is one of concern, a concern which should lead to engagement and action. Where Lukács' criticism has some justification, however, is in its pointing to the lack of guidance provided by existentialism concerning *how* to act. This is a point made by Rintelen, who comments that the existentialist notion of transcendence 'evidently does not allow us to pass beyond the frontiers of finiteness to unconditional, timeless truths with their valid meaning and intentional content. Non-committal resolve thus makes us like men on a diving plank who do not know in which direction to jump.'[40] This justifiable criticism, however, does not undermine existentialism as such, but merely indicates that existentialism cannot function as a self-sufficient philosophy. The problem is that, although it requires the human being to act and to become an authentic self, existentialism provides no guidance to the individual on how to act and on what self he or she should become. Rintelen draws from this insight the conclusion that, 'The task of existential thought can be fully successful only if it does not confine itself to the merely human sphere, but comes into contact with that part of being which is directed towards God.'[41] This is a valid critique. The lack of direction provided by non-theological existentialism creates a vacuum which can be filled by all sorts of unpleasant things, as Heidegger's brief involvement with National Socialism proves. This indicates not the inadequacy of existentialism as such, however, but only the untenability of non-theological forms of existentialism.

Macquarrie's Defence of Existentialist Theology

Thus far we have been concerned with critiquing arguments against the use of existentialism in theology. This does not of itself show, however, that existentialism provides a viable and useful tool for doing theology. In the remainder of this paper I wish to consider Macquarrie's arguments for the viability of existentialist theology.

The necessity of existentialist theology

Theological language is no longer the natural idiom of modern, secular human beings. According to Macquarrie, the reason for the loss of relevance of the language of the Bible is that, 'we today have quite a different way of looking at the world from that which belonged to the writers of the New Testament. Their ideas and ways of speaking are so foreign to us because they come out of a different world from our own' (*Studies*, p. 101). The result of this shift from a mythical to a modern world-view, Macquarrie points out, is that, 'The general picture which the New Testament offers is a strange and almost fantastic one to any-body with a modern outlook. What do we make of the stories of wonders and miracles, of voices from heaven and angels sent from God?' (*Studies*, p. 100). Consequently, if Christianity is to speak to modern human beings, it must find a point of contact with the secular world. This, Mac-quarrie writes, is 'a first principle of hermeneutics, namely, that there must be at least some basis of common ground between an interpreter and his audience if the interpretation is to get under way' (*Studies*, p. 4).

If Christianity is to be intelligible to secular human beings, it is necessary to find some common ground upon which the religious and the secular mind can meet and converse. This common ground, Macquarrie claims, is provided by our humanity. There are two justifications for this claim. First, 'Whether we are Christians or secularist, we share our humanity' (*Studies*, p. 4). Second, 'Christianity is a doctrine of man as well as of God' (*Studies*, p. 4). Statements about God always raise questions about the human being's existence in relation to God. It is here that existential-ism can provide a useful resource for the theologian, for it provides a tool for articulating the understanding of existence concealed in theological language. The questions existentialism prompts us to ask of the Bible are in Macquarrie's words: 'What does this [text] mean for my exist-ence? With what possibility of existence does it present me? Into what understanding of my own being does it bring me?' With such questions, Macquarrie comments, 'we have the core of the existential approach to the New Testament, and to the questions of theology in general' (*Studies*, p. 104).

For Macquarrie's argument for the usefulness of existentialism to the-ology to be convincing he must show two things. First, he must show that there is an affinity between existentialism and theology. Second, he must show that existentialism can shed light on theological statements.

The Existential Character of the Bible

The existential mode of expression of the Bible

Macquarrie notes that, 'there is a great gulf fixed between the basic concepts of the New Testament, taken over principally from Hebrew thought, and those of Greek philosophy, and therefore of the western philosophy which is descended from it' (*Existentialist*, p. 17). This gulf is also evident in the *form* of the biblical writings, which do not have the systematic, philosophical presentation of Greek and Western thought. The fact that the form of the biblical writings differs from that of Western philosophy does not mean, however, that the Bible does not convey knowledge, but rather that, 'the biblical writers communicate a different kind of knowledge – the knowledge of individual human existence before God, which defies the kind of classification and generalization which are appropriate only to the knowledge of objects in nature' (*Existentialist*, p. 17). Macquarrie suggests that Hebrew thought grasped the distinction that Western thought has generally overlooked, namely, 'the fundamental distinction between *Existenz* (the being of man) and *Vorhandenheit* (the being of things) as different ways of being' (*Existentialist*, p. 18). Thus in contrast to the systematic, scientific presentation customary in Western philosophy, the biblical writers 'employed poetry, prophecy, histories of national heroes and men of God, myths, and so on, to convey knowledge' (*Existentialist*, p. 18). For Macquarrie, the biblical authors 'did not make general statements, but confronted their readers with individual human beings in *existentiell* situations'(*Existentialist*, p. 18). Macquarrie draws two conclusions from the distinctive style of biblical writing. First, such a style 'is understandable if their approach to the subject was existential' (*Existentialist*, p. 18). Second, the style employed in some existentialist works has affinities with the style of the biblical writers, notably Sartre, who 'has used the forms of the novel, the journal and the drama to convey his existential teaching through existentiell situations' (*Existentialist*, p. 18).

The existential character of the biblical understanding of human being

Macquarrie holds that existentialism 'is the philosophy which, more than any other philosophy, expounds an understanding of the being of man which has affinity with the understanding of his being implicit in the thought of the biblical writers' (*Existentialist*, p. 18; cf. 24). This can be seen in the biblical doctrine of the *imago Dei*, which indicates that '. . . on the biblical understanding of his being, man is not simply a part of nature'. Macquarrie points out that this biblical understanding of the human being differs fundamentally from Greek, Cartesian, and modern scientific conceptions of the human being, all of which attempt in various ways to interpret the human being as a phenomenon of nature (*Existentialist*, pp. 18–19). In contrast to these philosophies but like the Bible, however, existentialist philosophy speaks of human beings as possessing a mode of being that is qualitatively distinct from the natural world. The existentialist distinction between *Existenz*, that is the qualitative type of existence possible only for human beings, and *Vorhandenheit*, that is the type of existence possessed by non-human objects in the world, parallels the biblical affirmation of the human being as created in the image of God and therefore distinct from the rest of creation. Consequently, according to Macquarrie, 'The philosophy of existence does not depersonalize man, as any philosophy which objectifies must do,' but 'does justice to the claims of the individual personal "I"' (*Existentialist*, p. 19). Macquarrie concludes that, 'in this important respect we are entitled to say that there is a definite similarity between existentialism and the understanding of the being of man in biblical thought' (*Existentialist*, p.19).

Macquarrie sees his argument for an affinity between biblical thought and existentialism as confirmed by the similarity between the main themes of the biblical teaching about the human being and that of the existentialists. Macquarrie cites the following common themes: 'individual responsibility before God . . . man's fall from his true destiny into concern with the creature; his consciousness of guilt; the call for decision; the fleeting nature of man's temporal existence, and its termination by death' (*Existentialist*, pp. 19–20).[42] For Macquarrie, these biblical themes

> are remarkably similar to the main themes of existentialist philosophy. The responsibility of the individual confronted with the possibility of being himself and the possibility of losing himself, fallenness, guiltiness, resolve, temporality, death – these are prominent among the phenomena which such a philosopher as Heidegger considers to be constitutive structures of the being of man. (*Existentialist*, p. 20)

Existentialism and the teaching of Jesus

When Macquarrie turns to the teaching of Jesus he finds further affinities with existentialism. He draws parallels between Jesus' protest against tradition and his call for inward obedience, and the existentialists' protest 'against the blind acceptance of the traditions and customs of collective humanity – *das Man*, in Heidegger's expression – and insisting that the individual must understand and decide for himself' (*Existentialist*, p. 22). A further parallel between the teaching of Jesus and that of the existentialists is Jesus' warning that the human being who strives after worldly things risks losing his soul, but renunciation leads to salvation (Mark 8.36; Luke 15.17; Matt. 10.39). This, Macquarrie claims, has affinities with 'the existentialist teaching that man is confronted with the basic possibilities of an authentic existence, in which he finds himself, and an inauthentic existence, in which the self is lost and scattered in concern with the world' (*Existentialist*, p. 22).

Jesus' eschatological teaching also has affinities with existentialism. Both Jesus and the existentialists teach the need for a radical decision. Jesus teaches the need for the human being to choose, in Macquarrie's words, 'between being his true self in a life of obedience to his Creator, and losing himself in serving the creaturely' (*Existentialist*, p. 22). In existentialist teaching, Macquarrie claims, there is a similar emphasis on radical decision, which is understood as 'resolve which unifies the self and makes its existence authentic' (*Existentialist*, p. 22).

The Existentialist Interpretation of the Bible

For existentialism to provide a viable way of doing theology it is not enough to show that existentialism and theology are compatible; it is also necessary to show that an existentialist approach can shed light on biblical and theological concepts. Macquarrie comments, 'We must test the existential approach to theology by asking how far it is likely to reveal to us the authentic thought of the New Testament writers' (*Existentialist*, p. 15). We would today probably be less confident than Macquarrie of ascertaining 'the authentic thought of the New Testament writers', but Macquarrie's basic point remains valid, namely that one of the criteria for deciding whether existentialism can be legitimately applied to theological concerns is whether existentialism can contribute anything to our understanding of the foundational texts of the Christian faith.

For Macquarrie the task of Christian existentialism is 'that of setting down in an explicit or thematic way the conception of Christian existence contained in the New Testament writings'. This will require translating the mythical, historical, and dogmatic forms of discourse employed in the New Testament 'into statements which explicitly relate to our human existence' (*Studies*, p. 117). This translation of the New Testament into existential statements, Macquarrie claims, 'must be done in accordance with definite hermeneutical principles'. For Macquarrie, 'the main principles in this enterprise are that we should ask questions which related to existence, and that we should seek to formulate answers in existential categories' (*Studies*, p. 117). The significance of the existentialist approach to theology can be best seen by considering what light it sheds on the three basic theological categories of myth, history, and dogma.

1. There are many texts in the Bible that are couched in a mythical language that is alien to modern human beings. The creation narratives, for example, have little significance if we interpret them literally, first,

because the biblical account conflicts with our scientific knowledge of the origins of humankind, and second and more importantly, because 'there would be no religious value in a literal interpretation, and no reason for including this myth in a book that is concerned with religious ideas' (*Studies*, p. 106). According to Macquarrie, it would also be a misunderstanding to interpret the myth 'as a primitive metaphysic, the view that man consists of an immaterial soul-substance and a material body-substance', for this would again be 'an interpretation with no specific religious value' (*Studies*, p. 106). For Macquarrie the creation myths make sense only when they are understood as 'vehicles for the communication of the existential understanding of the living God – the saving knowledge of God, if we may so speak – which belonged to the sacred writers and was disclosed or revealed to them in the experience of faith' (*Existentialist,* p. 64). In *Studies in Christian Existentialism* Macquarrie summarizes the existential meaning of the creation accounts as follows: '. . . the myth brings [the reader] to understand himself as a being who is at once finite and free, a being who is circumscribed, tied down, limited, yet at the same time a being of possibilities, responsible for his existence. This is not a detached understanding, but an understanding of oneself that is presented in the myth, an understanding which one may accept or form which one may turn away. And as such, this is an understanding with religious significance' (*Studies*, p. 106).

Another example of myth is eschatology. According to Macquarrie, we 'no longer look for a supernatural cataclysmic end to the world . . . it is the existential significance of the myth that remains as the element of permanent value in it' (*Studies*, p. 121). Reading eschatological texts in terms of their significance for human existence gives the following interpretation: 'Every individual does indeed stand before the imminent end – his own death; in his everyday decisions about the existence for which he is responsible, he is working out his own judgment; here and now, he either lays hold of his true being or he loses it' (*Studies*, pp. 118–19). By means of this existential interpretation, Macquarrie points out, 'eschatology ceases to be merely a curious belief that has survived from a remote and superstitious past. It can be understood as a way of facing our own human existence, a way marked by the note of urgency and the summons to responsible decision' (*Studies*, pp.118–19).

2. Existential interpretation is able to address the problem of Lessing's 'ugly ditch', namely the problem of how the long-past events of Jesus' life and death can be of significance for human beings today. For Macquarrie, 'The past becomes relevant and illuminating for our present existence when it is in some sense "re-enacted" in our own present history,

when it is understood as disclosing a possible kind of existence for us now' (*Studies*, p. 119). Thus the historical events of the crucifixion and resurrection become relevant and meaningful when we grasp the understanding of human existence they contain and interpret our own lives in the light of this understanding. For Macquarrie,

> We really 'believe' in the cross of Christ when we ourselves 'take up the cross' and in so doing experience a 'rising' from the death of sin into a new life of the spirit. This constitutes atonement, reconciliation with one's true being and so with God. In this way the merely past even acquires a new dimension that makes it a contemporary and saving event. (*Studies*, p. 119)

3. The meaning of dogmas becomes apparent when we interpret them in terms of what they tell us about our existence. For example, according to Macquarrie, 'the titles given to Jesus by the earliest Christians were not attempts to define his metaphysical status,' but to express 'the significance of the crucified and risen One for their existence' (*Studies*, p. 122). Similarly, the two-natures doctrine is a statement not only about the person of Christ, but also about the believer's relationship to Christ. Macquarrie comments:

> Prior to all metaphysical speculations on the natures of Christ and on his relation to the Father came the existential commitment of the believer to Christ, and this is what is expressed in the disciples' confession of his divinity. To acknowledge Christ as Lord and God, as St Thomas the Apostle did, is not only to say something about Christ but to say something about oneself, to declare one's attitude to Christ, to recognize in him one's 'ultimate concern'. (*Studies*, p. 120)

Existentialism is also able to highlight the necessity of grace, and in doing so to help us to move away from the magical conceptions that have bedevilled this doctrine. By means of an existential analysis of the human condition, Macquarrie claims,

> We are directed toward a transcendent source of grace. This is neither a senseless nor a speculative idea, but rather a question of life and death that arises directly out of the structure of our own existence. It is the question of God, for 'God' is the word which the religious man uses for the transcendent source of grace . . . The quest for grace allows the word 'God' to find its place on the map of meaningful discourse; and with it, other theological words find their places – 'finitude' may be equivalent to 'creatureliness', and 'sin' may acquire its full signification as 'separation from God'. (*Studies*, p. 9)

The Abiding Significance of Existentialism for Theology

It is difficult to understand, in view of the light existentialist theology can shed on apparently obscure, irrelevant, and meaningless theological concepts, why it should no longer be regarded as a significant theological resource. We need to find a balance between expecting too much and too little from existentialism. Existentialist theology is not the answer to all theological questions, but is a way of drawing out the significance of the Christian faith for the personal, individual existence of the human being. It is not the only valid way of doing theology, however, and needs to be supplemented by other theological approaches. Macquarrie himself makes this point, commenting that, 'Any particular way of presenting Christianity begins to look merely foolish if it is presented as the *only* way' (*Studies*, p. 123). Macquarrie holds that existentialism cannot do full justice to the historical element in Christianity and to the ontological implications of dogma (*Studies*, p. 124). He further points out that, '. . . a purely existential approach to theology is almost impossible, even if it were supposed to be desirable' (*Existentialist*, p. 25). This is because, 'Consciously or unconsciously, other influences from the long tradition of theological and philosophical thought will enter into any presentation of the Christian faith' (*Existentialist*, p. 25). A good example is provided by Bultmann, whose existentialist theology is coloured by his Lutheranism and liberal modernism.

On the other hand, the outright rejection of existentialism on the grounds that it is outmoded or incompatible with Christianity is based on a caricature of existentialism and the identification of existentialism with atheism. Employing an existentialist approach to theology does not entail accepting the ideologies accompanying some versions of existentialist philosophy such as Heidegger's philosophy of being or the atheism of Sartre and Camus. Rather existentialism is a hermeneutical tool that is able to clarify the categories according to which human beings structure and live out their lives. As Macquarrie puts it, it is a *style* of philosophizing rather than a coherent philosophy in itself. Macquarrie holds that, 'Like logical positivism, existentialism is not a body of doctrines but a way of doing philosophy. It is the way which begins by interrogating existence, where by "existence" is understood the kind of being that belongs to man in his concrete living, acting and deciding' (*Twentieth-Century*, p. 351). As such it is value-neutral and is not committed to any specific ideology. This neutrality is both its strength and weakness. The strength of existentialism is that it provides us with a powerful terminology for articulating the character of human existence. The weakness of existentialism is that it fails to give more than general guidance on the nature of the self which human beings are called upon to choose and realize. This is, of course, due to the existentialist emphasis on freedom, but as Heidegger's brief involvement with National Socialism shows, this can create a vacuum which can suck in pernicious world-views. Thus existentialism can never be an independent, self-sufficient philosophy or theology, but it can continue to provide a tool in the theological toolbox for making clear the transforming power of the gospel, throwing light on biblical concepts, and articulating the distinctive form of existence that is Christian faith.

Notes

1 Heinemann claims in *Existenzphilosophie: Lebendig oder Tot?* (Stuttgart: Kohlhammer, 1954, p. 11) that he coined the term *Existenzphilosophie* in his book *Neue Wege der Philosophie*, Leipzig: Quelle & Meyer, 1929.

2 Karl Jaspers, *Philosophy of Existence*, trans. with introduction by Richard F. Grabau, Philadelphia: University of Pennsylvania, 1971, p. 95.

3 Jaspers, 'Philosophical Autobiography,' in Paul Arthur Schilpp (ed.), *The Philosophy of Karl Jaspers*, augmented edition, La Salle, Ill.: Open Court, 1981, p. 28. *Psychologie der Weltanschauungen*, Berlin: J. Springer, 1919.

4 Jaspers, *Philosophy of Existence*, p. 96.

5 Jaspers, *Philosophy of Existence*, p. 96.

6 See, for example, Thomas Seibert, *Existenzphilosophie*, Stuttgart, Weimar: J.B. Metzler, 1997.

7 Simone de Beauvoir, *La Force des Choses*, Paris: Gallimard, 1963, p. 50.

8 Heidegger, 'Letter on Humanism', in David Farrell Krell (ed.), *Martin Heidegger: Basic Writings*, London: Routledge, revised edn 1993, pp. 217–65, esp. p. 232.

9 Jaspers, *Philosophy of Existence*, p. 96.

10 Jaspers, *Philosophie*, Munich: Piper, 1994, 3 vols; Vol. I, *Nachwort*, XXIII.

11 A glance at survey works on existentialism is sufficient to confirm this. An extreme example is provided by Robert C. Solomon's reader on existentialism, which lists as existentialists not only Kierkegaard, Heidegger, Jaspers, Sartre, and other generally recognized 'existentialist' thinkers, but includes writers such as Turgenev, Frankl, Márquez, Becket, Borges, Heller, Roth, and Arthur Miller. Robert C. Solomon (ed.), *Existentialism*, Oxford, New York: Oxford University Press, 2005².

12 De Beauvoir, *Force des Choses*, pp. 157–8.

13 Jean-Paul Sartre, *Existentialism and Humanism*, trans. and introduced by Philip Mairet, London: Methuen, 1955, pp. 25–6.

14 Mary Warnock, *Existentialism*, London: Oxford University Press, 1970, p. 1; David E. Cooper, *Existentialism: A Reconstruction*, Oxford: Blackwell, 1999², p. 5

15 Heidegger introduces the terms 'existentiell' and 'existential' in *Being and Time*, p. 33. For Macquarrie's discussion see *Existentialist*, p. 34, and *Existentialism*, p. 77.

16 For the sake of clarity, we shall write the English noun 'Existential' upper-case, while retaining the lowercase form for its adjectival use.

17 Heidegger himself dislikes the term 'category' to describe the 'Existentialia', because of the connotations it has acquired in the history of philosophy; *Being and Time*, p. 70.

18 It is presumably for this reason that Jaspers prefers to describe Heidegger's philosophy as *Existentialphilosophie* rather than *Existenzphilosophie* (Jaspers, *Philosophy of Existence*, p. 96).

19 Leopold Malevez, *The Christian Message and Myth: the Theology of Rudolf Bultmann*, trans. Olive Wyon, London: SCM Press, 1958, p. 157; quoted in Macquarrie, *Studies*, p. 117.

20 See, for example, Gareth Jones, 'Existentialism', in Alister McGrath (ed.), *The Blackwell Encyclopedia of Modern Christian Thought*, Oxford: Blackwell, 1993, pp. 200–7.

21 Fritz-Joachim von Rintelen, *Beyond Existentialism*, London: Greenwood Press, 1978, p. 9.

22 See Georg Lukács, *Existentialismus oder Marxismus?*, Berlin: Aufbau-Verlag, 1951; *The Destruction of Reason*, trans. Peter Palmer, London: Merlin, 1980; Theodor Adorno, *Jargon of Authenticity*, trans. Knut Tarnowski and Frederic Will, London: Routledge & Kegan Paul, 1973; Manfred Buhr, 'Existentialismus', in Georg Klaus and Manfred Buhr (eds), *Philosophisches Wörterbuch*, Leipzig: VEB Bibliographisches Institut, 1974, 10th revised and extended edn, 2 vols; Vol. 1, 390–2; p. 392.

23 Jaspers, *Philosophy of Existence*, p. 3.

24 Emmanuel Mounier, *Existentialist Philosophies: An Introduction*, trans. Eric Blow, London: Rockliff, 1948; Frederick Copleston, *Existentialism and Modern Man*, The Aquinas Society of London, Paper no. 9, London: Blackfriars, 1951; Werner Brock, *An Introduction to Contemporary German Philosophy*, Cambridge: Cambridge University Press, 1935, pp. 109–17.

25 David E. Cooper, *Existentialism*, p. 16.

26 Cooper, *Existentialism*, p. 16.

27 Robert Solomon, *Continental Philosophy since 1750: The Rise and Fall of the Self*, Oxford: Oxford University Press, 1988, pp. 1–2.

28 Solomon, *Continental Philosophy*, p. 172.

29 Solomon, *Continental Philosophy*, p. 175.

30 Heidegger, *Being and Time*, pp. 149–53.

31 Gabriel Marcel, *Being and Having*, London: Fontana, 1965, p. 32.

32 Cooper, *Existentialism*, p. 16.

33 Søren Kierkegaard, *The Sickness unto Death*, ed. and trans. Howard V. Hong and Edna H. Hong, Princeton: Princeton University Press, 1980, p. 13.

34 Cooper, *Existentialism*, p. 14.

35 Cooper, *Existentialism*, p. 14.

36 Buhr, 'Existentialismus', p. 392.

37 Dietrich Bonhoeffer, *Letters and Papers from Prison*, abridged edn, London: SCM Press, 1981, pp. 114, 121–2.

38 Bonhoeffer, *Letters and Papers*, p. 124.

39 Cooper, *Existentialism*, pp. 13–14.

40 Rintelen, *Beyond Existentialism*, p. 13.

41 Rintelen, *Beyond Existentialism*, p. 22.

42 Macquarrie cites as evidence for this claim Gen. 3.6; Ps. 51.3; Josh. 24.15; Ps. 103.15–16 (*Existentialist*, p. 20).

4 Translating Heidegger

GEORGE PATTISON

As John Macquarrie and Edward Robinson note in their preface to their 1962 translation of *Being and Time*, Heidegger's early masterpiece 'has often been called "untranslatable"'.[1] Nevertheless, just as Diogenes famously refuted the Eleatic denial of motion by walking up and down, the Macquarrie-Robinson translation offers an enacted refutation of this alleged untranslatability. But how was this refutation achieved? Simply by virtue of a facility in the German language? This would not seem to be enough, since, as they also note, 'It is a very difficult book, even for the German reader.' Just knowing German is therefore not a sufficient condition for understanding Heidegger's text, and one must presumably understand a text in order to translate it – or, to put it another way, any given translation of a text is, in effect, the exposition of how one understands it, it is the translator's primary interpretation of the text in question. What, then, is the understanding of the Heideggerian text that is embodied in the Macquarrie–Robinson translation?

Heidegger, of course, had his own views as to what it means to understand a text composed in a foreign tongue, and, especially in his translations of sentences, fragments, and words from early Greek sources, was himself a translator – often a controversial one. In the following, therefore, I shall begin by looking at a *locus classicus* of Heidegger's own practice as an interpreter-translator, before turning to see how this might apply to our interpreting-translating of Heidegger.

In the lecture series published as *What is Called Thinking?* Heidegger devotes Lectures 6–11 to the question as to how to translate a fragment of the 'Presocratic' thinker Parmenides (and, indeed, one can also read the preceding lectures as primarily introductory to this sustained meditation on the eight Greek words χρὴ τὸ λέγειν τε νοεῖν τ' ἐόν ἔμμεναι (*chre to legein te noein t'eon emmenai*). 'According to the usual translation,' Heidegger tells us (only, of course, he actually *said* this in *German,* not English), this means '"One should both say and think that Being is."'[2] Very near the start of his attempt to challenge this translation and to arrive at a more adequate alternative, Heidegger warns against the presumption that 'we', that is modern Western readers, 'are approaching Parmenides' saying in an objective manner and without presuppositions when we take cognizance of it without any intimations and even without giving it thought'.[3]

With these words we are already embroiled in problems stemming from the fact that we are now attempting to follow Heidegger's reflections in English, rather than in the original German. 'Take cognizance of it without any intimations' is, at the very least, inelegant and, at first glance, seems somewhat vague. We might be tempted to jump straight to 'without giving it thought', which could, fairly, be said to summarize the thrust of the sentence as a whole – although when one encounters such a phrase in a work entitled *What is Called Thinking?* one should, perhaps, pause for thought. Nevertheless, the word 'intimations' is worth reflecting further on, since it gives us some clue as to what reading or hearing the saying in a thinking way might involve.

Heidegger's German word *ahnen,* like the English 'intimation', carries rich associations of philosophical and literary meaning, not least from the era of romanticism and idealism, where it has connotations similar to those of such English phrases as 'intuiting' (in a non-philosophical sense), 'having a sense of or feeling for', 'having a premonition of', or, indeed, 'intimation of' – as in Wordsworth's 'intimations of immortality'. Having an 'intimation' is the sense of there being something more to a phenomenon, an experience, or a feeling than can immediately or definitively be said concerning it, something that eludes us, even as we are drawn towards it. To have an 'intimation' concerning the saying of Parmenides would, then, be to sense that it is conveying or addressing something more than what is given in the 'usual translation'. Without such a sense, indeed, the phrase becomes precisely a piece of 'idle chatter' in the sense of *Being and Time*, that is, something that's put into circulation and passed around without any more notice being taken of it than we usually notice the design of a coin, since all that matters, we assume, is its 'cash-value'. But merely to repeat 'what is known' about (in this case) Parmenides' saying and not to try to think for ourselves what it is that the saying itself is intimating is, precisely, to hear it and appropriate it without giving it any thought. In these terms the saying cannot, of course, add anything to the depth, clarity, or value of our own thought.

As he goes on to make clear, Heidegger's criticism is not merely or even primarily directed against the kind of 'thoughtlessness' one might expect from non-philosophers, but 'where every seemingly pertinent and apposite citation from all of the world's philosophical literature is indiscriminately thrown in' (*What is Called Thinking?*, p. 176). That is to say, we do not understand what Parmenides meant by the term 'Being' by saying (for example) that 'Parmenides introduced the idea of Being into Western philosophy; thereafter it was taken up and further developed by Plato and Aristotle, passing into the vocabulary of scholasticism, where, according to Aquinas, Being became a primary feature of the Deity, etc.' The meaning of Being – whatever that is – cannot simply be read off from some such grand narrative of the history of ideas. Nor could we understand Parmenides' meaning by applying some ready-made definition of Being derived from some other philosophical source (Aristotle, perhaps), and still less by assuming the view of some philosophers that 'Being' is a meaningless piece of metaphysical mystification. In any case (and as Heidegger already noted in the pre-Introductory page of *Being and Time*), we moderns have for the most part lost the capacity to be 'perplexed at our inability to understand the expression "Being"', a perplexity to which, as he points out, Plato already owned up. But such a perplexity would, Heidegger avers, be a necessary precondition for even beginning to think about what the meaning of 'Being' might be. Before we can slot Parmenides' saying into a given narrative of the history of ideas or use it to contribute to the construction of a doctrine of Being – can we say 'an ontology'? – we ought, therefore, to pause for long enough to admit to some perplexity as to what anything said about 'Being' could possibly mean. And, as Heidegger goes on to show, if we do so, we will soon find ourselves wondering whether Parmenides did, in fact, say anything about *Being* (or *Sein*) in the sense in which that term is used in modern – or even post-Aristotle – ontologies. In these terms, philosophers who think they know what Parmenides must have meant by saying 'One should both say and think that Being is' are likely to do far more damage than the non-philosopher who openly admits that all he knows about what Parmenides meant is what he read in such and such an encyclopaedia article.

So, we have to stop and think. And, in stopping, and 'without regard to later philosophy and its achievements in interpreting this thinker, we shall try to listen to the saying, so to speak, in the first bloom of the words – *aus der Frische der Worte*' (*What is Called Thinking?*, p. 176).[4] Over fifty pages of text on, it becomes clear that the issue is not how to translate or to justify translating the Greek words ἐὸν ἔμμεναι into their modern German or English equivalents, but, as Heidegger says, 'it is necessary for us to translate these words finally into Greek' (*What is Called Thinking*, p. 232). But isn't this merely to restate the problem, which is precisely that we don't understand the Greek words and therefore need them to be translated? How can we listen to the saying 'in the first bloom of the words'? Isn't this just what has been lost, irretrievably lost? And isn't this loss itself a decisive factor in Heidegger's own larger philosophical picture, since he repeatedly portrays the shift that occurred in the eclipsing of the early, Pre-Socratic Greek experience of truth by the subsequent rise of philosophy (as we know it) as a necessary element in the destiny of the West, the evening-land that is cut off in its very foundations from the first morning glow of the primordial experience of truth?

Yet, at least in *What is Called Thinking?*, Heidegger does seem to hold out some hope that we might be capable of translating these words – our philosophical vocabulary – back into Greek. He acknowledges that this won't be easy, not least if we've become habituated to learning our philosophy in the mode of idle chatter, of repeating and disseminating only what everybody agrees is the case. 'Such translation is possible', he says, 'only if we transpose ourselves into what speaks from these words. And this transposition can succeed only by a leap, the leap of a single vision which sees what the words ἐὸν ἔμμεναι, heard with Greek ears, state, or tell' (*What is Called Thinking?*, p. 232).

Something odd seems to be happening here. Heidegger has been asking us to *listen* to the saying, to *hear* the words in their first bloom. Now, however, there has been a metaphorical shift, and we are being told that we have to *see* what Parmenides is saying. However, Heidegger seems to know what he is doing, since he immediately asks 'Can we see something that is told?' His answer appears to be unequivocal: 'We can, provided what is told is more than just the sound of words, provided that seeing is more than just the seeing with the eyes of the body' (*What is Called Thinking?*, p. 232). We are once more, it seems, in the realm of 'intimation', of seeing, or sensing, a 'more', a surplus in Parmenides' words that reaches beyond what a simple verbal translation into a modern and (over-)familiar language could possible give. What we now have to do is to look in the same direction as Parmenides was looking, to be aware of what Parmenides was aware of, and what he sought to 'say' in his saying. And this, Heidegger says, is simply the presence of Being: that when we speak truthfully we speak with regard to the way in which what we speak of is present to us.

> The word says: presence of what is present. What it says *speaks* in our speech long before thinking gives attention and a name of its own to it. When thinking is expressed, this unspoken something is merely clothed in a word. It is not an invention but a discovery, discovered in the presence of the present already expressed in language. (*What is Called Thinking?*, p. 235)

Heidegger would be the first to acknowledge the difficulty of what he is asking of his readers. 'Leap and vision', he says, 'require long, slow preparation . . .' (*What is Called Thinking?*, p. 233). Yet he would also want to insist that we do not confuse this difficulty with the kind of difficulty usually associated with philosophical problems, It is not a conceptual difficulty, not a matter of juggling abstract ideas, and, therefore, not the kind of thing that only certain specially gifted intellectuals can do. On the contrary, habits of abstraction may be damaging to what is being attempted here. The problem is not to stretch our already over-developed capacity for abstraction still further, but to step out of our habitual abstraction and distraction into a direct acknowledgement of what, basically, is the most obvious but equally most overlooked thing of all.

At a much earlier stage in the lectures, attempting to interpret the word 'idea' Heidegger has spoken about another leap, the leap we take when we, quite simply, stand and face a tree in bloom.

> The tree faces us. The tree and we meet one another, as the tree stands there and we stand face to face with it. As we are in this relation of one to the other and before the other, the tree and we *are* . . . Let us stop here for a moment, as we would catch our breath before and after a leap. For that is what we *are* now, men who have leapt, out of the familiar realm of science and even . . . out of the realm of philosophy. (*What is Called Thinking?*, p. 41)[5]

In such an encounter with a tree (or the sky, or a rock, or a river . . .) we – any of us, any time – can experience what it is to stand in the presence of Being, to encounter the beings we encounter as they are in their Being-there. And, in so encountering them, we perhaps also become aware of what it is for we ourselves to be: we *are,* as Heidegger emphatically puts it, when we stand in a face-to-face relation to the tree.

Parmenides is inviting us to just such a leap, Heidegger seems to be saying – with the difference that, after all, a tree is a tree, and Parmenides' saying is a saying, a word, a call voiced in language. The importance of this is that we do not, as a matter of experience, live primarily in a word-less world of silently encountered entities. As the human beings we are, our world, our experience, our life, is mediated by language. The world we actually inhabit, the world in which our lives can be experienced as meaningful, is a linguistically-shaped world. This being so, Parmenides' word serves a somewhat different function from the injunction simply to stop and look at the tree in front of us. Such an injunction would, of course, also be a word, a saying, in language. What Parmenides' word does that the injunction does not do is to draw our attention back to language itself and to the miracle that can happen when – if – language too may become a mode of our being present to the presence – the Being – of beings. As such, Parmenides' word is not a word that we simply act upon. It is a word we have to listen to, to understand, to interpret, to translate – and then to translate back into Greek and to *see*. And, note, it is paradigmatic for Heidegger's approach to translating Parmenides that it is only after a 50-page preparation that he invites us to leap back into the seeing of the original Greek vision of the presence of Being. From where we are now, and as we are now, we cannot simply by-pass the whole history of translation and interpretation that lies between us and this original experience: before we can make the leap there are assumptions that need to be challenged and habits that need to be unlearned, and there is a whole history of what Heidegger variously calls 'metaphysics' and 'the forgetting of Being' that needs to be reckoned with. In these terms, the translation of a single saying of Parmenides is inseparable from the whole strategy of Heidegger's later philosophy, with its multiple readings and re-readings of key texts from the history of Western philosophy and, indeed, from Western art and poetry. Yet, as we noted at the beginning of this discussion, this history does not *explain* Parmenides' saying, and if we are to understand it, we have to hear it in its own terms as saying just what it says and nothing besides. To understand Parmenides is, in this perspective, essentially to repeat the word and the thought of Parmenides. It is to stand, once more, in the presence of Being to which his word points us.

Once more? We inheritors of the Western tradition have, on Heidegger's reading, long since lost our sense for Being, our intimation of the Being of beings, our capacity for presence. Yet 'once more' in that, although we are late arrivals in the long history of the forgetting of Being, Parmenides' original experience of the truth of Being adjoins our history, and indeed inaugurates it. Therefore it still in some way belongs to us and to our possibilities of thinking. And there is more. For us, who have lost the original radiance of the truth of Being, who – prior to undertaking the work of interpretation – have lost our sense for the bloom of the words, such a repetition can even be spoken of as salvific, since it opens a possibility of thinking that our own habits of mind and our culturally institutionalized forms of education (and even the Latinized vocabulary of our conventional attempts at philosophizing) have largely eclipsed. As such it opens a prospect onto a history that is other than the history now realized in the universal hegemony of planetary technology that Heidegger sees as the outcome of Western philosophy.

We have, perhaps, been learning something about what translation meant for Heidegger – but how does this relate to the translation *of* Heidegger?

Clearly (we might assume) whatever problems there might be in translating Heidegger, they cannot be quite as formidable as those of translating a thinker who wrote in an ancient language and whose work is preserved only in fragments. German may be somewhat different from English, and German philosophy may be very different from Anglo-Saxon philosophy, but these differences surely occur within a horizon marked by many shared features – not least the history of philosophy itself, from the Presocratics to Kant. And, if the philosophical ways have diverged since then, there are many features of the modern experience that echo on in both more recent traditions. Whatever may be involved in leaping back into a vision of the primal unveiling of Being seen with Greek eyes, the experiences of which Heidegger himself wrote in *Being and Time* are experiences still close – all too close, some might say – to our own. The average everydayness that is the life of *Das Man*, immersed in a stream of idle chatter (including idle philosophical chatter), haunted by anxiety, and confronted by the nothingness of an ineluctable death – all these are experiences that, whatever the awkwardness of rendering a given German word or phrase by an English equivalent, are experiences we instantly recognize as our own. Even allowing for the historical events and cultural shifts that have intervened between 1927 and our own time, Heidegger, surely, speaks to us of what we know. Perhaps today we are more inclined to be bored rather than anxious (though Heidegger had something to say about that too), and perhaps we are less optimistic as to the possibilities of becoming authentic (though Heidegger himself never claimed to have become authentic and, if read closely, is extremely reserved and hesitant about the feasibility of such an achievement), yet the overall configuration of Dasein's self-awareness as set out in *Being and Time* would seem to be considerably closer to us and therefore considerably easier of access than the text and the world of Parmenides. We still stand within what a pupil of Heidegger's would come to designate its 'effective history'.

Yet our very proximity to Heidegger (strange and difficult as we might at first find him) pinpoints a problem that makes translating Heidegger very different from translating Parmenides. On Heidegger's own account, we do not live, as Parmenides lived, in the pure radiance of an original disclosure of Being. We live in that state of estrangement so powerfully detailed in *Being and Time*. We can scarcely be presumed even to understand the point in raising the question of Being in the first place. It follows that whereas we might fairly easily be persuaded of the virtue of suspending our critical faculties and submitting to the word of Parmenides, laying aside our habitual language and hearing-seeing the saying 'in Greek', we might be more resistant to doing that in relation to the 'word' of *Being and Time*. If Parmenides' saying offers a kind of salvation, Heidegger's vision seems to offer anything but that. For where

Parmenides (according to Heidegger) offers an open view on to the revelation of Being, Heidegger himself promises no more than an approach to a question, an approach on which we are not offered anything like a self-authenticating view of the matter at issue, but only a deepening sense for the perplexity that the question generates. And the more deeply that perplexity takes root, that is, the better we understand Heidegger, the more questionable the offer of a moment of authentic vision becomes. If the human condition – or, at least, the modern, Western condition – is as Heidegger describes it, how can we ever come out of it by our own power? But, then again, if we cannot come out of it, if we do not have a vantage point from which to evaluate the swirling fogs of life lost in the 'They', can we really know whether Heidegger is talking any sense at all? Can we even understand him?

One of the best-known events of Christian theology in Western Europe in the twentieth century is, of course, the attempt by Rudolf Bultmann to deploy Heidegger's existential analysis of human being as a means of explicating what is involved in the proclamation of the Christian message. Bultmann, though accused of selling his theological inheritance for a bowl of humanistic pottage (or, as Barth put it, of allowing the anthropological tail to wag the theological dog) is insistent on this point: that in the actual circumstances of human existence, the transition to authentic life is possible only on the basis of grace. Authenticity is not a factical possibility for human beings as they are. This would suggest that while the purely formal possibility of authenticity is understandable to anyone capable of philosophical reflection, what it could actually mean to a really existing person would only be knowable by one who had heard and responded to the call of divine grace. Would that then mean that only a Christian could understand Heidegger and, therefore, that only a Christian could translate him?

That would be over-rash. As Heidegger's own reflections on Parmenides indicate, he did not himself look in the direction of Christian faith for a revelation of the truth of Being in order adequately to ground his presentation of human existence. The strong presence of such Christian sources as Augustine, Luther, and Kierkegaard in *Being and Time* – not to mention the New Testament – make it plausible to see Christian faith as a privileged vantage point for understanding it. But, even in his most generous moments *vis-à-vis* theology, Heidegger could only allow this as one possible factical realization of the formal reflections offered in *Being and Time*. Later, it seems, he would, in his own mind at least, withdraw that possibility, preferring to look back to the Pre-Socratics, to the poetry of Hölderlin, or else to the thinkers of East Asia for points of reference in seeking redemption from the West's 'forgetting of Being'.

Equally, however, a Christian experience of authenticity – faith – would also seem to call into question many of the perspectives of *Being and Time* itself. For, as John Macquarrie's critical appreciation of the Bultmannian 'translation' of Heideggerian existentialism into Christian theology makes clear, the view of human existence that Heidegger offers is too thin, too reduced, to do justice to all that Christianity itself wants to say, not just about God, but about human existence (*Existentialist*, esp. pp. 233–46).

If, then, a Christian theologian is to translate Heidegger (and whether or not we write down or publish our translations, every theologian who engages with Heidegger's thought is to some extent also engaged in translating him) he will first have to understand him; but that understanding cannot, as Heidegger's own recommendations for translating Parmenides suggest, simply consist in submitting ourselves to Heidegger's word and hearing it with his German ears. Christian theology's translation of Heidegger – understanding the term 'translation' both in its conventional sense but also as translation-interpretation – will always be a critical and argumentative encounter with Heidegger's own text. This, to answer the question asked at the start of this essay, is the only possible understanding of the text that can provide an adequate basis for the venture of translation. In this connection it is perhaps no accident that *An Existentialist Theology* was John Macquarrie's first publication with SCM Press since this was precisely a critical exposition of how far Heideggerian anthropology and ontology could be incorporated into the world of Christian theology. And, with reference far beyond Heidegger, we may conclude that only one who is capable of such critical reading will also be capable of translating any significant theological or philosophical work.

Notes

1 In M. Heidegger, tr. E. Robinson and J. Macquarrie, *Being and Time*, Oxford: Blackwell, 1962, p. 13.

2 M. Heidegger, *What is Called Thinking?*, ed. J. Glenn Gray, New York: Harper and Row, 1968, p. 171.

3 Heidegger, *What is Called Thinking?*, p. 177.

4 See also M. Heidegger, *Was Heißt Denken?* Tübingen: Max Niemeyer, 1984, p. 109.

5 For a further discussion of this passage see A. Rudd, *Expressing the World*, Chicago: Open Court, 2003, pp. 221 ff.

5 John Macquarrie at Union Theological Seminary in New York City

RONALD H. STONE

John Macquarrie arrived at Union Theological Seminary in 1962. His commitments to existentialism found a ready welcome in the department dominated seven years earlier by Paul Tillich. Reinhold Niebuhr, who also learned from Martin Heidegger, had retired two years earlier, but Roger Shinn was writing on existentialism and John Knox continued the Rudolf Bultmann tradition in New Testament hermeneutics. His arrival coincided with the publication of Heideggers's *Being and Time* (1962) which he and Edward Robinson, with much sweat and tears, had translated. His earlier works, *An Existentialist Theology* (1955) and *The Scope of Demythologizing* (1960), had introduced him to Union and evoked deep appreciation for the quality of his thought. The translation certainly established him along with Paul Tillich as a leader in existentialist theology. But like Tillich, and earlier Heidegger, he was not just an existentialist. His phenomenological study of humanity, using Husserl via Heidegger, was set in classical ontological reflection on being. His reading of Heidegger on human existence, criticized by Joan Stambaugh, another translator of *Being and Time* (Albany: State University of New York Press, 1996), as almost mystical, led him to move through philosophical theology towards a revelation of Being as holy. Human existence itself, interpreted by Heidegger, was more open to a religious interpretation than even Heidegger knew. His move from human nature's openness to a revelation of meaning and grace was similar to Paul Tillich's but it was more of one piece. For Macquarrie the theology of symbols rose out of the ontological-existentialist commitments to the phenomenological analysis of the human, whereas for Tillich the gap remained and answers were correlated. In 1965 both Tillich and Macquarrie had courses listed in the Union catalogue. Tillich's death that year prohibited his return to New York. Macquarrie succeeded Robert McAfee Brown in teaching the introduction to theology while Paul Lehmann developed the required doctrine course previously taught by Daniel D. Williams. Macquarrie's elective courses included courses on eschatology and atonement as well as nineteenth- and twentieth-century religious thought. His regular offering under the systematic theology listing of courses in *Being and Time* and on Heidegger's later writings showed his commitments. His remarkably clear exposition of *Martin Heidegger* (1968) was the fruit of both his classroom explanations and his earlier translation.

His years at Union were the time of his most existentialist writings. His inaugural lecture in 1962 (reprinted in *Theologian*, pp. 43–56) was a dialogue with Sartre on the meaning of human life. Following both Heidegger and Tillich he analyzed life to show that a possible response to the human condition was to say that Being itself was gracious. Beyond the nihilism of Nietzsche or Sartre, he thought he could present logically and coherently a view of life that human faith could affirm. His own definition of God from his inaugural lecture has always remained in my mind as one of the real options for God-talk: 'God is the religious word for Being, understood as gracious' (*Studies*, p. 11). This anthology of his technical writings from the first half of the 1960s provides more technical arguments for his interpretation and application of Heidegger. His identification with the spirit and project of his predecessor Paul Tillich echoes throughout the arguments. When making the choice of ontological insights he more frequently turns to the early Heidegger. In so doing he makes more clear than Tillich his dependence as a theologian on Heidegger's ontology.

For me, if not for other students or Macquarrie himself, approaching theology from Heidegger's phenomenology of death was difficult going at Union in the 1960s. I remember an occasion when Macquarrie, the lecturer, had to admonish students to listen carefully to serious reflection on death. It was too dark and too Teutonic for students whose natural inclinations inclined them to think of human existence as either love or politics. For those students was human existence, even if it were thrown, really thrown toward death? Maybe as the Vietnam War heated up under President Johnson, and the body bags coming home became a symbol of America, some of the students could focus on death. But my memory of those days is of a deeper response to Reinhold Niebuhr's ironic reading of the politics of the 1960s, and of great appreciation for Daniel Day Williams' course on love. In *Principles of Christian Theology* (1966), Macquarrie presented a typology of world religions in order to open intra-religious conversation. I wonder what the results would have been if Heidegger had focused on human existence being that of a religious response rather than on it as an authentic being toward death. Or maybe the religions could have been analyzed as a human response to death. Of course, there was an optimistic naiveté in many students in the 1960s. They thought the world could be changed through the Church. Many thought democratic protest would end the war. Macquarrie knew better. Both he and Heidegger had their reasons for looking at death, but it was hard to convince American students to look with them. Macquarrie's organizing of ministry to tens of thousands of German prisoners of war in North Africa had confronted him with human brokenness and fallenness which the students of the 1960s had not known.

In reviewing my copy of *Studies* for this essay, I noticed it was autographed by John Macquarrie. He would often present his students with one of his own books – an act of generosity which inspired others later to do the same. The whole Union faculty knew Union had to live by its wits, and the ethos encouraged continual research and frequent publication. Shortly after John Knox's book, *The Church and the Reality of Christ* (1962), appeared, the seminary president, John C. Bennett, told me how grateful he was for such a productive faculty. He said 'it was encouraging to know that by the time he was brushing his teeth in the morning, John Knox had been up and had written another chapter for Union.' The connection between Christ and the Church as the body of Christ in that book undergirded part of John Macquarrie's retort to the secular theologians of the 1960s.

Principles of Christian Theology (1966)

Macquarrie's *Principles* appeared in the middle of his tenure at Union. I had assisted him the previous year in the first course in theology, Systematic Theology 101. When *Principles* was published, I was studying philosophy at Oxford and collecting readings for his *Contemporary Religious Thinkers* (1968) and so did not feel the full force of the book. It is remarkable in showing how far a secular philosophy could be pulled into Christian theology, and how one brought up a Scottish Presbyterian could move towards Roman Catholicism.

The references to John Calvin and Calvinism are almost all negative. It is both Macquarrie's deep commitment to human freedom and his *via media* temperament that disinclined him from continuing in the Calvinism that brought him into ordained ministry. Not quite able to go with Pelagius' optimism, he affirms his freedom and resolves for a semi-Pelagian position which is more at home in Catholicism, Methodism or Anglicanism than in Calvinism. Macquarrie is quite at ease with human movement, and his own migration into relatively high-church Anglicanism would be for him, I would think, a move toward greater fulfillment of his personal vocation.

There were at the time of the book's publication no Roman Catholics teaching at Union. The seminary was enjoying the high-water marks of ecumenical, Protestant Church success. The move of Woodstock College to partnership with Union would come a few years later. Robert McAfee Brown's pioneering *rapprochement* with Catholicism had faded from Union with his return to Stanford. I myself would visit Vatican II and help with some translations, but concentrating on social ethics after returning to New York did not see how far John had moved towards Catholicism.

Interestingly, Macquarrie does not refer to Paul Lehmann in the volume. He was critical of Lehmann's mentors, Karl Barth and John Calvin, but silent about Lehmann himself. Daniel Day Williams had asked me to tutor theology for the year 1964–5. I anticipated working with Dr. Williams, but the lot fell on Macquarrie to teach semester one, Systematic Theology 101, on Method and the Doctrine of God. Paul Lehmann taught the second course on Christ, Spirit, humanity and the Church. Macquarrie built his philosophical or natural theology out of Heidegger's humanistic ontology and perspective on death. Lehmann started semester two, supposedly building on semester one, by rejecting humanistic apologetics and non-theistic ontologies. He began with biblical revelation from his perspective on Calvin, and the second semester was Lehmann's interpretation of and apology for Calvin, the text used being Calvin's *Institutes of the Christian Religion*. The contrast between two terms of what was to be a year-long introduction to theology was too much for many of the students. Three years later these students, now seniors, would lead the student revolt at Union while one of them served as student body president of Columbia during its 1968 revolt. Without mentioning each other's names except in debates in the *Union Seminary Quarterly Review* there was a theological war going on between Macquarrie and Lehmann in the minds of 140 very bright students. Beverly Harrison and George Boyd joined me for the second semester assisting Lehmann and I think their compassionate leadership of discussion sections on the *Institutes* helped the students understand what was happening in their theological education.

Meanwhile, Macquarrie was moving. He told me that the Episcopal Church in the USA was closer to the Church of Scotland than the Presbyterian Church in the USA, but his move was deeper and bolder. The friendship with and counsel of the New Testament Professor John Knox helped him in the transition to the Episcopal Church. *Principles* is dedicated to Knox and it consistently tears down barriers that would prevent convinced Protestants from uniting with Roman Catholicism or, going two-thirds of the way, by joining the Anglican Communion. Bringing the episcopate into his four foundations of the Church along with Scripture, creed, and tradition he makes room for a papal foundation even though preferring a conciliar form of governance. Finishing the course with him, I was present at his ordination as deacon in the Cathedral of St John the Divine. Paul Lehmann took the empty seat beside me. As the service concluded, Paul said, as the incense drifted around his head, 'All I can say, Ron, is Thank God for John Calvin.' The students in those theology courses did not perceive in 1964–5 that the English Civil War was being fought in their heads. If *Principles* had been published before I assisted in those courses I would have been more aware. Michael Walzer's *The Revolution of the Saints* (1965) would have also been of great assistance.

As one would expect, Paul Lehmann, the Calvinist, was the theologian of the three systematic theologians most enthralled by the student revolt. Daniel D. Williams, the liberal process theologian, was the one most tortured by the radical absoluteness and confrontational style of the radical students of 1968. Macquarrie understood the revolt, but was less drawn into it. He had found his *via media*, and his theology was floated more freely of student politics. I remember his more withdrawn role in a panel discussion on the revolution in which he criticized the reduction of everything to politics. He objected to this over-politicization by suggesting the absurdity of thinking of politicizing love or sexuality. I remember, also, a week later seeing a placard announcing for the 'free' curriculum at Columbia a course entitled 'Sexual intercourse in a political context'.

Macquarrie's own review of his career in 1980 and again in 1986 (*Theology*, pp. 1–9) saw *Principles* as his transition from 'the rather dreary evangelical Protestantism in which I had been reared' (*Theology*, p. 1) to Catholicism in its Anglican form. His own conviction that to become Catholic meant to take the whole system into oneself explains even further how he managed to consider topics like the virgin birth, Mariology, infallibility, the episcopacy, marriage as a sacrament, and other topics usually foreign to Protestant consideration. Beyond that, his attraction to the thought of Karl Rahner as he exposited Heidegger on death provided another bridge noted in his Festschrift *Being and Truth* (1986). *Principles* is a transition book in which Macquarrie moved in his ecumenical way beyond the Union Theological Seminary of that time. He even specifically criticized the Protestant attempts at ecumenicity which were building national union churches. His vision was of a restored world Church where the Pope would have a 'certain' primacy among bishops and respect would be given to Rome as the most illustrious of ancient sees. Subsequent years have confirmed how millions became 'cafeteria Catholics' without swallowing the whole meal of Roman Catholic teaching.

Philosophy of Language

God-Talk: An Examination of the Language and Logic of Theology (1967) is the most technical book from Macquarrie's time at Union. It integrates his lectures on language from 1962 to 1966 into one thorough argument. Here the thought of Ian Ramsey is integrated into Macquarrie's system completing the coupling of Oxford discussion of linguistic philosophy to Heidegger's phenomenology. No one else has done this so powerfully and clearly. Macquarrie's thought is an original synthesis. If a contemporary philosopher of religion were to read only one book of Macquarrie from the 1960s this should be the volume. I do not know whether Gilbert Ryle ever read Macquarrie, but I remember him tripping over his lamp cord and cursing after advising me not study with Ian Ramsey in 1965. I profited from my study with Ramsey and I wish I had read Macquarrie's book when it first appeared, for together those two were powerful antidotes to the positivist atheism underlying some of Oxford's philosophy of language in the 1960s. The volume analyzes theological language in Athanasius, Bultmann, Barth, Tillich, and Heidegger while examining mythology, symbols, analogy. paradox, and empirical language. He is persuaded by the language of existence and ontology as the central language for theology. Given human openness he argues that faith and ontological language can be persuasive. The language can stand up to critical analysis and defend, he believed, its truth claims. He provided language about God that was helpful in protecting my faith when it was challenged by philosophical positivism. Again one can note that Macquarrie was contending with the secularism of the United Kingdom, Germany, and France in his arguments. A more primitive religious language and uncritical mythology was more alive in America than he seemed to note. Today, 40 years removed from this linguistic work of the 1960s, millions of Americans apparently live in a religious-mythical world that was regarded by Macquarrie as an impossible habitation.

Against Secular Theology

An earlier suggested title for this volume, a tribute to John Macquarrie, was *The Eirenic Theologian*, and that captures much of his spirit as a writer of theology. He has no taste for polemics. The scholarly consensus has been that in his exposition of others' work he has been fair. His history of modern thought, *Twentieth-Century Religious Thought: The Frontiers of Philosophy and Theology, 1900–1960* (1963) and the reader, *Contemporary Religious Thinkers* (1968) which he edited were both praised for judicious selection and non-polemical discussion.

Another facet of Macquarrie was that he was a theologian of the Church. When theologians, professors of religion, or bishops produced theological works that undermined the Church's central perspectives, he reacted vehemently. One whom he criticized, Gabriel Vahanian, dismissed Macquarrie's God and Secularity (1967) as 'unfertile polemic'. This book on the death of God theologians, exponents of religionless Christianity, and Christian apostles of the secular, was certainly the most critical work about other theologians from his years at Union. He could find things to affirm in their writings, but his response to those who would try to do Christian theology without God was severe. It did not make sense to try to focus Christianity on Jesus, whose life was focused on God, without focusing on God. Christianity was a religion, not only an ethic. Christianity without prayer, sacraments, ritual, and religious community was very thin. To stay at a secular level was boring and unfruitful. Faith properly understood was to Macquarrie 'an utterly convincing reality' and atheism was a highly improbable option for the world humans lived within. The secular was better understood through the doctrines of creation, incarnation, Church, sacraments, and eschatology than in terms of human autonomy. In view of God and Secularity a full description of Macquarrie's work would need terms like 'tough reasonableness as well as eirenic. I do not recall Macquarrie ever using the term 'heresy' in these arguments, but the emphasis on death of God, religionless Christianity, and secular gospel, were all emphases which threatened to break the 'theological circle' of Church teaching.

Christian Ethics

In the latter half of his tenure at Union, Macquarrie turned to ethics. This turn represented by A Dictionary of Christian Ethics (1967) was a return to his partners in British scholarship. He said that it was coincidence that of the contributors 'half belonged to the Old world and half to the New' (Dictionary, p. vi). Now there was no entry on Heidegger and the essay by Carl Machaleson on existentialist ethics only mentioned his thought briefly. The topics covered represented the interests of scholars in the United Kingdom as much as they did American interests. They also expressed, as did his follow-up book Three Issues in Ethics (1970), how affected Macquarrie was by secular philosophy as a source for Christian ethics. He took the secular and non-religious thinkers more seriously than his counterparts in Christian ethics at Union did. Religion in Great Britain did not command the influence and respect that it easily assumed in the United States. Great Britain was becoming more hedonistic and non-Christian while the United States was becoming more hedonistic and Christian. The *Dictionary* appeared in 1967, the year I became an instructor at Union, and so I was able to refer students to it for my next 36 years' teaching Christian ethics. It provided good value both in its first edition and the later revised edition with Professor James Childress (1986).

The discipline of Christian ethics owes Macquarrie substantial thanks for his labour eliciting 366 pages of diverse writings by ethicists. Contemporary ethicists are not all good writers, and Macquarrie's volume is full of solid prose. Many who promised him essays could not deliver them by the publisher's deadlines, and rather than forego needed entries he laboriously wrote them himself. Macquarrie's statement in the preface: 'An editor's lot is not always a happy one, but to edit a book of this kind is an exciting educational experience,' was a substantial understatement.

A further word is needed about *Three Issues of Ethics* (1970) which concluded his stay at Union. It reflects both the Union ethos and the state of the debate about philosophical and Christian ethics in the United Kingdom of the late 1960s. It is dedicated to John C. Bennett, President of Union from 1963 to 70, during Macquarrie's tenure. Roger Shinn, Union's Professor of ethics is often quoted positively and Paul Lehmann, Macquarrie's colleague in theology is thoroughly critiqued. It is interesting that Reinhold Niebuhr, the dominant though retired, figure at Union is mentioned only once and that critically in a reference by the British philosopher W. G. Maclagan. Macquarrie does not like the influence of St Augustine and John Calvin in Christian theology, particularly regarding human freedom, and Niebuhr reflects these influences, though on freedom his position is essentially that of Macquarrie.

Niebuhr's ethic differs from Macquarrie in its shape on account of its reliance upon the love-justice axis for ethics. But on the three issues Macquarrie discusses in 1970 their positions are similar. (1) Both use their anthropology as a foundation for their ethics, though Niebuhr makes more of sin than Macquarrie while he also draws upon Heidegger who is assumed rather than named in *Three Issues*. (2) Both affirm a limited use of natural law or human reason in Christian ethics opening their reflections to the use of philosophical ethics. (3) Both hold that morals and religion are historically related, but that one could be moral without being officially religious. Together they taught that religious ideas enrich ethical discourse. In addition, both were critical of the misnamed 'new morality', and both relied on Christian hope while avoiding utopianism in their ethics. The absence of Niebuhr on human nature, history, or sin would not have been as surprising to British readers in 1970 as it was to American readers. Niebuhr was not very influential in the ethical discourse of Oxford in the 1960s. But the BBC produced a movie and a TV programme on him. Isaiah Berlin knew and respected Niebuhr and welcomed a paper on him in his graduate philosophy seminar. Tony Benn and others in British government had a Niebuhrian strand in their political thought. Niebuhr's paradoxes were not so welcome to the analytic philosophy of the time nor to Macquarrie, who was also wrestling with British analytical thinking.

Leaving Union

The Macquarries had settled into Union and America. I naturally consulted Mrs Macquarrie, a school teacher, about my own son's education. John learned to drive on the right-hand side of the road, practising in my 1960 Falcon for his New York State driver's licence examination. His later book *The Concept of Peace* (1973) reflected the turmoil of Union Seminary in New York City during the Vietnam War. On the other major American crisis, that of race relations, he did not write a book. But his family quietly and without announcement worshipped at St. Mary's Church of Manhattanville, a nearby predominantly Black Episcopalian church. Christopher Niebuhr told me (in October 2005) that John Macquarrie was particularly loved by the black teenage boys of Harlem who worshipped in that congregation. Practically they dealt with New York City, Union, and America, but particularly in the realm of mind and spirit John Macquarrie was a very contemporary British philosopher, though enriched by continental existentialism.

I spent the best year of my life in Oxford in 1965–6. So a couple of years later when John asked me about accepting his invitation to Oxford, I could only encourage him to accept. I had no idea then that as a student he had turned down an opportunity to study at Cambridge, in order to enter the parish ministry. The Lady Margaret chair of Divinity at Christ Church was an offer too good to refuse and to my uninformed American eyes that was particularly true for a Scot of relatively humble origins. A visit to the Macquarrie family at Christ Church in 1972 confirmed, for me at least, the wisdom of the choice. My son was delighted both by the rabbit in the priory and Mrs Macquarrie's pointing out the hole under the tree for the rabbit of *Alice in Wonderland*.

It was not only that Oxford was such an enchanted place. Union had been shaken by the events of 1968 and its increasing radicalism and more democratic governance introduced elements of discord into the community. Union was suffering both financially and spiritually by the time Macquarrie left in 1970. As late as 1967 when I joined the faculty as instructor, respect, cordiality, academic excellence and consensus characterized the community's life. The need for reducing the budget by not replacing faculty and the reality of a few faculty members beginning to be lured away affected morale. But to my mind, most of all there was a revolt by students and some young faculty against the 'fathers'. Beverly Harrison has told me that in her days as a student they treated the faculty 'as gods'. In the late 1960s that changed with students challenging the curriculum, the status quo, and the Union consensus. The college students coming to Union in the late 1960s brought social utopianism and a cynicism about their elders which were direct challenges to the Union ethos of Christian realism. The short-lived attempt at more democratic governance under the pressure of the student revolt allowed all sorts of dissidence to emerge. The discord continued for years, but even by the time Macquarrie needed to respond to the offer from Oxford, Union had changed. The few glimpses I had of John Macquarrie in the later years of the 1970s and the 1980s when I visited or lectured at Oxford persuaded me that the Union years had been good for him, but that he belonged in Oxford.

6 A Roman Catholic Response to *Principles*

AVERY CARDINAL DULLES S.J.

In 1966 Professor Macquarrie published yet another work of extraordinary interest to me, his *Principles of Christian Theology*.* This too was an amazing performance, showing the author's wide-ranging interests and manifold competences. Nearly any major synthetic work on systematic theology takes decades to compose. One thinks of Barth's efforts from the early 1930s until his death in the late 60s, or Paul Tillich's three-volume work which was some two decades in the making. Macquarrie's work is somewhat shorter – a little less than 500 pages – but almost equally comprehensive. In the introduction he speaks of a four-year interval between the publisher's invitation and the completion of the work. But anyone acquainted with even the broad outlines of Macquarrie's activities must be aware that he could not have been by any means exclusively taken up with this work during these four years, and so the book is a remarkable demonstration of the speed and efficiency with which he evidently works.

The approach here, as in Macquarrie's other work, is highly ecumenical. He himself expresses the hope that his presentation will be helpful 'to readers of a wide range of Christian traditions' and there is no question but that in this he has succeeded. He has kind words about the theological leadership presently being given by certain Roman Catholics, especially Karl Rahner, whom Macquarrie says he has found 'the most helpful among contemporary theologians'. Not surprisingly, therefore, Macquarrie's *Principles*, in paperback, has found its way into many Catholic colleges as a textbook.

As a theologian concerned with revelation, I was particularly pleased by the manner in which Macquarrie handles this subject. Drawing

---

* This is an extract from an unpublished lecture delivered at the Trinity Institute in New York City on 14 May 1970. Page references are therefore to the first (1966) edition.

extensively on modern phenomenology, he distinguishes between two types of revelation. By primordial or classic revelation, he understands a disclosive experience of the holy which offers a model (or paradigm) for the subsequent experience of the holy within a given community. The subsequent re-enactment of the disclosive experience within such a community he calls 'repetitive revelation', a term more or less equivalent to Tillich's 'dependent' revelation. In his analysis of the experience of the holy, Macquarrie closely follows Rudolf Otto. The *mysterium tremendum et fascinans* is in Macquarrie's view the grasp of the transcendent as gracious. Faith, which perceives the divine reality as gracious, is always a particular, concrete experience; it comes to the individual or to the community as a gift. Hence all revelation is special. There is no such thing as general revelation.

The content of revelation, Macquarrie maintains, is the dimension of depth found within the realities present to us in experience. Thus revelation has no particular content that can be directly expressed in verbal statements. Rather, it is the self-communication of being itself, which seizes the whole of man and penetrates his entire life. But believers must make use of particular symbols in order to speak of the ways in which the divine has become manifest to them. Symbols drawn from personal life have the highest adequacy. Christ, in this perspective, becomes the supreme revelation of God. The formulas of faith that come down from apostolic times or from the early Church are not themselves revelation, but they point to the event of revelation as it was experienced by the primitive Church, and call for reappropriation in later ages. Christians today are not bound to adhere to the letter of primitive formulas, but must re-express the divine self-manifestation as it comes to them through 'repetitive revelation', which continues to take place with the tradition.

Macquarrie's doctrine of revelation seems to me to be in line with the best theology of our time. It safeguards the value of tradition as a vital source of contemporary ecclesial experience and retains sufficient flexibility so that tradition is not felt to be a straightjacket which might impede authentic religious experience in the Church today. While I agree with Macquarrie that revelation is primarily a depth experience, I would perhaps emphasize more than he does that revelation has a distinctive content – namely that which the experience discloses about God and his gracious purposes.

When Macquarrie turns to the sources and channels of revelation, which are of crucial importance for his theological method, I have no difficulty in accepting his general position. In addition to revelation and experience, of which I have already spoken, Macquarrie lists four other 'formative factors in theology': Scripture, tradition, culture and reason.

He regards Scripture and tradition as necessary to preserve the memory of the revelations from which the Christian community derives its identity. Many Christian theologians from different denominational traditions would be inclined to feel that Macquarrie, in his very valid concern to avoid biblicism, tends to minimize unduly the positive value of the Bible. In reading his book as a whole, I am impressed by the infrequency with which he settles questions by recourse to Scripture. He seems to be extremely selective in the passages which he does cite, and almost never, to my knowledge, grapples seriously with the total testimony of the Bible with regard to any given problem – for example the creation, the attributes of God, the nature of life beyond death.

While Macquarrie obviously works within the broad stream of Christian tradition and especially Christian tradition as it today exists in the Anglican communion, he does not make it very clear what authority he attributes to the documents of tradition. In this respect his approach differs from that common to Roman Catholic theology – and a comparison with Rahner would, I think, make the difference clear. Rahner is very careful, in his discussion of any theological problem, to square his statements with the binding teaching of the Church, which he tries to ascertain by careful exegesis and appraisal of papal and conciliar documents. When I read Macquarrie's systematic work, my reaction – which is that of a moderately conservative Roman Catholic, and therefore one which I would not expect most Protestants and Anglicans to share – my reaction, I say, is that his theorizing seems arbitrary, and therefore somewhat impoverished. When all is said and done, one can say only: that is what Macquarrie thinks. Even where he clearly adheres to the tradition, as he does on most doctrinal points, Macquarrie does not seem to take the pains that most Roman Catholic dogmaticians would take to show that his views are indeed those which the Church must and does profess. Some occasional references to creeds such as the *Quicumque* do not seem to anchor his conclusions sufficiently in the Tradition, especially since Macquarrie never clarifies exactly what authority he attributes to the *Quicumque*. The greatest methodical deficiency in Macquarrie's work, as it would appear from my own point of view, is its comparatively feeble grounding in positive theology.

Turning from considerations of method to substantive doctrine, there would be much to say about the positions Macquarrie takes on various questions. The most original, and surely the most controversial, section of the book is that which deals with the doctrine of God. And it is here, I must confess, that I have the gravest misgivings. Appealing explicitly to Heidegger's doctrine, Macquarrie rejects the God of 'traditional theism' which would view God as a particular being, and substitutes a new doctrine which he labels 'existential-ontological theism'. According to this doctrine God is to be understood not as a being but as 'Being', or, in some sentences, as 'holy being'.

Although I am sure there are weaknesses in traditional theism, I do not see that they are the weaknesses that Macquarrie finds in it, and consequently I do not concede that they call for the radical solution he proposes. He gibes at traditional theism for holding that God is a person, 'but a strange metaphysical kind of person without a body'. I have to confess that this is the belief to which I have always adhered, unless one wishes to object somewhat pedantically that God is not a person but three persons. However that may be, it seems to me quite evident that God is personal; if he were not I do not see how he could know or love, forgive or answer prayers. If he did none of these things, I do not see how he could be the God made known to us through the Bible, the God of Jesus Christ, and the God of traditional Christianity. I am disturbed by Macquarrie's apparent reluctance to assign personal attributes to God. On finishing Macquarrie's book I felt some doubt about whether he believes in a God who is a free and conscious subject. If he does not, I am afraid that I have to separate myself very markedly from him at this point. Unlike many contemporary Christian thinkers, some of them Roman Catholic, I continue to hold that the term 'person' is properly attributable to God, though of course one must add that the attribution is by way of analogy, and that man has no positive and direct concept of what it means for God to be personal (or anything else). Our knowledge of God is achieved through the ascending dialectic of causality, negation and eminence – a method too complicated and subtle to describe in a brief critical survey of this kind.

I see no serious objection, then, to saying that God is personal. Macquarrie, however, seems to think that God should not be conceived as a person without a body. Such a person, he maintains, would have to be a 'strange metaphysical person'. Now I admit that it may be difficult for us, who are persons of a bodily kind, to conceive of persons who do not have bodies, but I see no rational grounds for denying that God could be personal in this way. I do not know any Christian who believes that God by nature does have a body (a view that would lead almost inevitably to pantheism or some other unhappy consequences).

Does traditional theism, then, hold that God is a 'strange metaphysical kind of person'? That God should be strange to us is not really strange; being God he could hardly be otherwise than strange to our way of thinking. Is he metaphysical? Not in the strict sense of the word. Metaphysics is a highly abstract mode of human thinking. God in himself is not metaphysical, though some human thought about God is metaphysical.

In the same crucial passage Macquarrie goes on to say that according to traditional theism God 'was another being in addition to the beings we know in the world'. This seems to me to be more false than true; at least, it is a caricature of what was taught in the theology that I learned. God is not *added* to the beings of the world because one cannot add to one another things that are not in the same category or genus. But I would say that God is a being, analogous with creaturely beings. In saying '*a* being' I am not making him one of a number or class, but I am insisting on the concreteness of God. God is not an abstraction, nor is he an incomplete being, nor is he part of the world; he is a single and complete being, subsisting in himself. He is of course intimately present to all his creatures, but he is not any part of the created world, which owes its existence to him.

To this traditional doctrine Macquarrie has two objections. First, that 'science has shown that the world can get along as a self-regulating entity and we do not need to posit some other being beyond it'. To this I can only say that seems to me to be entirely beyond the capacity of science to judge whether the world regulates itself without being regulated by another, or whether its very capacity to regulate itself is given to it by another. This is a philosophical or theological, not a scientific, question. Second, Macquarrie objects that if God were a being he could not be ultimate 'because we could always ask about *his* being'. Or as we read on another page, 'transcendent being would be more ultimate than our supposed absolute, for it would be the condition that there may be an absolute, or any being whatsoever'(p. 100). These assertions seem to me to be gratuitous, even false. If by transcendent being Macquarrie means the abstract idea of being, I would say that this is posterior to, and dependent on, real, concrete being. If there is an absolute, self-subsistent being, it would be the source not only of all other concrete being but also of the abstract, transcendent idea of being. While we *could* ask about the source of the being of the absolute, the question would on examination turn out to be based on a misunderstanding, namely a failure to perceive that absolute being is self-explanatory, and does not need to derive from anything else.

While defending traditional theism against the charges that Macquarrie makes, I should like to ask a little more closely about the being that Macquarrie identifies with God. God, he says, is holy being. To this I ask, is all being holy, or only some? Is the holiness in question created holiness, or uncreated? Is God the collection of all the beings that are holy, or the source of their holiness? Is God dependent for his existence on beings other than himself? Is he free, is he sovereign, is he conscious, and is he personal? While I can see much merit in what Heidegger has to say about 'Being' (with a capital B), Heidegger makes it clear that when he talks about 'Being' in that sense he does not mean what Christians have in mind when they talk about God. If Heidegger understands his own position correctly, Macquarrie should probably explain more fully than he has yet done (in the writings familiar to me) how his notion of holy being differs from Heidegger's notion of *Being (Sein)*.

The ambiguities in Macquarrie's doctrine of God would be the source of most of the other difficulties I find in his book. When he speaks of 'revelation' I have to ask myself whether he is speaking of the free and conscious self-disclosure of that singular and utterly exalted being whom biblical and Christian faith designates by the name of God. When he speaks of the 'Word of God' and of the 'Incarnation' is he speaking of the action in history of that God, or simply of the presence of Being within beings?

The doctrine of prayer is certainly very difficult to discuss, and I should not myself be prepared to say much about it. But I did check rather carefully what Macquarrie has to say on prayer, because I felt that it might indicate to me whether he does after all think of God as free, conscious, and personal. I am afraid that I found here the same ambiguities. Dr Macquarrie has authored a small pamphlet entitled *Prayer is Thinking*, which contains many beautiful thoughts on meditation which I should gladly make my own. But the shortcoming of the pamphlet, from my own point of view, is revealed by the title. Is prayer essentially thinking? In the Judeo-Christian tradition prayer has always been conceived as speaking or conversing with our heavenly Father. In an atheistic universe there could be thought, contemplation, and reflection; there could even be worship of a sort; but there could not be that inter-personal exchange which the Christian (or for that matter nearly any religious believer) knows as prayer.

From these reservations it might appear that my judgement on Macquarrie's *Principles of Christian Theology* is basically negative. On the contrary, I hold that it is a remarkable book, which treats admirably of many subjects. Even in its doctrine of God, I find much to commend Macquarrie's work. When he insists that the transcendence of God does not exclude, but rather demands, his immanence, I heartily agree. In that sense I can accept Macquarrie's 'panentheism'.

He has some fine statements on the presence of God as *Logos* in the whole of creation, since the beginning of the world. His treatment of miracles is, by and large, acceptable to one of my theological persuasion. About his Christology I have some reservations, because it does not seem to me to give sufficient status to Jesus in his earthly life. The doctrine of the Church in Macquarrie's *Principles* comes very close to what many Roman Catholics, including myself, would accept. As he is no doubt aware, his objections against infallibility are directed more against certain interpretations of the Catholic position than against that position itself. I found very moving what Macquarrie has to say about the role of the pope as *primus inter pares*, and about the necessity for all the Churches to be in communion with 'the most illustrious of the apostolic sees'. Further, I would agree with Macquarrie on the subordination of the Church to the Kingdom of God. Finally, there is profit to be gleaned from Macquarrie's speculations on heaven, purgatory, and hell. While I am not as confident as he in about the non-existence of hell, I find his position on the point worthy of serious consideration. Perhaps I shall someday be able to agree, but before I do so I shall have to see more clearly than I now do how to handle the enormous weight of the tradition in favour of the eternity of hell. I find that he resolves the question too hastily, though perhaps not wrongly . . .

7 Principles of Christian Theology

JOHN WEBSTER

I

Principles of Christian Theology (1966; revised edn 1977)[1] is one of a handful of enduring texts of Anglican divinity from the 1960s, and the only comprehensive account of Christian doctrine of any substance written by an Anglican in at least the last 60 years. That so even-tempered and untroubled a book should emerge at a time when Anglican theology was almost entirely taken up with mannered and shallow radicalism indicates the remarkable theological robustness of the project and its author. Though the book has enjoyed wide admiration and long use as a text for theological formation, it has been discussed relatively little by doctrinal theologians, and less so as Christian existentialism fades from view. Where it has evoked commentary, attention has often focused on the natural or philosophical theology which makes up its first part (rightly so, because this part is in some respects the most energetic and well-profiled section of the book).[2] The dogmatic themes in the sections on symbolic and applied theology have a less secure place in the literature; yet they evoke some of Macquarrie's best writing, and no *laudatio* of his achievements should pass them by.

One clue to the book is its style. There can be few more lucid accounts of Christian doctrine. The prose is not self-conscious or clotted, but transparent and apparently effortless: simple, short sentences for the most part (any exceptions are in the treatment of philosophical theology), an uncluttered line of argument, very few forays into distracting detail, remarkable economy of reference to historical and contemporary discussions. There is an almost complete absence of the high seriousness of Tillich or Rahner, even in the opening chapters; the book already displays Macquarrie's formidable skills as an expositor of ideas. *Principles* is, indeed, an extraordinarily pacific account of its subject matter. Neither in its overall design nor in its details does it position itself polemically. The few sharp words in the book – they are very few – are reserved for Calvin and his followers (on the mind's fallenness: 'to hold that our intellect is so perverted that we just cannot think straight is to fall into a skepticism so bottomless that further discussion becomes pointless' (*Principles* p. 50); on election: 'This fantastic exaggeration of the divine initiative into a fatalism is repugnant not merely because it dehumanises man but also because it presents us with a God who is not worthy to be worshipped' (p. 341)). Calvinism irritates Macquarrie, because it fails to respect a fundamental rule announced in the preface: 'There is a kind of dialectic that operates in theology and that arises, I believe, out of the polarities of human existence itself. The effect of this dialectic throughout the history of theology has been to exclude extreme and exaggerated points of view' (p. xii). For *Principles*, balance, clarity and coherence are the supreme intellectual virtues, and imbalance is at the heart of theological disarray. The calm surface of the book is unbroken by anxiety. Barth began his first lectures on dogmatics by announcing his terror at the prospect of talking about God, an undertaking which, he said, puts 'a pistol at the breast of theologians'.[3] There is no such drama in *Principles*. Certainly Macquarrie can speak in Heideggerian tones of the way in which, in 'primordial' thinking and revelatory experience, 'the initiative passes to that which is known, so that we are seized by it and it impresses itself upon us' (p. 94). But the *bouleversement* is temporary, the checks and balances quickly making sure that stability is restored.

The tranquil character of the book is related to its generally non-dramatic conception of Christianity. As with many theologies with a strong philosophical orientation, the presentation is predominately conceptual and topical rather than historical. Macquarrie certainly lays some emphasis on the divine dynamism, and the account of symbolic theology is organized in such a way as to reflect the divine economy of creation, reconciliation and consummation. But a dramatic dogmatics (Barth or Jenson) requires for its execution a powerful sense of irreducible, nameable particulars, without which it will fail to achieve a sufficiently dense presentation of its *dramatis personae*: God and God's creatures in their common history. Macquarrie has learned from Heidegger to replace the metaphysics of substance with the metaphysics of existence in time, but is less concerned to emphasize the element of the unsubstitutable in the scriptural narrative, and more naturally turns to conceptual analysis and restatement. In part this may reflect residual disquiet about excessively lavish language about divine action learned from Bultmann. By the time he comes to write *Principles*, Macquarrie has already articulated a sympathetic criticism of Bultmann's reticence over the matter, but he himself remains nervous of speaking of being as energy or act, fearing 'too much flavour of physical forces' (p. 113). However, the preference for the non-dramatic is a sign that in *Principles* the particularities of the Christian faith sometimes threaten to resolve themselves into something anterior, available for conceptual reconstruction. Mythology is 'a matrix for theology, rather than a form of theology' (p. 131). This is not a matter of decoding doctrine: the doctrines of the Trinity, the incarnation and the Church have too much real work to do in the book for them to become mere contingent expressions of underlying themes. But it is an account of the Christian faith in which the moral drama of the covenant and its agents does not figure quite so large as does the immanence of holy Being.

Principles does not conduct its presentation by extensive discussion of texts. Biblical exegesis is only lightly scattered throughout the book, as are references to classic authors; and only rarely does Macquarrie place himself with respect to the other leading systematicians of his day, such as Tillich or Barth. No doubt this is in part a way of securing clarity of exposition, undistracted by side references. On occasions the unintended effect is to give the impression that interesting tracts of Christian doctrine are not in fact worthy of attention and can safely be dropped (the dismissal of the doctrine of justification by faith as 'neither indispensable nor specially illuminating' (p. 342) is a case in point: surely a closer reading of the matter is required). Partly, also, this feature of *Principles* is to be explained by the fact that, unlike systematic theologians in the Reformed, Lutheran and Roman Catholic traditions, the Anglican Macquarrie cannot look back over a long list of precedents with whom he is bound to converse. Further, Macquarrie conceives of Christianity as a cumulative set of experiences and ideas. He does not betray a strong 'canonical' sense – whether of biblical or traditional texts – and often works with somewhat distilled versions of Christian doctrines, closer to ideal types than to the more refractory assemblages of exegesis and argument that make up most classical formulations. The treatment of the theology of the atonement is a case in point: heavily reliant on Aulén, it accords a great deal of weight to 'motifs', and concentrates on an issue (the relation of objective and subjective) which has often dominated soteriology since Socinus but which does not really get under the skin of premodern texts on the theology of salvation. This is not to say that Macquarrie drastically oversimplifies doctrines: his versions are a good deal more complex than those to be found in some styles of philosophy of religion, which skate over historical forms of Christian teaching and their textual carriers. But he does not feel the need to do much by way of biblical and historical exercises, and his expectations of the constructive contribution of these 'special ways of considering theological questions' (p. 40) are relatively low. *Principles* is not *ressourcement* theology; for all its investment in a

theology of tradition, it is tradition as *re*interpretation rather than retro-
spective attention: 'the function of tradition ... is interpretation, and
interpretation needs to be done over and over again' (p. 13).

The arrangement of the material is instructive. An introductory chapter
gives an account of the tasks of theology and of its sources, method and
divisions (though not, note, of its norms, though there are the beginnings
of a discussion of the matter in chapter 25 on 'The Question of Truth',
added to the second edition). The lengthy first section on 'Philosophical Theology' is part prolegomena, covering topics such as revelation
and theological language, part philosophical anthropology, part metaphysics, the whole understood as 'an inquiry into the possibility of any
theology whatsoever' through which 'the foundations of theological
discourse' (p. 43) can be shown and described, if not demonstrated, in
relation to the realities of human existence. After this, the rest of the
work is devoted to doctrinal topics, with the material distributed into
'symbolic theology' and 'applied theology'. The first of these sections has
a conventional trinitarian structure; the outlines of trinitarian teaching
are sketched, followed by an account of the divine attributes, creation,
providence and evil, though with only a light treatment of anthropology,
which has already been handled under philosophical theology. This in
turn is followed by Christology, soteriology, pneumatology, the theology
of the Christian life and eschatology. Ecclesiology and its entailments are
held over until the third part on applied theology – a curious move which
does not quite secure the linkage of ecclesiology to the rest of the corpus
(despite the attempt in chapter 69 to establish the linkage of the doctrine
of the Church to creation, Christology and eschatology – pneumatology
is left unmentioned). The sequence ends with a brief treatment of moral
theology.

What can be learned from the distribution of material in the system?
Some of what might be worked out doctrinally is in fact worked out at a
prior stage, in the section on philosophical theology – most of all, theological anthropology, treated at some length in Part One but quite briefly
in Part Two (chapter 39) which simply recapitulates earlier discussions,
a move which indicates Macquarrie's (qualified) kinship with those revisionist theologies in which anthropology plays a foundational role and
is less directly shaped by christological and soteriological considerations.
In the treatment of symbolic theology, the transition from creation to
Christology without a theological account of the election of Israel tends
to reinforce the sense that the context for specifically Christian doctrine
is less the economy of salvation and more a universal anthropology. In
applied theology, the expansiveness and detail of the ecclesiology are
worthy of note: with the exception of its slight treatment of ethics, the

entire third section demonstrates considerably greater fluency and ease with conventional doctrinal material than, say, the earlier section on the atonement, and less concern to illuminate the topics in terms of descriptive phenomenology.

II

The 'new style natural theology' to which the first part of the book is devoted establishes the possibility of theology by displaying the correlations between 'ordinary situations' and 'the situations of the life of faith' (*Principles*, p. 57). Its importance is as much material as it is foundational and methodological, however, for it already sets out primary doctrinal moves which shape the course of the book in its entirety.

The philosophical theology invests heavily in Husserlian descriptive phenomenology – that 'careful descriptive analysis' of the human situation which 'begins in the right place, with the phenomena themselves' (p. 35). It soon becomes clear, however, that the kind of existential anthropology which is generated is not simply method but source and norm; it is here that we have an investigation of 'the conditions that make any theology possible' (p. 39). The conditions are anthropological, in that 'the starting-point of philosophical theology is man himself, the common humanity that is known to each of us men existing in the world' (p. 58). On this basis, an account of the human condition can be built up in which authentic selfhood (described as 'the attaining of a unified existence, in which potentialities are actualized in an orderly manner and there are no loose ends or alienated areas' (p. 77)) is threatened by 'disorder' and 'imbalance' (p. 69). Authenticity can only be attained by 'faith', which 'looks to the wider being within which our existence is set for support' (p. 80). To this anthropological quest there corresponds 'the *gift* of a sense for existence' (p. 84), that is, revelation as 'the self-giving or self-communication of being' (p. 104).

The guiding hand here is, rather obviously, Rahner, shorn of the technicalities and a number of his dogmatic commitments. The results are a privileging of a general anthropology (particular human self-descriptions do not figure in the account), and a rather relaxed affirmation of the continuity between natural existence and life in Christ. Barth or von Balthasar would judge the proposal a christological disaster: too abstract and generic, nameless. Perhaps the most important effect of beginning here is that it already encloses the specific history of God's economy of grace within a wider context, in such a way that the events of that economy, though they 'focus' (a favourite term) the wider reality of human being

87

in the world, do not have absolute force. As the symbolic theology will show, in their particularity they are representative but not constitutive.

Similarly, the account of the relation between being and God lays much of the ground for subsequent doctrinal construction. The critique of ontotheology in chapter 21 is remarkably deft, accomplishing in a few paragraphs what others never quite achieve in hundreds of pages of gesticulating: 'The assertion "God exists" is not to be taken as meaning that there is to be found a being possessing such and such characteristics' (p. 120). Perhaps: but one casualty is the language of personal agency, quietly laid aside as mythological here and in most of the rest of the book until it makes its return in ecclesiology and sacramental theology. Rather than agency, Macquarrie prefers 'letting-be' (p. 118), a curiously passive and disengaged term which lends an explicitly panentheistic idiom to the account of God in what follows. The qualifiers are there, admittedly; holy Being is transcendent, asymmetrically related to the world, not simply its depth dimension. But once again the effect is to de-emphasize the dramatic in favour of 'an "organic" model of the God-world relation' (p. 121), that is, 'not a confusion between God and the world, but . . . a recognition of their intimate relatedness' (p. 121) – a relatedness, we should note, which is more mutual interpenetration than it is active encounter.

Macquarrie conceives of the move from philosophical to symbolic theology as one from 'general structures and concepts' to 'the explication of the particular faith' (p. 177). This move involves working through the symbols of faith, that is, those forms of verbal expression of the Church's faith that are the vehicles through which primordial revelation is transmitted. In Christian symbolism 'there is a preference, though not an exclusive preference, for the dynamic and dramatic, the temporal and historical, over generalised timeless truth' (p. 182). The way in which Macquarrie conceives of the relation of this material to his philosophical foundations is deeply informative. The transition from philosophical to symbolic theology is described as a move from description to interpretation. Doctrinal symbols 'interpret' in the sense that they give a particular configuration to what has been described through phenomenology. This does not mean that they are merely ornamental; but it does entail that they are not irreducible. It is phenomenology, not symbolic theology, that is concerned with facticity. Symbols 'enrich and vivify' (p. 184) what is presented in existential-ontological analysis; but that analysis forms the 'frame of reference' (p. 184) within which the symbolic language responding to a particular revelation has its place. The effect here is that the dynamic, dramatic, temporal and historical aspects of Christian symbols are more form than content; they do not indicate a discrete order of being so much as look in a different way at what has been rendered in phenomenological analysis. It would be quite wrong to think of Macquarrie as falling into the kind of reductionism in which Christian symbols can be resolved without residue into an anterior metaphysical scheme. What is indicated is a measure of unease about direct language of divine historical agency, an unease which goes a long way towards explaining the near-complete absence of extended reference to the biblical depiction of the *magnalia dei*.

A case in point is the treatment of the doctrine of the Trinity. The high expectations that Macquarrie entertains of this doctrine is one of the most remarkable features of *Principles*, and says a good deal about Macquarrie's distance from doctrinal critics like Maurice Wiles who ten years previously had found no gainsayers to his argument that the doctrine of the Trinity is devotionally useful but theologically arbitrary and inessential. Macquarrie has a secure grasp of the dynamic character of trinitarian theology, though his statement is cautious, and well before social trinitarianism became *de rigueur* he already anticipates its unsatisfactory features. For all this, the account of the doctrine that he offers is tugged back towards the generic, largely because he is unwilling to relinquish the 'convergence of the doctrine of God as Being with the doctrine of God as Trinity' (p. 198). An early summary of the doctrine runs: 'He is a God who embraces diversity in unity; who is both transcendent and immanent; who is dynamic and yet has stability' (p. 192) – all true, no doubt, but not particularly trinitarian unless set out in a more extended account of the divine persons and the enactment of their identities. Such a description Macquarrie is very reluctant to provide. Accordingly, there is a distinct preference for functional rather than nominal language to differentiate the three modes of God's being: primordial, expressive and unitive being do much more work in *Principles* than Father, Son and Spirit. That the differentiations in the community of faith's experience of holy Being correspond to some kind of real distinctions in God Macquarrie does not question; but he has quite slender investments in the language of person, and his text could be rather easily manipulated towards some variety of modalism. This is compounded by reticence about the doctrine of the immanent Trinity. The account of trinitarian theology is almost exclusively economic in orientation. There is no presentation of the sheer spontaneous plenitude of the triune life, no account of paternity, filiation and spiration (the procession of the Spirit, for example, is thought of as his presence in the world, not his inner-triune relation to Father and Son). 'Holy Being . . . has let itself be known in the Christian community of faith under the trinitarian symbolism of Father, Son and Holy Spirit, one God' (p. 198). If there is a danger here, it is that *malgré tout* trinitarian considerations have not penetrated to the depth of the Christian doctrine of God – that holy Being might be other than the symbolism of trinitarian faith, that the (admittedly clumsy) language of person, procession, relation and the rest might in the end prove unnecessary, that trinitarian faith might survive without talk of God's self-enactment and self-naming.

Some of the same issues can be traced in the presentation of the doctrine of creation. Holy Being is letting-be, and so creativity.

> A being is a being by virtue of the fact that it is, but Being is not something that is but rather the letting-be that is prior to any is-ness. So while Being may be inseparable from beings, it is nevertheless the *fons et origo* of all beings. The beings are subordinate to and dependent on Being, which lets them be. This letting-be is the creativity of Being, and the dependence of the beings is their creatureliness. (*Principles*, p. 211)

The language is that of co-ordinated states, not of events. And, characteristically, divine creativity and human creatureliness are thought of as symmetrical realities. Certainly Being is *fons et origo*, beings are subordinate; yet there is no extensive depiction of the freedom of the divine act of creation. *Creatio ex nihilo*, for example, is expounded in terms of the fact that created being stands 'between nothing and being' (p. 215), not in terms of divine originality. The reason is, of course, a laudable desire to differentiate the Christian doctrine of creation from a mythical conception of creation as production by a supersensible agent. But the effect is a retraction of talk about divine action and an inflation of anthropological considerations: the question to which the doctrine of creation is directed is 'What does it mean to be a creature?' (not, note, 'Who is the creator?'): 'To know oneself as creature is to see oneself in the light of being, that is to say, not as an autonomous being, but as a being who is at once answerable for his being and empowered to fuller being, at once the subject of a demand and the recipient of grace' (p. 213).

With Part Three, 'Applied Theology', we enter a rather different world; the reticence about talk of divine action is set aside somewhat, and talk of the agency of Christ and the Spirit flows more easily. In part, no doubt, this is because for the first time in the book we have entered more directly into the world of action in time. Like others indebted to existentialist philosophy, Macquarrie finds ecclesiology (rather than, say, Christology) to be the point of real concreteness – something which made Donald MacKinnon lash out in fury on more than one occasion. For all that, the ecclesiology is undergirded by a sense that the Church is not simply a symbolic culture but a sphere of the operations of grace. 'The church represents Christ in the sense of making him present to the world' (p. 447); but it does so, not because he is absent until ecclesially realized, but on the basis of the fact that Word and sacrament 'become the places where Being makes itself present-and-manifest in and through particular beings' (p. 449). Behind this is a conviction that Christ as revelation is 'not only *original*, but also *originative*' (p. 448). This is one of the places in *Principles* where the reader is left wishing for some more description; to speak of Christ as 'originative' could mean simply that he is the precipitating occasion for the Church to do its work in response to a distant stimulus; but the larger context of Part Three of *Principles* suggest a rather more vivid sense of 'God's making himself present' (p. 455). With this, Macquarrie certainly moves beyond the attenuated theology of the resurrection in the symbolic theology; this in itself may suggest that the re-incorporation of ecclesiology into symbolics would have had a salutary effect on the whole.

III

The most important thing to say about *Principles* is that it was written: simply to attempt an overall account of Christian doctrine in such a bleak period of Anglican divinity is an act of considerable courage and commitment. At the time of its first composition, the best minds of Anglicanism in England and North America were either on the episcopal bench or engaged in biblical, patristic or liturgical studies; such constructive doctrinal work as was undertaken tended to be at the hands of those engaged in ecumenical work. In *Principles*, Anglicanism (as well as the other Christian traditions) were handed a text in which doctrine has real work to do. The heavy presence of existentialism ought not to eclipse the fact that in many respects the book is an act of resistance, far from the ironic treatments of Christian theology then fashionable, and which later drew Macquarrie to protest over *The Myth of God Incarnate* (see below, pp. 99–100).

Moreover, there is a permanent lesson to be learned from his 'existential-ontological' handling of the material. At first blush, this seems to be one more instance of the 'balance' which *Principles* values so highly. In fact it is an attempt to keep together the reality of the objective and the subjective which threatened to fly apart at the hands of existentialist-minded theologians like Herbert Braun and Fritz Buri and their Barthian opponents like Helmut Gollwitzer. Here Macquarrie's aversion to exaggeration stands him in good stead: he refuses to surrender metaphysics and allow theology to implode into spirituality or morals, retaining a sense of the intentionality of the act of faith and a confidence in talk of God, Christ and the Spirit's work. He does so with a quite slender arsenal of weapons, for his distaste for the Reformed tradition means that he is not able to feel the power of Barth's dogmatically-driven response to Christian existentialism in the 1950s or of the vigorous theological realism which T.F. Torrance was expounding in New College while Macquarrie was at Union, and he never quite escapes from an inhibiting set of anxieties about mythology. Yet whatever reservations might be held about bi-polar or dialectical theology, it offered a tether against the drift into immanentism. Others such as Michael Ramsey or Donald MacKinnon might be considered to have greater dogmatic penetration; but it was left to Macquarrie to produce a comprehensive account of the field.

Principles has not been superseded. Classroom texts such as Owen Thomas's *Introduction to Theology* or McGrath's *Christian Theology* are pedestrian by contrast and have nothing of Macquarrie's constructive grandeur or philosophical acumen. Anglicanism still awaits another attempt of similar stature. The eclipse of existentialist philosophy has gone hand in hand with loss of confidence in deploying a theory of common human experience as theological prolegomena, a loss felt acutely by revisionist theologians. Theologians are more likely to look for conversation partners among literary and cultural theorists, and to demonstrate a great deal more metaphysical hesitancy. Alongside this, the field of systematic theology has changed almost beyond recognition, perhaps most of all because many now have stronger historical interests, and approach the classical traditions of Christian theology as a resource rather than a set of problems to be overcome, and so have found their way back to 'positive' theology not constantly on the back foot. Undertaken today, *Principles* might look very different: shorn of an extensive prolegomena, more biblically and historically dense, perhaps more cheerfully mythological, certainly less even-tempered. But aspirants to authorship of a new *Principles* should be under no illusions: Macquarrie has set the bar very high.

Notes

1 Page references in the body of the article are to the revised edition.
2 E.T. Long, *Existence, Being and God: An Introduction to the Philosophical Theology of John Macquarrie*, New York: Paragon, 1985; G. Morley, *John Macquarrie's Natural Theology: The Grace of Being*, Aldershot: Ashgate, 2003.
3 K. Barth, *The Göttingen Dogmatics. Instruction in the Christian Religion* I, Grand Rapids: Eerdmans, 1991, p. 6.

8 John Macquarrie in Oxford

ROBERT MORGAN

The Macquarrie family move to Oxford in 1970 was neither sought for nor expected.[1] Jenny was happy teaching mathematics in New York, and their son John had just gained a place at Manhattan College; and even if he found the politics at Union Seminary a distraction, Macquarrie himself was not a quitter. He had not applied for the Oxford chair, nor known that his name was being considered, but in May 1969 the offer came, together with an attempt at persuasion from Henry Chadwick, the Regius Professor of Divinity and Dean-elect of Christ Church.

The death in 1968 of the patrologist F. L. Cross who had been Lady Margaret Professor since 1944, and also of Cuthbert Simpson the Dean, leading to the translation of Chadwick and the search for a new Regius, signalled a time of change in Christ Church. Two other Regius Professors were also on the brink of retirement: S. L. Greenslade in ecclesiastical history and V. A. Demant, Professor of moral and pastoral theology since 1949. The faculty remained strong in patristics, but with its two luminaries now heads of colleges (J. N. D. Kelly at St Edmund Hall, and Henry Chadwick at Christ Church) rather than professors, the new Regius Professor would have to be a patrologist. However, the traditional undergraduate pattern of Oxford theology as 'the history of true religion from the Garden of Eden to the Council of Chalcedon' was clearly obsolete, and there was general agreement that modern theology would become more central to the syllabus. The need for a systematic theologian rather than another historian was underlined by the death, also in 1968, of Oxford's most distinguished philosophical theologian, Austin Farrer, and also the earlier departure in 1966 of Ian Ramsay to be bishop of Durham.

The Lady Margaret electors were accordingly instructed to look for a systematic theologian. Since he (and for canonical reasons in those days it could only be 'he') had to be an Anglican priest, the author of *Principles of Christian Theology* (1966), and a consultant at the recent Lambeth Conference, was clearly the ideal choice in a rather small field. A new joint degree in philosophy and theology had also been established in 1969, and while that was mainly the responsibility of Basil Mitchell who had succeeded Ian Ramsey in the Nolloth Chair 'of the philosophy of the Christian religion' there were obvious advantages in having a theologian also well qualified in modern philosophy.

The appointment was made too late for the Macquarrie family to leave New York until 1970, and by then Maurice Wiles had been appointed as the new Regius Professor. Wiles's primary expertise was in patristics, but as Professor of Christian Doctrine at King's College, London (1967–70) he had been teaching modern theology. Oxford thus gained in 1970 two distinguished doctrinal theologians who were very different in background and training, and therefore complemented each other in what would today be called a dream ticket, balancing a historical theologian with a systematic one, an expert on the early Church and recent English theology, with a specialist in German post-Enlightenment philosophy and theology. But the differences ran deeper: Macquarrie was an Anglo-catholic, Wiles a liberal Anglican from an evangelical background; Wiles a son of the establishment, Macquarrie the son of a skilled worker on Clydeside; Wiles a natural leader of the faculty (where the Regius Professor is *primus inter pares*) and later chairman of the Doctrine Commission (on Macquarrie's suggestion), Macqarrie a teacher and scholar who avoided the limelight. He was active locally, nationally, and internationally in the Church, but unlikely to lead any fight to reform the institutions which he served unselfishly and reliably. They could easily have not seen eye to eye. In fact they worked together as harmoniously as doctrine professors as they prayed together daily in the cathedral as canons.

In his letter encouraging Macquarrie to accept the invitation to Oxford, Dr Chadwick wrote about both the faculty and the college. The university consists of thirty-odd independent colleges, the largest of which is unique in having a cathedral at its heart. Every professorial chair in Oxford is tied to some particular college, but four (until recently five) of the divinity chairs have since the Reformation been tied to cathedral canonries and provide houses within the college. The colleges are the reality in Oxford, especially in subjects where tutorial teaching as well as teachers' and students' social life is centred. In comparison, the faculties exist mainly on paper, for administrative purposes such as co-ordinating lectures, organizing examinations and graduate studies, and relating to university bodies. They are less immediate and demanding and sociable than the colleges. For a canon-professor worshipping daily in the cathedral, and living on its doorstep, the college is still the key to Oxford happiness, as it was for bachelor dons until the late nineteenth century.

In fact the faculty has its own reality, especially for professors, who have less contact with undergraduates but some responsibility for the academic discipline they profess. Power is still widely dispersed throughout the community of scholars in the collegiate university, but most senior professors have some moral authority in the faculty and help shape the syllabus and lecture on it at a safe distance.

The theological faculty in particular has one kind of reality which transcends most of its college bases and component parts: its ecumenical character. Theology in Christ Church has a predominantly (not exclusively) Anglican flavour, due to the cathedral and college statutes, whereas the faculty, its syllabuses and its personnel (teachers and students) are all strongly ecumenical, insofar as they are confessional at all. No Oxford college, for example, has so many university theological students as Regent's Park College, a permanent hall with a Baptist foundation, represented in this volume by its Principal, Paul Fiddes. Mansfield College is an originally Congregationalist foundation with Roman Catholic and Anglican priests now among its teachers.

The ecumenical potential of the faculty was illustrated when Henry Chadwick and the late Edward Yarnold S.J. of Campion Hall guided the Anglican–Roman Catholic International Commission, and Campion is represented here by Philip Endean S.J. The faculty also includes other institutions and personnel, notably Blackfriars (Dominican), St Benet's (Benedictine), Greyfriars (Franciscan), three Anglican theological colleges with different shades of churchmanship, and the originally Unitarian foundation Harris Manchester College with its mature students' scheme which has educated some impressive second-career theologians. Greek orthodoxy is represented by its bishop, Kallistos Ware, and there are a number of research institutes such as the Ian Ramsey Centre for Science and Religion. A faculty membership of over 100 teachers, plus many more not listed, offer unusual possibilities for collaboration and collegiality. With the recent establishment of a religious studies' track this ecumenical breadth now extends to the study of Judaism, Islam, Buddhism and Hinduism.

Both the inner-Christian ecumenism, with its strong Roman Catholic participation, and the inter-faith component which feels under no pressure to make converts from other religions, are close to Macquarrie's lifelong concerns. Like Wiles he was warmly welcomed by such venerable colleagues as Greenslade, Demant, Kelly and Nineham, and unlike Wiles was rapidly co-opted as a governor into the Anglo-catholic institutions Pusey House and St Stephen's House, and into such informal groupings as the Saturday lunch. They were both elected in 1970 to the Theological Wine, though two less likely to be called a glutton and a wine-bibber are hard to imagine.

For the Macquarries themselves it was a transition to a very different world from New York, and quite unlike the old one they had left behind eight years previously. North American and European social and intellectual life were further apart in 1970 than through easy air-travel and now e-mail they have since become, but in matters of religion and theology England and Scotland were in some ways even more separate. There are philosophical links between Glasgow and Oxford, but as the intellectual centre of the High Church party of the Church of England Oxford must have seemed 'something completely different', even for a recently ordained Anglo-catholic who had long felt some affinity with the Episcopalian church in his native Scotland, and who (as a good royalist) had never taken American citizenship. In a world where everyone seemed to know everyone else, at least from student days if not from school, he was something of a foreigner with a distinctive accent, but the whole family soon made themselves at home, and Jenny taught mathematics at the cathedral school for ten years and helped open the stall as a volunteer at the cathedral, and also became the first woman governor of the theological college at Cuddesdon before it was united with the modernists from Boar's Hill. The younger children eventually returned north, but Ian and Jenny and John have remained in Oxford, now some 36 years. The suggestion that he might return to his Celtic roots by becoming Bishop of Argyle and the Isles was humbly and wisely resisted.

Inhabiting the three-fold world of college, cathedral and faculty, in a system where authority is dispersed, involves more committee meetings than can be good for a scholar's mental health, but the books continued to flow, if not on quite the scale of those written at Union. Unlike the cathedral, the faculty has no dean or head of department. The chairmanship of its governing body, the faculty board, rotates, professors alternating with non-professors for a period of two years. Some teachers are for ever tinkering with syllabuses, or even wanting serious reform; others are content to let things tick over a little longer, provided the framework is flexible enough to allow everyone to do what is right in their own eyes. Macquarrie was not a revolutionary. Of the 24 consecutive years the present writer sat on the board, the two years of Macquarrie's chairmanship were the most peaceful and least memorable. One burning issue concerned library heating. There was no faculty centre in those days and the faculty library was in Pusey House, combined with that establishment's own library. The Principal of Pusey House was a delightful churchman, keen to minimize global warming. The librarian was a forthright young woman from Glasgow who, unlike the Principal, did not enjoy the warmth of a worsted cassock. Macquarrie's friendly association with Pusey House ensured a compromise, but when his period of office ended the stove again subsided, and in due course the libraries were sadly separated. Behind this simple narrative stands some weeping and gnashing of teeth, no trace of which was ever seen to darken Macquarrie's countenance.

More important than his contributions to the administration of the faculty was his teaching. Wiles and Macquarrie supervised a large number of graduate students, and both gave memorable lecture-courses, two of which are recalled by Stephen Platten in this volume. A new undergraduate syllabus was established in the 1970s after public debate about how much Greek was still essential had entertained the wider university. In the university parliament or 'Congregation' scholars eminent in other fields held forth, with arguments such as that if Galilean fishermen could learn Greek then so could Oxford undergraduates. The new syllabus was partly taught by seminars on 'doctrine and interpretation', led jointly by a biblical and a doctrinal theologian. As a junior partner to both Macquarrie and Wiles in several of these pairings the present writer can testify to their value in helping to educate biblical scholars theologically, whatever they did for students. The new syllabus also involved courses on 'special theologians' and Macquarrie's speciality was always Schleiermacher, a fact that has some bearing on the essay on his Christology later in this book. His graduate seminars sometimes studied a book for a term, and one choice which is also relevant to his Christology was Schillebeeckx's *Jesus* (ET 1979).

Oxford gives its professors considerable freedom to do their work as they see fit. Their statutory duties are minimal and the system depends on everyone being willing to do much more than their contract stipulates. This gives freedom and flexibility to serve on national bodies, and it gives (less now than formerly) time to write. And Macquarrie wrote. His monument is his remarkable *oeuvre*, and Oxford gave him the space to continue doing what he did best. His much praised lucidity was a feature of his writing, no less than of his lectures. Books, articles, reviews, pamphlets continued to flow from his pen.

Some books had been commissioned and started in New York. One of them, pursued by Paul Wignall in Chapter 24 below, was *The Faith of the People of God* (1972), written in response to a request by Scribner for a more popular version of *Principles*. It was more creative than that. Intended for the laity it made the 'people' (*laos*) of God its central motif and principle of organization. The doctrines and practices of Christianity are related to that. Most of Macquarrie's writing has the appearance of popularization, thanks to his gift for writing simply when writing profoundly, but Scribner's request was answered more directly a few years later in *The Humility of God* (1978). These 'meditations' originated in addresses given at Christ Church but can be used as an introduction to Christian doctrine by those who would find *Principles* too long or too philosophical to read straight through. This work was revised in 1977, just before *Humility*, and the second and third parts are more accessible than most systematic theologies, and can be read piecemeal by anyone wanting instruction on a particular doctrinal topic, but *Humility* is even more accessible. Its echoes of Barth's *Humanity of God* show how much closer these two theologians had moved since the 1940s. Both books, and many of the articles from this time, express a pre-eminent concern to address the Church as well as the academy, and some of them have a quite narrow church readership in mind.

Existentialism (1972) had also been commissioned and begun in America. Its second edition (1973) became a best-seller with Penguin, read widely by non-theologians. Whereas *Twentieth-Century* had focused on thinkers, this is thematically arranged. Macquarrie's early interests persisted, and his early enthusiasms are not repudiated.

Paths in Spirituality (1972, enlarged edn 1992) is referred to by Rowan Williams in the Foreword to this collection and is called 'one of my own favourites' by Macquarrie himself (*Theologian*, p. 67). The close relationship of theology and spirituality is a feature of Macquarrie's work, as it is of Greek Orthodox theology. This book comes from a period when others were beginning to recover the importance of spiritual practices as the 'secular' and 'religionless' Christianity of which Macquarrie had long been critical (*God and Secularity*, 1968) had proved ways out of the Church rather than ways into a deeper engagement with God. *The Concept of Peace* (1973) followed, and *Christian Unity and Christian Diversity* (1975), the latter a product of his engaging in ecumenical conversations and some disquiet about where the ecumenical movement was headed. His more substantive contribution to ecumenical thought came later in *Mary for All Christians* (1991). Several earlier essays were brought together in *Thinking about God* (1975), the second of four such collections, the others appearing in 1965, 1986, 2003, each roughly covering a decade, and *Christian Hope* followed in 1978.

These books were short, but they fed into the more substantial *In Search of Humanity* (1982) which was soon matched by his Gifford lectures, *In Search of Deity* (1984). The two books are less symmetrical than the titles suggest, because *Humanity* is entirely thematic, whereas *Deity* returns to Macquarrie's other preferred approach for nearly half the book, developing his own position through a sympathetic exposition of other thinkers, here from Plotinus to Heidegger. These are the ripe fruits of the Oxford years in post. They have their roots in his earliest work in natural theology, and their shoots were nourished by the ongoing study of Rahner, discussed in the next two essays of this collection. Rahner's visit to London and Oxford in 1984, shortly before his death, and Macquarrie's lecture on Rahner's eightieth birthday, and the photo of them both in Tom Quad are iconic of these Christ Church years when Rahner's theology was a constant inspiration.

The still riper fruits of his retirement are above all the works on Christology which form an arc or an ellipse spanning the two poles on humanity and deity in an account of Jesus human and divine, perfectly human and the incarnate Word of God. Both the importance of the theme and the distinctive way it is tackled require separate treatment (below, Chapters 20–21). Macquarrie's relationship to Schleiermacher is less direct than his relationships to Bultmann, Heidegger, and Rahner, but it is no less seminal. Years of pondering the christological part of *The Christian Faith* with the small groups of Oxford undergraduates who chose Schleiermacher as their 'special theologian' left a mark on his Christology, but the raw materials were gathered in his earlier conceptual work. What is remarkable here is a philosophical theologian successfully negotiating the dangerous currents of New Testament scholarship. Maurice Wiles was comfortable with the discipline (he had been a lecturer in New Testament at Ibadan and written at length on biblical interpretation), but unlike one or two of his other Oxford colleagues who could seem naive when they spoke of the New Testament Macquarrie now showed he could swim effortlessly with the sharks. Coming into academic theology through Bultmann was of course a help, because although Bultmann's philosophical theology was the focus of his research, the interpretation of Paul was its substance, and in any case it is impossible to read the master closely without getting a theological grasp of the New Testament.

This perhaps surprising turn to Christology may have been partly sparked by *The Myth of God Incarnate* controversy of 1977 into which he waded with something closer to passion than is typical of his writing. There is a tradition of Oxford collections of essays causing controversy in the Church, from *Essays and Reviews* (1860), *Lux Mundi* (1889), *Foundations* (1912) and beyond, but the SCM paperback which caused this 1977 controversy was not an Oxford collection. It was edited by John Hick, a philosopher of religion from Birmingham, and mostly written by two of his Birmingham colleagues, Frances Young (a pupil of Wiles) and Michael Goulder (a former clergyman). But the participation of Maurice Wiles was enough to give it an Oxford association and one quick-fire response and a later set of reflections on the theme were Oxford-based, the first edited by a local evangelical vicar,[2] and the second by a distinguished Oxford New Testament scholar.[3]

The controversy did not flatter either English church life or its theological culture. Macquarrie's reviews (1977 and 1978) and articles (1979 and 1982), partly reprinted in *Stubborn*, pp. 78–93, were motivated by his obligations as a teacher of the Church and that included taking account of the harm it seemed to have done by its sensationalist title and publicity. It was of course embarrassing for Macquarrie that his close colleague and neighbour at Christ Church was involved, but in 1978 he distinguished Wiles's 'cautious and tentative discussions' from 'the confident, sometimes highly polemical deliverances of some of Dr Wiles's less judicious collaborators', and 'without seeking to prove that Dr Wiles is an "anonymous incarnationalist" I think that his view does fall within the broad boundaries which I suggested (in 1977) as the basic structure of an incarnational doctrine in contemporary terms' (*Stubborn*, pp. 86–7). He did not at that time know that Wiles had strongly opposed the title, but had accepted collective responsibility for the book.

On the subject of 'myth' Macquarrie was more of an expert than any of the contributors, having written two books on Bultmann and demythologizing and much more on religious language (*God-Talk*, *Thinking*, etc.). He found little materially to disagree with in Wiles's contributions and despite their being on opposite sides in this debate their two positions were close. Both wanted 'myth' recognized as myth, not taken literally, and the way Wiles spoke of the significance of Jesus seemed to Macquarrie pretty much what he himself meant by incarnation. Quoting in 1993 what Wiles had published in 1979 (and delivered in some 1977 lectures), that Jesus 'had lived a life that embodies God's character and action in the world . . .', Macquarrie again thought this 'an adequate statement of the Church's faith in Christ, and I would personally find it acceptable as saying all that was of importance in the Chalcedonian formula, or all that is implied in the notion of an incarnation' (*Stubborn*, p. 161).

That comment might be said to reflect a minimalist interpretation of Chalcedon[4] which perhaps goes to the heart of their differences. Wiles was enough of a historian to feel he was in a different world from Chalcedon, and saying something different in theology, even if expressing the same Christian religion at a different period in its development. He thought it close to dishonesty to use the traditional language in a way that suggested one shared the theological beliefs of the early Fathers, and thought the Church had to be educated sufficiently to be free of doctrinal fundamentalism. For Macquarrie as a catholic theologian what mattered was preserving the essential continuity with the tradition which he believed Wiles preserved, but which some of the *Myth* contributors clearly did not. He thought the Chalcedonian definition 'truly God, truly man' and the *doctrine* (not its mythological expressions) of the incarnation essential to a doctrinal structure that preserved authentic Christian faith.[5] Continuing to use ancient formulations in the Church's worship helps maintain the continuity of Christian faith over the centuries and a sense of belonging to the one holy catholic Church, even though we understand the world differently today and therefore understand the ancient formulations differently. The ongoing task of theology is continually to rethink and reappropriate the Christian language, proposing new formulations but not attacking old ones which remain evocative for many Christians.

Many Christians, or most, or only some? Part of the missionary and apologetic impulse behind the *Myth* symposium was a desire to move on from language that was misleading (if myth was literalized), damaging (if it hindered respect for other religions), or meaningless to many Christians in the modern world. Macquarrie shared all those concerns and had advocated them strongly, if less sensationally than the iconoclasts. It was the element of shock tactics and the media event (more the responsibility of the publisher than the contributors) that he found pastorally unwise, and in this too he could find common ground with Wiles. The argument that academic discussions needs to be better known among the faithful was important to them both and led them to expend much energy on writing for the larger constituency and engaging in extra-mural teaching. Wiles was not afraid of controversy, and perhaps gave greater weight to the positive potential of a media event, but as a pastorally sensitive theologian he was equally sensitive to the negative aspect of this and went to great lengths to minimize it.

In his initial review of *Myth* Macquarrie pays only brief attention to Wiles's profound reflections on pp. 161–5 of that collection. They are so similar to his own later christological reflections that one can imagine the two professors resolving their differences over a pint or the port. But it was not that kind of a relationship, and one may wonder how much they actually discussed the issue, if at all. Their collegial relationship was always cordial and became warm, but their very different backgrounds, expertise, and churchmanship meant that they pursued similar theological goals while ploughing rather different furrows, co-operating in their teaching and examining, but belonging to different discussion groups and partly different friendship circles, such as the Anglo-catholic Saturday lunch in Macquarrie's case. Academics who first meet in mid-life as distinguished professors do not usually enjoy the same kind of relationship as those who were students together, or who move in the same religious circles. Twenty-eight years after the *Myth* controversy Maurice Wiles died and Macquarrie wrote one of the signed obituaries (in *The Independent*) and preached at the memorial service in Christ Church in a way that left no doubt about his affection and admiration for his younger colleague. He followed this by a long article on 'The Theological Legacy of Maurice Wiles'[6] which together with Rowan Williams's contribution to *The Making and Remaking of Christian Doctrine* (1993) are the outstanding memorials to the *primus* of the Oxford Faculty in the 1970s and 80s.

It has seemed worth pausing on this national controversy even though Macquarrie's involvement in it was tangential, as revealing something about 'Macquarrie in Oxford', and the conversations that did and those that did not take place. If this account suggests a degree of detachment from the passions often aroused by theological controversy that is probably accurate. But he evidently thought something vital was at stake in this unwanted controversy, and Chapter 19 below on his christology will try to clarify that.

Macquarrie's Oxford years divide into his 16 years in Christ Church (1970–86), and his longer period of retirement on Headley Way, an unpretentious part of Oxford, convenient for the coaches to London and Heathrow, and for the hospitals, and served by one of several East Oxford churches in the catholic Anglican tradition. Both periods involved plenty of travel, giving lectures around the world as well as all over Britain and Ireland, most importantly to give the Gifford Lectures at St Andrew's in 1983–4. The first part also involved regular preaching in the cathedral and college chapels, the second part in his own parish church at Headington.

One incident reveals a certain nimbleness. Invited to preach on 'gluttony' in a series at St John's on the seven deadly sins he mislaid the topic instruction and arrived with a sermon of more general relevance prepared for the Queen at Sandringham the previous week. Learning of his error from the notices during the service he was left with four minutes to retrieve the situation. Reflecting on Philippians 2.7 and kenotic Christology he explained how 'he emptied himself' in the incarnation was quite the reverse of the gluttony of which the Son of Man was wrongly accused . . .

A cathedral chapter decision in which he played a decisive part was the decision to reserve the blessed sacrament. He had in 1965 published an article in support of the devotional service called Benediction and these arguments were supplemented by some 'new thoughts' in 1975, but the cathedral was never in much danger of following that particular path in spirituality. His work in the cathedral also had a practical side. He was for several years canon-treasurer, and colleagues speak of the care he took over his administrative duties, as well as the spiritual depth of his preaching.

His participation in the life and worship of St Andrew's, Headington, since retiring has a memorial in the little book, *Invitation to Faith* (1995), given as Lent lectures there in 1994 and first published locally in that year as *Starting from Scratch*. Beyond that, Fr Michael Brewin, vicar since 1987, kindly sent an account of his regular sharing in the principal weekly celebration, regular preaching (at least once a month, and always on the gospel reading for the day) and his taking responsibility for the Monday morning Eucharist for some 15 years following his retirement. In 2002 a life-threatening illness curtailed his activities, but he has recently been able to resume a small part of them. Both *The Mediators* (1995) and *Two Worlds* (2004) began as Lent courses in the parish, as did some of his writing on Mary and on the Eucharist. In addition he spoke at parish Quiet Days and gave Advent addresses after compline. He spoke on occasion to groups of local clergy, but the diocese cannot be said to have made as much use of his gifts as it might have done. He still assists the vicar with sick communions and visiting the housebound, and has shared in the ministry of his parish in many ways, including hearing confessions, anointing the sick and dying, and offering pastoral care and counselling. Perhaps above all, he has given loyal support, advice, and friendship to a vicar caught up in the pain and aggravations of the Church of England over the ordination of women.

These disagreements (see below) have become more acute since Macquarrie's retirement. Earlier this year (13 Jan 2006) he wrote for his local vicar (a strong opponent of womens' ordination) some notes on the Roman Catholic response to the Rochester Report on women bishops. In his Point 4 he agrees 'that the decision to admit women to the priesthood would seem to imply that they might thereby qualify to be consecrated as bishops' (para. 7), but finally concludes 'that any move to consecrate women as bishops at this time in the Church of England would be premature. Much more study and reflection is needed' (8). Because 'what common humanity embodied in sexual differences means within the Church is something still needing exploration and not likely to be settled for a long time' (5).

If ever, one might add. Some theological questions are never finally settled, and some are clarified in practice before they are resolved in theory. Demanding more theological clarity is sometimes a delaying tactic, and sometimes delay is prudent, and sometimes it is not. Judgements have to be made and the decision not to proceed may be as decisive (and divisive) as moving ahead in faith, hope, and love. Macquarrie thinks 'it would be wrong to consecrate women Bishops as if the question were already settled, just as it would also be wrong to say that it would be impossible *ever* for a woman to become a bishop'.

The 'principle of the unripeness of time' has a long history in academic politics. Its application to the life of the church might seem less than prophetic, but swimming with the secular tide is not particularly prophetic, or costly either. Macquarrie's main argument, taken from the Roman Catholic response, is that this move is in practice irreversible and should not be taken before there is a real consensus that it is right, and 'I don't think that the votes in the General Synod are truly representative of the mind of the Church of England'. He wants to 'know whether the mind of the Church is really moving toward the change proposed (which might suggest that indeed the Spirit is guiding us that way) or whether a well-organized minority is manipulating the church' (3). There are certainly well-organized minorities on both sides of this debate, but they are both committed, in theory, to listening to 'what the Spirit is saying to the churches'. Macquarrie's main concern in this is that premature action 'may create schism within the Church of England and will widen the distance already separating us from the great Catholic churches of both East and West (8).'

These are all surely weighty comments, especially as coming from one who has been happy to assist a woman celebrant at All Saints convent in East Oxford, and sees no theological arguments against the ordination of women, and has no personal problems with what has been done (see above), only with how (in the United States) it was done, unlawfully and uncharitably. Not that the lack of charity has been all on one side. Those who read these informal reflections are likely to be encouraged in views they already hold rather than converted one way or the other. 'Premature at this time' might be less premature in five years' time and the wheels of ecclesiastical law turn slowly. Granted that the consecration of women bishops is tied to the ordination of women as priests the main theological question is surely whether this was a mistake, and should be stopped. That is not a view which would find much support in the Church of England. It may have been 'premature', or it may have been rather late, but was it right? Here a consensus does seem to be forming, despite the strong opposition of a determined minority and despite some bad arguments on both sides. Debate continues and not all contributions are as eirenic as Macquarrie's.

The local context of a community of faith is important for many theologians' work, and the ecclesial and apologetic orientation of Macquarrie's writings was mentioned in the Introduction. In his letter dated 13 September 2005 about 'Ian Macquarrie's contribution to the parish' of St Andrew's, Headington, Michael Brewin recalls one of their earliest conversations in which Macquarrie said 'that he would want to be remembered above all else as an apologist for the Christian faith'. That is not something his fellow-Scot, the layman Donald MacKinnon could easily have said, but any clergyman might say the same, including Schleiermacher, Barth and Bultmann, Wiles and every other reputable canon of Christ Church.

One other product of retirement deserves mention because it bears some relationship to this volume. Among the many North American friends and frequent visitors to Headley Way is John Morgan (above, p. 1), the instigator and part-editor of *On Being a Theologian* (1999), Macquarrie's autobiographical reminiscences with four reprinted lectures, and his lectures given in Moscow in 1989, and Beijing in 1995, and a Roman Catholic response on the papacy. Georgina Morley outlines 26 of his books up to his eightieth birthday in 1999, but excluding the *Dictionary of Christian Ethics* (1967) and *Contemporary Religious Thinkers* (1968) as edited and only part-written by him.

Dr Morgan writes in a personal communication dated 8 October 2005 how he 'boldly proposed to host a conference in the southwest of Ireland, at the historic seat of early Christianity, namely, Ardfert in County Kerry, a favourite site of Macquarrie's, as I came to learn later, owing to the magnificent role St Brendan played in the early days of the Church in that wild and glorious region of the world'. He recalls how as a young Quaker seminarian he was himself alerted to the significance of Macquarrie's work by John Knox (the other one) in 1968. Years later he came to know Macquarrie and heard from the other side about that very significant friendship which began with the gift by Knox of *The Church and the Reality of Christ* (1962) to his new colleague at Union. Thirty years after being guided by Knox to *Principles* Dr Morgan brought Macquarrie to Ireland 'to talk about being a theologian and doing theology', which he did 'with grace and magnanimity'. He says he 'felt somewhat uneasy about the way I had managed to persuade Macquarrie to do the conference. He had always said he would not write an autobiography.' He adds,

Of the words of insight and counsel, one stands clearly and boldly before me now. It had to do with advice to would-be theologians. And the remarks came in response to a question regarding how best to launch a teaching career in theology and how best to manage one's aspirations with regard to actually being or becoming a theologian. His response was short and direct. He said, 'Know someone and know something!' By knowing someone he meant knowing thoroughly the thought of someone already established. For him, it was Heidegger. By knowing something he meant knowing thoroughly a theory or doctrine or theological and/or philosophical position. For him, it was existentialism.

Finally, he looks back (as do others) 'on my years of friendship with John Macqarrie and the hours of intimate conversation in the quiet comfort of his home made so nurturing by Jenny Macquarrie, his wife and companion for over fifty years . . .' and the inspiration he has offered to many others seeking to do theology.

It is perhaps appropriate to end with that 'personal reminiscence' of an American friend because it represents the appreciation felt by a long succession of transatlantic visitors to the summer schools Macquarrie has continued to address when age and ill-health might have bid him rest. Meetings of Congregation in Oxford end with one word: *Continuamus*. We hope that he too will continue 'until' (to quote the prayer of another great Oxford theologian who also was, when it mattered most, a catholic Anglican) 'the shades lengthen, and the evening comes, and the busy world is hushed, the fever of life is over, and our work is done. Then, Lord, in thy mercy, grant us safe lodging, a holy rest, and peace at the last; through Jesus Christ our Lord'. Amen.

Notes

1 See *Theologian*, pp. 38–42, 57–75, 103–13.

2 Michael Green (ed.), *The Truth of God Incarnate*, London: Hodder, 1977, included Macquarrie's revision of his review of *Myth* in *Theology*, Sept. 1977.

3 A. E. Harvey (ed.), *The Incarnation: Story and Belief*, London: SPCK, 1981 contained two short essays by Macquarrie.

4 John McIntyre, *The Shape of Christology* 2nd edn, London: SPCK, 1998, pp. 259–83, offers a sympathetic portrayal of Macquarrie's Christology but doubts it is quite what the conciliar fathers had in mind.

5 In 'The Theological Legacy of Maurice Wiles' (forthcoming, *Anglican Theological Review*, 2006) he demurs at Wiles' view, expressed in *The Remaking of Christian Doctrine* (1974) p. 43, that 'we have no right to treat (the Church's traditional belief in Christ as both God and man) as an unquestionable axiom'.

6 See n. 5.

9 John Macquarrie and Karl Rahner

PHILIP ENDEAN S.J.

Among contemporary theologians, I have found Karl Rahner the most helpful. In saying this, I am acknowledging that the leadership in theology, which even ten years ago lay with such Protestant giants as Barth, Brunner, and Tillich has now passed to Roman Catholic thinkers. Among them, Karl Rahner (himself a penetrating student of Heidegger) is outstanding. He handles in a masterly way those tensions which constitute the peculiar dialectic of theology . . . faith and reason, tradition and novelty, authority and freedom, and so on. (*Principles of Christian Theology*, p. viii)

This warm tribute to Rahner, at the outset of one of the major English-language contributions to systematic theology in the twentieth century, may now appear in some respects dated. It was written in 1966, and it may have been influenced by Macquarrie's recent transition from Presbyterianism into the Episcopal Church. It may also reflect the sense of hope and openness generated among Catholics and the ecumenically minded by the event of the Second Vatican Council. But we must nevertheless take it as a strong statement from Macquarrie about a felt intellectual influence.

That said, it is not easy to document the influence that Rahner had on Macquarrie. After his initial, ground-breaking book on Heidegger and Bultmann, Macquarrie's major works were wide-ranging affairs, focusing less on the close detail of any theologian's writings than on the general sweep. He became noted for the sheer range of his engagements, and for his gift of making lucid, reader-friendly summaries. Hence references to Rahner in Macquarrie's major works are often merely passing, and even the more extensive discussions of Rahner rarely extend beyond a few pages.

In Search of Deity is, if anything, critical of Rahner. Macquarrie notes Rahner's failure, in his seminal essay '*Theos* in the New Testament'[1] to move beyond 'the transcendent monotheistic deity of the Old Testament' in the direction of Macquarrie's preferred 'dialectical theism'; he also throws off a sharp aside dismissing the idea of the 'anonymous Christian' as 'arrogant pretension' (*Deity*, pp. 44, 228–9). *Jesus Christ in Modern Thought* is more positive and typical. Here Macquarrie writes appreciatively of Rahner's transcendental Thomism, and of how it provides a grounding for theology in 'an affirmative sense of the infinite possibilities of transcendence'. On this basis, Macquarrie then praises Rahner's approach to dogmas as 'truths which open the way to the – ever greater – Truth', and his retrieval of a christological approach taking the full humanity of Jesus Christ seriously (*Jesus Christ*, pp. 304–8). Both in this later work and in *Principles of Christian Theology*, Macquarrie shows particular appreciation for Rahner's 1951 essay marking the jubilee of the Chalcedonian definition, 'Current Problems in Christology'.[2] He clearly approves of the close connections which Rahner draws between Christology and the theology of humanity at large, and of its vision of Christology as 'self-transcending anthropology' and anthropology as 'incomplete christology'.[3] So Macquarrie can appreciatively quote a key sentence from that essay:

> Only someone who forgets that the essence of humanity . . . is to be unbounded . . . can suppose that it is impossible for there to be a human being who, precisely by being human in the fullest sense (which we never attain) is God's existence into the world. (*Jesus Christ*, pp. 369–70)[4]

However, the most obvious source for what Macquarrie thought of Rahner must be the lecture he gave at Heythrop College in February 1984, marking Rahner's eightieth birthday. Delivered in Rahner's presence, the lecture was entitled 'The Anthropological Approach to Theology', and amounts to a learned, urbane, well-crafted defence of an approach to Christian theology beginning 'investigations from the human end'.[4] Macquarrie takes Aquinas, Calvin and Barth as examples of a 'classical approach', one that places 'the doctrine of God at the forefront of theology' (*Theology*, p. 50). For Macquarrie, such an approach, for all its venerability, has 'become simply inappropriate'. Theology couched in these terms will not meet the mentality of today's atheists, or indeed of today's believers, given that 'the mood of godlessness . . . has moved within the Church' (p. 52).

After briefly dismissing objections arising from analysis in terms of Feuerbachian projection and from a doctrine of universal sinful depravity, Macquarrie then developed his own approach more positively. Quite apart from pragmatic pedagogical considerations, Macquarrie's preferred approach to theology 'can be seen as theological obedience to the incarnation, in which God came into the human condition and stood beside human beings in solidarity with them' (pp. 55–6). Though the question of God may have become otiose in modern technical culture, there remains an 'urgent and irresistible' question about the true nature and destiny of human freedom (p. 56). Particularly if we adopt the dialectical theism advocated by Macquarrie, there are convergences between this question and the question of God that a contemporary theology can exploit. Moreover, it can also draw on versions of the traditional cosmological argument, and on the ancient idea, as developed by Leibniz, of humanity as 'microcosm', summing up the whole of the created order in relationship to God. Human beings are 'images of the deity' in so far as they are 'capable of knowing the system of the universe and, to some extent, of imitating it through their own inventions' (p. 59).

At the very end, Macquarrie's argument shifts quite explicitly into revealed theology, by which he sees his contention about starting theology with the human as 'extraordinarily strengthened'. The case against the atheist's argument from projection is sealed by the fact that 'God himself has descended into the created order . . . there is already a humanity in God'. And so Macquarrie concludes:

> At this point we can pay Karl Barth his just due, but while he was right in affirming the ontological priority of God in this as in everything, and we would have no desire to differ from him on this point, it leaves unchanged our own contention that in the order of knowing, there is a legitimate and indeed compelling way that leads from the knowledge of the human to the knowledge of the divine. (p. 60)

After the lecture, Rahner spoke of his 'almost unreserved agreement' with Professor Macquarrie, although even then he could not resist making a qualification. Then he raised three topics for Professor Macquarrie's comments (*Theology*, pp. 60–5). The first was Rahner's view that, in a graced world, 'it is impossible to speak of a purely natural theology', because every man or woman, whether they like it or not, is 'standing under the effective call of God's revelation' (p. 61). The second was the implications of the fact that Barth's position on natural theology had appeared to move closer to Thomism. The third was about 'the minimalization of sin in modern society', and Rahner's own view that this trend, far from simply indicating 'the godlessness of our contemporaries' might actually be 'a sign of God's grace at work' (p. 65).

It was a guest lecture on a Friday evening, and the audience, though delighted by Rahner's own participation, was not in a mood for refined conceptual distinctions. Macquarrie caught the mood of the occasion well as he began by remarking on 'the honour of getting a *viva* from

Dr Rahner', and on how 'those of us who teach at Oxford try to make things a little easier' (p. 61). What came across to the audience – I write from personal recollection – was a sense of polite convergence and consensus; we were among friends, and all were agreed that theology had somehow to draw on an analysis of the human condition. However, as I read the text now, more than 20 years later, and after some years of research work on Rahner (for which, indeed, I was honoured to have Professor Macquarrie as an examiner), I am struck also by what it tells us about the differences between the two distinguished theologians who were speaking at Heythrop that night. It would be fruitless to attempt a full summary or exegesis of the exchange because it wanders. Macquarrie was presumably having to think on his feet, while Rahner's questions, especially in translation, come across as rather obscure and convoluted. But some significant contrasts can, at least tentatively, be discerned. Perhaps we can say that Rahner and Macquarrie are united on the legitimacy and necessity of an 'anthropological approach' to theology, but that there are some significant differences in how they understand what the theological enterprise is.

Above, Below and Within

A good place to start comes in Rahner's second question. He begins by alluding to the alleged shift (one that Barth specialists today would tend to deny) between Barth's earlier and later writings, and to the claim that later Barth is closer to accepting a version of natural theology. It was on these biographical issues about Barth that Macquarrie's reply focused. But Rahner formulated his concern also in another way, one that was more systematic. If 'God's grace and self-communication are always *a priori* at work' among human beings, then surely we cannot simply endorse Barth's claim that any human attempt to reach God is 'sinful or even blasphemous'. Then comes a revealing sentence:

> Need one conceive the problem in terms of God descending vertically from above to humanity below, or of humanity ascending to God above, if God is already present below, at the very beginning of humanity's search, in the form of grace-with-humanity? (p. 63)

There are issues here about grace and nature to which I will shortly return. More significant than these, however, is Rahner's sense that the dilemmas between starting with God or starting with creation, between a theology 'from above' and a theology 'from below', are somehow to be avoided.

The opening, perhaps programmatic essay in *Theological Investigations* 3, the volume bringing together Rahner's early papers on the spiritual life, is entitled 'Reflections on the Problem of the Gradual Ascent to Christian Perfection',[6] and was first published in 1944. The 'problem' that Rahner identifies is the question of how to make sense of Christian talk about ascent to God, growth in the life of God, if we exclude merely 'gnostic' or 'mystic' conceptions of the ideal. Even now, we may have to pause before we recognize the problem for what it is, so influential are the metaphors of spiritual ascent. What sense can we make of the idea of growth in the Christian life if we exclude ways of thinking that imply an escape from the human condition?

A crude summary of the argument is enough here: Rahner suggests that we need to understand spiritual growth in terms of what we now call life-cycle theory, and also in terms of growth in freedom or existential depth. The important point for our purposes is not so much the details of Rahner's answer as the insight determining his question: both the logic of the incarnation, and indeed a philosophical analysis of what it is for *humans*, spirits in the world, to know God demand a close integration between human and religious development. The theological enterprise for Rahner is to gain insight into the graced world as it is, to help us appropriate what is 'always already there' (*immer schon gegeben* – the phrase is almost a refrain in Rahner's philosophical writings). We may stand in permanent dynamic relationship to what grounds our inevitable questioning as spirits in the world, to the *woraufhin* of the *Vorgriff*. But we do *not*, for Rahner, ever in any literal sense move towards it – despite what some of the conventional translations of *Vorgriff* and *woraufhin* inevitably suggest. Rahner's theology is radically uninterested in going anywhere. If God is with us, then the theological enterprise must be of the kind so memorably expressed at the end of Eliot's *Four Quartets*:

> Our life is a constant exploration that culminates, paradoxically, not in reaching some longed-for destination but in coming to know our very starting-point 'for the first time'.

Because theology cannot even begin unless God is in relationship with humanity – quite apart from the radical account of this relationship implicit in Christianity, according to which God-in-Godself (the immanent Trinity) is identical with God-for-us (the immanent Trinity) – Rahner can sit lightly to the arguments about whether theology is better done 'from above' or 'from below'. What is at stake is an incomprehensible mystery of interaction that we can approach only through figures of speech. Thus a good Christology, say, will draw freely on both 'ascending' and 'descending' motifs, and recognize that the right use of such figures of speech depends on our not employing them beyond a certain point. The Chalcedonian definition places limits on the extent to which it is legitimate to use the metaphor of divine descent in connection with Jesus Christ. Rahner's Christology is not written programmatically 'from below' in the manner of Pannenberg's; it is only redressing, not replacing, a mainstream ecclesial Christology over-determined by Alexandrian approaches 'from above'.

By contrast, the conclusion of Macquarrie's 1984 lecture suggests that his elegantly expressed learning serves a rather different intellectual project. The language is significant: Macquarrie speaks of 'a legitimate and indeed compelling way that leads *from* the knowledge of the human *to* the knowledge of the divine' (my emphasis). Macquarrie's commitment to the metaphor of an epistemological journey is notably stronger than Rahner's. Though his rhetoric is gentle and typically eirenic, and though he sometimes presents 'the anthropological approach' simply as a legitimate, newer alternative to the classical one, Macquarrie effectively regards this approach as the only legitimate possibility, at least within the order of knowing. It alone enables us to start with something familiar, something accessible and non-controversial; from that, we can move on to the altogether more problematic business of talking about God. The alternative approach, 'from God's side' as it were, can be criticized devastatingly for the formal contradictions that at least wholesale versions of it involve. How can you have *human beings* talking about something which is allegedly from God *alone*? The weight of Macquarrie's argument lies, however, on the claim that talk of God is no longer generally intelligible or acceptable. Hence the idea of God can no longer serve as a foundation upon which to build an edifice of knowledge. Metaphors of transportation play a larger role in Macquarrie's project than in Rahner's. In the 1984 lecture, theology appears as a kind of intellectual engineering moving us from the known to the unknown, from the created world to God.[7]

Reason and Revelation

Once we recognize this central difference between how Macquarrie and Rahner imagined the theological enterprise, the other points of difference politely and indirectly expressed in the Heythrop exchange fall into place. Though Rahner endorsed Macquarrie's contention that natural and revealed theology were of a piece, he qualified his agreement:

> Of course, in this connexion, I would not use the term 'apologetics' but rather 'fundamental theology'. I regard the latter not so much as a

presentation of Christian dogma which should authenticate itself, but rather I would say that it is an *argumentative* effort of humanity in its approach to God. (*Theology*, p. 61)

Rahner's talk of 'argumentative effort' here – whatever the German was for 'argumentative' – is hardly clear, but we can probably gloss it in terms of the appeal to the unbeliever made in *Foundations of Christian Faith*. Christianity is presented in terms of the 'inescapable circle' between human 'horizons of understanding' and 'what is said, heard and understood'. Rahner is clarifying those connections, and then making an appeal to the non-believer's freedom, an appeal rooted in the universalism of the gospel and of any coherent doctrine of creation:

> ... everyone is then asked whether they can recognise themselves as that person who is here trying to express their self-understanding, or whether, in responsibility before themselves and their lived existence, they can regard as their truth the conviction that they are not a person of the kind that Christianity promises for them.[8]

What Rahner is *not* doing is to build a justification for a problematic Christianity on the basis of a supposedly uncontroversial account of human nature. Nor is it central to his strategy to claim that the unbeliever is guilty of some kind of intellectual mistake (even though some version of a proof for something less than Christian faith, namely for God's existence, is an element within a more complex whole).

For Macquarrie, the tradition of 'classical theism' was in multiple ways religiously inadequate; *In Search of Deity* is an attempt to replace that tradition with a more adequate 'dialectical theism', on the basis of which the doctrine of the Trinity can be at least adumbrated, and with which the idea of incarnation is somehow more compatible (*Deity*, pp. 231, 233). Responding to the first of Rahner's questions at Heythrop, Macquarrie also spoke of a 'common grace', a grace given in creation, with which 'the grace that we know in the Christian faith is continuous'. But the continuities that Rahner concedes are only part of the story, and the other part is all about disjunction. Rahner was uninterested in epistemological continuities between grace and nature; in his view, there are elements in the Christian message which it is a mistake to justify by any means other than an appeal to grace. Quite apart from the questions to be raised about just how classical Macquarrie's 'classical theism' actually was, it was self-evident for Rahner that Christianity relies on 'an ontological ultimate which a merely rational ontology would perhaps never suspect' (*Foundations*, p. 222), and hence there is no need to render philosophical theology more 'dialectical'. Rahner moves within Vatican I's teaching of

twofold order of knowledge of God (*Dei filius*, chapter 4).[9] The knowledge derived from natural reasoning and the knowledge which comes
from grace both refer to the same creation under God, but otherwise they
remain severely distinct.

Rahner's 'fundamental theology' parts company with the rationalism
of its predecessors. Rahner complies with Vatican I's rejection of fideism,
not by refining the strategy of developing a philosophical foundation
on which subsequent theology can build; such an approach leads to
an irresoluble dilemma between extrinsicism and intrinsicism. Rather,
Rahner understands the philosophical moment of theology in purely
formal terms, in terms of a fundamental correlation between what is the
case and what can be known. Thus central to his project is simply a sense
that there must be a correlation between the uniqueness of Jesus and the
capacity of humans to receive his revelation. This strategy makes a claim
about human reason at large and the intrinsic intelligibility of whatever is
the case, and thereby respects Vatican I's prohibition of fideism. But at the
same time, it leaves the material question about what reality consists in
unadjudicated by philosophy; this account of the openness of all human
persons for God thus remains open for the kind of radically gratuitous,
outrageous initiative that Christianity proclaims. Thus Rahner remains
uninterested in exploring further the hinterland between what is sheerly
gracious and what might be the case in some hypothetical world of 'pure
nature'; neither admirers from English-language natural theology such as
Macquarrie, nor theological critics such as de Lubac and (ironically) the
early von Balthasar, draw Rahner into this territory.

Rahner's cosmos is far from anarchic, but its order comes from a God
who is beyond human comprehension. His version of an 'anthropological approach' proceeds from a sense that the subjective and the objective
must somehow fit together, even if the principles on which they do so
remain permanently a matter of ongoing discovery. He avoids epistem-
ologies that take either the subjective or the objective as foundational, as
absolute; in particular, many of Rahner's most distinguished critics are
simply wrong to read Rahner as straitjacketing God's revelation within a
particular philosophical account of human subjectivity.

In this connection, it may be significant here Macquarrie's answer to
Rahner's third question developed into quite a sharp criticism of the idea
of the anonymous Christian. Both Barth and Rahner, Macquarrie says:

> . . . take the view that the whole human race already is embraced by
> the salvific will of God, and that in a sense the decisive salvation has
> already taken place, although this has all got to work itself out in
> history. What I think worries me is the idea that human beings can

somehow be already recipients of salvation and yet not be aware of it ... the human being is so much constituted by consciousness and responsibility and self-understanding ... that the concept of salvation cannot really mean very much until he begins to understand it and appropriate it into his own being. (*Theology*, p. 66)

For Macquarrie, the idea that what is most important in our identity under God might elude our reflective awareness is seriously problematic. What the human subject knows is foundational for Macquarrie's account of humanity under God. For Rahner, what we know about ourselves and our God, though in its way necessary, is always grounded in a reality that is mystery, beyond human understanding. What really matters may well lie beyond our reflective awareness.

Concluding Spiritual Postscript

During the Heythrop lecture Rahner's well-known impatience and mental energy got the better of his politeness. He gave up listening to a lecture that he had already read being delivered in a language which he could not understand orally. To the amusement or edification of the gathering, he pulled out his rosary, sitting as he was on the podium, and began to pray it as the lecture continued.

Within the intellectual framework of Macquarrie's lecture, this incident is a pious triviality – it is no doubt nice that Rahner practised conventional Catholic devotion, but such devotion is fundamentally incidental, decorative. But within Rahner's own way of thinking, his impatient gesture at one of his last public appearances is significantly symbolic. Rahner's 'spirituality', the experience of being drawn into a reality beyond our grasp, is central, rather than incidental, to his theological creativity; his creativity depends on his having taken the witness of the mystics, not as the object of some arcane and marginal specialism within practical theology, but as a stimulus to renew the whole range of theological disciplines.[10]

There is a rather irresponsible tendency in contemporary Rahnerian literature to *contrast* Rahner the mystic with Rahner the philosophically acute theologian – a tendency with its roots in anti-intellectual prejudices about the nature of the devout life. But it remains true that prayer and spirituality are central to Rahner's work, in a way that is and was quite revolutionary both within his own Roman Catholic world and beyond. Rahner's 'anthropological approach to theology' is not an apologetic strategy starting from the self-evident realities of everyday experience and moving to the more difficult reality of God, but rather an attempt to articulate more fully how the mysteries of salvation – which remain mysteries permanently – interact with human experience here and now.

One might be tempted to describe the use of the expression 'anthropological approach to theology' in Macquarrie and in Rahner as itself a *coincidentia oppositorum*. That would, however, be to trivialize Macquarrie's use of that richly traditional term. It would be better to say that Macquarrie drew on Rahner selectively in order to develop his own distinctive theology – one that functioned powerfully within cultures largely unknown to Rahner himself. And if Rahner's work has stimulated others to work along lines very different from himself, this is all of a piece with his thought.

Notes

The quotations from Rahner vary in places from the published translations, notably in avoiding translating 'Mensch' as 'man'.

1 Karl Rahner, *Theological Investigations*, Vol. 1, ET London: Darton, Longman & Todd, 1961, pp. 79–148. German 1954.

2 *Theological Investigations*, Vol. 1, pp. 149–200.

3 *Theological Investigations*, Vol. 1, p. 164.

4 *Theological Investigations*, Vol. 1, p. 184.

5 *Heythrop Journal*, 25 (1984), pp. 272–87. Reprinted in *Theology*, pp. 48–60.

6 Karl Rahner, *Theological Investigations*, Vol. 3, ET London: Darton, Longman & Todd, 1967, pp. 3–23.

7 Cf. N. Lash *Easter in Ordinary: Reflections on Human Experience and the Knowledge of God*, London: SCM Press, 1988, pp. 69–70.

8 Karl Rahner, *Foundations of Christian Faith*, ET London: Darton, Longman & Todd, 1978, pp. 24–5, translation corrected.

9 *Dei Filius*, as cited in Norman P. Tanner (ed. and tr.), *Decrees of the Ecumenical Council*, London: Sheed and Ward, 1990, pp. 804–11.

10 Philip Endean, *Karl Rahner and Ignatian Spirituality*, Oxford: Oxford University Press, 2001; 'Spirituality and Religious Experience: A Perspective from Rahner', in Declan Marmion (ed.), *Christian Identity in a Postmodern Age: Celebrating the Legacies of Karl Rahner and Bernard Lonergan*, Dublin: Veritas, 2005, pp. 201–19.

10 'The Task of Theology Is Never Finished'

John Macquarrie and Karl Rahner on the Challenges and Limits of Doing Theology

MORWENNA LUDLOW

My title comes from the first chapter of *The Faith of the People of God: A Lay Theology*, in which John Macquarrie sets out with his customary clarity his views on the nature and purpose of Christian theology. It is, he writes, 'the attempt to state as clearly as possible the beliefs or doctrines that belong to the Christian way of life'.[1] This task of 'clear statement' includes, however, some constructive work explaining how Christian beliefs 'cohere among themselves' and to what extent they are 'compatible with all the other beliefs that we hold in the modern world' (*People*, p. 1). Both of these tasks together ensure that the work of theology is never complete, because the community of the Church and its historical context are constantly changing, calling for a continuous process of restatement and new explanation. In this perspective on theology Macquarrie is very close to Karl Rahner and indeed he cites Rahner as a good example of a theologian who realizes the ongoing nature of theological reflection.[2] In my paper I will compare these two theologians and try to outline very briefly how their shared conception of theology stems partly from their reaction to Rudolf Bultmann's demythologizing and their common interest in existentialism, but partly also from similar understandings of Christian history. Without claiming that Macquarrie has the ecclesial stature or the historical importance of Rahner, the comparison perhaps throws light on his aims and methods.

Rahner was more directly influenced by Heidegger than by Bultmann. However, in his writings on the development of doctrine it seems clear that Rahner is responding to the challenge laid down by Bultmann. This is particularly clear in his writings on eschatology. Thus, although Rahner is decidedly more critical about the results of Bultmann's approach, it is fair to say that Rahner and Macquarrie both agree about the fundamental problem that Bultmann identifies – Macquarrie, for instance, seems fond of quoting Bultmann's thought that:

> It is impossible to use electric light and the radio, and to avail ourselves of modern medical and surgical discoveries, and at the same time to believe in the New Testament world of demons and spirits. We may think we can manage it in our own lives, but to expect others to do so is to make the Christian faith unintelligible to the modern world.[3]

Both men share with Bultmann the hope that by making Christian beliefs more intelligible, they will not only help Christians understand what they believe, but will enable their beliefs to becomes more meaningful in an existential sense, in every aspect of their lives.

However, both Rahner and Macquarrie disagree with some apparent implications of this programme of 'demythologization'. Whereas some existentialist interpretations of Christianity seem to imply that it is possible to abstract timeless truths from the myth-laden text of Scripture, Rahner and Macquarrie both assert that *any* theological statement is historically conditioned and couched in the terminology of its own day.[4] This immediately views the task of the theologian as constructive rather than as abstractive. Rahner in particular is keen to emphasize that the sort of restatement that is called for from the theologian is not merely a kind of theological window-dressing: 'we must not suppose that the differences we are looking for need and can consist of a merely literary, verbal or rhetorical adaptation of an old theology to our time, in new "applications", "outlooks" or corollaries in the practical order.' Rather, Rahner is looking for a dogmatic theology that tries to be truly adequate to reality – that is adequate to its own time.[5]

It is precisely because the historical context in which Christians live their lives and in which theologians do theology is always changing, that Rahner and Macquarrie emphasize that theology is not only a constructive, but also a never-ending constructive task: these two characteristics always go together, making theology a thoroughly future-oriented exercise.

> Tradition, as everyone knows, can become dead and mechanical, so that all growth and healthy development are inhibited . . . The function of tradition that has been stressed here is interpretation, and interpretation need to be done over and over again. (*Principles*, p. 11)

Theologians are never spared the task of prompt renewal. Anything which is merely conserved or which is merely handed down without a fresh, personal exertion beginning at the very sources of Revelation, rots as the manna did.[6]

In this common emphasis on the historically-conditioned nature of all theology and on the constant task of the theologian to reinterpret for each generation, we can find in Macquarrie and Rahner a balance between Scripture and tradition. For whereas Bultmann's comments were addressed to Scripture, primarily of course the New Testament, Macquarrie and Rahner are calling for a demythologizing (or more properly a 'remythologizing') of the Christian faith encapsulated in Scripture and a reformulation of later doctrinal statements. They assume that one should go back to Scripture as well, but their remarks reveal an understanding that the reformulation of doctrine is not just what modern theologians are called to do now, but what all (good) theologians of the past have done. Thus, one is able to see, for example, the Greek technical terminology developed in the fourth and fifth centuries as historically conditioned attempts to restate or make intelligible an earlier faith in and experience of God as Father, Son and Spirit. This frees the theologian from the necessity of viewing such doctrinal formulations as either false philosophical accretions to the Christian gospel or, on the other hand, as normative definitions in addition to which nothing more can be said. Rahner challenges the kind of overly pious deference which arises from the latter perspective: the central doctrines of Christianity 'simply bristle with formulations which no one examines but towards which everyone makes a reverential bow'. This mistaken deference is in fact an intellectual laziness which treats the thought of earlier generations as 'a sort of couch for the thought of later generations'. Rather, 'definitions are much less an end than a beginning'.[7] Using a different metaphor, Macquarrie argues that conciliar definitions rule some interpretations out as 'dead ends', but that ideally the Church is incited by them 'to pursue more promising ways in the hope of gaining a fuller version of the truth'. Chalcedon, for example, 'is an important milestone in the church's progress toward a deeper understanding of Jesus Christ, but it left plenty of scope for further reflection'.[8] It is not surprising if his views echo Rahner's here, for he quotes him, and indeed seems fond of quoting Rahner particularly on this topic of the development of doctrine. It has to be noted, however, that Rahner is far more deferential to doctrinal definitions than is Macquarrie, and that naturally their different confessional loyalties come into play here.

Because of their emphasis on the constructive aspect of theology and the never-ending nature of the theological task, both men are rather critical of a certain kind of writing that reduces historical theology simply (in Rahner's words) 'to showing how what prevails today came into being'.[9] Against this, rather, Rahner argues that what one should look for in historical *theology* (as opposed simply to history) is 'a route which we today can follow into a territory not yet explored'.[10] Despite the danger of reading our own modern preoccupations into past writings, the aim should be to do theology *with* or *alongside* the writers of the past.[11] Similarly, Macquarrie criticizes a tendency (which he detects especially in Anglican theology) to read the theology of the past in a way that does not look forward to the future: '[the rise of the critical historical method] has led to a type of theology which is parasitic, in the sense that it criticizes the tradition but makes no contribution of its own to what ought to be a growing expanding tradition' (*Theology*, pp. 99–100).

It must be stressed, however, that there is another reason for the never-ending nature of the theological task, besides the continually changing contexts in which Christian believers find themselves. Both Macquarrie and Rahner acknowledge that theology is *never* adequate – that is, it does not simply become inadequate as one set of circumstances overtakes another, but no theology can ever be adequate to what it is trying to describe. In Rahner's theology this view rests on his overarching emphasis on the concept of God as mystery. From this perspective, it would be blasphemous to suggest that any theology could be adequate even to such divine revelation as humans have been granted.[12] Similarly, Macquarrie writes that all theological formulations are approximate as a result of the nature of faith and of revelation: 'Faith is the response of the whole man to God, and this cannot be completely transcribed into words. Likewise the Christian revelation has been given in the person of Jesus Christ, not in words.'[13] This leads him on some occasions to describe revelation as giving rise not to a body of dogma, but rather to a group of 'fragments' (*Hope*, p. 104).

The result of the emphasis on the idea that the task of theology is never complete is, as I have already suggested, that Macquarrie and Rahner both have a very fluid and forward-looking concept of Christian doctrine. Rahner comments to the effect that the development of a technical terminology in theology – as in science – is a sign of the inherent fertility (and thus forward movement) of the discipline.[14] Macquarrie sometimes suggests that the inevitable tension between 'fragments' of doctrine gives Christian doctrine an internal drive to development:

> The various theological interpretations of the Christian hope, some individual, some social, some cosmic, some this-worldly, some other-worldly, some evolutionary, some revolutionary, some looking to the

present, others to the future, are not so much rivals to each other as fragments of an inclusive vision that escapes us. We cannot synthesize all these theologies, but neither can we choose one of them and reject all the others. We have got to let them confront one another, correct one another, even conflict with one another, and in this dialectical procedure, both the strengths and the weaknesses of the different positions will come to light and we may hope to come closer to the total vision. (*Hope*, pp. 103–4)

However, it will be already evident that doctrinal change is construed by neither Rahner nor Macquarrie as some automatic readjustment or organic development by 'theology' abstractly conceived. There is no theology without theologians and no change without a believer to own it. Thus, their reflections often highlight the task of the theologian as an active one, and they are demanding about the task required: no one can rest, to use Rahner's vivid image, on the 'couch' of the theology of the previous generation, because that couch will quickly become worn out and sagging. To put it in Macquarrie's words (from the preface to his *Principles of Christian Theology*):

> The fact that every theology will have some flaws is not a reason for turning away from the theological task or for underestimating the place of theology in the Church's life. Theology is indispensable to the Church, and where theology fails, we must take this as a demand for better theology and certainly not as an excuse for turning away from it or for imagining the Church can get along without it. (*Principles*, p. vii)

The idea of the challenge of theology is expressed by both theologians, I suggest, from three perspectives: that of judgement, of risk and of responsibility.

The idea of judgement – making critical choices between different expressions of a doctrine – is implicit in the notion that the task of the theologian is an active one, not just the passive reception of tradition, but the transmission of it with the necessary modifications.[15] The element of judgement is important even when it is a case of making decisions between various options within the Christian tradition. Thus, both Macquarrie and Rahner take eschatology as an example of a case where there are conflicting traditions, even in Scripture. It is part of the job of a theologian to make judgements on which parts of the tradition should override others, or – more properly – which should be highlighted. Sometimes the grounds for making judgements between different parts of the Christian tradition are to do with internal coherence, at other times coherence with modern scientific understandings of the universe. Despite the demand for intelligibility, however, ultimately neither theologian is seeking a bland uniformity across all contemporary theology: in the 1950s Rahner indeed bemoans the fact that contemporary textbooks of dogmatics demonstrate the 'graveyard calm of weariness and boredom'; they are apparently oblivious of the theological disagreements of centuries before – disagreements which, he stresses, were within the bounds of orthodoxy (Prospects, p. 11). Rahner even structured one of his writings on purgatory in dialogue form, allowing two (unnamed) theologians to debate traditional and radical interpretations of the doctrine without Rahner the author obviously coming down on one side or the other.[16] Another example of the avoidance of a perfectly harmonious theology for the sake of truth is also found in Rahner's eschatology: although he expresses the belief that one should hope that all people will be saved he is unwilling to let go of the concept of hell completely.[17] Similarly, in the last chapter of his book *Christian Hope* Macquarrie argues that hope is not hope if it does not acknowledge 'an element of fallibility and uncertainty', while not wanting to go so far as to say that history as a whole might fail, and God's purposes for the world might be totally denied (*Hope*, pp. 110–11).

For Macquarrie, this attitude to tension in theology applies even when the tension is caused by views which might be considered heretical:

> Theology is a dialectical science, so that every minority view, yes, even every heretical and schismatic view, has its elements of truth and justification, so that the majority view needs the constant stimulation and correction of the minority view if one is to move along the path that leads to deeper truth.[18]

Macquarrie reminds his readers that 'almost every member of the church and every theologian' has probably at one time or another believed something that is, strictly speaking, heretical, but that the only really *dangerous* heresy is that which has 'a systematic and deliberate quality' (*Thinking*, p. 47). Both Macquarrie and Rahner are too good historians to forget the role of heresy in the development of early Christian doctrine, so it is no surprise to find Macquarrie quoting Rahner to the effect that the best response to heresy is not to try to suppress it 'by administrative means', but to respond to it by a positive declaration of what the theologian believes to be the truth (*Thinking*, p. 49). Discussion is the best antidote if the alleged heretic is ready for discussion. In any case the Church must be prepared to accept some responsibility for the emergence of heresy, which often arises as the result of the poor articulation of doctrine by the Church (*Thinking*, p. 48).

Such an attitude to heresy underlines Macquarrie's forthright attitude to risk in theology, which demands that even 'drastic reformulations' should be made if they are necessary:

> In the search for such reformulations, some mistakes are bound to be made. Truth is occasionally sacrificed in the interests of a supposed relevance, and sometimes novelty is prized for its own sake. Yet it is better that such risks should be taken than that the church should be left only with the formulations of earlier times, often couched in antiquated terminology and conceptuality. Even the mistakes can be helpful as exercises in experimental thinking, for it may only be after a position has been explored that one becomes aware that it leads to a dead end or is subversive of some vital Christian truth. In general, the Church is able to contain such aberrations, and may even be stimulated by them to find new and more adequate formulations of doctrine. (*Thinking*, p. 48)

Of course, one person's attitude to risk differs very much from that of another and Macquarrie's writing for the 1978 Lambeth Conference on the question of whether women should be ordained, for example, demonstrates a fair degree of caution and emphasis on the need for consensus – despite the fact that he outlines a very similar view on the benefits of heretical and schismatic opinion in the course of his argument (*Theology*, p. 91). Rahner, similarly, is sometimes accused of developing doctrinal propositions which appear more traditional than his protestations about the need for doctrinal reformulation might suggest. Part of this is a matter of genre and perspective – his entries in the encyclopedia *Sacramentum Mundi*, for example, are more focused on relatively traditional formulations of Roman Catholic dogma, while many of his articles in *Theological Investigations* are much more exploratory. Nevertheless, although some of the results may occasionally seem tame from the perspective of the beginning of the twenty-first century, one should not underestimate his perception of the risk involved in reformulation: one must be prepared to be wrong. He sometimes speaks of the 'danger' of such a task, and firmly criticizes those theologies that are 'very orthodox' but 'not very vividly alive'.[19] (Although Rahner is writing mainly about an intellectual danger – the danger of being wrong, misleading, unintelligible, of distorting the truth – he was clearly aware of other dangers, having himself been placed under pre-censorship early on in his theological career.) Particularly in his writings on the development of doctrine, Rahner is strongly opposed to those who draw up an all-inclusive theory of doctrinal development with the express purpose of using it to discard developments of which they disapprove. In answer to the imagined anxious query as to whether his position is leaving the door wide open to 'the rankest proliferations of pseudo-theological speculation and callow visionary enthusiasm', Rahner replies:

> The danger of the human factor [in the development of doctrine] simply remains a danger, and no precautionary measures exist which can exclude it unambiguously at the very start. Any attempt to protect oneself by human sharpsightedness against such a danger, so that it is simply not possible for anything to 'slip through', is itself radically false. It is the promise of the Spirit and that alone which prevents the final realization of an ever-present danger.[20]

So one should trust in the Spirit and not resort to doctrinal policing. As a result, Rahner's theology is often difficult to place on the usual conservative–liberal spectrum: he is deeply committed to the need for re-expressing theology for today, and yet equally deeply faithful that the results will be in quite a close continuity with the past. As Karen Kilby has insightfully put it, the truth seems to be that 'at his best and most creative Rahner shows that theology is not a zero-sum game, so that the more one is orthodox the less one can rethink the faith in changing circumstances'.[21]

For both Rahner and Macquarrie, the riskiness of doing theology is also insured against by a strong sense of responsibility to the Church. By this I mean, of course, the Church broadly conceived: the 'faith of the people of God' in Macquarrie's words, or the faith of the ordinary believer, whom Rahner often has in mind in his projects of doctrinal reformulation.[22] Both theologians also clearly feel a sense of responsibility to the Church, historically conceived. Hence Rahner admits that doctrine, although it develops, is always bound in some way by the past, and Macquarrie notes that radical discontinuity in doctrine is nonsensical: 'there are limits to what [Christianity] can become without losing its identity.'[23] This sense of responsibility to the whole of the Church, across time and space is important to these two theologians, not least because it counters the individualism which is obviously one of the most pressing dangers of an overly open approach to the development of doctrine.[24]

In reflecting on the nature of theology and the tasks of the theologian, Rahner and Macquarrie stress its demands and challenges: the need to re-express doctrine in terms that are meaningful to one's audience; the need to undertake this task constantly, with an awareness both of responsibility to the truth and of the riskiness of the enterprise. Regardless of what we might think about each theologian's success, one of the most attractive aspects of their thought is their common recognition of theology's finitude. The theology of each man is characterized by writings and re-writings, not as if they are searching after an elusive 'perfect' formulation, but because they recognize that different situations demand different kinds of response. It is not a coincidence, I think, that some of the best theology from each writer is the most occasional; nor is it surprising that each took very seriously the theologian's duty to communicate beyond the academy. Furthermore, their shared belief that answers to theological questions require refining and reformulating over the course of a career presents a challenge to their academic readers, both historians of doctrine and systematic theologians. To the former, they present a warning against reading a theologian's corpus as one homogenous mass with no lines of development or changes of mind; to the latter, they continually present a reminder of the necessity, but also the inevitable finitude, of doctrinal reformulations. Thus, for both the historian and the systematician, Rahner and Macquarrie remind us that 'the past can only be preserved in its purity by someone who accepts responsibility for the future'.[25]

Notes

1 *People – A Lay Theology* (1972), p. 1; cf. *Principles* p. vii: 'The theological task needs to be done over and over again, as new problems, new situations, and new knowledge come along.'

2 'The Anglican theological tradition' (1975), reprinted in *Theology*, pp. 92, 99.

3 'Development of doctrine' (1993), reprinted in *Stubborn Theological Questions* (2003), p. 153, quoting Bultmann's contribution in H.-W. Bartsch, (ed.), 1953, *Kerygma and Myth*, London: SPCK, p. 5.

4 '. . . the multiple ways in which tradition speaks of the last things cannot be simply and on principle reduced to one and the same "demythologized" meaning' (Karl Rahner, 'Last Things', in Karl Rahner *et al.* (eds), *Sacramentum Mundi*, New York: Herder & Herder, Vol. III (1970), p. 275). Macquarrie is in agreement with Rahner on this point, but is more prepared to defend Bultmann in particular against the accusation that he made the error: see, for example, his comment on Bultmann's demand for the existential interpretation of eschatology: 'Existential truths are not timeless generalizations, but concrete expressions of self-understanding that have to be appropriated and applied in particular situations' (*Hope*, p. 100).

5 'The Prospects for Dogmatic Theology' (German 1954), *Theological Investigations*, Vol. I, London: Darton, Longman & Todd, 1961, pp. 6–7.

6 Rahner, 'Prospects', p. 10.

7 Rahner, 'Prospects', p. 10.

8 *Jesus Christ*, pp. 165–6; see also *Principles*, p. 12 and *Stubborn*, p. 160.

9 Rahner, 'Prospects', p. 7.

10 'Prospects', p. 8; cf. pp. 9–10: [good historical theology] 'is the art of reading texts in such a way that they become not just votes cast in favour of or against our current positions (positions taken up long ago), but say something to us which we in our time have not considered at all or not closely enough, about reality itself.'

11 Rahner, 'Prospects', pp. 8–10.

12 See, e.g. 'Prospects', p. 5; 'The development of dogma', in *Theological Investigations* Vol. I, pp. 43–4.

13 'Some thoughts on heresy' in *Thinking*, pp. 45–6.

14 'When a scientific discipline loses its power to forge concepts it becomes sterile ... Technical concepts are necessary if a science is to develop, because accumulated experience can only become fruitful for the achievement of a new, exact and various understanding when what has been acquired is made available for further employment by resolution into a determinate concept. Hypostasis, the supernatural [et al.] and many others are concepts of this kind, which have emerged as the condensed results of theological work which has often gone on for centuries, and so could and still can each form a point of departure and a conceptual tool for further development.' 'Prospects', pp. 4–5.

15 See e.g. 'Development', p. 152.

16 'Purgatory', *Theological Investigations*, Vol. 19 (1980) for a discussion of Rahner's stance as author in this article, see Morwenna Ludlow, *Universal Salvation*, Oxford: Oxford University Press, 2000, pp. 197–8.

17 'The hermeneutics of eschatological assertions', *Theological Investigations*, Vol. 4, 1968.

18 'The ordination of women to the priesthood' (1978) in *Theology*, p. 191; cf. 1986, 'Liberal and radical theologies compared', in *Thinking about God*, (1975), pp. 71–2: 'In the foreseeable future, Christian theology is likely to be pluralist. New truths will be won out of the constructive confrontations of the different points of view. The conflicts will sometimes be sharp. But they need not be bitter, and in subjects like theology, the truth is never found entirely in one position.'

19 Rahner, 'Prospects', pp. 7, 13.

20 Macquarrie, 'Development', p. 43.

21 Karen Kilby, 'Rahner', in Gareth Jones (ed.), *The Blackwell Companion to Modern Theology*, Oxford: Blackwell, 2004, p. 343.

22 See e.g. the beginning of 'Remarks on the theology of indulgences', *Theological Investigations*, Vol. 2, 1963, p. 175.

23 'Development', p. 160 (citing Maurice Wiles, and shortly afterwards Rahner).

24 *Principles*, pp. 10–11; compare Rahner's comments on the interplay between the individual theologian and the magisterium, 'Considerations on the development of dogma', *Theological Investigations*, Vol. 4, p. 15.

25 Rahner, 'Prospects', p. 7.

11 John Macquarrie: Creativity and Criticism

STEPHEN PLATTEN

Thomas More, Henry VIII's sometime Chancellor and author of *Utopia*, has occasioned more biographies than most, even against the background of that fascinating period of uncertainty and change marked by the politics of the early sixteenth century. Alongside these biographies stands Robert Bolt's acclaimed play, *A Man for All Seasons* (London: Samuel French, 1960). It does not purport to be a straightforward biographical dramatization, but it does seek to penetrate the mystery which surrounds the character of this most complex, political, and intelligent man. In the preface to the play, however, Bolt offers a more straightforward insight into the character of Thomas More.

> At any rate, Thomas More, as I wrote about him, became for me a man with an adamantine sense of his own self. He knew where he began and left off, what area of himself he could yield to the encroachments of his enemies, and what to the encroachments of those he loved. It was a substantial area in both cases, for he had a proper sense of fear, and was a busy lover. Since he was a clever man, and a great lawyer, he was able to retire from those areas in wonderfully good order, but at length he was asked to retract from that final area where he located his self. (p. xii)

Here, then, is Bolt briefly attempting to engage in descriptive biography. Later, as the play unfolds, Bolt sets out again in pursuit of the truth of More's character, but this time in a more obviously creative mode. This contrast may act as a metaphor in outlining the intentions of this chapter. In his extraordinarily productive life as a theological teacher, John Macquarrie has offered to the scholarly community two rather contrasting strands. Sometimes he has been more obviously an expositor and critic; elsewhere he has endeavoured to offer a systematic theology. On occasion his theological exploration might also be described as speculative. In the light of this distinction, then, when do we encounter him acting primarily as a descriptive critic and expositor, and where has he seen his task as that of being a more explicitly creative theologian? Macquarrie's range is vast. From systematic theologian to writer on spirituality, from ethical analyst to apologist for the Christian faith – all of these are there and more. In different ways various of his writings are patient of being placed at different points along that spectrum, then, which has description and criticism at one end and more explicit creativity at the other.

All this is clear not only from his writings, but also from his university lecturing. In the 1970s, early in the period when he was Lady Margaret Professor of Divinity in the University of Oxford, he offered two parallel series of lectures, on 'God and Human Nature' and 'Christology from Schleiermacher to Ritschl'. They demonstrated both the descriptive and the creative aspects of Macquarrie's work, and also the difficulty of attempting too sharp a distinction between the two. The series of lectures on Christology was a model of historical theology. This second series did explore its subject matter using Macquarrie's distinctive existential-ontological approach, but, at the same time, it engaged both descriptively and critically with contemporary theologians. So there were references to the work of Alistair Kee, one of Macquarrie's pupils, on theism; to Dennis Nineham, a colleague in Oxford, on the subject of cultural relativism; and to John Robinson, in this case on the issue of panentheism, as discussed in Robinson's *Exploration into God*. On one occasion he quipped: 'Write that down – you won't often be hearing me recommend you to read *John Robinson*.' His unmistakable Scottish tones rang out clearly as he emphasized the name which through *Honest to God* had become almost notorious. The lectures were in every case a model of clarity, spiced with humour, and interjected with the Professor's inimitable and piercing glance which would terrifyingly alight randomly upon the face of one student within the audience. But how does this mixture of exposition and creativity work itself out as one investigates Macquarrie's entire *oeuvre* written over a period of some fifty years?

In his first monograph, *An Existentialist Theology* (1955), Macquarrie stands most clearly within the stream of existentialist theological thought, which includes not only Bultmann, but also Paul Tillich. Macquarrie uses existentialist categories (and notably those of Heidegger) to establish both a theological epistemology, and also a common language or grammar within a culture that is not naturally theologically articulate. As Macquarrie's thought develops, however, there is a shift, already clear in *Principles of Christian Theology* (1966). An emphasis on both existentialism and ontology is now clear, as it was later in the Oxford lectures on 'God and Human Nature'. The aim is to rediscover authentic 'God-talk', beginning with humanity, and this means that the two key doctrines of God and humanity are entwined. Theology and anthropology became part of one and the same process of intellectual exploration. As Macquarrie critically engages with Bultmann, so he begins to seek a less individualistic existentialism, and a theology with more defined ontological roots. He admires Tillich's use of the terms 'ground of being' and 'ultimate concern' as he develops his systematics.

Macquarrie's dialogue with the American Episcopalian theologian John Knox, during his time at Union Seminary in New York had led him to a new engagement with the public domain, as he finally became an Anglican. Knox influenced him in formulating a more corporate (and so less individualistic) understanding of the 'Christ-event'. On the historical basis in the New Testament for Jesus' life he goes further than Bultmann's scepticism had warranted, and he adopted a new-style natural theology, a philosophical-theological approach that rejects both Barth's hostility to natural theology and Bultmann's one-sidedly existentialist theology. He is also keen to avoid a Barthian over-emphasis on transcendence, at the expense of an appropriate immanence. In his Oxford lectures he pointed out how a number of 'death of God theologians' had started out life as Barthians, and how an extreme emphasis on God's transcendence obstructed any understanding of God's engagement with humanity, and so any clear sense of divine initiative. Macquarrie prefers to describe God as *holy Being* and to see God as a deity who *lets be*. God, then, is both being in itself and the source of being for creation. There is a clear engagement of the divine with creation. Before tracing the development of this creative theology in the 1980s trilogy we turn to the descriptive work characteristic of all his teaching.

Twentieth-Century Religious Thought (1963) surveys a wide range of authors and material, from systematic theology through the philosophy of religion to more general critiques of religion. In concise descriptions and critical assessments authors on 'the frontiers of philosophy and theology, 1900–1960' are placed in 20 chapters and 66 groupings, each chapter and the whole book framed by introductions and conclusions. The 1971 edition contained a postscript on the latest decade, which was subsequently expanded into 'The Fourth Phase' (pp. 373–446), and the 2001 (fifth) edition included a chapter on postmodernism. The theological development of the century is very broadly divided into four phases, and a conclusion confirms the author's determination to view Christian theology from the perspective of philosophy and in particular reflection on religion. Since religion is concerned with truth, our understanding of religion should be reasonable, contemporary, comprehensive – but also 'on the way', in the process of development. We do not possess absolute truth and must live with a degree of relativism.

This early interest in setting Christianity in the broad context of the philosophical and empirical study of religion is complemented by one of his latest books, *The Mediators* (1995). This introduces nine 'spiritual geniuses', including Moses, Buddha, Socrates and Muhammed, encouraging beginners to enter the dialogue among the great religions of the world. The pen-portraits are not left starkly to hang in an austere and uninterpreted gallery. The conclusion considers how inter-religious dialogue may develop. It acknowledges the need for 'a long period of dialogue before we begin to see the shape of a future relation among the religions that will satisfy the competing claims of unity and diversity' (p. 150), and calls for 'a new openness and respect of one another among the adherents of the separate traditions' (*ibid.*). These reflections, partly stimulated in Egypt, Libya and Palestine at the end of the war when as an army chaplain he 'learned quite a lot about Islam' and 'learned more about human nature than one can learn in a classroom' (*Theologian*, p. 14), anticipate the new relevance of relations between Christianity and Islam, and illustrate the broadening canvas of Macquarrie's own theological journey.

A New Dictionary of Christian Ethics (1986) names Macquarrie as co-editor because it develops and replaces the original dictionary edited by Macquarrie alone in 1967. Although edited mainly by James Childress it retains about seventy contributions from Macquarrie while omitting all articles on individual thinkers. Again Macquarrie's ability to offer concise descriptive and critical introductions to individual authors and key theological, philosophical and ethical topics, is put to good use. The dictionary then stimulated him to gather together a selection on ethical issues, *Three Issues in Ethics* (1970). His critical, revisionist account of different natural law traditions within this collection remains a good starting-point for those embarking on a better understanding of the natural law tradition within Christian thought. As usual, the chapter begins with a broad overview characterized by a generous attitude to a wide range of traditions. It leads to the recurring theme of setting the discussion of Christian theology within the wider context of human nature. Macquarrie's theology is always anthropological. He begins by considering whether 'at least under present circumstances, the most appropriate way of doing Christian ethics is the way that sets out from the nature of man, rather than ways that begin from distinctively Christian concepts. The next step, after our discussion of contemporary human nature, is to consider the notion of natural law' (pp. 82–3).

This whole approach stands in clear contrast to that of Karl Barth and his various inheritors who are again prominent in Christian theological debate. Macquarrie's philosophical and descriptive method leads to a consistent generosity and breadth, and is bound to embrace a form of *natural* theology. One criticism of this approach is that it underplays Christian distinctiveness and fails to offer contemporary culture the riches of the tradition. But Macquarrie has throughout his teaching career written descriptively on the Christian churches and on different aspects of worship and spirituality, as well as doctrine and ethics. His introductory apologetics for lay people, *The Faith of the People of God* (1972) is a fine example:

> As lay people are being called upon to play an ever increasing role in the life of the church, it is important that better provision should be made for their theological training. But it is also important to understand that lay theology is not a simplified or watered down version of academic theology, but a distinct theological *genre*, with a character and dignity of its own. (p. vii)

In that same decade *Christian Unity and Christian Diversity* (1975) contributed to the ecumenical debate with the hallmarks of Macquarrie's own Anglo-catholicism, looking for Christian unity with a sacramentally based ecclesiology.

Alongside Macquarrie's ecclesiological reflections stand books that describe different aspects of the Christian spiritual tradition. Continuing to draw from the Catholic tradition, *Paths in Spirituality* (1972, 1992²) notoriously included a chapter which justifies and promotes the practice of Benediction of the Blessed Sacrament. Macquarrie writes: 'Benediction is very much an act of waiting on God, of letting him make his presence known, of letting him speak to us' (p. 101). Elements of a systematic theology, rooted in God's *holy Being* and *letting be* are evident even there. In a more academic theological presentation, *A Guide to the Sacraments* (1997) addresses issues of sacramentality and draws on the work of Oliver Quick and Edward Schillebeeckx in seeing Christ as the primordial sacrament. Macquarrie again begins as broadly as possible by reflecting upon a sacramental universe. His philosophical training helps him to engage with language about sacraments, and provides critical instruments to analyse Christian sacramentality. His most recent book, *Two Worlds are Ours* (2004), investigates the long tradition of mysticism in the same way. A brief analysis of the meaning of mysticism is followed by some description of the classical world and the ancient Hebrew tradition, before he sets out to reflect upon the New Testament and the patristic material. All these works stand foursquare within the mainstream Christian tradition, and there is no compromising the distinctiveness of the Christian faith, contrary to the criticism mentioned above. They exemplify a catholic and natural theological approach which is itself constantly engaging with the wider culture. The existentialist influences have been developed, but have never been obliterated.

Returning now to the later books which in effect comprise a revised systematic approach to Christian theology, *In Search of Humanity* (1982) renews Macquarrie's quest for a systematic engagement with the Christian theological tradition. Again humanity is, so to speak, his raw material as he seeks an anthropological argument for the existence of God. In this third systematic endeavour Macquarrie broadens the project still further, gathering together a number of his earlier reflections about humanity in a series of short thematic essays. The initial essay is titled *Becoming*, the concluding essay is on *Being*. The other chapters investigate a number of key themes, including freedom, transcendence, language, alienation, love, and religion. At the end of the book, Macquarrie reflects:

> The concept of God which has emerged in this last chapter conforms, I think, to what may be the only valid procedure for forming such a concept, that is, 'by treating the universal properties of created things' – in this case, the human being, the highest known created thing – 'as inferior forms of that which, in supremely excellent form, constitutes the divine nature'. (*Humanity*, p. 261)

That final quotation from Hartshorne and Reese (eds), *Philosophers Speak of God* (1953), p. 137, is followed by the concluding claim that 'a God so conceived as deeply involved with his creation is no oppressive God, but one whose transcendence is a goal and encouragement to the transcendence of humanity. But at this point the search for humanity merges into the search for deity, and would call for another book.' It is thus a 'launch pad' for the second part of the project, which issued in the more integrated form of *In Search of Deity* (1986). The danger of over-emphasizing transcendence is again in mind and leads him to argue for a dialectic in talk of God. Adapting the familiar model of Hegelian dialectic, Macquarrie argues that the initial thesis of transcendence (classical theism) is fundamental in establishing a balanced concept of God and God's relationship with us, that is with our human nature. But he at once follows this with a critique of classical theism and engages with a number of philosophers and theologians beginning with Plotinus and Dionysius, who represent an alternative tradition to both classical theism and to its atheistic and pantheistic rivals. One of his most interesting engagements is the dialogue he conducts with his fellow Celt, John Scotus Eriugena, which concludes that God is in that which he makes, and therefore that

God can be enriched. This is consistent with his earlier language in *Principles* where God is *holy Being* and *lets be*. It is also consistent with a lifelong critical dialogue with the theological tradition of panentheism. It is out of this dialogue, which continues into the modern period, engaging Leibniz, Hegel, Whitehead and Heidegger, that a dialectical concept of God emerges. From this dialectical concept, Macquarrie moves on to look at the implications of this for ethics, theology and also for Christianity's relationship with the other world religions.

Anyone critical of this programme of natural theology might well protest about the non-christological nature of the project up to this point. That follows in the third book of the trilogy, *Jesus Christ in Modern Thought* (1990). What Georgina Morley describes as Macquarrie's concept of the *grace of being* has its embodiment in the self-giving love of Jesus Christ (Morley, 2003, pp. 121–42). The *grace of being*, identified in the concept of God, is present throughout Macquarrie's work, but more focused in the two *Search* volumes, and now focused finally in the person of Christ. In Christ the dialectic reaches perfection. Humanity's self-transcendence and God's giving and self-transcendence meet. As in Macquarrie's earlier writings there is dialogue with the early tradition, and with a range of later theologians. Some have argued that Macquarrie's Christology, as set out in this book, errs in the direction of adoptionism, but in twelve theses Morley counters this claim.

The penultimate chapter of *Jesus Christ* posits two different possible endings to the christological story, which he designates as the standard *happy ending* and the *austere ending*. The happy ending is enshrined in a series of mysteries, dominated by the resurrection and with the ascension drawing out a further meaning of the resurrection. It includes the final mystery of his coming again, and here 'the clouds of mythology thicken, and preoccupation with the expectation of Christ's return has been the source of many superstitions and has led to the growth of many deviant Christian or quasi-Christian sects' (p. 410). Macquarrie clearly dislikes this part of the happy ending and draws on modern New Testament scholarship to suggest it may have originated in the disciples misunderstanding Jesus' intention. He refers to Moltmann's attempt to revive a futuristic eschatology, but is not enthusiastic:

> I suppose that one might say in a very general sense that if Christ is the revelation of God and of the divine purpose for the creation, then in the end the spirit of Christ which is also the Spirit of God will bring all things to their destined fulfilment. But this would come about by the gradual processes of history, not by the dramatic return of a heavenly judge . . . (p. 411).

The biological view of the virgin birth and also the descent into hell receive equally short shrift but both are quarried for the theological truths they express. Macquarrie thinks all these traditional ideas 'can make sense and be acceptable in the context of modern thought'. The austere ending is exemplified by Rudolf Bultmann for whom 'faith in resurrection is really the same thing as faith in the saving efficacy of the cross' and who asks 'whether all this mythological language about resurrection and ascension is not simply an attempt to express the meaning of the historical figure of Jesus and the events of his life' (pp. 43f.). Macquarrie defends the austere ending as broadly true to Johannine theology and conserving 'the essential truths of Christianity', but leaves the reader to make his or her own choice. He doubts whether they can be combined into an intelligible unity, but his own account of the 'happy ending' and his defence of Schleiermacher's essential orthodoxy (p. 386) may be considered steps in that direction.

This rapid survey suggests a further conclusion. Granted the validity of the distinction with which we began, exemplified by the way in which Robert Bolt treats his subject both descriptively and dramatically, then Macquarrie's work also exemplifies this contrast. Further discussion of his many monographs and articles would confirm that some are largely descriptive, expository and critical in both form and intention. Other works are clearly more creative works of theology, seeking to make systematic sense of the Christian tradition and God's engagement with creation and our human nature. We have cited some of the most significant of Macquarrie's endeavours in systematic theology, and also acknowledged that there are other works of a more hybrid nature. A further conclusion, however, can be drawn from Macquarrie's contribution as a whole, when seen both historically and in its developing integrity. This is that the very clarity in exposition and criticism which has made John Macquarrie such an excellent teacher has also contributed to his achievement as a creative theologian. For his 1980s' trilogy has applied his expository/critical method to his own creative thinking. Gone is the deliberately systematic approach of *Principles* which has some similarities with Tillich's approach to Christian systematics. In its place, we encounter a critical dialectic which echoes the Hegelian model. Macquarrie's method of beginning with humanity structures the argument in the first volume by providing a critical focus on specific issues. The second part of the dialectic is a dialogue with the tradition. The final volume issues from the dialectic and sees the self-giving Christ in terms of that dialectic. Even the two alternative endings of the Christology preserve the critical/expository method. So these two rich strands in Macquarrie's theological work are clear at every stage. But in his later creative systematic they come together in a dialectic which leads from an analysis of the human condition, through encounter with God to the self-transcendence discovered in Jesus Christ.

12 John Macquarrie and the Lambeth Conference

ROBERT JEFFERY

It was a warm sunny day in August 1968 at Church House Westminster. The Lambeth Conference was taking place. The bishops were engaged in a theological debate and some of the American bishops were finding it rather tedious. One of them suggested to Archbishop Ramsey, in the chair, that they might move on to another topic. The Primate's reply was typical of him. 'No, we are having a very interesting discussion and after we have had coffee we will listen to Professor Macquarrie.'

John Macquarrie was acting as a consultant to the Lambeth Conference. He had only been an Anglican for three years but his international reputation as a leading theologian was such that he had to be there. Commenting on this experience he wrote, 'I served as a consultant at the decennial Lambeth Conference and felt that 500 bishops, many of then rather mediocre, when gathered in one place are just too much for comfort' (*Theologian*, p. 39).

This was the first conference where consultants were invited and publicly acknowledged. There is a cautious remark in the 1958 report that the ecumenical delegates attended the public worship but were not otherwise present. In 1968 there were 26 consultants. Five of them were from the USA, sixteen of them from the United Kingdom, three from Africa and only one from India. The ecumenical delegates also participated.

Three volumes of preparatory essays were prepared for the bishops and John Macquarrie's contribution was entitled 'The Nature of Theological Language'.[1] In nine tightly argued pages, he appraised the state of theological language in the post-A. J. Ayer world. Theological language has its own nature and relates to the wider practices of religion. The basic word is 'God' which has become meaningless for many. But theology must have its own discipline and integrity. The writings of different theologians belong together in the framework of discourse about God within distinct polarities. The first of the three main polarities is the 'confessional-critical' polarity, inside which we see tensions between the experience of the individual and the history of the community. The confessional faith had to respond to critical questions and none is totally distinct, thus 'Barth is not uncritical and Tillich is not non-confessional'.

The second polarity is the 'existential-ontological'. Theological language keeps God and man together. It is essential not to talk of faith in isolation. Thus he affirms Ian Ramsey's description of situations of faith requiring both commitment and discernment and Tillich's description of God both as ultimate concern and being itself.

The third polarity is the 'symbolic-conceptual'. The mystery of God will require the use of images, symbols, analogues, and models.[2] Such language is also used in contemporary physics. All these polarities 'converge in the idea of the God-man'. Jesus Christ is the manifestation of the truth that theology tries to put into words. There is an urgent task to establish the logic of theology in today's world even though this task can never be completed.

One can imagine that some of the bishops did not find this an easy read, but Resolution 3 of the conference reflects his words: 'The conference recommends that theologians be encouraged to continue to explore fresh ways of understanding God's revelation of himself in Christ, expressed in language that makes sense in our time. It believes that this requires of the theologians respect for tradition, and of the Church, respect for freedom of enquiry.'[3]

The section of the conference looking at this topic was chaired by Bishop Leonard Wilson of Birmingham and called for the use of picture, poetry and parable as well as honest attempts to meet the secular thinker on his own ground. Exhortation, parables, and traditional phrases will not be enough. The section warned that people mistrusted the word 'myth', which they defined: 'The essence of religious myth is not its lack of historicity but its disclosure of a truth having an abiding significance which cannot be wholly conveyed in abstract terms; a faith which is too real and too powerfully present to be expressed literally.'[4]

The 1968 conference narrowly voted that the arguments for the ordination of women were 'inconclusive'.[5] It is not clear whether John Macquarrie had any input into that.

At Canterbury in 1978, John Macquarrie was again a consultant. This was the first campus-based conference and it affected its dynamics. There were 20 consultants. John Macquarrie was only one of three who had also been a consultant ten years earlier. (The other two were David Jenkins and Henry Chadwick.) By this time John had been at Christ Church as Lady Margaret Professor for eight years. John again wrote a preliminary paper, this time on 'The Bishop and Theologians'.[6] In a typically lucid paper, he begins by saying that ideally the bishop and theologian should be one and the same thing. Often in the early Church theologians had been bishops, but the work of a bishop has changed. Today a bishop's theological thinking will derive from a conversation with the theologians but there is a serous divide between theology and the life of the Church. Equally the secular world has put academic theologians under considerable pressure to justify their existence in the academic world. Even as a churchman, a theologian wishes to defend vigorously his academic freedom. Moreover all knowledge is under great question with the result that there is no one theology which can appeal to all. He approves of Rahner's view that we experience 'a number of theologies juxtaposed in a pluralist way, not contradicting each other, of course, but not susceptible of being positively incorporated into a higher synthesis' (*Theology*, p. 184).

Hence there was a need for continual theological exploration. But the role of the bishop cannot just be to encourage innovation. He quoted from an earlier American working party on the subject (of which he had been a member) that 'The bishop's role is the calm enabling of the theological dialogue.' The bishop is to encourage enquiry. In such dialogue there is potential division between conservatives and progressives, but the bishop must not be partisan and must try to prevent polarization. Theologians can be tempted to think they have obtained a 'gnosis' well beyond the ordinary believer. There cannot be a theological elite; theologians need spiritual sensitivity. Truth is as much a matter of prayer as it is of belief. Christian theology is too important to be left to the theologians; it is the responsibility of the whole Church. So 'doing theology' is a corporate experience where all bring their own expertise to enlighten each other. The bishops need the theologians but they also need the laity. This is the process of 'co-theologising'.[7]

There is little echo of this essay in the report, but this was probably because the conference had been dominated by the issue of the ordination of women which, in spite of the caution of the 1968 Lambeth Conference, had become a matter of fact in Hong Kong, Canada, New Zealand and the USA.

This subject was the subject of a major 'hearing' at the conference. The speakers giving the opening addresses were John Macquarrie and Bishop Cyril Bowles of Derby. The speeches were considered sufficiently important to be summarized in the final report.[8] Macquarrie's address is full of clarity and charity. He attempts not to rehearse the arguments for and against, but to categorize the nature of them. Then he defines the nature of the necessary consensus and finally considers, as women priests were now a fact, how the rest of the Communion should respond.

He points out that all thought is historically and sociologically conditioned and this raises questions for the defenders of a purely male priesthood. But there also has to be a critique of the sociology:

> it does seem to me that some of those who have been most forward in criticizing the tradition on the grounds of its cultural bias have themselves been operating in terms of an uncriticized secular ideology, characterized by egalitarianism, relativism, immanentism and sometimes too the alleged need for confrontation – characteristics which are all very questionable from a Christian point of view. I make these points to show that although some churches have already come to decisions on the question of women's ordination, the argument is by no means over and ought to be pursued in greater depth and with more critical acumen in those churches where no decision has yet been taken . . .' (Theology, p. 191)

Consensus does not mean that everyone should think alike. A measure of pluralism is acceptable but 'sheer pluralism would mean the dissolution of the Church'. The ordination of women requires a very wide consensus of at least two-thirds of the bishops, clergy and laity and where that happens most will end up accepting it. But is national or religious consensus enough? There is no such thing as an autonomous church. Given that some provinces had acted before the 1978 conference and had not taken ecumenical relations into account, how is it to be handled? He then points out that there is a hierarchy of truths and in that light the ordination of women is a peripheral and not a central issue. The Christian faith does not stand or fall by it. Hence there is no need for schism. There needs to be a 'modus vivendi' (cf. Theology, p. 191) worked out for those of very different positions, but 'it will be sad indeed' if this is being done at the price of a rapprochement with the Roman Catholic Church (Theology, p. 195). He ended with a question:

> If indeed women in the priesthood is a genuinely disputed question belonging to that peripheral area where pluralism is legitimate, is it not possible for our two Communions to continue to grow togther on the basis of the many things that they have in common while respecting difference of discipline on matters which surely do not make or unmake the Church? (Theology, pp. 195–6)

The resolutions of the conference reflect some of these concerns. The bishops have the task of maintaining and strengthen the fellowship of the Church. The unity of the Anglican Communion is to be preserved and worked for with mutual acceptance of each other in one Communion. It hoped that the ordination of women would not affect the ongoing dialogue with other churches. The resolutions were carried by 316 votes to 37 with 17 abstentions. There can be little doubt that the pressure for harmony was greatly assisted by John Macquarrie's contribution.[9]

By the time the 1988 Lambeth Conference took place John had retired from Christ Church and his successor (Rowan Williams) became a consultant. Here we see the man with a passion for theological truth and a respect for both enquiry and tradition. Not any way a campaigner, he was someone for whom everything is tempered by charity. Michael Ramsey was right – the Lambeth bishops did well to listen to John Macquarrie.

Notes

1 A.M. Ramsey (ed.) *Lambeth Essays on Faith*, London: SPCK, 1969, pp. 1–10. Revised in *Thinking*, pp. 3–14.

2 He had expanded on this in *God-Talk* (1967).

3 *The Lambeth Conference 1968 Resolutions and Reports*, London: SPCK, and New York: Seabury Press, 1968, p. 29.

4 *Lambeth*, p. 68

5 *Lambeth*, p. 39, Resolution 34.

6 *Today's Church and Today's World: The Lambeth Conference 1978 Preparatory Articles*, London: CIO, 1977, pp. 248–54.

7 A word he had coined in *People*, p. 18, and repeated in *Principles*, p. 441.

8 *The Report of the Lambeth Conference 1978*, London: CIO, 1978, Appendix, pp. 116–24.

9 He had expressed his views on Christian Unity in *Unity* (1975) but opposed the proposals of the consultation on Christian Unity in the USA.

13 Professor Macquarrie in China

HE GUANGHU

Professor John Macquarrie has been one of the few contemporary theologians who inhabited the Chinese mind after such a long time when more than one generation of the Chinese people had absolutely no idea of Christian theology. He is also one of the few Western theologians with a high reputation among, and an increasing influence upon, today's Chinese teachers and students who are interested in theology or religious thought. Furthermore I believe he will be one of the few Christian theologians to be studied, understood and admired by Chinese scholars, across the humanities and by academics studying different religions. In the following three sections, I will elaborate these three points.

I

During the period from 1949 to 1978, as the result of the driving out from China of all the Western missionaries and the clearing out from people's minds all religious influence since the Communist takeover, most of the Chinese people and all the young had had no idea about, or knowledge of, Christianity, not to mention Christian theology, except the idea that the missionaries were all foreign spies and that their influence was only to make the Chinese slaves to the Western mind.

My personal experience is a good example. I was born in 1950 and grew up in Guiyang, the largest city in Guizhou Province. My mother was a school teacher and my home was by the school yard, which used to be a part of the compound of the largest and most prestigious Catholic seminary next door to the Guiyang Cathedral. Most of the compound was occupied by some factories, storage space, administration blocks and even a police station from the 1950s to the 1980s. During my childhood, I used to see some pictures posted by the local administration on the cathedral wall or hanging on ropes between posts in front of the cathedral gate, facing the busy street. I could read the captions under those vague pictures or photos of jars or something like that. These jars were said to contain eyeballs gouged out of Chinese children by the Western priests and missionaries for their drug concoctions; and also hearts taken out of Chinese babies for their meat concoctions! Under the influence of such propaganda and the teachings and textbooks supporting it in the school, many schoolmates and playmates of mine used to go to the garden of the seminary to steal the fruits and even to destroy the fruit trees there, and go to the doors of the cathedral to shout rude and insulting words, even in imitation of some hymn melody, to the old people at Mass, until the garden and the cathedral were completely closed in late 1950s, like all Christian and other religious institutions, ranging from churches to Buddhist temples all over the city and throughout China.

Over these 30 years, outside the shrinking church there were no publications or public media disseminating a knowledge of Christianity. The only two books on Christianity which appeared during the period were about how imperialism used Christianity to invade China. So it was nearly impossible for Chinese people born in the 1940s–1960s to get any positive impression or knowledge of Christianity and theology during the years when they were raised and educated.

After Deng Xiao-ping's restoration in 1978 of the higher education system in China, which had been destroyed by Mao Ze-dong in 1966, Nanjing University (with the aid of Nanjing Union Theological Seminary newly restored) and the Graduate School of the newly established Chinese Academy of Social Sciences enrolled about ten students for a Masters Degree in the study of Christianity. They were the only students in the field in China for several years and I was among them. A few of us decided to make the works of such theologians as Reinhold Niebuhr, Bonhoeffer, and Moltmann our thesis topics. My choice was experienced, and described in my afterword to my Chinese translation of *Principles of Christian Theology*, as guided by the Holy Spirit.[1] So even if we count Niebuhr and Bonhoeffer as 'contemporary' theologians like Moltmann and Macquarrie, only a few of them entered the Chinese mind after an interval of more than 30 years. I recall that after the publication of the abstracted version of the MPhil theses mentioned above in some small circulation professional journals, only my thesis was published in full and in a quite popular series.[2] My first Chinese translation of Macquarrie's work appeared in the 1980s[3] while the Chinese versions of works of Niebuhr, Bonhoeffer and Moltmann did not appear until the 1990s. Professor Chen Ze-min, the deputy dean of Nanjing Union Theological Seminary which was then the only, and is now the largest divinity school in China, took my draft translation of Macquarrie's *Principles* and circulated it among the graduate students from as early 1982.

II

In the July 1989 issue of *Dushu* (Reading), a monthly periodical with at that time the largest circulation in China, my article 'What This World Needs Most Is Agape' appeared and made so deep an impression on many young people's minds that some of them still mention it to me after 16 years. I believe that is not only because the article appeared imme- diately after the bloody Tiananmen Square Incident, but also because it introduced some Christian ideas, hence some alien but fascinating thought and hope to young intellectuals in despair. In the same month, my translation of Macquarrie's *Twentieth-Century Religious Thought* was published, and sold out very quickly. It was like a shower of rain falling down to some plants in a vast desert. That is, I think, because, as I said in the translator's preface to the book: 'As a history, a diction- ary and an encyclopedia in the field of religious thought, to the Chinese readers who have not seen any material in this field for decades' this book offers 'a plentiful and panoramic picture of the development of western religious thought in our time.'[4]

The popularity of this book in the Chinese-speaking world can be seen in the fact that in 1992, my translation was published in Taiwan, with terminological amendments to adjust it to the Chinese terms which are common in Taiwan but different from those on the Mainland, and in 1997, another Chinese translation (by Portia Ho) appeared in Hong Kong and went into a second edition in the following year, with com- mendations from some top theologians in Hong Kong. And two of the theologians, Professor Dr Yu and Professor Dr Yeung wrote about how the book had become their companion since their youth.

When I read on the back cover of the Hong Kong edition that 'this book is . . . like an encyclopedia of twentieth-century theological thought', it struck me that the same description of the book had sprung into the minds of two translators who had never met each other. The two transla- tors happen to have the same surname ('Ho' is another spelling form of 'He'), as the editors of *On Being A Theologian* and the present volume (who have met only once – ed.) happen also to have the same surname.

In 1992, three years after its completion, the Chinese translation of another work of Macquarrie's, *God-Talk*, was published by Sichuan People's Publishing House, in the 'Religion and the World' series which I edit and which remains the oldest and largest translation series in China in the field of religion. The translation (by Zhong Qing) was revised by myself and my wife, Professor Gao Shining (she is also the reviser of *Twentieth-Century Religious Thought*). This translation was given the title *Shenxue de Yuyan yu Luoji* (*The Language and Logic of Theology*), its original sub-title. The English title was omitted, because the publisher thought it might get the book banned in a situation where it might be seen as politically incorrect to talk about God. I was very unhappy about this so I mentioned the original title in the first sentence of my preface. Fortunately, a few years later, the original title (*Tanlun Shangdi*) began to appear on the front cover of a new edition because the publisher found that they had not got into trouble with my mention of it, and the book needed reprinting to meet Chinese demand.

This is why when Professor Macquarrie gave his lecture on 'The Ebb and Flow of Hope: Christian Theology at the End of the Second Millennium' (*Theologian*, pp. 128–41) in October 1995 at Beijing University, as the first Western theologian to lecture on theology at Beijing since the Communist revolution of 1949, he 'was impressed by the questions asked, which showed that the audience, mostly students, were certainly not ignorant of the subject' (*Theologian*, p. 112). He does not mention in his narrative the moving fact that, during his lecture and the discussion with him in the packed lecture-room, there were many students crowding at the doors, standing and listening for as long as three hours.

Professor Macquarrie's lecture on 'Dialogue among the World Religions' (*Theologian*, pp. 132–55) at the Chinese Academy of Social Science, and the following discussion also lasted three hours. My Chinese translation of it appeared in *Shijie Zongjiao Yanjin* (*Studies of World Religions*) issued by Institute of World Religions, 1995, and my translation of the lecture delivered at Beijing University was published in *Tao Fong Hanyu Shenxue Xuekan* (*Logos and Pneuma, Chinese Journal of Theology*), No. 5, Autumn 1996, and reprinted in *Christianity in Modern and Postmodern Context*, Ming Feng Press, 2004.

In 1998, 16 years after its completion, my translation of Macquarrie's *Principles of Christian Theology* was published by the Institute of Sino-Christian Studies (ISCS) in Hong Kong. Although the publishers' efforts to publish it in Mainland China have not been successful, it has circulated in Taiwan, and since academic visitors from the Mainland can easily get a copy from the Institute (ISCS), and the Institute has kept close contact with nearly all the academics in Christian studies in China, I believe that nearly every teacher in this field has the book. In fact the director of ISCS, Mr. Daniel Yeung, told me that many theological seminaries have made it their student textbook. In my own university, a study group of academics from different disciplines has selected this book for reading and discussion.

In the summer of 1999, when I had to say good-bye to Professor Macquarrie in his car driven by Mrs Macquarrie to the railway station, after a stay of two days at their home in Oxford, I said that I hoped to see a new edition of his *Twentieth-Century Religious Thought* covering developments in its final decade, making it a full history of the century. Saying that, I also had another thing in my mind, a hope that he would get much healthier in the new century, for I saw he was at that time not in a very good physical condition. I was surprised and happy to receive from him the new edition of the book in July 2001. I admire very much his efficiency in working and his strength of character. He finished the fifth edition, which he said 'must be the last, since we have now come to the end of the century' (*Twentieth-Century*, 5th edn, p. 14), in November 2000 on the eve of the new century, and sent me a copy of the new chapter as early as September 2000. With some shame for being late and lazy, I translated into Chinese all the added and revised parts in the new edition (in comparison with the edition of 1981, the sections on E. Underhill, M. Polanyi, I. Ramsey, A. Camus and chapters XXIII and XXIV), a total of nearly 100 pages. However, this translation of the new edition has not been published. The reason is that the Chinese Christian Literature Council Ltd in Hong Kong, which is said to have obtained the exclusive copyright for Chinese (including traditional and simplified Chinese) versions of the book, told my publisher that they have just allowed the Chinese Christian Council (CCC), the official national Christian organization, to publish a Chinese translation (by Ms Ho, of the 1988 edition). But I can take comfort that more Chinese can now get the book after my translation was sold out 15 years ago, though all the publications of CCC and the Church in China have limited circulation outside the official churches and their bookstores.

Since writing the above paragraphs, I have heard that the publisher of the Chinese translation of *Principles* is much nearer to getting it published on the Mainland, and that another book of Macquarrie, *An Existentialist Theology* (1955), has been translated into Chinese by a Professor at Sichuan University.

III

The third point mentioned at the outset was the suitability or appropriateness of Macquarrie's thought for the condition and mentality of Chinese scholars and thinkers across the humanities and for students of different religions. Among the hundreds of thousands of Chinese researchers (in academies of social sciences in Beijing and all the provinces) and teachers (in universities and colleges) in humanities, there are just some hundreds, including the non-professionals, in religious studies.[5] That is to say that among every thousand Chinese scholars in the humanities there are at most one or two who are familiar with the works of religious thinkers or writers. If we take into account that within religious studies about a quarter or a third are active in Christian studies,[6] we should say that even fewer scholars are familiar with the works of Christian theologians.

As for their influence upon college students (the number of the students in religious studies is even smaller than that of teachers because of the restrictions from above on the development of the faculties and departments in this field) and their influence on the public (which though growing is still quite limited, on account of the restrictions on publication in the field), it should be kept in mind that most of these share certain traits in their way of thinking. These traits have been inherited from the past 2000 years of Confucianism and from the influence over the past century of a narrow kind of rationalism. These traits are to stress:

1 rationalism over fideism;
2 philosophy over theology;
3 humanity over divinity, hence, the anthropological over the theological.

All these emphases by scholars have left and will leave their mark on their audience and on their readers' understanding of Christianity.

While many in religious studies think in this way, the number is a thousand times larger in the humanities as a whole. After all, among all the several thousands of universities and colleges there are no more than twenty with departments or faculties engaging in religious studies. As for those studying religions other than Christianity such as Buddhism, Taoism, Confucianism and so on, few of them have a balanced or true-to-life knowledge of Christian theology. Many of them look at and think about Christianity only against the background of West–East (or Western–Chinese) confrontation or opposition and with the mentality of competition or rivalry between Christianity and Eastern (or Chinese) religions. Therefore, it would hardly be possible for them to understand the kind of Christian theology associated with Karl Barth. It is more likely they would have an antipathy or even hostility to those Christian works that take on exclusivist attitude towards other religions.[7] On the other hand, in Professor Macquarrie's work, we can clearly see such features as the full recognition and appropriate use of reason. He puts forward a powerful defence of reason as one of the 'formative factors of theology' (*Principles*, pp. 15–8), and he says that 'fideism in any form' is a 'very shaky basis for religious belief' (*Deity*, p. 4). This attitude could draw Chinese readers and scholars much closer to Christian theology, while they, in the perspective of rationalism, used to think of it as no more than fideism which cannot stand long in the face of reason.

Another feature we can find in Macquarrie's thought is his stress on the place of philosophy. Since he takes as an aim of theology to 'think the Church's faith as a coherent whole' (*Principles*, p. v) it is natural that he makes use of the work of contemporary philosophy to express Christian faith (*Principles*, p. vii). And he urges the theologian to make a positive relationship with philosophy (*Principles*, pp. 21–5). Furthermore, in the structure of his systematic theology, what he calls 'philosophical theology' has taken the first place, at least with respect to epistemology. This feature makes Macquarrie's view more acceptable to the Chinese scholars who are approaching Christianity and other religions mostly from a philosophical perspective.[8]

The third feature of Macquarrie's theology which corresponds to our third characteristic of the Chinese intellect is his existential or anthropological approach which could be understood by the Chinese mind as some kind of humanist one. Macquarrie called his approach 'existential-ontological', and did highly commend existentialism among contemporary philosophies when he wrote his first book (*Existentialist*, p. ix). Such a high valuation can be found in the 'Conclusion' appearing in all the editions of *Twentieth-Century Religious Thought*. On the other hand, Chinese scholars are mostly supporters of humanism in some broad sense. Those of them who are interested in Western humanities and philosophies are familiar with existentialism, including its claim that existentialism is humanism. In fact, M. Heidegger, J. P. Sartre and P. Tillich are among the several modern Western thinkers whose major works have been translated into Chinese. Nearly every Chinese philosopher today knows of Heidegger, and the popularity of Tillich in China is close behind.[9] So not only the popularity of the Chinese version of humanism (the overwhelming stress on human existence or human life), but also the popularity or reputation of Heidegger and Tillich among Chinese scholars, will certainly make Macquarrie's thought much more widely studied, understood and admired by the Chinese. Of course, he has not only inherited and explained most clearly the thoughts of these two thinkers, but has also developed his own theological thought on the basis of the thought of these and other Western thinkers who have been and are becoming more familiar to Chinese scholars, among them Plotinus, Dionysius, Eriugena, Cusanus, Leibniz, Hegel and Whitehead.[10] I should add here another coincidence. Macquarrie's own concept of God is described as 'dialectical theism'[11] and is put forward as an alternative to classical theism, while the Chinese scholars have been greatly influenced by Marxist-Leninist materialist criticism of theism and have some very affirmative attitudes towards any concepts and approaches described as dialectical, for the philosophy they have had to learn from secondary school to university is called 'dialectical materialism'.

Last but not least is the attitude of Macquarrie toward other religions. As we can find in so many works ranging from *Twentieth-Century Religious Thought* (1963) through *Principles* (1966) to *In Search of Deity* (1984) and his lecture 'Dialogue among the World Religions' in the Chinese Academy of Social Sciences, Macquarrie's attitude towards other religions and religion in general is quite open, balanced, affirmative and dialectical, so his thought is quite appropriate for the Chinese scholars, especially for the scholars of religions different from Christianity, who are mostly enthusiastic for so-called inclusivism (in their understanding), at least in words and in consciousness, and at the same time are very antagonistic to all kinds of Christian exclusivism (in their misunderstanding).

Of course, these three features cannot characterize even a small part of Macquarrie's work, which is so rich, broad, profound and concise that not even ten further articles could cover all its features. But as I wrote in my 'Introduction' to the Chinese translation of *Principles*, the comprehensiveness and ecumenicity of Macquarrie's work, 'his attitude of openness, generosity and seriousness in seeking truth, has brought about a result that may exceed his expectation, that is that his work will be beneficial not only to readers in various Christian traditions, but also to readers outside the Christian traditions'.

Notes

1 *Jidujiao Shenxue Yuanli* (Principles of Christian Theology), Hong Kong: Institute of Sino-Christian Studies, 1998, p. 672.

2 'A Comprehensive Contemporary Christian Theology: John Macquarrie's Systematic Theology', in Wenhua, *Zhongguo yu Shijie* (*Culture: China and the World*), Beijing: Sanlian Shudian, Issue 4 (1988), pp. 54–114.

3 *Ershi Shiji Zongjiao Sixiang* (*Twentieth-Century Religious Thought*), Shanghai: People's Publishing House, 1989.

4 *Ershi Shiji Zongjiao Sixiang*, p. 3, p. 4.

5 The largest association of academics in the field, the Chinese Association of Religious Studies, has just 217 council members. (Cf. *Zhongguo Zongjiao Yanjiu Nianjian*, Yearbook of Religious Studies in China, 2001–2002, ed. Institute of World Religions of CASS, Zongjiao Wenhua Chubanshe Press, 2003, pp. 562–4.) The number of the scholars whose names are not included in the list is very unlikely to exceed 217 by two or three times.

6 The largest symposium on Christian studies in China is the annual meeting co-organized by Institute of World Religions and Regent College in Vancouver. This is widely attended by scholars in the field. Every year it enrols about 100 participants.

7 For example, in the discussion about Alan Torrance's Christian exclusivism in the *Regent Journal* (Spring Issue, 1999, Chinese Studies Programme, Regent College), all the Chinese contributors except me attacked or criticized his position severely.

8 As Professor Zhao Dunhua observes: the 'Heat for Christian culture' in today's China tells us that 'the Chinese people are rather apt to understand and accept Christian thought in the perspective of philosophy, but are quite unfamiliar with Christian theology'. ('Christian Philosophy in the Eyes of the Chinese', in Edwin Hui and Zhao Dunhua (eds.) *Christian Philosophy in China*, Beijing: She Ke Wen Xian Press, 2000, p. 13.

9 The Chinese translations of *Being and Time* by Heidegger and *Being and Nothingness* by Sartre were published in late 1980s, but my translation of Tillich's *Systematic Theology* was published in the late 1990s.

10 Discussed in Macquarrie's *In Search of Deity* (1984). We should concede that some of the names are familiar only to scholars in this philosophical field.

11 *Jidujiao Shenxue Yuanli*, P. xviii.

14 John Macquarrie and SCM Press

JOHN BOWDEN

When John Macquarrie had his PhD thesis on *An Existentialist Theology: A Comparison between Heidegger and Bultmann* accepted for publication by SCM Press in 1954, he embarked on a relationship which to date has lasted for more than 50 years and has produced 29 books.

The SCM Press that he approached was a remarkable creation, one of the consequences of the famous Edinburgh Missionary Conference of 1910. The Publications Department of the Student Christian Movement from which it arose was created by Hugh Martin (1880–1964), who proved to be a gifted publisher over many years; he retired in 1952. Three books which he published during World War One, *The Manhood of the Master* and *The Meaning of Prayer* by the American preacher Harry Emerson Fosdick, and the *Jesus of History* by T.H. Glover, made so much money between them that the Publications Department unusually became a major source of finance for the Movement. It was logical to make it a separate business concern, and this happened in 1929 with the creation of the Student Christian Movement Press Ltd. During the 1930s and throughout World War Two the Press published not only works of theology but books on the social and political situation of the time.

The next Editor and Managing Director of SCM Press, Ronald Gregor Smith (1913–68), was perhaps even more gifted, and a leading theologian in his own right. Gregor Smith had studied theology in Germany before World War Two; he served in the Army during the war and then returned to Germany to work as a member of the Allied Control Commission on the de-Nazification of the universities. At the same time he was associated with SCM Press, for which he discovered the latest developments in German theology and reported them back. For example, he discovered that a theologian called Dietrich Bonhoeffer, imprisoned by the Nazis, had written some remarkable theological documents which were smuggled out – the classic *Letters and Papers from Prison*; he was also a strong advocate of the translation of Barth, Bultmann and many others. Thus began the Press's involvement in Continental theology which was to produce so many classics.

An Existentialist Theology appeared in 'The Library of Philosophy and Theology', one of the pioneering series which Gregor Smith had introduced (another was 'Studies in Biblical Theology' which eventually numbered more than 80 volumes). The Library contained works of both German and Anglo-American philosophy and theology, and John Macquarrie's next book, *The Scope of Demythologizing: Bultmann and His Critics* (1960), was also to appear in it. However, undoubtedly the most important volume in the series with which he was involved was his translation of Martin Heidegger's difficult book *Being and Time* (1962), which he completed with an American philosopher friend, Edward Robinson.

In 1957 John Macquarrie was invited to lecture at Union Theological Seminary, New York, and after a long period of discussion and negotiation he was appointed Professor of Systematic Theology there in 1962. This led to a change in his relationship with SCM Press for a time. The President of Union, Henry van Dusen, had a son Hugh who was an editor at the publishers Harper and Row in New York, and Harpers were not slow to approach this rising talent. Even before John Macquarrie took up his post at Union they approached him to write a book discussing the major developments in theology and philosophy in the twentieth century. He accepted, and the book eventually appeared in 1963 as *Twentieth-Century Religious Thought*; it has gone through five editions, the most recent published in 2001.

So while John Macquarrie was in the United States, Harpers became his publishers. Nor was that all; Charles Scribner's, another famous New York publishing house, invited him to write a one-volume systematic theology. Again, after some hesitation, he accepted, and this book became *Principles of Christian Theology*, which appeared in 1966.

However, this did not mean that SCM Press had been abandoned. At that time, and until the rise of the big international publishing corporations, American publishers recognized that they could not sell American books effectively in the British Commonwealth, and British publishers recognized that they could not sell British books effectively in the United States. So it was customary for American publishers to sell British rights and vice versa. When John Macquarrie signed contracts with his American publishers, with characteristic loyalty he stipulated that SCM Press should be the English partner, and so the link continued, albeit for the moment more indirectly.

Ronald Gregor Smith left SCM Press in 1956 to become Professor of Divinity at Glasgow University. His two successors, briefly David

Paton and then from 1959 David L. Edwards, were very different from him, and were concerned to bring a more popular touch to a publishing house which perhaps had begun to lack its former popular appeal. David Edwards concentrated on publishing paperbacks, justifying his not always financially successful programme with John A. T. Robinson's *Honest to God* in 1963, and discontinued many of Gregor Smith's translation projects. During his time in office he maintained warm relations with John Macquarrie, but did not approve of *Being and Time*. When the opportunity arose, he sold off the rights in it on the grounds that it was not an appropriate book to be on the list of a Christian theological publisher. (*Being and Time* is still in print with the fortunate purchaser, for whom it must have made a small fortune!) But this period saw an invitation to John Macquarrie to become editor of the highly successful *Dictionary of Christian Ethics* (1967), and the publication of *Studies in Christian Existentialism* (1965), a collection of lectures and articles from the previous ten years.

John Macquarrie was at Union Theological Seminary for eight years, from 1962 to 1970. They made a deep impact on him: in particular he became an Anglican, impressed by the worship and pastoral concern of the Episcopal Church, and he joined in its activities in Harlem. This was also to leave its stamp on his writing from then on.

As he happened to be in Britain on a visit from the United States, John Macquarrie was the first author I met when I came to SCM Press in August 1966 as Editor and Managing Director. At that time the Press occupied two gracious buildings in Bloomsbury Street, on the corner of Bedford Square, the then heart of publishing. It had been there since the 1930s, and my office, which looked out on the wall of the British Museum, would not have been out of place in a London club. It was an ideal place for relaxed conversation before or after lunch, and many friendships were forged there. My friendship with John Macquarrie was one of these, and from then on we kept in regular touch. I went twice to Union Theological Faculty, in 1968 and 1970, and enjoyed the warm Macquarrie hospitality there; on my first visit John Macquarrie had arranged a party with a group of his colleagues and I have a vivid memory of a long conversation with James Cone, which opened my eyes to American Black theology and later liberation theology.

Two more books, in which Harper and Row was still the originating publisher, appeared during these years: *God-Talk* (1967), subtitled *An Examination of the Language and Logic of Theology*, and *Three Issues in Ethics* (1970), which was highly critical of the situation ethics and new morality current at the time. John Macquarrie also edited a volume entitled *Contemporary Religious Thinkers* (1968) in an ambitious series entitled 'Forum Books', which set out to cover every aspect of Christian theology.

When John Macquarrie returned to England in autumn 1970 to become Lady Margaret Professor of Divinity at Oxford, SCM Press immediately seized the opportunity to invite him to become a director, and he attended his first board meeting in October of that year. The directors of SCM Press played a particularly important role, so to speak, as guardians of the tradition. Up to World War Two the Student Christian Movement, the owners of all voting shares in the Press, had been strong, but after the war the Movement had declined to a shadow of its former self. Indeed, with the upheavals in the student world after 1968, it came to consist of a relatively small group of radicals totally focused on the present, with no awareness of their heritage. The role of the board was to ensure that SCM Press continued to publish books of high quality in the broad SCM tradition and to make sure it was not adversely affected by the new character of the Student Christian Movement. The Editor and Managing Director was given complete freedom, but the Board was there to provide advice and support. Dealing with SCM required a great deal of tact, and for a number of years John Macquarrie found himself sitting on the Board beside SCM student directors. Here his gentleness and the openness which his time in New York had brought him paid dividends.

The Chairman of the SCM Press Board at that time was Alan Richardson, then Dean of York, the personification of the SCM tradition; his *Creeds in the Making*, the text of lectures given at an SCM Swanwick Conference in 1935, remained in print for more than fifty years, and he had written a series of popular books on biblical topics. The Vice-Chairman was Ronald Preston, equally closely associated with the SCM, who taught at Manchester University. Other members represented the academic and ecumenical world. The challenge in selecting directors was to balance the old guard with creative new members, and John Macquarrie proved an ideal choice.

SCM Press was a commercial company and had to make a profit to survive; to do this it needed to publish not just the distinguished but specialist books with which had made its name, but also scholarly yet popular books which could command a wide audience. Here around 1970 it was particularly fortunate: not only had its chairman written such books, but it had on its list the Scottish New Testament scholars A.M. Hunter and William Barclay, together with John A.T. Robinson, the Anglican bishop whose *Honest to God* had made such an impact and who continued to write a number of provocative sequels. John Macquarrie effortlessly added himself to this list, over the years producing books on an amazingly wide range of topics, all of which were eagerly awaited and read.

I found John Macquarrie the easiest of authors to deal with. First and foremost, he knew what he wanted to write and when, and he kept to his deadlines. While his first two big books had been commissioned, from then on he chose what he wrote. There was no reason, indeed no room, to suggest possible projects to him; they seemed to flow from him effortlessly. What made his books so valuable was that so many of them arose out of his varied activities in the university and the church. Thus *The Concept of Peace* (1973) contained the Firth Lectures given at Nottingham University; *In Search of Deity* (1984) the Gifford Lectures given at St Andrews; and *Heidegger and Christianity* (1994) the Hensley Henson Lectures given at Oxford, and many of his other books, such as *God-Talk*, had their origin in a lecture series. Several of his books are collections of papers and lectures about Christian life and the life of the Church given on particular occasions: for example, the *Humility of God* (1978) consists of meditations largely given at Christ Church, Oxford, and *Invitation to Faith* (1995) contains Lent lectures given in his own parish in Oxford; *A Guide to the Sacraments* (1997) and *Christology Revisited* (1998) also arose in such circumstances.

A Macquarrie typescript requires virtually no editing. Even his PhD thesis, a genre which is notably unreadable, needed little alteration to make it a good book. John Macquarrie has never advanced into the computer age, but his typescripts were exemplary long before PCs came to be used and have remained so: clearly set out and with no corrections – doubtless, to judge by comparison with other more murky contemporary typescripts, another legacy of his years in the United States.

In 1972 came the last of the Macquarrie books that originated in the United States; this was *The Faith of the People of God* (1972). Scribner's had commissioned it while John Macquarrie was still at Union as a popular version of *Principles of Christian Theology*. From then on his books have come to SCM Press first, and SCM Press has arranged the US publisher. A tiny handful of books went elsewhere, for example *Christian Hope* (1978), which was published by Mowbrays, and *Mary for All Christians* (1991) published by Collins, but these were slim volumes, and very much the exception.

To ensure change on the board, SCM Press directors were invited to serve two three-year terms, after which they had to take a sabbatical, so in 1976 John Macquarrie resigned. This period had seen the appearance of *Paths in Spirituality* (1972), *The Concept of Peace* (1973), *Christian Unity and Christian Diversity* (1975) and *Thinking about God* (1975). However, he was too valuable to lose permanently, so in 1983 he was again invited to join the board; he served until 1988. Meanwhile the list of his books had continued to grow with *The Humility of God* (1978) and *In Search of Humanity* (1982).

By this time there had been major changes at SCM Press. The long and favourable lease of Bloomsbury Street had finally expired and the new rent asked was impossibly high; in any case the picturesque and venerable building had been proving incompatible with computers because of the inevitable dust. The decision was made to move out of central London and buy rather than rent premises from which the Press could continue to distribute its own books as it always had done. The new location was Dalston, which had a bad reputation for crime and social deprivation; however, in practice it proved to have a character of its own, though the journey for staff and directors was more onerous.

Again the Macquarrie bibliography grew with *In Search of Deity* (1984) and *Theology, Church and Ministry* (1986). However, the origin of much of his work in lectures, talks and meditations, and their orientation often on topical issues meant that of all his works, two of the earliest, *Twentieth-Century Religious Thought* and *Principles of Christianity*, which had been specifically commissioned, still remained unequalled. This was to change in 1990 with the publication of *Jesus Christ in Modern Thought*. Long in the preparation, it was originally conceived of as the third volume in a trilogy, the first volume of which would be a study of the human being in modern theology (it became *In Search of Humanity*) and the second a study of God (*In Search of Deity*). Its roots probably even go back to the publication in 1977 by SCM Press of the controversial collection *The Myth of God Incarnate* edited by John Hick. I remember having lunch with John Macquarrie after the press conference for the book which generated so much interest; of course we had a long discussion of it. He was highly critical but conceded that there were problems with the doctrine of the incarnation, and he addressed these and much else in *Jesus Christ in Modern Thought*. It was awarded the Collins Religious Book Prize and came to stand alongside *Twentieth-Century Religious Thought* and *Principles of Christian Theology* as one of his three *magna opera*.

Towards the end of the 1980s SCM Press was faced with another important change. Its shares were still owned by the Student Christian Movement, now reorganized but minute in size, and it seemed risky to have ultimate control vested in such an unpredictable body. So the complicated process was embarked on of buying the shares and transferring them to a trust whose members would be solely concerned for the future well-being of SCM Press. The buy-out was achieved, but it left SCM Press with a burden of debt, and trading conditions for small firms were becoming increasingly difficult. In due course the debt was paid off by selling the premises in Dalston and moving to the smaller ones in Islington which the Press still occupies, but this left the Press weak in capital funds and with no obvious means of raising more.

In retirement John Macquarrie continued to write with his customary regularity: this period saw seven new books, several of which have been mentioned already. In addition to them *The Mediators* (1995), a study of nine figures ranging from Zoroaster to Krishna, was a contribution to inter-faith dialogue. *On Being a Theologian (1999)* rounded off the decade. It consisted of personal reflections on his life by John Macquarrie together with a series of milestone lectures, an outline of each of his major books, and a comprehensive bibliography of all his published writings and translations. It is an invaluable reference work.

I retired from SCM Press in 2000, so *On Being a Theologian* was the last book with which I was associated with John Macquarrie professionally. So far two books have appeared in the twenty-first century, *Stubborn Theological Questions* (2003) and *Two Worlds are Ours. An Introduction to Christian Mysticism* (2005). They have all the characteristics of his previous works and show that his gifts have not declined.

Part II

Philosophy and Symbolic Theology

Part II

Philosophy and Sociological problems

15 Self and Other

*Some Reflections on John Macquarrie's Philosophical
and Theological Anthropology*

EUGENE THOMAS LONG

I

In a volume intended as a tribute to John Macquarrie and a celebration of
his achievement of publishing over fifty years with the SCM Press I hope
it is appropriate for me to begin with a few personal remarks. When I
arrived in Glasgow in 1960 to begin my postgraduate studies, John Macquarrie was at a relatively early stage in his career. It was a time when
philosophical theology was beginning to recover from the onslaught of
logical positivism on the one hand and the positivism of revelation on
the other hand. Faculty and students alike seemed to share a sense of
excitement while focusing on new currents from the Continent and the
English-speaking world that promised new approaches and perhaps even
solutions to traditional philosophical and theological problems. In my
undergraduate training I had been particularly interested in the ideal-
ists and the American philosophical tradition, but in my early studies in
divinity I found little in contemporary theology that interested me. Often
to the dismay of my adviser, I took refuge in courses in the philosophy
of religion, American thought, the history of philosophy and comparative religion. I had, however, been reading Karl Jaspers on my own and
I was particularly struck by his concern with a sense of transcendence
within ordinary experience, his freedom from religious orthodoxies and
his openness to diversity. In my senior year I enrolled in a seminar on
Paul Tillich where I felt almost immediately at home. Because of this
background, perhaps, I have always had a sense of being privileged to
have been at Glasgow at the time I was, and to have come under the
direction of Macquarrie. Although he left Glasgow for New York before I
could complete my dissertation, my research programme was established

under his direction. I have many fond memories of our quiet and for me exciting conversations regarding my work, his help finding part time employment to supplement my wife's teaching salary, the generous use of his office with the gas heater that helped penetrate the damp cold of Glasgow winters and the trips to the Macquarries' home in Scotstoun on our BSA, where my wife and I often arrived with skid-lid marks on our foreheads. Glasgow was our first home together and it is a result of the kindness of the Macquarries and other teachers and friends then and through the years that we count our time there among our best and always look forward to trips 'back home'.

In 1955 Macquarrie published his first book, the well-received comparison of Heidegger and Bultmann, *An Existentialist Theology*, that placed him on the map, so to speak. A follow-up to that book, *The Scope of Demythologizing*, appeared during my first year in Glasgow. At that time Macquarrie was also with Edward Robinson completing the English translation of Heidegger's *Sein und Zeit*, published in 1962, and he was preparing the Hastie Lectures which were delivered in Glasgow University in 1962 and later expanded and published in 1967 under the title, *God-Talk: An Examination of the Language and Logic of Theology*. Macquarrie describes this period as his 'existentialist period', but there were already signs of his developing dialectical view of the self, his existential-ontological approach to philosophical theology and the symbolic and analogical character of religious language, themes that later became influential in my own development.

II

One of the topics in Macquarrie's work that attracted me from the beginning was his philosophical and theological anthropology which is developed most fully in his 1982 book, *In Search of Humanity*. In this brief essay I cannot discuss the whole range of Macquarrie's anthropology. Rather, I will focus attention on two aspects of his anthropology that are of particular importance for recent discussions in continental philosophy of religion concerning the self and its relation to the other: first, his analysis of what he calls 'the egoity and sociality of the self' and second, his analysis of suffering. In his insistence on the tension between egoity and sociality or the individual and the social poles of the human Macquarrie avoids some of the pitfalls of those philosophers who tend to emphasize either the individual or the social order. Like Heidegger, Macquarrie challenges the Cartesian model of the unembodied rational self in the interest of revealing a self that is a worldly or embodied being already existing in relation to persons and things in the world. On this view persons are not primarily theoretical knowers, although they are that, and certainly not timeless and bodiless knowers standing in independence of a world out there. They are agents engaged in a world in which there are no artificial gaps drawn between subjects and objects or between subjects and subjects. Subjects are never locked inside their minds seeking a world outside, and they cannot know themselves and their worlds independently of their involvements with other persons and things.[1]

Both Heidegger and Macquarrie shift the focus of our attention from the *what* to the *who* of the self, from the essence or nature of a thing which in Descartes' terms was a thinking thing, to the self as a concrete and historical being who asks the question of the being of the self. In his analysis of the who of the self Macquarrie is much influenced by Heidegger. However, he goes beyond Heidegger particularly in his discussion of the sociality of persons. Of fundamental importance in Macquarrie's analysis of the self as a narrative of polarities (including possibility and facticity, rationality and irrationality, and responsibility and impotence) is the polarity between egoity and sociality. In his first book Macquarrie argues that, although Heidegger recognized our being-with-others as a basic existential of human existence, he curiously left that side of his analysis of human existence undeveloped. Macquarrie insists on the importance of the sociality of the self, but not to the exclusion of the individual. He insists on the importance of the individual while recognizing the tendency for that to harden into a harmful egoism. He also insists on the importance of sociality, but recognizes its tendency towards collectivism. Thus it is important at one and the same time to acknowledge the individual and the other, the polarity between the self and the self's transcendence towards the otherness of the other person. It is the polarity between the individual and social poles of the self that I am inclined to say is the most fundamental for Macquarrie. As he puts it:

> But perhaps it would be no more correct to say that society is prior to the individual in an ontological as distinct from a chronological sense, than to say that an individual is prior to society. Both the social and the individual poles seem equally original in the being of man, and their tension is there from the beginning as one of the factors contributing to the dynamics of human life. (*Humanity*, p. 85)

Macquarrie provides us with a dynamic temporal narrative of the self as a dialogical, living being in the world realizing itself in relation to others in freedom, sociality, cognition, language, commitment, love and so forth. Each individual is engaged in carving out his or her own identity, his or her unique life-story. But this cannot be done apart from the historical and social context of which the individual is part and which both makes possible and sets limits to his or her fulfillment of self. He rejects the substance notion of the self, as was said above, but he also rejects the more extreme position of such contemporary French thinkers as Jean-François Lyotard, who seems in his over-emphasis on difference and diversity to lose any traces of a unified and self-identical self. In addition, Macquarrie also argues that the picture of the self that emerges from his analysis might allow us in some sense to think of the human being as a miniature cosmos and that our ordinary everyday human being might be understood to provide on the finite level some clue, however distant, to absolute being or within the context of religious faith, the being of God. This puts him at odds with the Barthians but also with the more recent French thinker, Jean-Luc Marion, who seems to so emphasize the discontinuity between finite and infinite, divine and human, and to so separate philosophy and theology that he can speak of the divine only by reference to the authority of revelation.[2]

Among the European thinkers currently in vogue, Macquarrie seems to share most in common with Emmanuel Levinas. He is sympathetic with Levinas's emphasis upon our encountering a genuine other in our relations with the infinite other. And he is sympathetic with the notion of an immanent suffering divine reality in contrast with the serene monarchical image of the God of traditional theism. However, Macquarrie insists that there are other possible ways of encountering the infinite other. I also believe that he would be critical of Levinas's emphasis upon an asymmetrical relation between the self and the infinite and his refusal of all efforts to conceptualize the infinite on the grounds that such efforts necessarily deny alterity. Macquarrie would agree that in some sense all knowledge of the infinite is beyond conceptualization. He might even agree that in some sense all knowledge of the infinite depends on revelation as Levinas himself seems to suggest at times. But if the divine is 'wholly other' in the strictest sense, Macquarrie argues, God would remain a completely unknown quantity and anything like an incarnation or revelation would be impossible.[3] One might add that we would also be left without any possibility of justifying, or perhaps better, making understandable the reality that religious language is supposed to reflect.

A related problem arises with reference to the relation of the self and other persons. Macquarrie agrees with Levinas on the importance of recognizing the otherness of the other person. He argues that a genuine relation to another person depends upon an openness to the other in his or her own being, a listening and receiving, as well as a giving. But Macquarrie's effort to re-think the natural law tradition of ethics as a movement towards the fully human, towards the fulfilment of self in community does not fit well with Levinas's more asymmetrical understanding of the relation between self and other and what appears to me at times to be a passivity of self or even emptying of its being in response or responsibility to the other. Levinas seems to leave little room for consideration of those very ways of being that tend to make possible and/or limit our capacity to be responsive or responsible to the other person. This, I suspect, is in part what Macquarrie has in mind in saying that it is difficult to understand how Levinas 'can recommend an asymmetrical relation of service to the other as if it comes naturally, whereas in the real world human beings attempt to dominate one another' (*Twentieth-Century*, p. 465). For Macquarrie ethical norms are located in nature, so to speak, including both human nature and the wider range of being, and ethical norms are in principle available to any rational being. Ethical norms, however, have in the final analysis to do with the formation of persons and the building of human community. This is not to ignore the importance of responding to the call of the other, of being just, of feeding the poor and so forth. It is to say that ethical norms direct us beyond fairness and justice towards a transformation or conversion of our relations with others in our personal, social and political orders, towards a community of persons in which we are liberated from self-centredness and freed for each other in our differences.[4]

III

Closely related to the issue of egoity and sociality is the issue of evil and suffering. On Macquarrie's account, as was suggested above, in reflecting upon the various polarities of human becoming we gain an initial impression of being itself because 'our becoming derives from being and already bears an initial impression of being. As and if that initial impression is developed and made explicit in a transcendent becoming, then in that becoming there occurs a disclosure of being' (*Humanity*, p. 253). It is in the description and interpretation of the various dimensions of human becoming that we catch some clue or glimpse of being as spiritual reality. And together, he argues, the several aspects of human life may be understood to provide an anthropological argument for the existence of God. He has in mind a kind of cumulative case argument that points not towards God understood as an absolutely transcendent monarch standing in the way of human freedom and transcendence but towards 'a God working and suffering in and with his creation, leading and inspiring human transcendence rather than standing over it' (*Humanity*, p. 256). Belief in a monarchical God, one might add, is not only incompatible with our experience of suffering in the world. It may even turn us away from involvement with those who suffer.

It is one thing to seek in the more positive dimensions of human experience such as our cognitive and spiritual powers, our language, our trust, our loving relations, and our freedom, clues to what in religious terms is understood to be divine reality. It is another, as Macquarrie recognizes, to deal with what might be called the more negative dimensions of human experience, for example, our being-towards death and what appears to be useless human and non-human suffering. Suffering, of course, is not unique to contemporary life, but suffering has had a particularly powerful impact upon Western philosophy and theology since the early twentieth century. Human suffering took unique form in the Holocaust, but one might want to add other events including 9/11, the Boxing Day Tsunami, the world AIDS and hunger crises, and the recent disasters in the Gulf coast of the United States and in Pakistan. In some of these cases it seems difficult to separate moral and natural evil as philosophers are often inclined to do.

In recent Continental philosophy the problem of evil and suffering has been at the heart of both secular and religious discussions. In Anglo-American philosophy this problem has manifested itself for the most part in the philosophy of religion where it is often connected with the so-called evidential argument in which some non-theists argue that at least some suffering cannot be adequately explained in traditional theistic belief. In defending the rationality of traditional theism against such critics some theists have extended the notion of defence to include efforts to provide theodicies or rational accounts of why an all-powerful and all-benevolent God allows evil in the world. At the root of many of these arguments is the belief either that evil is useful or necessary to a greater good or that eventually, whether in time or eternity, evil will be overcome or transformed by a greater good. In response, some non-theists as well as many continental philosophers and theologians, some of whom consider themselves to be theists, have argued that some evils are so destructive of any conception that humans might have of the good that no instrumental or future notion of the good could reasonably be held to account for such evil. These philosophers often speak of the 'end of theodicy'. Although Macquarrie does not himself speak of the end of theodicy, he does argue that even when we take into account the instrumental notion of soul-making, excessive and senseless evil remains. In this context he says, 'I have no new wisdom to offer on these topics, and do not believe that human wisdom can find a solution', and that in the face of the excesses of suffering, 'there would be a kind of insensitivity in even seeming to "explain" them' (*Humanity*, pp. 222, 231).

Suffering, argues Macquarrie, is not primarily an abstract philosophical or theological problem. Suffering is part of our being in the world, a chilling fact, as he says, of which we are all aware if not in our own experience, then in the experience of the suffering of someone else. Suffering tempers our joy and challenges the more positive dimensions of human becoming witnessed in our commitments and beliefs, our love and our religions. Yet, he argues, suffering even in its most destructive and pointless forms need not nullify the worth of human life. What then is suffering? Suffering, according to Macquarrie, is the opposite of my freedom and action in which I initiate a chain of events that enables me to achieve some desired state of affairs. Suffering is not something that I desire. It is something that happens to me. Action and suffering stand opposite each other, in tension with each other, the one pointing in a direction sought in our freedom and the other standing over against this as if seeking to destroy our goals.

Suffering takes many forms, argues Macquarrie. First there is the suffering associated with physical pain. Some physical pains may be moderate and temporary and not too difficult to accommodate into our way of being. Indeed, some pains may be understood in positive ways in the sense that they alert us to some dangers or perhaps help us appreciate the pain of others and in this way contribute to our solidarity with other persons and animals. We often speak of such suffering as helping us to develop character – 'soul-making', as some philosophers and theologians call it. Yet, as Macquarrie acknowledges, some physical pain is so intense and the suffering so great that it makes little sense to speak of gratefully accepting it or integrating it into human life.

Closely related to the suffering associated with physical pain is the suffering associated with mental and spiritual pain. Such suffering may have benefits for humankind in leading us to accept and integrate our finitude into our becoming persons in the fullest sense. But here too, Macquarrie argues, we may at times suffer mental deprivation and anguish so overwhelmingly destructive that we are unable to justify them and can only fall silent. Guilt is another form of mental pain, but Macquarrie considers the suffering arising from this sufficiently distinctive that he classifies it as a third form of suffering. He recognizes that guilt may often be exaggerated and blown out of all proportion to the wrongdoing to which it is a response resulting in mental paralysis. He also argues, however, that guilt may often be a warning that something has gone wrong with personal being, somewhat analogous to the way pain works in the body, and that guilt may be transformed by the experience of forgiveness. Finally, among what he calls the more obvious forms of human suffering Macquarrie mentions vicarious suffering which, he argues, may be the most acute of all. Even those of us relatively untouched by personal suffering must confront the suffering of other persons and animals. And here again we find both that suffering can contribute to our development as persons in awakening in us feelings of compassion and solidarity and that some forms of innocent suffering are so severe that we can only be silent.

On Macquarrie's view then, by contrast with the process of becoming in which we seek to realize some state of affairs that we desire and through which we seek to realize our fullest possibilities of being, suffering brings us up against what we might call a boundary to our human transcending. In this sense suffering may play a positive role in helping us become aware of our finitude and may clear our world of the gods of self-deification including, one might add, religions in which suffering appears at times to be purchased at the price of higher rewards. In its more limited forms suffering may be accommodated into our human becoming. Whether religious or not we may find ourselves saying that although we would not have sought suffering we are better persons for having undergone the experience of suffering. Here we find at the experiential level the truth of traditional theodicies in both secular and religious forms in which it is argued that persons are not ready-made, that persons are the result of long processes of self-transcending, of soul-making, to use the language of one of the widely held theodicies.

If experiences of suffering were always of the form that we seem to be able to accommodate into our way of living, the problem of evil would not be the mystery it is for humankind. In some cases, however, evil seems to be other than what can be accommodated within the context of soul-making. Such evil is often said to be gratuitous and the suffering which follows unjustified and unjustifiable. It is in this context that some Continental philosophers speak of the end of theodicy, the end of efforts to provide rational theories or explanations to make sense of gratuitous evil and suffering. Such evil, Levinas argues, is non-integratable and non-justifiable.[5] It makes little sense to speak of persons directly or vicariously experiencing the Holocaust choosing to bear their suffering or justifying their suffering in relation to some future human or eternal good. For those who suffer the most, it often makes little sense to speak of soul-making or moral progress. Speaking of the victims of Auschwitz, Hans Jonas writes, 'Dehumanization by utter degradation and deprivation preceded their dying, no glimmer of dignity was left to the freights bound for the final solution, hardly a trace of it was found in the surviving skeleton specters of the liberated camps.'[6]

Macquarrie makes it clear that he is not trying to solve the traditional problem of evil. However, in acknowledging the uselessness of some suffering and the insensitivity associated with trying to explain such suffering, he comes near to some Continental philosophers who speak of the end of theodicy. In his talk of inexplicability and silence, and of a silence that recognizes a 'more' which is inexpressible, Macquarrie focuses his attention on what might be called the ontological dimensions of suffering and the mystical dimensions of the spiritual and some might challenge him for inadequately treating the ethical. I am inclined to believe, however, that he would go at least part of the way with Levinas and others who emphasize the ethical dimensions of the experience of evil and suffering. This is suggested in his unwillingness to separate the theoretical and the practical, his argument that there is no absolute disjunction between being and the ideal, his insistence on the importance of both the mystical and the prophetic elements in religion, and his belief that moral experience points towards a deeper reality.

Implicit in the experience of useless suffering, I would argue, is a summons to a kind of moral outrage and a summons to overcome or transform such suffering at least within the limits of our abilities. A full discussion of this issue in Macquarrie's thought would require that we investigate his understanding of being and creation. It would also require us to explore in more depth his existentialist account of a natural law ethic, a topic that I touched upon above and a topic that deserves more discussion than it has received. I cannot undertake those discussions here but I do want to suggest, and I believe that Macquarrie would agree, that there are both ontological and moral dimensions in the experience of useless suffering. Macquarrie would agree with Levinas in rejecting traditional ontology to the extent that it fails to grasp the difference between being and beings. This need not mean, however, that the ontological is displaced by the moral for, as Macquarrie himself has suggested in his brief discussion of Levinas, 'before anything can be good or beautiful it must in some way or other *be*' (*Twentieth-Century*, p. 465). One might even argue that Levinas's ethical implies an ontology, that the sense of responsibility of which he speaks belongs to the very nature of things. At a minimum it seems to me, the ethical and the ontological would have to be equi-primordial. To put this another way, in Macquarrie's view, moral values belong to the nature of being or reality, including human being and the wider range of being. This is not to say that the moral life is restricted to the religious. It is to say that particular religions provide a context of belief and formation that is supportive of the moral life.

Most of us discover in experiences of useless suffering, whether suffered on our own or vicariously, I would argue, an absolutely certain condemnation, a deep sense of being undeserved, an 'absolute no' which seems to transcend all human and cultural boundaries and point us towards the wider range of being itself. I say most of us because while one might believe that there is something deficient about a person who does not condemn the experience of suffering in Auschwitz, there does not seem to be a necessary connection between the experience of suffering and the experience of condemnation even in this case. In the experience of absolute condemnation we seem unable to find any justification. This is beyond the pale of soul-making and we can find no usefulness for such suffering either in this life or another. I am inclined to speak of this as a transcendent dimension of ordinary human experience that may lead us to confront our finitude, our nullity, but may also suggest a solidarity with others that calls forth our love and compassion for others which at times at least seems to transcend the dimensions of any morality of rational calculation. Vicarious suffering in particular seems to call us to put our own being at risk, so to speak, to suffer with others, to become actively involved in relieving the suffering of others where we can and in changing those conditions that bring about senseless suffering. In such experience, one might argue, we come up against a limit or boundary situation, to use the language of Jaspers, one that may point us towards transcendent reality. This reality, however, is not adequately described in the language of traditional theism. As Macquarrie argues, in continuously creating, in conferring being or letting-be, in calling beings out of nothing God puts God's self at risk. God takes the risk that being may be dissolved into nothing. Because of this, faith in God's providence, in God's overcoming nothingness by positive beingness, must be held in tension with God's self-spending (*Principles*, ch.11). Indeed, God's self-risking or self-spending may also be said to be the strength of God in that God transcends or goes out of God's self in self-giving, in loving.

To speak of God being at risk need not result in one saying that God is overwhelmed by the risks, the suffering of this world, in the way that human beings at times are. Macquarrie expresses sympathy with Whitehead's talk of God as 'the great companion – the sufferer who understands' (*Deity*, p. 150). But he also insists that, as the ultimate reality, God cannot be annihilated or overcome by suffering and that in this way the suffering of God differs from human suffering. God, argues Macquarrie, 'has an infinite capacity for absorbing suffering , and even transforming it, though we cannot know how this transformation takes place' (*Deity*, p. 181). Macquarrie does not draw a sharp distinction between creation and providence. Creation means the dependence of beings at all times on the creativity or letting-be of being, and providence is a way of speaking of the on-going creativity or energy of divine reality. Understood in this way faith in the providence of God is not a way of avoiding the reality of evil and suffering. On the contrary, 'in its highest manifestations providence enlists free co-operation of responsible creaturely beings' (*Principles*, p. 245). I believe that Macquarrie might agree, were we to add at this point, that the capacity of God to absorb and even transform evil and suffering cannot be understood apart from the call to human beings to put their own beings at risk, to suffer with others and to be freely involved in relieving the suffering of others where they can and in changing those conditions that bring about such suffering. To put this in another way, in the experience of senseless suffering persons are called not only to condemn such evil and suffering and suffer with those who suffer, but also to assume responsibility for creating or responding to new possibilities for good.

Notes

1 Macquarrie is not a realist in the sense of one who begins with the intuition that there is some reality that exists independently of our attempts to know it and then argues that our factual statements may be assessed as true or false depending on whether or not a fact exists independently of our cognition. He is a realist in the sense of one who understands that reality has to do with what stands over against or transcends us, that what is other, whether a thing, person or God is given, but that it is understood in virtue of its place in our being in the world in relation to persons and things, in our world of intelligibility and meaning.

2 In the case of Jean-Luc Marion, knowledge of God appears to be restricted to the Christian revelation and the church dogmas. It may even be restricted ultimately to the dogmas of the Roman Catholic Church where, as he says, theologians must let the Word speak, where the Word makes itself present in the eucharistic task, where only the celebrant receives the authority to go beyond the words to the Word, where the priest, who alone is invested by the *persona Christi*, stands in for the bishop and where 'one must conclude that only the bishop merits, in the full sense, the title of theologian'. Jean-Luc Marion, *God Without Being*, Chicago: University of Chicago Press, 1995, p. 153. Although Macquarrie has not discussed this point in detail, he does suggest that Marion allows no place for natural theology and no non-Christian theology. *Twentieth-Century*, 4th edn, pp. 473–6.

3 *Humanity*, p. 255. A full discussion of this would need to take into account Macquarrie's reluctance to speak of ontology or metaphysics in the sense of attempts to grasp reality in rational terms, his understanding of the anchorage of language in experience, the dialectic between symbolic and analogical language and the dialectic between the language of religion and the language of metaphysics. See in particular *God-Talk*.

4 For his discussion of natural law and ethics, see *Issues*, pp. 82–110 and *Deity*, pp. 212–24. Macquarrie's aim is to get beyond ethics understood as the performance of right actions and to reinterpret natural law as a way that allows for flexibility and movement towards a fuller existence or the fulfillment of the fullest human potentiality in community.

5 Emmanuel Levinas, 'Transcendence and Evil', in Phillipe Nemo, *Job and the Excess of Evil*, Pittsburgh: Duquesne University Press, 1998, p. 173.

6 Hans Jonas, *Mortality and Morality: A Search for the Good After Auschwitz*, Evanston: Northwestern University Press, p. 133.

16 Trailing Clouds of Glory: John Macquarrie on Being Human

GEORGINA MORLEY

> If human beings appear on this earth 'trailing clouds of glory' (Words-
> worth), from where do these clouds mysteriously come?[1]

Is it *good* to be human, in the Christian tradition? This is the question, pastoral and practical, which teases at all my theological thinking,
emerging as it does in countless conversations with those who are on the
margins of the Church and struggling to stay – or to leave. Can we talk
about being human in such a way that its sheer, delicious glory is celebrated? And in such a way that its maddening, shaming, soul-destroying
difficulties are admitted and raged against, but without inducing persistent self-flagellation? Or do we find ourselves guarding our backs, hedging
our bets, curbing our joy lest we claim too much for ourselves, clinging
to our weaknesses in the hope that God's view of us will thereby be
ameliorated?

Can we talk about God and about human being in the same sentence,
without one or the other being diminished? Suppose someone was drawn
to the practice of faith by a sense of the mysterious 'otherness' of God.
Seeking space for awe and wonderment, suppose they find instead a different sort of otherness – a distant, jealous monarch whose capricious
majesty requires human dignity and worth to be circumscribed lest they
trespass on divine prerogative. Or suppose someone was drawn to seek
God amid the sheer pleasure and pain of being human but finds that, in
order to safeguard the glory of humanity, God has been reduced to little
more than a cipher: a Feuerbachian projection reclaimed and tamed. Is
it possible to give an account of God and of human being so that God is
'big' enough, 'other' enough, to summon us into self-giving allegiance,
and at the same time is 'like' enough that that summons is an intimate
and demanding sustenance of becoming more truly human?

These questions, achingly genuine, no straw men here, were what I brought to my first systematic reading of Macquarrie, and I found in him a rich resource and an ally. From the very first of his published writings, Macquarrie has insisted that talk of God and talk of being human must go hand in hand. In a non-theological age, talk of God best begins from our experience of what it means to be human because here, at least, is common ground. Our experience of what it is to be human leads us to enquire of the possibility of God, both as the focus of human aspiration and worship, and as the source, sustainer and goal of all that is. So intertwined are Macquarrie's talk of God and of human being that his mature work culminates, in *In Search of Humanity*, in an explicit *anthropological argument for the existence of God*. This takes the form of traditional cosmological arguments for the existence of God: 'If the universe is like *this*, it points us to a God who is like *that*.' But it focuses solely on human being, as the highest point of the cosmos, to direct us towards the possibility of God. At the heart of the argument, then, is the claim that human being, in a number of interrelated ways, points us to a particular way of understanding God.

The anthropological argument for the existence of God[2]

1 Human being has brought to light more than anything else that we know the astonishing potentialities latent in the physical universe.

Macquarrie's argument starts from the understanding that human being is *microcosm,* bearing within itself the whole hierarchy of being within the universe, and bringing to light 'the astonishing potentialities latent in the physical universe' (*Humanity*, p. 257). If the universe has produced these extraordinary beings who in and through their embodiedness are nevertheless more than simply physical, then the universe is itself 'far more than matter and force or collocation of solid atoms or however old-fashioned materialism expressed it' (*Humanity*, p. 257). If human being, as a product of the universe, is sentient, percipient and cognitive, then it represents these latent potentialities in the cosmos made actual. Then we are directed towards a sacramental view of the universe, rather than a purely material and mechanical view, and to questions about the possibility of some sort of divine immanence in the created cosmos which establishes and supports its development and evolution.

2 Some aspects of our humanity suggest a transhuman spiritual source.

Some aspects of human life and nature point to a spiritual source which transcends the physical world. Although many aspects of human being are held in common with animals, or are explicable as developments for survival, there are intellectual, moral, personal and spiritual aspects which transcend the survival of the species. These include language, conscience and moral obligation, and the kind of knowing appropriate to the knowledge of persons rather than of things. 'The highest reaches of human life, what is in fact most distinctively human in us, seem to posit an origin in a level of being not less than personal and spiritual transcending both ourselves and the world' (*Humanity*, p. 259). That this is not an argument for a dualist origin for human being is already established: human being is the universe bringing itself to personal and spiritual expression and enquiry; it is the whole, then, which has its origin in a transcendent source of being, focused and brought to expression in human personhood.

3 The human being in certain respects transcends nature, in such a way as to provide an analogy of divine transcendence, and to suggest that the goal of humanity is participation in the life of God.

It is apparent that human beings in some respects transcend nature, rather than merely summing it up. Human being has a role in shaping the cosmos. Although finite and creaturely, human beings stand out from the world and act creatively upon it. Even – especially – in their own being, they are a space in nature where fresh creation is still possible, where the possibilities in the cosmos can be explored and brought towards fulfilment. They ask questions, they are bearers of reflective thought, they shape the world. This is not *discontinuity* with the cosmos, although it is a critical epoch and a point of absolute novelty.[3] This kind of transcendence over the immediate situation is the best evidence, Macquarrie argues, for a transcendent God. If the cosmos does not point beyond itself and its present condition, there is no reason to raise the question of a transcendent source or goal. But if there is a being in the world who is both immanent in the world and transcendent of it (or, better, who *is* the transcendent aspect of the cosmos), then such a being might point us towards the kind of transcendence we might understand in relation to God and, further, might be a sign that this is the point at which we are growing into the divine likeness.

4 Human beings show a natural trust in the wider being within which their existence is set.

This is a contestable claim, with palpable evidence to the contrary, and Macquarrie concedes that 'reality presents us with an ambiguous face. There are evidences that are supportive of faith in God . . . while there are others which suggest that reality is godless' (*Humanity*, p. 260). Nevertheless, he argues that human beings tend towards trusting reality, evidenced in the undertaking of commitments which rest on a basic trust in the order of things, and the persistence of hope and of faith in certain values or in the worthwhileness of life. This might be deemed a natural disposition towards faith, even where it falls short of religious faith and, as such, hints at the natural affinity between divine and human being as it arises in human experience.

5 There are some negative factors in human existence which can be understood as limit-situations, impressing on us our own finitude and at the same time evoking the idea of absolute being.

Negative factors in human experience function as limit-situations, 'imposing on us our own finitude and at the same time evoking the idea of absolute being' (*Humanity*, p. 260). Suffering, death and various kinds of alienation may not be unremittingly negative: 'recognition of finitude and guilt dispels illusions of grandeur and self-conceit' (*Humanity*, p. 261). Coming to the limits of human capacity may, as Jaspers has suggested, be the point of openness to and encounter with transcendent being.

6 Finally, many of these strands of human experience come together in religion, in which men and women claim to experience in various ways the reality of God, and this claim has a prima facie case for its validity as one deeply rooted in the human condition.

Many claim that they find themselves in communion 'with a gracious reality which gives a new depth and significance to their lives' (*Humanity*, p. 261). This cannot be disproved, nor proved, but Macquarrie insists that the persistence of religious practice (or its substitute, notably art, amongst those who seek the sublime and a measure of transcendence) is rooted so deeply in the experience of being truly human that it should be taken as evidence for the reality of God as the source, support and goal of human life.

Whence the clouds of glory?

Macquarrie's anthropological argument depends on two fundamental claims about human being: that it is in continuity with the cosmos and that it displays an openness, a transcendence, which points beyond the merely physical. The particular shape of these claims derives from the communities of dialogue in which Macquarrie's thought is honed, and from the way in which his theology develops, maintaining the strengths of early perspectives, counteracting weaknesses and incorporating new insights to reframe the whole.

The openness of human being is a key theme in Macquarrie's earliest work, and takes the shape of the existentialist concerns which occupied him when working in Glasgow. In dialogue with Heidegger, Macquarrie explores the questions of what it means to be human, not in traditional categories of substance but under the rubric of temporality. Human beings know that they exist and that they must become who they have the capacity to be. They stand out from other entities and enquire about their existence, and about their responsibility for their existence. They must embrace the possibilities of existence that are truly theirs – or lose themselves in the world of entities, ignoring their possibilities and being inauthentically human. In other words, being human is an 'unfinished project which may or may not become "human" (in the sense of "truly human") and therefore must be *made* so' and, indeed, be *kept* so (*Humanity*, pp. 12, his italics). The fundamental openness or freedom which this implies is more profound than a simple freedom of choice. It is more akin to the nothingness out of which God has created the world: it is 'the empty space, the room that is left for manoeuvre and has not yet been filled up and determined . . . We only know it through our own exercise of freedom' (*Humanity*, p. 13). This exercise of freedom is genuinely co-creative with God. Humanity is not a finished product, and we have a share in determining what it will become. We also shape the world in our engagement with it: through agriculture, science, technology, recreation, the natural world is absorbed into the human realm and 'humanized'. At a finite level, human beings bring into being a definite shape where things are as yet undetermined or at least are determinable.

This quality of freedom may equally be expressed as transcendence because of its dynamic character. It 'goes beyond', it is the 'becoming more', it 'exceeds limits'. This is not necessarily akin to a doctrine of progress, because we may choose not to exercise our freedom and co-creativity, and things may slip back towards shapelessness and nothingness, but it certainly amounts to a doctrine of hope. A key dimension is that it has directedness, a leading edge, which is located not in biological determinism or in the will to power. The leading edge is a unified feature of the whole 'conscious, discriminating and purposeful' ego, the 'mineness' of existence in Heidegger's language, which nevertheless is only fulfilled in going beyond the individual in community, and in commitment (the development of stable attitudes and policies of action).[4]

The scope of human freedom, however, is partial and limited. Although human beings are called to freedom, 'summoned to go beyond whatever condition they find themselves in to a fuller mode of personal and social being', freedom is also threatened and hedged in by any number of givens (*Humanity*, p. 19). In existential language, the facticity of the human condition as the context for the summons to freedom causes anxiety and flight from the very freedom which characterizes true humanity. For some, this tension is evidence of the absurdity of the human condition. But for Macquarrie it is the point at which we begin to re-understand God. If human resources alone are inadequate to overcome the tension between freedom and facticity, then maybe here we are directed to the possibility of a source of grace which will overcome the tension between openness and limitation. This is the point at which we begin to see God as the protector of human freedom, rather than its usurper. God is the ground of freedom, the author of freedom as the one who has left openness within what has been created, and the one who summons human being into the continuing work of freedom.

In order to understand Macquarrie's understanding of human being, it is essential to recognize that human facticity and limitation are not equated to human being's continuity with the cosmos. Such an equation would produce a fatal dualism which is wholly absent in Macquarrie's thought. Facticity is simply the given of human existence, and is value neutral. It is the context in which freedom is to be exercised. Embodiedness, both in the physical body and the social body, may be limiting to the exercise of freedom, but only in so far as it sets the specific arena within which freedom is exercised, and not because embodiment is *per se* inimical to freedom. Facticity and freedom do not correspond to matter and spirit, but to immanence and transcendence as two aspects of a single reality (as, for example, convexity and concavity) rather than as two opposing ideas to be held together in paradox. This means that divine immanence may also be spoken of as subject to limitation – to operating within a given sphere. That this is so is, ironically, part of the divine transcendence: the capacity to go beyond divine freedom into limitation and risk.

The articulation of continuity with the cosmos is arrived at by Macquarrie through a quite different route to issues of facticity and limitation. Even in his early existentialist days, he is concerned to safeguard his work against dualism. A rubric of temporality rather than of substance is the first bulwark in the defence. Human being in *all* its aspects is temporal and cannot be divided into various kinds of 'stuff', material and spiritual. But existentialism does tend toward an accidental dualism between human beings and other entities, because it emphasizes that human uniqueness consists in standing out from (*ek-stasis*) the world of entities. As the human existent enquires about the world in which he finds himself, he engages with it much as a workshop full of equipment. Things are functional, instrumental, and are harnessed to his world not as items in a shared realm but as tools for his tasks. This accidental dualism arises not least because existentialism starts from the individual – the 'I' and the 'mineness' of all experience of the self and the world. Macquarrie's work is never as individualistic as pure existentialism because his insists from the first on the historical and social groundedness of human existence.[5] This opens his thought accordingly to a less narrowly instrumentalist approach to the relation between human beings and material things and to a significantly social approach of shared ownership and responsibility.

Combined with the existential-ontological approach developed in *Principles of Christian Theology*, a broader sense of the role of human beings in relation to the material realm begins to emerge. The awareness of 'my' existence extends to awe that anything exists, that there is something rather than nothing. This 'awareness of being' is tantamount to a revelation of 'there being *being*' in the beings. Human being is seized by an awareness of 'being' in and through everything that *is*, and of being responsible as a guardian of that being – that it should not fall back towards nothingness but flourish towards fullness of being. A shift is made from a self-oriented instrumentality to a participation in the flourishing of being. By the time this is placed in the more cosmically focused framework of *In Search of Humanity*, the human task in relation to the cosmos works both ways: as well as bringing to bear the consciousness and the voice of the universe in enquiring about its own being, human being as personal being, as a centre of freedom and self-transcendence, shares in the divine task of bringing-into-being the cosmos. Two movements meet in human being, the transcendence of the cosmos bringing itself to personal and spiritual expression, and divine transcendence summoning human being into responsible, directed freedom within the cosmos.

Speaking of God and of human being in the same sentence

Where does Macquarrie's theology take us, in relation to my initial questions? Is it good to be human, with Macquarrie's theology under our belts? Indeed it is. Can we speak of God and of human being in the same sentence, without one or the other being diminished? Yes, this is how we must speak in order to avoid diminishment.

In the first place, Macquarrie allows us to speak of the radical immanence of God in human experience. In our being human, and in the context in which our being (and becoming) human is set, God is present and manifest. Everything that has being participates in God as the dynamic source of being. The very fact that there is something rather than nothing directs us to an infinitely great bringer-into-being, and our awareness of being – all the beings and the particular character of our own being – summons us into a responsible and generous being human in the cosmos. If God can be this immanent, and in this generous way, he is no distant monarch ruling from afar, and we can neither be oppressed by his otherness nor can we model our being human on his detached tyranny. Rather, we are summoned into responsible awe and generous embodiedness.

At the same time, Macquarrie's anthropological argument insists on transcendence alongside immanence. It allows us a very different model of transcendence from that of classical theism, one based on temporality rather than substance and spatiality, and on complementary rather than oppositional dialectic.[6] If divine transcendence is glimpsed through the human capacity to go beyond the present situation, to choose for what is truly human in the context of delineated possibility, and to share in the creative freedom of bringing latent possibility into being, then divine transcendence has the character of the protection, support and summons of human freedom, and is not its rival. The divine otherness is not located in distance, stasis and will, but in a greater capacity to go beyond the self and to summon into being. Truly human being consists in participation in this openness and creativity, both in relation to the divine person and in relation to the human person embodied in community and cosmos.

The brilliance of Macquarrie's understanding of human being lies in his overcoming of the polarity of divine transcendence and divine immanence by viewing them through the experience of being human. This is tantamount to a synthesis of revealed theologies and natural theologies. What is revealed, with an insistent dynamism worthy of any kerygmatic theology, is the immanence of divine being in all that is. What is 'natural' (that is, given in nature) is the self-transcendence of the cosmos culminating in human being which enquires about and is summoned into transcendence in order to be what it truly is. To be human is to be summoned by God, grasped by grace for a truly human way of being which nevertheless would not be possible with the resources of human experience alone. And yet this grace, this gift and summons, is immanent, rooted in being, and only known in the factical conditions of human life. We cannot be truly human without God, but we find God – are seized by God – only in the task of becoming human. It is in the very nature of being human that God gives himself to be known, and calls us into new horizons of humanity. The concept of God which emerges from Macquarrie's study of human being, 'a God so conceived as deeply involved with his creation is no oppressive God, but one whose transcendence is a goal and an encouragement to the transcendence of humanity' (*Humanity*, p. 261). Human being so conceived is invited into joy and generosity, risk and possibility.

Notes

1 *In Search of Humanity*, London: SCM Press, 1982, p. 255.

2 *Humanity*, pp. 257–61. It is not an argument for the 'existence' of God as such, but for the possibility of God and the ways in which human experience directs us to this possibility.

3 See Georgina Morley, *John Macquarrie's Natural Theology: The Grace of Being*, Aldershot: Ashgate, 2003, for an exploration of this distinction, pp. 132–4.

4 *Humanity*, pp. 45–6, 140. On the 'mineness' of existence, see Martin Heidegger *Being and Time*, Oxford: Blackwell, 1973, pp. 67–8.

5 The 'what and how' of history, the factual content of the gospel, was an early concern of Macquarrie's in opposition to Bultmann, and his writings in Glasgow and New York take up the question of the corporate nature of human existence.

6 That is, 'X is A and B' (where A and B are characteristics apparently difficult to reconcile) rather than 'X is A' and 'X is not-A' (where not-A is the negation of A).

17 On God the Incomparable: Thinking about God with John Macquarrie

PAUL FIDDES

Who ever addressed a prayer to necessary being? (*In Search of Deity*, p. 23).

With this question, placed mischievously in parentheses, John Macquarrie takes a side-swipe at what he calls 'classical theism', and points us to the heart of any project of talking about God. All God-talk has to be adequate to the practice of prayer. We learn from Macquarrie that spirituality and the experience of God are primary in the religious life, with theology as a 'second-order enterprise' for analysing, conceptualizing and evaluating what is already there: 'Spiritual discernment leaps ahead in its intuitive perception of God' (*Deity*, p. 191). But what then is perceived? Here Macquarrie reaches for a word that occurs often in his work, which he draws from two typical sources of his thought – the Bible and Martin Heidegger. What discloses itself – for Macquarrie agrees with Karl Barth that the human mind without God's initiative cannot know God – is 'incomparable'. In an early work he refers this term to one of Heidegger's expressions for the mystery of Being,[1] while in his magisterial *Principles of Christian Theology* (p. 203) he also traces it to the prophet Isaiah: 'To whom then will you liken God, or what likeness compare with him?' (Isa. 40.18). In a nutshell, God is 'the incomparable that lets-be, and is present-and-manifest' (*Principles*, p. 115).

In this essay I want to explore the potential of describing God as 'the incomparable', both for exegeting various aspects of John Macquarrie's own doctrine of God, and for taking the argument in some different directions from those which Macquarrie himself has chosen to tread. At the same time I intend to test these exploratory journeys against the criterion that Macqarrie himself has posed – that of prayer and spiritual experience. In doing so, I gladly write in tribute of a deeply spiritual theologian and a truly catholic father of the Church in our time, to whose work and personal encouragement I owe a greater debt than I can express here.

Existence and Being

The experience to which theology applies the term 'incomparable' is, for Macquarrie, characterized both by wonder at being and by intuition into the unity of things. With regard to the first aspect, Macquarrie quotes Wittgenstein, 'Not how the world is, is the mystical, but that it is'[2] and places this alongside the wondering question from Leibniz which is also cited by Heidegger, 'Why are there beings at all, rather than just nothing'?[3] For the second aspect, Macquarrie refers to a long line of Christian mystics who have had a visionary sense of things in their unity and interconnectedness, and who have found this to be a situation in which God is present and self-disclosing.[4] Being and oneness are both by definition incomparable, unique, *sui generis*. Indeed, in a long tradition of reflection from Plotinus to Heidegger, being and oneness have been found to be two sides of the same concept.

Macquarrie draws on the view of Heidegger that 'Being' is incomparable because it cannot be placed in any class of 'beings' or existing entities with which we are familiar in the world. Beginning from our experience of 'being there' in the world *(Dasein)*, we discern and postulate the prior enabling condition for 'beings', and this must be Being itself. Human existence demands an ontology as a precondition. Escaping all categories, Being is the incomparable *transcendens*, a unity that precedes all beings, and yet Being 'gives itself' *(es gibt)* and is nothing unless it is present and manifest in beings in the world.[5] Being is both transcendent and immanent at the same moment, a duality for which Macquarrie coins the lapidary phrase 'Being that lets [others] be' *(Principles*, p. 113). The spiritual experience of wonder and intuition thus demands a kind of theology that Macquarrie calls 'dialectical theism', in which both the transcendence and immanence of God are taken with equal seriousness, and in which many other oppositions are also held within the oneness of God. It is 'dialectical' in two senses: first because polarities (such as transcendence and immanence, eternity and time, impassibility and passibility), are held together in God as Being; and second because Being moves out beyond itself into other beings, and returns to itself in a newly enriched unity. As Macquarrie himself freely acknowledges, this movement is discernible in the *exitus* and *reditus* of Neo-Platonist thinking about the One and the many, and is reflected – though in too remorselessly rational a way – in Hegel's philosophy of Absolute Spirit.[6]

Macquarrie calls this a 'natural theology', since it is a concept of God that can be mediated through all persons, things and events in the world; it can be appropriated by universal human faculties without appeal to special religious traditions, though it is specially focused in the Christian story of Jesus. But unlike older styles of natural theology, this know-ledge depends on a dynamic and gracious 'letting be'. Because Being is an 'incomparable *transcendens*' there can be no question of permanent human ownership of some endowment giving access to a knowledge of Being; an *analogia entis* has to be continuously created by the self-giving and self-unveiling of Being which can withdraw as well as approach.[7] To know Being as God also requires a human attitude of trust. The word 'God' does not simply denote Being, since non-religious philosophers can acknowledge and talk about Being as the mysterious origin and source of all beings. 'God' is 'holy Being', where the word 'holy' points to an atti-tude or affective state of the believer towards Being. To call Being 'holy' has the existential connotations of valuation, faith, commitment and wor-ship. This is why Macquarrie calls his theology 'existential-ontological' – it is talk both about Being and about our trust in Being as letting-be in a way that enhances life and love.[8] Again we see that, for Macquarrie, philosophical theology is essentially spiritual, even mystical.

Macquarrie's doctrine of God thus presents us with a masterly integra-tion of natural and revealed theology, blurring the boundaries between them.[9] Indeed, it might be better to call it a theology of 'general revela-tion', given the need for 'holy Being' as incomparable to 'seize' hold[10] of human thought and language for any knowledge of God to happen. At one point Macquarrie calls his scheme 'a universal *possibility* of revela-tion', declining the title 'general revelation' (*Principles*, p. 89). But if Being is always letting-be, always self-giving and always creating symbols of itself in the world then it seems that – as Karl Rahner suggests – the very state of being human is that of receiving primordial revelation or being a 'hearer of the word'.[11] The 'possibility' is surely for any event, thing or person to become the bearer of *more* intense, more focal or more noticeable revelation. Such general revelation would not, of course, carry the older sense of 'natural revelation', which implied revelation was some kind of endowed knowledge rather than an activity of God's self-revealing in the here and now.

We should, however, pause at one point in this phenomenological description of a self-disclosing 'incomparable' which is Being and One. Macquarrie is surely right to point to the need for some sense of unity to bring stability into the flux of life with its many entities and diverse images. In his advocacy of a 'henological argument', he comments that 'if we were confronted with a sheer multiplicity of phenomena . . . we could know nothing at all', and judges that Plotinus was right to think that 'unity is just as fundamental or even more so than the idea of being' (*Deity*, p. 203). This stress on the 'One' does, however, seem to run into the danger of a 'totalizing' approach to the world against which

Emmanuel Levinas warns. To adopt a metaphysical scheme of a 'whole', whether called Being, Reason or Spirit, may result in submerging persons into some common ground, and losing their difference from each other.[12] As Levinas puts it, we see others simply as an extension of 'the same kind of thing' as we are (as instantiations of Being), and we blunt the impact of their mystery and strangeness to us, so failing to recognize the infinite moral demand they make upon us.

Macquarrie is well aware of this danger; he stresses that oneness is not a mere arithmetical unity, and implies an intrinsic plurality; his eschatological vision is of a new level of unity in which the diversity of creation is not lost. But the question is whether equating the 'whole' with Being can altogether avoid a dominating totality to which people can appeal as a sanction for oppressing others. How to think of a 'whole' which does not dominate is an issue I intend to pick up again in thinking about persons and relations in God.

Being and Nothing

As incomparable, God (or holy Being) cannot be classified with any beings in the world (*Principles*, p. 108). This fundamental truth leads Macquarrie, however, to two rather different accounts of the relation of Being to 'nothing', and – at least implicitly – to set a challenge as to how to reconcile them.

In the first place, the concept of 'nothing' stands in stark contrast to Being. Macquarrie observes that since holy Being is incomparable it is elusive and we fail to notice it; what we notice are particular beings. Following Heidegger, Macquarrie affirms that there is, however, a mood that predisposes us to recognize the approach of Being. This is the affective state in which we become aware of 'nothingness'. That is, we have an awareness of the precariousness of existence which may at any time lapse into nothing and which may cease to be in death: 'We become aware of the very nullity that enters into the way we are constituted.'[13] The world sinks to nothing, and is stripped of the values and meaning we normally assign to it. This is characteristically a state of anxiety, which is generated when we feel the tension in which we are caught as finite persons, suspended between our freedom and our limits, between our possibilities and our facticity. Now, it is by contrast with sheer nothingness that we notice Being, and hear the invitation to trust Being in the midst of the tensions of life. It is against the foil of this 'nothing' that our eyes are open to the wonder of Being, and we know it as presence and manifestation.

In the second place, again following Heidegger, Macquarrie presents 'nothing' as a way of referring to Being itself. Since holy Being is incomparable, we cannot strictly say that 'Being exists', and so in a sense it is nothing. In *Was ist Metaphysik?* Heidegger suggests that the positive sciences divide up among themselves the total realm of particular beings to be encountered in the world, leaving 'nothing' for the philosopher as a subject of study, but that this 'nothing' is more beingful (*seiender*) than any particular being. The concern of philosophy is ontological – directed towards Being itself which is 'nothing' in so far as it is not an existent entity in the world, but which is the source of all beings. *Ex nihilo omne ens qua ens fit*, asserts Heidegger: 'out of nothing every being, as a being is made.' The other sciences – including, in Heidegger's view, theology – are 'ontic', dealing only with a specific area of beings.[14]

Macquarrie strongly contests Heidegger's allocation of theology to the merely 'ontic' (or the 'onto-theological'); in the name of dialectical theism he is precisely rejecting the kind of theology that regards God as an individual being (or three beings), however superior to finite beings. He aligns Heidegger's language with that of mystical theologians such as John Scotus Eriugena and Johannes Eckhart who also say that God does not exist or that 'he is nothing' in the sense of 'not one of the objects in space and time'.[15] Aquinas, Macquarrie thinks, is truly affirming God's incomparability when he names God as Being itself (*esse ipsum*), but relapses into implying that God is an existent entity additional to the world with his designation 'he who is' (*Qui est*). Macquarrie prefers the more subtle statement of Eriugena who proposes that if one says that God exists one must match it by saying that God does not exist, and that God is rather 'He who is more than being' (*Qui plus quam esse est*) (*Deity*, pp. 31–2).

In summarizing Macquarrie's appeal to the two senses of nothing, I have brought together material distributed throughout his writings. In fact, in *Principles* (1966/1977), he deals almost entirely with the first sense, according to which 'nothing' is a foil and contrast to Being. He notes only in passing that Being 'refers to nothing in the world of particular beings' (*Principles*, p. 128), and that 'one can no more say that "God is" than that "being is"'; he adds that it is more appropriate to say that 'God exists' than to say that 'God does not exist', since God's letting-be is the condition of the existence of particular beings, and so this is a legitimate 'stretched' use of language (*Principles*, p. 18). In *Deity* (1984), on the other hand, Macquarrie omits the first sense of 'nothing' altogether, even when exegeting Heidegger, rather taking up the mystical tradition of God as 'nothing' in the service of countering any notion that God is an existent being: 'Existence, as we understand it in our everyday dealings . . . excludes God. Inevitably, he is nothing' (*Deity*, p. 173). Being and nothing are presented as the first two polarities within God to be held together by a dialectical theism. The 'nothingness' of God underlines his incomparability.

Much earlier, in a paper in *Studies in Christian Existentialism* dating from 1963, Macquarrie had noted both senses of nothing in Heidegger, but made no attempt to reconcile them (*Studies*, pp. 85–6). Finally, in a paper in *Stubborn Questions in Theology*, written in 1989, he returns to both senses as Heidegger deals with them. He asks how Heidegger thinks we can know the 'nothing' out of which every being is made, and answers that Heidegger appeals to the phenomenon of anxiety, when the world appears to fall to nothing: 'Angst reveals nothing', and so uncovers the ultimate reality which is Being. Macquarrie comments, however, that 'the relation between anxiety and mysticism is enigmatic and ambiguous' (*Stubborn*, p. 188). He perceives some connection in the feeling of awe and the numinous when confronted with 'nothing' in a mood of anxiety. There is some resonance between the way that all particular things lose their separateness and individual value in the sinking of the world to nothing, and the mystical experience of loss of identity in the unity of all things.[16]

But this ambiguous connection seems to underplay the element of *destructive* negativity that can be experienced in a mood of anxiety, or in the midst of the tensions of life. Here Paul Tillich has proposed another kind of divine dialectic, in which God as 'being-itself' eternally includes and overcomes non-being, while non-being remains eternally resistant to Being. Since the negative is always there to be coped with by Being, it is in effect the activating element in the divine life: 'Non-being drives being out of seclusion, it forces it to affirm itself dynamically.'[17] There are resonances here with the *Ungrund* of Jacob Boehme and the *Potenz* of Schelling's thought. Tillich has developed this speculative scheme because his concern is to speak of a God who 'participates in the negativities of our lives'. That which is of ultimate concern to us must be meaningful to those who are in 'the boundary situations of life'.[18] However, he too seems not fully to have connected the 'nothing' that arises in anxiety with the 'nothing' in God, since the confrontation between God and non-being in the form that Tillich describes it is not an exposure to real alienation. Non-being in God is aggressive only in the sense of vitality and creativity, while we experience non-being as threatening and destructive. Like the place of non-being in the life of Absolute Spirit in Hegel, it simply belongs to the divine. If God is really to participate in human suffering, it seems that actual estrangement and desolation must enter God's being.

Here both Hans Urs von Balthasar and Eberhard Jüngel take us, I suggest, a step further. For Jüngel, and somewhat like Tillich, the divine life is always characterized by a tendency towards 'nothingness', a kind of undertow or current against which God is struggling, and which is always resolved in the making of new possibilities. God is always creating out of nothing. As finite beings we experience this 'nothingness' not as creative but as a swirling current towards annihilation; but it is because God *already* exists in the tension between Being and non-being that God can take *our own* experience of deathly non-being into the divine life through the cross of Jesus, and overcome it in favour of life.[19] Similarly, for von Balthasar, God's triune being is always characterized by an 'abyss' or gulf of love between the persons. In their mutual self-giving, self-emptying and infinite difference from each other there is a kind of separation motivated by love. In this space there is room to take in and absorb the more vicious kind of alienation which is the result of human sinning in the course of history.[20]

Such visions of 'nothingness' in God, linking the nothingness of human anxiety to divine being, require a model of trinitarian relations in God which can be disturbed. I am going to leave a comparison of this with Macquarrie's own thought for the moment. But in general, Macquarrie's 'dialectical theism' certainly has room for the suffering of God in creation; indeed, he thinks that trust in holy Being as taking the risk of 'letting-be' and participating in the world of beings positively requires it. Only a vulnerable God who is touched by the sufferings of his creatures is worthy of worship. The other side of the dialectic, God's impassibility, needs also to be maintained, but Macquarrie thinks this means that God is never *overcome* by suffering. God has an 'infinite capacity for absorbing suffering and transforming it' (*Deity*, pp. 80–1). The way that Macquarrie handles the question of evil, moreover, would fit in with the kind of movement from one kind of 'nothing' to another in God that I have been commending.

Macquarrie proposes that the doctrine of *creatio ex nihilo* means that finite beings exist between being and nothing, and are always being sustained by God over the abyss of nothingness (*Principles*, p. 215). This is a neutral kind of nothing, simply non-being in contrast with being. But Macquarrie also understands evil, with Augustine, as *privatio boni*, as a turning away from the good. Graphically he describes created beings as slipping away from the good towards the non-being from which they have been created, a 'lapsing into nothing' which is 'a standing threat to all created beings'. It is this *slipping back* into nothing which is evil, as a 'reversal and defeat of the creative process' (*Principles*, p. 255). We might surely add that this slippage is another kind of non-being, more aggressive and hostile, more opposed to Being than the nothing out of which creation comes.[21]

In moods of anxiety we experience both the neutral non-being of finitude and the destructive non-being of evil; the experience of death is, indeed, a blend of the two. As Macquarrie says, we are anxious both about ceasing to be, and about the guilt that we *fail* to be (*Principles*, p. 86). In the divine life we might then envisage the presence of 'neutral' or creative non-being as a place where God can freely assume and confront a more virulent kind of non-being – that which has entered the universe as an alien factor as a result of the slipping of creation away from God's good aim. Would Macquarrie, I wonder, regard this as a legitimate extension of his thought about God the incomparable? Or would it bring God too much into the 'ontic' sphere of beings? Much depends, I suggest, on the place of personal images within a doctrine of God, to which we now turn.

Being and the Personal

God is the incomparable, and yet the presence and manifestation of holy Being in beings makes it appropriate to use comparisons drawn from the created world in talking about God. Among those comparisons or analogies, Macquarrie judges that the most appropriate are personal images, since persons share in God's own activity of letting-be (*Principles*, pp. 143–4). Holy Being discloses itself symbolically in beings, and is most clearly manifested in persons with a (limited) freedom and creativity. Moreover, as the source of persons, Being 'is not less than personal' and 'includes personality' (*Deity*, pp. 42, 242–8). All this gives Macqarrie good reason for believing that personal symbols do give us insight into the mystery of the holy as it relates itself to human beings. Personal images – such as God as father, friend and lover – belong especially within the language of prayer and spirituality, though here the final aim is towards silent adoration without any words or images at all.

Macquarrie maintains that both prayer and theology are cognitive, though in different ways. There is a 'personal knowing' or 'tacit knowledge' in prayer which uses the second-person language of address (*Deity*, pp. 188–9). Spirituality, as we saw at the beginning of this paper, precedes the third-person language of theology which aims at conceptualization. But when we *are* thinking carefully in theology, and reflecting on our experience, Macquarrie stresses that we need to be aware that personal language is a symbol for Being, and is 'stretching' human words to reach towards some reference to Being. For all his affirmation of the personal, Macquarrie is thus entering a claim for the greater accuracy or appropriateness of Being-language in the realm of theology. This becomes clear in his reflections on the human awareness of Being which happens in the mood of anxiety, against the foil of a sense of nothingness. In opposition to the I–Thou philosophy of Martin Buber, he considers that the experience of the self-disclosure of Being has can only have 'very remote' analogy to a personal encounter (*Principles*, pp. 92–4).

For this he advances three reasons. First, a personal meeting is mediated by physical objects and events, and holy Being has no body. Second, personal relations are characterized by reciprocity, or by 'give and take'. But in a direct revelatory experience, Macquarrie thinks that the person who receives the revelation is 'utterly transcended' and 'mastered' by the holy Being that discloses itself. Third, an 'I–thou' encounter is one in which two particular beings know each other, whereas holy Being is not a being. The kind of knowing which happens between persons Macquarrie designates as 'existential thinking', or a 'thinking into the existence of another subject'; a special case of existential thinking is 'repetitive thinking', an entrance into an experience that has been handed down by others, and he thinks that most of our reception of revelation actually happens in this way. The direct encounter with Being, which belongs to classic instances of revelation, is rather to be characterized as what Heidegger calls 'primordial' thinking, in which Being has an enhanced gift-like character and the knower is 'subjected to that which is known'.

However, I suggest that there are good reasons for finding personal features even in what Macquarrie calls a 'primordial' experience, and that a response to at least two of Macquarrie's objections might be made from the resources of his own thinking elsewhere. With regard to the first point, though God clearly *has* no body of God's own, God still *uses* bodies: all encounters with holy Being must be mediated through the physical world in which Being is present and manifest. As Macquarrie suggests elsewhere, in this sense the universe might be regarded as the body of God, and has a sacramental quality.[22]

Second, Macquarrie clearly recognizes that the relation between Being and beings is a reciprocal one, in which the created universe contributes to the richness of God's being in a process in which God's perfection is increased without ever being less than perfect. God does not evolve out of the world as the end of a process, but Macquarrie approves of Eriugena's view that, in making beings in whom God is present, God is continually 'making himself', and he compares this with Whitehead's vision of the 'consequent nature' of God.[23] Can this reciprocity be entirely excluded from moments of self-disclosure in which the relation of Being with beings is intensified? Moreover, there is an element of being 'overwhelmed' by the other person in any personal relationship, as the core of the subject is broken open by the ethical demand which the other makes. This was already recognized by Martin Buber, for whom reciprocity between persons is not a matter of comfortable give and take, and it has been accentuated by Emmanuel Levinas.[24] All this suggests that there is a closer analogy between a personal relation and the unveiling of incomparable Being to beings than Macquarrie maintains.

Macquarrie's third objection is the most telling. God as the incomparable is certainly not a being, or an individual person, and Macquarrie's whole project has been most successful in bringing this home to readers without undermining the reality of the spiritual life. But might it be possible to release personal language from the confines of individuality? Used in a fully relational way, transcending the boundaries of individual beings, the personal might be as capable of expressing both transcendence and immanence as the language of Being. As Buber himself suggests, what is truly personal in our own experience is what happens 'between' subjects, and this is essentially mysterious, beyond our control.[25] If we look for where we find the 'mystery in our midst' in human life, then the realm of the personal is the most obvious place to find it. It is just not the case that we know what it is to be personal, and that we project this on to God as the unknown. The fact that we treat each other in brutal ways, like mere objects, is evidence that the true meaning of personalness always eludes us, and it is just as cogent to say that we receive what is personal from God as to say that we make God in our personal image.[26] The potential for a doctrine of God of giving the 'personal' a fully relational sense must wait, however, for a consideration of the doctrine of the Trinity.

At this point we might enquire in what sense Macquarrie thinks that personal language is symbolic of Being. Can he mean that talk of Being is *literal* speech about the ultimate reality which is the source of all beings, and that it is the only non-analogical language for this mystery? Several times Macquarrie quotes the declaration of Paul Tillich that the only non-symbolic statement we can make about God is that he is Being-itself, implying that Being-itself is literal language, which 'does not point beyond itself'.[27] He is also careful to quote what seems to be a later modification by Tillich on the subject, when Tillich writes that the only non-symbolic assertion we can make about God is 'the statement that everything we say about God is symbolic'.[28] It is difficult to tell, however, whether Macquarrie agrees with the first or second opinion of Tillich, or neither. Perhaps the language of Being just does not function in this way, and Tillich is being clumsy in supposing that it does. At least we can say that Macquarrie declines to state overtly that the language of Being is either 'literal' or 'non-symbolic'. He approves the statement of Eriugena that God is 'more than being', and does not qualify this as 'more than *a* being' or 'more than *created* being' (*Deity*, p. 90). He finds himself in sympathy with the view of Plotinus and the whole Neoplatonic tradition that the One as nameless is 'prior to being', and he does not gloss this as meaning 'prior to beings' (*Deity*, p. 62). He maintains that the question of Leibniz, 'why is there something rather than nothing?' prompts us to trace the contingency of the universe back to 'a reality of another order which is a "nothing" within the universe and which is designated by such ciphers as "God" or "being" '. Using the term 'cipher' for Being comes from Karl Jaspers, and Macquarrie thinks it is significant that Jaspers quotes Eckhart to the effect that 'The Godhead is unthinkable . . . Being, God, Creator – these are already conceived in categories that do not fit the Godhead' (*Deity*, p. 206).

If 'Being' were indeed a cipher,[29] then Macquarrie would be suggesting, in effect, that personal images are symbolic of *another symbol* which is more appropriate for theology, namely that of Being. This would fit in with his appeal to the theory of theological language in Dionysius, where the positive and negative ways are resolved in symbols which qualify each other in pointing beyond themselves to the incomparable mystery which is 'God beyond God'.[30] We would have to conclude that Macquarrie is suggesting a kind of hierarchy of symbols, with that of 'Being' at the summit as the most capacious for expressing both transcendence and immanence, and for operating in both an apophatic and cataphatic manner. The way would then be open for us to suggest that personal language is by no means inferior to Being-language in these respects, so that it is as appropriate in theological reflection as in spirituality. It would be better to think of complementary symbols, that of 'Being' augmenting the personal, and vice-versa. In some circumstances, such as the disclosure that happens in an affective mood of anxiety, and in thinking about creation as emanation from God, the symbol of holy Being will be indispensable.

We might say that the symbols of 'personalness' and 'relationality' are derived from the experience of persons in relation with just the same logic as the symbol of Being is drawn from the experience of beings. All these symbols have the capacity to offer some comparison between created reality and the final mystery which is incomparable, because all participate in it. Talk of personalness and Being both 'stretch' language in order to indicate the final mystery which is incomparable. When Macquarrie asks, 'why should we use the language of "being" about God?' he replies that in face of the 'shock of being', woken by the wonder that things are at all, people 'stretch language to the uttermost' to point to the mystery (*Deity*, p. 173). It remains to show, of course, that the symbol of personal relations can be stretched in the way that 'being' can. We should agree with Macquarrie that a relation with God, who is incomparable, not only escapes a classification of subject to object, but must even transcend that of subject to subject (*Principles*, p. 94). It will have to be shown that the language of personal relations can express this transcendence as well as 'being' can, and that it can also express the same kind of hiddenness of God, who is veiled even in being unveiled.

If we are able to think the personalness of God in a way that does not reduce God to either one subject or three, then we can integrate the analogies and refer to God as 'personal Being', but not '*a* personal being'. This might well be a theology that is truly adequate to the demands of spirituality. A theology that uses the language of 'personal relations' and 'personal Being' will be more continuous with the prayerful address to God as 'a person' (as, for example, a father or mother) than a theological language of 'Being' only. The boundary or transition between imaging and conceptualizing will still be there, but the dividing line will be blurred.

Being and Trinity

From the basic perspective of God as incomparable, it is clear that what have been called 'persons of the Trinity' in Christian tradition cannot be conceived in the modern sense of a person. That is, there cannot be three psychological centres of consciousness in God, nor three personal subjects, nor even three personal agents. Macquarrie is surely right to be emphatic about this. Stressing the wonderfully intimate nature of individual persons in relationship (in a 'social' doctrine of the Trinity) will neither yield one God nor sufficiently express the otherness of God from finite beings in the world.

Macquarrie proposes that we should begin with the way that holy Being 'has let itself be known', as the energy or act of letting-be. He would agree with Karl Barth (though he does not explicitly appeal to Barth here) that 'with regard to the being of God, the word "event" or "act" is final'.[31] 'Letting-be' is Being as a verbal noun; Macquarrie dislikes Tillich's phrase 'ground of Being' because it makes Being too static.[32] But holy Being has also let itself be known in the Christian community under the trinitarian symbol of Father, Son and Holy Spirit, so we may say that this divine event has three modes, or better, movements. Three 'persons' thus refers to 'three movements within the dynamic yet stable mystery that we call "Being"'. (*Principles*, p. 198). Macquarrie points out that the traditional vocabulary for thinking about the Trinity – the generation of the Son, and the procession or spiration of the Spirit – is dynamic in the highest degree. Here he appeals to the insight of Eberhard Jüngel, who is himself building on the thought of Karl Barth, that the trinitarian doctrine implies that 'God's being is in motion, being in act'.[33] Macquarrie's identifying of the three persons in one God as three movements in one event is of the greatest importance, setting the direction for a cogent doctrine of the Trinity with a clarity not found in Barth's own thought.

At this point, however, Macquarrie offers an explanation of the three movements in God that moves away from the traditional trinitarian language of internal relations, in a direction reminiscent of Hegel. The first movement, or the Father, may be called 'primordial Being'. [34] This term points to 'the ultimate act or energy of letting-be, the condition that there should be anything whatsoever, the source of all possibilities of being'. Primordial Being is the 'depth of the mystery of God'. The second movement, or the Son, may be called 'expressive Being': 'The energy of primordial Being is poured out through expressive Being, giving rise to the world of particular beings in space and time.' In traditional concepts, the Logos is generated by the Father and is the agent of the Father in the creation of the world. The Logos expresses the primordial Being of the Father in created beings, and Christians believe that Being finds its highest expression in the finite being of Jesus.

The third movement, or the Holy Spirit, is 'unitive Being', restoring the unity of Being with beings which is constantly threatened. It is of the essence of God to let be, not to hoard being within himself, and so 'as Being goes out into the openness of a world of beings it involves itself in the risk of being torn and fragmented within itself'. The risk becomes acute when the universe brings forth beings who have a limited freedom, who are meant to be 'guardians of being'[35] but who 'forget Being' and are alienated from it. In this situation, unitive Being not only maintains and restores unity, but 'builds up a higher unity than would have been possible if Being had never moved out of primordial Being through expressive Being'.

In giving this description of the triune nature of Being, Macquarrie intends to offer both an 'existential' account of the community's experience of the approach of God, and an 'ontological' account that 'tries to express an insight into the nature of God' (Principles, p. 191). In the classical language of trinitarian theology, he is proposing both an economic and immanent Trinity. He is venturing to talk about the incomparable God in a way which does not reduce Being to a being, using the dynamic symbols of 'act' and 'movement'. In this project, he clearly thinks that personal symbols have a very limited function. In his discussion of theological language more generally, he asks how personal analogues – like God as father, king, judge, shepherd and so on – might illuminate Being for us, and answers that they do not disclose Being 'as it is in itself' but only Being 'as related to us' (Principles, p. 141). While I want to take a somewhat different direction at this point, his account of the way that a personal symbol of God operates to speak of the incomparable God is immensely helpful. He stresses, rightly I believe, that the analogy does not lie in expressing a similarity between Being and beings, despite some affinity. The analogy, we might say, cannot be between a human person and a divine person of the Trinity, though this is usually how it is employed. The analogy offered by the symbol is between the relations of beings to each other on the one hand, and the relation of Being to beings on the other (*Principles*, p. 140). We might put this into the formula:

being-being : Being-being

Macquarrie gives an example of this analogy of proportionality: 'as a father pities his children, so the Lord pities those who fear him.' Now, I suggest that we can extend this analogy of relations into personal talk about God, while still following its own logic:

being-being : Being-being : Being-Being

In this formula, the analogy lies between the hyphens in each pair of terms. That is, a comparison is being made between inner-human *relations* and inner-divine *relations*, but not between 'persons' who are relating to each other.

This kind of comparison is possible if we think of the 'persons' in the Trinity not as subjects who *have* relations, but as nothing more or less than relations themselves. Taking up Macquarrie's language of 'movements' within one act of Being, these are *movements of relationship*. They are movements that can be compared to the way that a human father relates to a son, or a mother to a daughter, in a spirit that continually opens up these relations to new depths and a new future. To some extent this proposal continues the tradition of 'subsistent relations' within trinitarian thinking. Augustine had asked what was denoted by the term 'person' and answered (in an experimental way) that 'the names Father and Son do not refer to the substance but to the relation'. Aquinas later gave formality to the idea by stating that ' "divine person" signifies relation as something subsisting'. Both these accounts must be read in the philosophical context of their time,[36] but they hint at an idea that can be opened up by an ontology of 'act' and 'event' such as is advocated by Macquarrie.

Speaking of God as 'three movements of relationship in one event of Being' gives equal weight to the language of persons and Being, as I proposed that we might do earlier. It also, I suggest, uses the language of personal relations in a way that avoids equating the incomparable God with created beings. It is an apophatic as well as a cataphatic form of speaking, no less than the idea of Being that lets-be. Three interweaving relations cannot be envisaged or observed as objects, even in the mind's eye. They cannot be painted on a canvas, sculpted in stone or engraved in glass. There is something elusive about the concept, which lends itself to speech and silence at the same time. The objection, 'but there can't be relations without individual persons who are related' is voiced precisely from the viewpoint of wanting to draw an analogy between human and divine subjects, and this fails to grasp the incomparability of God. Of course, human relationships require individual persons to exercise them, but here we are using symbols to speak of the uncreated. We are not speaking literally but analogically, with an analogy drawn from relations. In fact, it is a kind of speech that is not observational but participative: it only makes sense from the perspective of being *involved* in God. In a final section I want to focus on this idea of participation, but here we might consider the experience of prayer as an example of participating in relations that are already there, in God.

The New Testament portrays prayer as being 'to' the Father, 'through' the Son and 'in' the Spirit. This means that when we pray to God as Father, we find our address fitting into a movement like that of speech between a son and father, our response of 'yes' ('Amen') leaning upon a child-like 'yes' of humble obedience that is already there, glorifying the father.[37] At the same time we find ourselves involved in a movement of self-giving like that of a father sending forth a son, a movement which the early theologians called 'eternal generation' and which we experience in the mission of God in history. These movements of response and mission are undergirded by movements of suffering, like the painful longing of a forsaken son towards a father and of a desolate father towards a lost son. Simultaneously, these two directions of movement are interwoven by a third, as we find that they are continually being opened up to new depths of relationship and to new possibilities of the future by a movement that we can only call 'Spirit'; for this third movement the Scriptures give us a whole series of impressionistic images – a wind blowing, breath stirring, oil trickling, wings beating, water flowing and fire burning – evoking an activity that disturbs, opens, deepens and provokes.

Thus, through our participation, we can identify three distinct movements of speech, emotion and action which are like relationships 'from father to son', 'from son to father' and a movement of 'deepening relations'. They are mutual relationships of ecstatic, outward-going love, giving and receiving. Like patterns of a dance they interweave and interpenetrate each other (*perichōrēsis*). So far in describing them I have followed the form of address that Jesus himself taught his disciples, 'Abba, Father', offering the image 'from son to father' for the movement of response that we lean upon. Christians find that the relation of Jesus with

God exactly fits into the eternal movement within God which is 'like' the relation of a son to a father, so that we depend on the shape of this particular human life to participate fully in God ourselves. But the movements of giving and receiving in God cannot in themselves be restricted to a particular gender; in appropriate contexts they will give rise to a range of feminine symbols as well.

This account is, borrowing a term from Macquarrie, 'existential-ontological'. We cannot speak of God without also speaking of our involvement in God, for there is no God apart from the one who has freely chosen to be open to the world, making room to include us in the space which is created by divine relations. A significant departure here from Macquarrie's account, however, is that all these relations have aspects of primordial, expressive and unitive Being to them. The difference is between the relations, in which we participate; but all relations are mysterious in their primordial depth of Being, shape created beings expressively in the image of this mystery, and unite them in a fellowship of love. The first movement still has a primacy, as in the Eastern model of the Trinity, giving direction to the flow of the dance of love, so that all movements are to and from an ultimate source.

Here I venture to suggest that Macquarrie's scheme tends towards the danger of assigning different 'persons' of the Trinity to express transcendence and immanence respectively. It seems that Macquarrie does not intend this, for he speaks of primordial Being as 'a movement within the whole structure of Being', and stresses that we cannot think of primordial Being as ever dwelling in isolation from the other movements. However, he also writes that 'as the primordial "it gives", God is utterly transcendent and is separated by the ontological difference from the beings. But in the expressive and unitive modes of his being, God is thoroughly immanent in the world.'[38] This equates the dialectic of immanence and transcendence in God with the first movement on the one hand, and the second and third movements on the other. This has similarities to the distinction between the absolute transcendence of the One and the immanence of Mind and Soul in the trinity of Plotinus, and to the difference between the primordial and consequent natures of God in process theism.[39] But in the Christian vision of the Trinity, the whole of the three-personed God must be transcendent *and* immanent. If we think of the world as existing in God, as I have suggested, then there is no need for a mediatorial agent or expressive movement to bridge a gap between transcendence and immanence. All the divine movements of relation are transcendent in infinitely exceeding created relations in their richness and depth, and immanent in including all human relations in themselves.

With Macquarrie, we notice that the experience of spiritual writers and mystics is to intuit a whole, an overall shape (*Gestalt*) in all creation, or an interconnectedness of all reality. Macquarrie emphasizes that the whole is differentiated into modes, as Being moves out from itself into creation and returns in a new unity, but I suggest that the experience of prayer shows a discernment of a wholeness that is internally related within itself. Earlier I noted the danger of an oppressive totalization, but a relational whole is not oppressive for a number of reasons: because there are no subjects here to reinforce the power of human agents, but only relations; because the patterns of relation are those of mutual self-giving; because there is no synthesis but only a continual opening to the future; and because we can only know this whole by participating in it and so bringing something to it ourselves.

Being and participation

Macquarrie constantly affirms that all beings 'participate in Being'. This participation is the other side of the presence and manifestation of Being in everything there is. While God is incomparable, he is holy Being that lets be, and so in thinking about creation we need to use a model of emanation to complement the more personal model of 'making'. In an overflow of divine love and generosity, God 'puts himself into the world'.[40] Because Being is expressed in beings, symbols emerge that are capable of illuminating Being, which themselves 'participate' in the reality that they symbolize.[41] The incomparable thus allows itself to be grasped by comparisons, while still remaining veiled, and requiring language to be stretched to point to the mystery of Being.

But what can actually be meant by this 'participation' in God? Macquarrie is apparently going further in terms of a two-way engagement between Being and beings than is allowed by the Neoplatonist tradition which he otherwise values highly. According to Plotinus, the highest reality, the One, was absolutely transcendent, beyond being, and so could not be participated in by the many.[42] The One overflows into the many, and in the first place into mind (*nous*), proceeding as the radiance of light from light. The human goal is to become fully *nous*, and so to touch some higher level of being, but it is not possible to participate in the One Itself, which is ineffable, inexpressible and inactive. Macquarrie attributes a notion of 'participating in God' to Plotinus, by insisting that the One is not by itself the godhead: 'God' for Plotinus is a triad comprising the One, the Mind and the Soul, and a kind of sympathetic unity binds all individual souls to the World-Soul (*Deity*, pp. 66–8).

But this is a very qualified sense of participation, relying on distinct areas of transcendence and immanence in God. Macquarrie means more than this, and at least as much as Aquinas does in using the term 'participation'. For Aquinas, except for very rare and temporary anticipations of the final beatific vision, 'participation' does not mean direct vision or engagement in the essence of God during a person's lifetime. Creatures 'participate' in the pure being of God through an analogy of being, so reflecting aspects or properties of God, and in particular the likeness of the light of reason to the uncreated light of God. Particular entities thus participate in God in two senses: 'participation' means that they *resemble* God, and that they are *caused* by God who has created all forms.[43] In this earthly life, God can be known only indirectly, through seeing created things, as the light of the intellect shines upon them.

Macquarrie follows Aquinas in laying considerable stress on participation as an imitation of God. All things tend to imitate God, but the fullest imitation of God, and so participation in God, comes about when creatures in turn 'let be'. All living beings that reproduce themselves participate in letting-be more than do inanimate things; but on a far higher level is the human person with the capacity – however limited – for creativity and love, who brings the imitation of God on to an altogether new level, that of free co-operation in letting-be. Human destiny is to become a co-worker with God, as a 'guardian of Being'. The incomparable God freely allows creatures to be compared with God's own self. So human participation in God could never be interpreted as absorption, as in pantheism – that would be a nullifying of the whole process of creation (*Principles*, pp. 225, 232–3).

With this idea of a participating in 'letting-be', Macquarrie takes us further than Aquinas. He claims that, for Aquinas, imitation of God is a participation that is 'internal' to God, (*Principles*, p. 225), but this seems to be building on Aquinas's thought with the help of reference to Heidegger and the thought of some Christian mystical writers. For Heidegger, notes Macquarrie, it is in affective states such as anxiety that we become aware of our participation in Being (*Deity*, p. 185–6). So questions about Being are not asked by someone who merely 'beholds', but by those who are involved in Being (*Principles*, p. 107). As I have myself suggested for the language of relations in God, talk of Being is not observational, but participatory. A deeper sense of participation than Aquinas describes is also to be found in the mystical experience of Meister Eckhart, to whom Macquarrie appeals in thinking about the unity of the human person with holy Being: 'the Father gives birth to his Son without ceasing; and I say more; he gives birth to me, his son and the same Son.'[44] Though Macquarrie does not explicitly make a connection here with a human participation in the divine letting-be, we can surely say that as we share in that letting-be we are participating in the very movements that characterize the being of God as event.

This metaphor of sharing in the generation of the Son actually makes most sense, I suggest, with a more relational view of the Trinity. A truly 'internal' view of participation would be a sharing in the participation of the persons of the Trinity in each other. Human persons are involved, that is, in the interweaving, mutual relations in which the divine life consists. It is as if God 'makes room' within God's own self for created beings to dwell, in the midst of eternal relations of self-giving and other-receiving love that we name as Father, Son and Holy Spirit.[45] This is what we might call a 'panentheistic' vision, in which 'everything is in God'.

Macquarrie suggests that his own dialectical theism is a kind of 'panentheism', in so far as it steers a midway course between theism and pantheism, avoiding a one-sided emphasis on either transcendence or immanence.[46] However, despite his appeal to participation, he does not have much to say about the sense in which everything might be 'in God', which is surely an essential element of panentheism. It might be objected that if all things live, move and have their being within a relational space in God, then there is no place for the existential commitment to which Macquarrie refers. But there are degrees of participation in God, less and more willing. As Macquarrie himself says, human destiny is 'to participate in the fullest and most conscious way possible in God. All things indeed participate in God (Being) but man's destiny is to participate freely, responsibly, gladly, with love, to become a co-worker with God in creation' (*Principles*, p. 233).

As I have reflected on the incomparability of God during the progress of this paper, with the help of John Macquarrie, I have taken my thought in a more personalist and relational direction than he does. I believe that I have, nevertheless, been steering a course which is within the borders of his own thinking. Most of all I hope that I have followed, at least a little, the example he gives us: that theologians, in their own way, can be co-workers with God.

Notes

1 *Studies*, p. 89; cf. later, *Principles*, p. 113. In *Principles* p. 122 Macquarrie signals his intention only to capitalize Being when it is used as an alternative to God. In later writings he uses lower-case initial without distinction. In this paper I adopt the convention of Being (upper-case initial) wherever this is distinguished from beings.

2 *Principles*, p. 100; *Deity*, p. 173; he cites Wittgenstein, *Tractatus Logico-Philosophicus* (1922), London: Routledge & Kegan Paul, 1981, p. 187.

3 *Deity*, pp. 120, 158, 173, 206; he cites Leibniz, *The Monadology*, trans. Robert Latta, London: Oxford University Press, 1898, p. 415; and Heidegger, *Was Ist Metaphysik?*, Bonn: Cohen, 1930, p. 42.

4 *Deity*, pp. 189–90, 203–6; *Two Worlds*, pp. 27–9.

5 See Macquarrie, *Deity*, pp. 164–6; *Principles*, pp. 113–16; *Studies*, pp. 89–92, citing Martin Heidegger, *Brief über den Humanismus* (Frankfurt: Kostermann, 1947), pp. 22–24; Heidegger, *Being and Time*, trans. John Macquarrie and Edward Robinson, Oxford: Blackwell, 1973, pp. 22, 32–35. Cf. *Existentialist*, pp. 56–61.

6 *Deity*, pp. 174–5, cf. pp. 132–3, 68–70.

7 *Deity*, pp. 13–14, 197; *Principles*, pp. 94–5, 104.

8 *Principles*, pp. 116–17, 121–2, 127.

9 Macquarrie states that the idea of 'theophany' in Johannes Scotus Eriugena makes the borderline between natural and revealed theology a tenuous one: *Deity*, p. 94.

10 *Principles*, pp. 94, 104; the word is used by Karl Barth for the commandeering of human language by revelation: see Karl Barth, *Church Dogmatics*, tr. & ed. G.W. Bromiley and T.F. Torrance, Edinburgh: T. & T. Clark, 1936–77, I/1, p. 430.

11 Rahner, pp. 126–9. While Tillich, *Systematic Theology* I, p. 154, like Macquarrie, rejects the term 'general revelation', he uses the phrase 'universal revelation' in the same sense as I am using 'general revelation'. An influential advocate of the concept has been John Baillie, in e.g. his *Our Knowledge of God*, London: Oxford University Press, 1939, pp. 35–43.

12 Emmanuel Levinas, *Totality and Infinity. An Essay on Exteriority*, tr. A. Lings, Pittsburgh: Duquesne University Press, 1969, pp. 37–40, 48–52.

13 *Principles*, pp. 86–7. Cf. *Humanity*, pp. 119–22.

14 *Studies*, p. 89; *Deity*, pp. 156–8. Macquarrie cites Heidegger, *Was Ist Metaphysik?*, pp. 38–42, and Heidegger, 'Phenomenology and Theology' in *The Piety of Thinking*, Bloomington: Indiana University Press, 1976, pp. 5–21.

15 *Deity*, pp. 88, 160–1, 173; *Stubborn*, pp. 185–88.

16 With *Stubborn*, p. 188, cf. *Deity*, pp. 194–8.

17 Paul Tillich, *The Courage to Be*, London: Collins/Fontana, 1962, I, p. 174; cf. Tillich, *Systematic Theology*, Combined Volume, London: James Nisbet, 1968, pp. 210, 258–60, 280.

18 Tillich, *Systematic Theology*, I, p. 300; III, pp. 430–2.

19 Eberhard Jüngel, *God as the Mystery of the World*, tr. D. Guder, Edinburgh: T. & T. Clark, 1983, pp. 199–204, 217–19.

20 Hans Urs von Balthasar, *Mysterium Paschale*, trans. A. Nichols, Edinburgh: T. & T. Clark, 1990, p. ix; *Theo-Drama. Theological Dramatic Theory*, Vol. IV, *The Action*, trans. G. Harrison, San Francisco: Ignatius Press, 1994, pp. 323–5.

21 The distinction between *ouk ōn* and *mē ōn* made by both Plato and Plotinus expresses the difference between neutral nothingness and a negation which is hostile to being: Plato, *Parmenides* 160c–162a; Plotinus, *Enneads* 1.8.3.

22 *Thinking*, pp. 117–20; *Sacraments*, pp. 1–11.

23 *Deity*, pp. 93, 182; *Principles*, pp. 121, 208–9.

24 Martin Buber, *I and Thou*, trans. R. Gregor Smith, Edinburgh: T. & T. Clark, 1937, pp. 51–4, 111–12; Levinas, *Totality and Infinity*, pp. 194–201.

25 Martin Buber, *Between Man and Man*, tr. R. Gregor Smith, London: Collins/Fontana, 1961, pp. 244–7.

26 For this argument, see Wolfhart Pannenberg, 'The Question of God', in *Basic Questions in Theology*. Vol. 2, tr. G. Kehm, London: SCM Press, 1971, pp. 228–33.

27 Tillich, *Systematic Theology*, I, pp. 264–5.; *God-Talk*, p. 51; *Sacraments*, p. 29; *Two Worlds*, pp. 90–91.

28 Tillich, *Systematic Theology*, II, p. 10.

29 In *Principles*, p. 203, however, Macquarrie denies that God or Being is '*just a cipher*'.

30 *Two Worlds*, pp. 94–5. However, in *Deity*, p. 243, Macquarrie equates 'God beyond God' as 'reality beyond the personal'.

31 Barth, *Church Dogmatics*, II/1, p. 263.

32 *Principles*, pp. 109–10; cf. *Twentieth-Century*, pp. 367–8.

33 Macquarrie, *Principles*, p. 195. See Eberhard Jüngel, *God's Being is in Becoming. The Trinitarian Being of God in the Theology of Karl Barth*, tr. John Webster, Edinburgh: T. & T. Clark, 2001, pp. 14–15.

34 For the following, see *Principles*, pp. 198–202.

35 This recalls Heidegger's phrase, 'shepherd of being', in *Brief über den Humanismus*, p. 29.

36 Augustine, *De Trinitate* 5.6, was attempting to meet the alternative presented by the Arians, that 'persons' in God must be defined either by substance or accident. Augustine replied, using Platonic concepts rather playfully, that the persons fell into neither category, but were relations. Aquinas, *Summa Theologiae*, 1a.29.4, unfortunately explained the subsistence of the three persons in an Aristotelian way by their identity with one essence, so tending to lose the 'otherness' of the persons.

37 2 Cor. 1.20; cf. Rom. 8.34, Heb. 7.25.

38 *Deity*, p. 177. The movement of unitive being, he writes elsewhere, is the 'nearer-side of God': *Thinking*, pp. 130–1.

39 Macquarrie offers a qualified approval to the dipolarity of God in process theism: see *Deity*, pp. 150–1. His modification of Whitehead's scheme in a trinitarian direction does not overcome the distribution of transcendence and immanence among the persons.

40 *Deity*, p. 36; cf. *Principles*, pp. 218–19.

41 *Principles*, pp. 135–7; *Sacraments*, pp. 30–33. Here Macquarrie quotes from, and offers a critique of, Tillich in *Systematic Theology*, I, pp. 174, 266–8.

42 Plotinus, *Enneads* 5.1, 5, 6.

43 Aquinas, *Summa Theologiae* Ia.6.4, reply; Ia. 44.1.1; I.a.3.3.2 and reply; *Summa Contra Gentiles* III.97.3.

44 *Deity*, p. 195; he quotes from Edmund Colledge and Bernard McGinn, *Meister Eckhart: the Essential Sermons, Commentaries, Treatises and Defense*, Ramsey, N.J.: Paulist Press, 1981, p. 187.

45 Cf. von Balthasar, *Theo-Drama*, pp. 319–32; Paul S. Fiddes, *Participating in God. A Pastoral Doctrine of the Trinity*, London: Darton, Longman & Todd, 2000, pp. 28–55.

46 *Deity*, pp. 53–4; *Principles*, p. 120; *Thinking*, pp. 111–13.

18 John Macquarrie's Panentheism

MICHAEL W. BRIERLEY

Presumably we are standing only at the beginning of the revolution in the idea of God. Its application to particular Christian doctrines is something that has still to be fully worked out. That it will be more mature and more satisfying than the way of thinking of God that has been dominant in the past few centuries . . . I cannot doubt (*Thinking about God*, 1975, p. 109).

John Macquarrie is surely the 'Grand Old Man' of British panentheism. On its own, 'grand' would not be right, since Macquarrie is known for his modesty rather than for pretension or ostentation; but if the phrase means 'venerated', or regarded with deep respect, 'Grand Old Man' is appropriate. *Principles of Christian Theology* and *Twentieth-Century Religious Thought* have become classics, perhaps also his trilogy on anthropology (1982), the doctrine of God (1984) and Christology (1990), and the secondary discussion of his work (below p. 321) is only the tip of the iceberg of his influence. I suggest that he is most appreciated (whether consciously or not) for his panentheistic doctrine of God, and that this doctrine (with its particular style) is his most important legacy, and that such a legacy is of special significance at a time when panentheism is explicitly coming to the fore.[1] This essay therefore seeks to do three things: to identify the hallmarks of panentheism within his doctrine; to see how the influences on his doctrine add to what is known about the origins of modern panentheism; and to assess what the particular characteristics of his panentheism have to offer to contemporary discussion.

The Indicators of Macquarrie's Panentheism

The suggestion that Macquarrie's panentheism is his most important legacy is admittedly not helped by his own hesitations about the term. Recognizing it as a middle term between classical theism and pantheism, and asserting that panentheism is closer to the former than to the latter, he finds the term confusing, because its similarity to the word 'pantheism' suggests that panentheism tends towards this pole.[2] However, he himself observes that there are 'various forms of panentheism' (*Stubborn*, p. x) and not all these are as close to classical theism as his own.[3] It would therefore be more accurate to say that Macquarrie's version of panentheism rather than panentheism *per se* leans towards classical theism. Although in *Deity*, he prefers the term 'dialectical theism' to 'panentheism', in his later work he does not refrain from using the term 'panentheism'.

Regardless of the term itself, Macquarrie's work displays a number of characteristics that point in the direction of panentheism.[4] First, he holds that God is mediated 'in and through' the cosmos. God expresses Godself or appears or is present and manifest 'in and through' the world.[5] These prepositions are significant, as they imply the connectedness as opposed to the externality of God in relation to the cosmos. Indeed, the prepositions are intrinsic to the meaning of sacraments, those things 'in and through' which God comes; so the description of the cosmos itself as a 'sacrament' is another panentheistic trait of Macquarrie's work. Perhaps on account of his Anglo-catholic persuasion, Macquarrie is slightly wary about using the term 'sacrament' beyond the seven sacraments of the Church,[6] but is willing to use the adjective more broadly and speak of a 'sacramental universe' and the sacramental potential of all things.[7]

There are two further elements of panentheism related to the language of God being known 'in and through' the cosmos. One is that this language is applicable to the action of persons with regard to their bodies; hence the language implies the image of the cosmos as God's 'body'. Macquarrie prefers the term 'form' to body, and he is clear that it is a limited analogy, and he does not use it widely; nevertheless he states that this analogy (which Philip Clayton has called *the* panentheistic analogy) is not to be despised.[8] The other element of panentheism related to the prepositions is applicable to those theologies like Macquarrie's which hold evil to be privative, as a lack rather than existing in itself.[9] Such a position allows Macquarrie to say that the cosmos in and through which God works is fundamentally good; panentheisms which hold evil to be privative are distinctive in attributing intrinsic positive value to the cosmos.[10]

In the quotation at the head of this essay, Macquarrie stated that the application of new (that is panentheistic) ideas of God to other Christian doctrines (which presuppose and thus depend on the doctrine of God – *Secularity*, p. 14) still had to be fully worked out. It is nevertheless possible to identify the impact of his panentheism on his discussion of some of these other dependent doctrines. In his Christology, for example, which has received significant attention,[11] Macquarrie subscribes to the 'degree' type which is entailed by panentheism: Christ differs from the rest of humanity in 'degree' rather than in 'kind'.[12] With regard to miracle, Macquarrie seems to share the panentheistic understanding that 'miraculous' phenomena, while being disclosures of God, have natural explanations, since God works in and through nature, though those explanations may not be, nor indeed may ever be, known (*Principles*, pp. 250–1). With regard to eschatology, Macquarrie subscribes to the universalism implied by panentheism: if all things are 'in' God even in their current imperfection, it is difficult to see how any can be put permanently outside the divine life.[13]

The Foundation of Macquarrie's Panentheism

Beneath these surface features of panentheism present in Macquarrie's work, it is possible to identify the deep impulse that gives rise to them. This is the concept of Being which Macquarrie derives from Martin Heidegger and which Macquarrie identifies with God.[14] Analysis of human existence reveals individual entities ('beings'), and also existence itself in which the beings subsist ('Being'). Being is not a separate entity like the beings, but is rather their source in which they participate. God is Being experienced as gracious or holy. Thus God is not a separate entity alongside other entities, no matter how superior to them: as Tillich was fond of saying (himself influenced by Heidegger), God is the ground or power of being.

This conception of the relation between Being and beings is, theologically speaking, panentheistic. It suggests between Being and beings the deepest possible connectedness. As soon as Being is conceived as a being or entity, the element of separation that is essential to classical theism has been introduced. Eugene Long, an early commentator on Macquarrie, observes that the conception of God as Being itself is anti-dualist and thus 'the root of Macquarrie's break with classical theism'.[15] Without Being, beings would not exist; and conversely, Being needs beings in order to express itself, in order to be complete. The notions of Being as 'ground', and of beings as 'participating' in Being, establish the connectedness, and thereby establish the panentheism which follows when God is identified as (holy) Being.

The connectedness expressed by this conception of Being and beings is seen in three further panentheistic expressions. First, God and cosmos are regarded as distinct (they are not the same) but not separable: the language of 'distinct but not separate', or 'inextricable intertwining', is intrinsically panentheistic; and Macquarrie's work is peppered with it.[16] Second, Macquarrie is able to assert that because Being and beings need each other (though not in the same way), God is dependent on the cosmos. Macquarrie is perhaps over-cautious here: he affirms that it is God's *nature* to create, but resists the assertion that God *needs* the cosmos (*Thinking*, p. 151), or that the cosmos is *necessary* to God (*Thinking*, p. 118), on the grounds that this might imply that something outside God compelled this (*Deity*, p. 179) and of course there can be nothing beyond Being. He prefers to say that God 'freely creates', and to deny the unwelcome implication that God could have acted otherwise (*Deity*, p. 36). I think that since 'necessity' and 'freedom' in God can *both* be misconstrued by their respective implications, both terms may be used, with appropriate qualification: God freely needs the cosmos, with no other option and without any outside force. Indeed, the language of necessity is implied by talk of God's 'nature', so it can hardly be avoided. If 'liberty and necessity are one' in God, as Macquarrie agrees with Lossky (*Thinking*, p. 118), then this means that both are true; both are entailed by divine love.

Panentheism denies, on the one hand, that God is separate from the cosmos, and on the other, that God is identified with the cosmos. In between these two extremes, it asserts that to some extent God and the cosmos affect each other. Hence the mutuality, intimacy and reciprocity which Macquarrie recognizes in the 'organic' rather than the 'monarchical' model of God, and the third aspect of connectedness which pushes towards panentheism: God being affected by the cosmos, or divine passibility. This is one of the most commonly articulated features of panentheism, and Macquarrie's panentheism in this regard is no exception.[17]

The Origins of Macquarrie's Panentheism

Having described Macquarrie's panentheism, I consider now how the sources of Macquarrie's doctrine add to what is known about the stimuli for the rise of panentheism in modern theology, before turning finally to the benefits of Macquarrie's own style of panentheism.

Three main influences can be identified in Macquarrie's panentheism. Two are widely recognized as sources of panentheism in modern thought. The first is idealism. Macquarrie was greatly influenced as an undergraduate in philosophy at Glasgow (1936–40) by the Oxford idealist F. H. Bradley, whose *Appearance and Reality* he described as at that time his bible.[18] The influence of idealism was also mediated by Macquarrie's teacher C. A. Campbell.[19] It is true that existentialism brought Macquarrie to some extent 'back down to earth', but the persistence of his early assent to the overriding unity of reality, to which everything else related, should not be underestimated. Indeed, Macquarrie's reflection that 'perhaps Bradley's suprarational Absolute was still lurking [in *Principles*] in the new guise of Heidegger's Being' (*Theology*, p. 6) suggests continuity between this idealist influence and the ontology that Macquarrie drew from Heidegger and used to critique existentialism. As Georgina Morley observes, 'It may be, then, that this earlier interest in Bradley fostered [Macquarrie's] openness to Heidegger's later thought, for although Bradley's ultimate position is not congenial to Heidegger's work, there are a number of points of similarity.'[20] Philip Clayton has traced the connections between the idealist tradition and modern panentheism.[21]

The second source common to Macquarrie's theology and panentheism in general is religious experience.[22] Macquarrie confesses to a natural awareness of the immanence of mystery and the holy, which drew him away from cerebral Protestantism towards the Catholic tradition (*Theology*, p. 2). He associates this religiosity with his 'Celtic heritage' (cf. *Theologian*, pp. 1–11); and it is neither over-romanticized nor historically naive to say that 'Celtic spirituality' has become a recognisable type of spirituality, essentially panentheistic in orientation.[23] Furthermore, beyond the connection of Celtic spirituality and panentheism, mysticism has often been expressed panentheistically; and it is no coincidence that Macquarrie has an abiding interest in mysticism (cf. *Two Worlds*), noting its connection with panentheism or dialectical theism (*Deity*, pp. 193–200, 216, 237–8). Again, Georgina Morley points to the consonance of Macquarrie's religious experience both with Bradley's Absolute and with Heideggerian ontology.[24] She suggests that his religious experience made him receptive to Bradley, and that Bradley in turn made Macquarrie receptive to Heidegger.

The third and principal influence on Macquarrie's theology, then, is Heidegger and existentialism. This was developed primarily through his doctorate on the influence of Heidegger on Bultmann. Macquarrie studied existentialism as a philosophical movement, with a particular analysis of human existence; but existentialism also influenced him as an 'attitude',[25] the taking of human existence as the starting-point of thought. Like phenomenology, existentialism starts with what we know of ourselves. Macquarrie found that human existence implied an ontology: the question of human being raised the issue of Being in general, and the relation of Being to God. In this way, existentialism led to a 'new-style natural theology'. Hence Macquarrie's chief criticism of Bultmann was that Bultmann over-emphasized the subjective element in analysing existence: Bultmann gave insufficient attention to the ontology implied by human being,[26] an ontology that was supplied by Heidegger's own later work.[27] And hence Macquarrie's own position, his incipient panentheism, was what he himself called an 'existential-ontological' position, which in his one-volume systematics, *Principles of Christian Theology*, he systematically applied to the range of Christian doctrine.[28] There is a parallel between Macquarrie's *Principles* and the doctoral thesis of John Robinson:[29] both were attempting to formulate a metaphysics for structuring Christian belief, alternative to the 'substance' mode of classical thought, one on the basis of existentialism with its emphasis on temporality, the other on the basis of personalism, both of which can be regarded as panentheistic (cf. *Existentialist*, pp. 3–25). In the case of existentialism, the start with human existence and the following of its connections to a wider ontological sphere assume the continuity that panentheism enshrines. Some versions of existentialism stop at the subjective or reductionist level, and thus do not progress beyond atheism or pantheism; but the way is nevertheless open under existentialism to a panentheistic interpretation of reality. Three points emerge: that existentialism is inherently biased against a classical theistic conclusion; that existentialism has not been widely recognized as a source of modern panentheism; and that the work of John Macquarrie makes the connection between existentialism and panentheism plain. In this way, Macquarrie's work adds to the understanding of the origins of modern panentheism.

The Distinctive Style of Macquarrie's Panentheism

It remains to be considered how Macquarrie's style of panentheism contributes to discussion about the doctrine of God in contemporary theology. Panentheism is a major resource for modern theology, and Macquarrie's work shares in its potential.[30] What is distinctive about Macquarrie's contribution is his 'dialectical' mindset; he is 'possessed of the skill to think dialectically in an habitual fashion'.[31] This is clear in his preference for the term 'dialectical theism' over 'panentheism'. But the dialectical urge runs beyond terminology: Macquarrie is concerned to affirm an element of truth in all, not least extreme, positions. His conscious aim is for a middle path, in the awareness that one side never has a monopoly of truth. His criticisms of positions, while robust, are never total. Indeed, Macquarrie can be most severe about those who are in fact his natural allies as 'dialectical theologians' and panentheists: he is surprisingly critical, for example, of Tillich and Robinson, when they were pursuing similar aims with often similar resources.[32] It is significant that when Schubert Ogden criticized Macquarrie for a 'both-and' approach to theology, Macquarrie took it as a compliment.[33] They became friends.

Panentheism, located between classical theism and pantheism, is thus for Macquarrie a natural home. He regards it as a qualification or corrective of classical theism, rather than in opposition to it. Compared with the marked dipolarity of process panentheism, his dialectical style of panentheism is more integrative.[34] It has sometimes been the temptation of panentheists to caricature the classical theism against which they define themselves, and to see themselves, for example, in opposition to Thomism. It is characteristic of Macquarrie, by contrast, to try and consent to as much as he can in Aquinas, even stating recently that he now doubts that he did justice to Aquinas in *Deity*.[35]

This is why the term 'eirenic' is an appropriate one for Macquarrie, and one reason why this Grand Old Man is accorded such respect. Theologians can recognize in Macquarrie a consonance between the balanced *method* of his theology and its balanced *content*. He is someone who practices what he preaches: he exhibits the graciousness which he identifies as the essence of the Godhead. He embodies the eirenic nature of dialectics, the divine 'yes' and 'no' to every human situation, the 'self-critique' of the cross and the 'self-affirmation' of the resurrection.

'Presumably we are standing only at the beginning of the revolution in the idea of God.' Panentheism is indeed a revolution, a revolution which has hitherto been 'quiet'. The work of John Macquarrie shows how and why the revolution should be peaceful.

Notes

1 See, for example, the symposium on Philip Clayton's panentheism in *Dialog* 38 (1999); Philip D. Clayton and Arthur R. Peacocke (eds), *In Whom We Live and Move and Have Our Being: Panentheistic Reflections on God's Presence in a Scientific World*, Grand Rapids, MI, and Cambridge: Eerdmans, 2004; and *Science and Theology News* 5/9 (2005), pp. 34–41.

2 *Deity*, pp. 15, 54 and 171; Macquarrie, 'Panentheismus', *Theologische Realenzyklopädie*, Vol. 25, Berlin and New York: Walter de Gruyter, 1995, pp. 611–15 at 611. Cf. *Principles*, p. 120.

3 For varieties, see Michael W. Brierley, 'The Potential of Panentheism for Dialogue between Science and Religion', in Philip D. Clayton (ed.), *The Oxford Handbook of Religion and Science*, Oxford: Oxford University Press, forthcoming 2006. Cf. Niels H. Gregersen, 'Three Varieties of Panentheism', in Clayton and Peacocke (eds), *In Whom We Live*, pp. 19–35.

4 For these characteristics, see Michael W. Brierley, 'Naming a Quiet Revolution: The Panentheistic Turn in Modern Theology', in Clayton and Peacocke (eds), *In Whom We Live*, pp. 1–15; and Brierley, 'Norman Pittenger (1905–1997) and Panentheism', *Theology* 109 (forthcoming 2006).

5 For example, *Principles*, pp. 89, 114–5, 204; *Secularity*, pp. 62 and 116; 'God and the World: One Reality or Two?', *Theology* 75 (1972), pp. 394–403

at 398 and 403 (cf. *Thinking*, pp. 110–20, at 113 and 120); *Thinking*, p. 106; *Humility*, pp. 15–18; and *Deity*, p. 176.

6 *Sacraments*, pp. 12–14; cf. 'Incarnation as Root of the Sacramental Principle', in David W. Brown and Ann Loades (eds), *Christ: The Sacramental Word*, London: SPCK, 1996, pp. 29–39 at 34. Similarly, it may be his high doctrine of the Church that keeps Macquarrie from developing a distinctive panentheistic ecclesiology, in *Principles*, pp. 386–92.

7 *Sacraments*, pp. 1–11; cf. *Secularity*, pp. 136–7.

8 'God and the World', pp. 399–400, revised in *Thinking*, pp. 110–20 (cf. 117–19).

9 *Principles*, pp. 254–5; *Deity*, pp. 182–3.

10 *Secularity*, p. 132; cf. *Sacraments*, p. 6.

11 See below, p. 321, for details of discussions by Charles C. Hefling (1991), Marion L. Hendrickson (1998), John McIntyre (1998), Niall Coll (2001), and Stepen W. Need (2005).

12 *Jesus Christ*, pp. 346, 359 and 392; 'Current Trends in Anglican Christology', *Anglican Theological Review* 79 (1997), pp. 563–70 at 567–8; and *Christology*, p. 59 (cf. p. 74).

13 *Principles*, p. 361; cf. *Secularity*, p. 137.

14 See *Studies*, pp. 3–16, reprinted in *Theologian*, pp. 43–56, and also *Studies*, pp. 79–96.

15 Eugene T. Long (1980), pp. 215–26 at 218.

16 For example, 'God and the World', pp. 398 and 400, and *Thinking*, p. 111; cf. *Secularity*, p. 63, and *Sacraments*, p. 5.

17 *Secularity*, p. 127; *Thinking*, p. 114; *Humility*, pp. 4, 63 and 69–71; and *Deity*, pp. 41, 179–81 and 183.

18 'Pilgrimage in Theology', *Epworth Review* 7/1 (1980), pp. 47–52 at 48. The revision in *Theology*, pp. 1–9, is reprinted in Kee and Long (1986), ix–xviii.

19 Owen F. Cummings, *John Macquarrie: A Master of Theology*, New Jersey: Paulist Press, 2002, p. 7; Long, *Existence, Being and God*, New York: Paragon House, 1985, pp. 2–3.

20 Georgina L. Morley, *John Macquarrie's Natural Theology: The Grace of Being*, Aldershot: Ashgate, 2003, p. 72.

21 Philip D. Clayton, *The Problem of God in Modern Thought*, Grand Rapids, MI, and Cambridge: Eerdmans, 2000.

22 For panentheism and religious experience, see Brierley, 'The Potential of Panentheism'.

23 Cf. Donald Allchin, '"There Is No Resurrection Where There Is No Earth": Creation and Resurrection as seen in Early Welsh Poetry', in Mark Atherton (ed.), *Celts and Christians: New Approaches to the Religious Traditions of Britain and Ireland*, Cardiff: University of Wales Press, 2002, pp. 103–23 at 112.

24 Morley, *Natural Theology*, p. 74.

25 Gareth Jones, 'Existentialism', in Alister E. McGrath (ed.), *The Blackwell Encyclopedia of Modern Christian Thought*, Oxford: Blackwell, 1993, pp. 200–7 at 200. Cf. Paul Tillich, *Systematic Theology*, Vol. 2, London: SCM Press, 1978, p. 26.

26 *Existentialist* (3rd edn), pp. 228–30; *Scope*, pp. 122–8; *Principles*,

p. 134; *God-Talk*, pp. 238–48; *Secularity*, pp. 35–6 and 97–8; and 'Bultmann's Understanding of God', *Expository Times* 79 (1968), pp. 356–60 at 360, slightly revised in *Thinking*, pp. 179–90 (at 188–9).

27 *God-Talk*, pp. 147–67, and 'Heidegger's Earlier and Later Work Compared', *Anglican Theological Review* 49 (1967), pp. 3–16, revised in *Thinking*, pp. 191–203.

28 See, for example, *Principles*, pp. 107, 116, 167, 183–6; cf. Morley, *Natural Theology*, pp. 97–120.

29 John A. T. Robinson, *Thou Who Art: The Concept of the Personality of God*, London and New York: Continuum, 2006.

30 For the potential of Macquarrie's theology for feminism, see Georgina L. Morley, 'The Grace of Being: Connectivity and Agency in John Macquarrie's Theology', in Susan F. Parsons (ed.), *Challenging Women's Orthodoxies in the Context of Faith*, Aldershot: Ashgate, 2000, pp. 175–89.

31 Cummings, *John Macquarrie*, p. 128.

32 As Macquarrie occasionally recognizes, e.g. in *Theology*, p. 6.

33 *Studies*, pp. 156–60 at 157. I am grateful to Georgina Morley for this point.

34 But for perceptive comments on the relation of Macquarrie's doctrine to process theism, see D. William D. Shaw, 'Personality, Personal and Person', in Kee and Long (eds) (1986), pp. 155–67. See also the inclination of process theologian Norman Pittenger towards Macquarrie's theism, in W. Norman Pittenger, 'Christian Theology after the "Death of God"', *Church Quarterly* 1 (1969), pp. 306–14 at 312, reprinted in Pittenger, *'The Last Things' in a Process Perspective*, London: Epworth Press, 1970, pp. 106–17, and Pittenger, *Catholic Faith in a Process Perspective*, Maryknoll, NY: Orbis Books, 1981, p. 20.

35 *Theologian*, p. 74. Cf. Wayne J. Hankey, 'Aquinas and the Passion of God', in Kee and Long, *Being and Truth*, pp. 318–33.

19 The Triune God

KEITH WARD

Preparing this essay has given me the very great pleasure of reading John Macquarrie's work again. He is, in my view, the pre-eminent Anglican systematic theologian of modern times, and I would like to see his work used as the basis of all Anglican theological training in systematic theology. My own intellectual debt to him is immense, and this short essay is meant to be a small tribute to his immense creativity and imaginative power.

I wish to make some remarks about Professor Macquarrie's exposition of the doctrine of the Trinity. The kernel of this is found in a short chapter on 'The Triune God' in *Principles of Christian Theology* (1977 edition, pp. 190–210). The chapter centres on three main themes – the basis of Trinitarian doctrine in experience (the 'existential-ontological' method), the idea of God as 'letting-be', and the exposition of the triune God as primordial, expressive and unitive holy Being. I shall devote an all too short section on each of these themes in turn, for I believe they each have something very important to contribute to modern theological discussion. My own views on the Trinity can be found chiefly in *Religion and Creation*.[1]

Existential-Ontological Method

It was Friedrich Schleiermacher who first attempted to found Christian doctrine upon experience, and to derive all Christian doctrines from a primal experience of 'absolute dependence', qualified by the further experience of the redemptive efficacy of the new life that the community founded in the name of Jesus Christ makes possible. 'Christian doctrines are accounts of the Christian religious affections set forth in speech.'[2] In other words, doctrines are not the primary given data of theology. Those data lie in three main sources, scripture, tradition and personal experience.

As far as Christian revelation is concerned, the heart of Scripture is to be found in the Gospels. They provide four different presentations of the ways in which Jesus was apprehended by his followers. They directly express accounts of how people experienced the historical person of Jesus, remembered by his disciples, and presented in the light of the resurrection and further experiences of the risen Lord in the Church. They indirectly express the experience of Jesus himself, experience of God as Father and of the divine Spirit as the energizing and creative power of his own life.

Christian tradition has been built up over centuries, as the primary experience of redemptive encounter with God in Jesus has been placed within the ever-changing contexts of more general understandings of the universe and of human history.

Personal experience witnesses to the fact of present encounter with God through the person of the risen Christ in the community of the Church. Such experience is always limited by the psychological and social situation of the disciple. That is why it needs to be controlled by some awareness of wider communal traditions that include many different personal perspectives, and can distinguish between the ephemeral and the enduring in matters of worship and devotional understanding. It needs to be controlled also by the normative canon of Scripture, which provides the personal paradigm and the general parameters of Christian understanding.

On this understanding, the primary data of theology thus lie in forms of experience – the normative experience of the apostles, the historical experience of the Church, and the personal experience of the individual disciple.

There are two major misunderstandings of such a stress on experience as the basis of doctrine. One is that experience is somehow objectionably subjective, or that Schleiermacher is just talking about 'inner feelings' that do not relate to objective reality. On the contrary, for Schleiermacher and those who follow him, experience is precisely *of* objective reality. In the case of religious awareness, that reality has a unique status, which is very hard to pin down conceptually. But it is objective, it is real, and it is knowable. To put it bluntly, if no one ever apprehended, had direct experience of God, why should we talk of God, except as an abstract hypothesis?

Yet 'knowing God' has a peculiarly personal character. It is possible only by a form of personal commitment to goodness, and its vehicle is a total affective response to the world. Experience of God is not dispassionate or speculative. It is immediate and self-involving at the deepest level. In that respect, it is something like knowledge of another finite person, which can only be achieved by an initial empathy and concern, and only discloses what our own reactions enable us to perceive. So with God we must be prepared to be in a relation of absolute dependence if we are properly to apprehend such a relation, and we can only interpret it in accordance with our own presuppositions and expectations.

This leads on to the second misunderstanding, which is that primary experiences of God carry no interpretation with them, that they are wholly non-cognitive or non-reflective. That is clearly false. We could not have a feeling of absolute dependence, for instance, if we lacked the concept of 'dependence', and if we could not distinguish conceptually between the relative and the absolute. Apprehensions of God are necessarily interpreted in terms of the concepts available to us. But those concepts do not control the apprehensions. Concepts give form and shape to our apprehensions, but without the apprehension concepts would be purely abstract. And we will probably have to amend or qualify our initial concepts in the light of new apprehensions that occur to us.

Christian doctrines may be founded on experience, but such experience is not a matter of purely personal subjective and wholly non-rational feeling. It is controlled by the normative experiences of Jesus and the apostles, it is tested by the long and changing experience and reflection of the Church, and it is given intellectual content by the concepts and values that we bring with us to all new experience.

When John Macquarrie, standing in this general theological tradition, speaks of an 'existential-ontological' approach, he stresses two things. First, that religious experience is not just a matter of individual feeling. Authentic religious experience must be rooted in an authentic appreciation of the conditions of human existence as such, and involves an understanding of what it is to exist as a human person, an understanding that the life of Jesus and subsequent reflections on that life can illuminate profoundly. Second, that religious experience is not just a matter of subjective feeling. Religious affections are the appropriate modes of access to the objective, ontological, reality that we name 'God'.

When we apply an existential-ontological approach to the doctrine of the Trinity, we discover something negative and something positive. The negative thing is that some traditional thought about the Trinity seems to have lost touch with the existential altogether. We may not want to go as far as Harnack in saying that Orthodox speculations about internal relations within the Trinity belong to 'the lowest class of religion'. But we may well think that some questions about the relations of the divine persons to one another are so abstrusely philosophical that they could be of interest only to scholars who have a greater faith in the perspicacity of Neoplatonism than is possible for most modern philosophers.

The positive thing is that it is proper not to pursue our investigations into the inner nature of God further than the Bible and our own experiences of God in Christ suggest. As Isaiah 45.15 says, 'Truly, you are a god who hides himself', and we know of God only what God reveals of the divine in its relation to us and to our salvation. So when Karl Rahner claims that the immanent Trinity is the economic Trinity, we need to pause and ask, 'How do you know?' If all that is meant is that the divine being in itself must be such that it is appropriately related to us in a Trinitarian way, we need not hesitate to agree. But if this tempts us to say that we actually do know what the divine being in itself is like, we may need to read Isaiah 45.15 again.

The existential-ontological approach can lead us to say: 'This is what God is truly like, as God turns to the world in love.' But it will gently forbid us to say that now we understand with our pitifully impoverished minds what the divine being essentially is.

God as 'Letting-be'

Professor Macquarrie follows ancient tradition in saying that God does not exist in the way that any finite being exists. As Thomas Aquinas put it, God is *esse suum subsistens*, an ungrammatical phrase that points to God's transcendence of all particular beings. But Macquarrie utilizes the first Genesis creation account (Gen. 1.3) to add that God 'lets be' all particular things that are.

I detect in this an echo of Leibniz's thought that possibilities press into being, as though they were not content with just being merely possible, but had a sort of inner urge towards actualization. For traditional theists, God, who is the 'source and horizon of all possibilities', to some extent controls the outpouring of possibilities, perhaps ordering and structuring them in accordance with principles of valuation rooted in the divine being.

A new element of Macquarrie's thought here is that the power of Being must express itself in the actuality of particular beings. Pure Being in itself – what Macquarrie calls 'primordial being' – has a sort of indeterminacy and incompleteness that calls out for some form of actualization. The letting-be of particular beings is in this sense a completion of the potency of primordial Being.

Whereas Thomas Aquinas's God is pure actuality, containing no potentiality at all, Macquarrie's God is more like pure potentiality, requiring some form of particular expression if it is to become actual. Yet God is not just potential. God is beyond the dialectic of actual and possible.

I myself would say at this point that God is actual, but not in the way that finite beings are. Yet God contains the whole realm of possibility, and I at least have lost the sense that God could rest content in the contemplation of possibilities that, because they are in the mind of God, are more real than individual beings (a view stated by Anselm, for instance). I share the modern prejudice that the actual (even the physically actual) is more real than the merely possible (even the possibility in the mind of God). So if God is going to contemplate ideas in a satisfactory way, they must be actualized.

All possible worlds remain only potential in God, unless and until God creates them in actuality. In that sense, God must let possibilities be actual, if God is to know and appreciate them as actual. God may evaluate merely possible states. But if God is to appreciate and enjoy them, God must make them actual.

The crucial difference from the Thomist view is that there are many potentialities in God (God is not pure actuality). Actualizing some of them (letting them be) makes a difference to God, for only then can God appreciate them. And perhaps God necessarily actualizes some of them, as a condition of actualizing the divine perfection of enjoying the contemplation of many sorts of finite beauty, which otherwise would have remained only potential.

This is beginning to sound as abstract as the patristic arguments I have protested about. So I need to bring it back to experience, and point out that 'the God who lets-be' is a God who respects the autonomy of the created order, who delights in and enjoys it, and who is affected by it in a dynamic and truly relational way. The experiential basis for this lies in the sense that God encounters us in Christ as one who enjoys and suffers, who lives through time and is present and manifest in history, who does not control history by the exercise of overwhelming force, but who shares the limits of finitude in order to draw the finite into the divine life by the power of love.

The Triune God

It is this central Christian narrative of the entrance of the Eternal into time, in the person of Jesus, that gives rise to a doctrine of God as Trinity. The primordial being of God is the ultimate source of all things, unknowable and transcendent, beyond the reach of human understanding. This sense of God as transcendent mystery is rooted in a basic experience of a presence that transcends all understanding, a 'sense and taste for the infinite', as Schleiermacher put it, disclosed in and through finite beings.

For some forms of religion, that remains the one definitive experience of God. But Christians find God present and manifest in a unique way in the person of Jesus. The eternal enters into time. As it does so, it expresses itself in a dual way. Macquarrie speaks of the expressive being of God as that form through which God begins to express the divine nature in the beings of time. The *logos* is God as wisdom, as structured and intelligible being, as the archetype and pattern of creation (Col. 1.15), as the conceptual structure of all possibility.

Christians speak in this way only because the person of Jesus is believed to express in human history the character and action of God. It follows that God is truly expressed in time. Following the suggestion of the prologue of the Gospel of John, this temporal expression is seen as a true human expression of the eternal Word. Jesus realizes in an exemplary way the archetypal possibility of a union of humanity and divinity. The form of the divine being that is so united to humanity, but that eternally exists as a form of God, even before humans exist, is the divine Word.

With the incarnation the ineffable source of all things becomes Father, related in a personal and interactive way to the eternal Wisdom, embodied as the Son.

An element of much patristic thought that is best avoided here is the thought that the Son is an identical copy of the Father, a 'second God' of the same sort. The transcendent origin and the eternal wisdom are different forms of being, the former beyond all conceptual thought and the latter defining the parameters of conceptual thought. Their characteristics are quite different. Yet they are forms of the same being, who thus exists in two different forms, not reducible to one another.

With incarnation, the human person (in the modern sense) united to the eternal Wisdom in Jesus, becomes Son to the Father who is the transcendent origin of all things, but has now taken up a specific relationship of personal care and compassion to this individual life.

Macquarrie speaks of primordial being and expressive being as 'movements' or 'modes' of Being. I use the term 'form of being', to avoid any suggestion of temporal succession. But I believe that Macquarrie is right in seeing in the divine Wisdom an inner tendency to incarnation in the finite cosmos, and so in seeing 'the Son' as always tending to express in visible form the invisible and conceptual possibilities that are part of the Son's eternal being. Incarnation affects both Father and Son, giving them a particular personal relationship that could be realized differently in different realms of created being.

That is to say, the Word could be incarnated in principle in many different finite forms of being, not just the human. In that case the relation of such an incarnate being to the transcendent form of divine being might well not be that of 'Son' to 'Father'. For some finite persons might not have such filial genetic relationships. Any divine embodiment would always, however, be a relation of the transcendent form of the divine being to an expressed, incarnate, individualized form of the divine being.

The Christian narrative is not simply of the manifestation of the eternal in time, at one particular time and place. The narrative is completed only when the temporal is taken into the life of the eternal. In Christian experience, this is known and felt as the work of the Holy Spirit acting within human lives to unite them in the Body of Christ, and give them the firm hope of participating in the divine nature, in eternal life (2 Pet. 1.4).

Macquarrie fittingly speaks of the Spirit as unitive Being, as that form of the divine that is present and active in human lives to unite them to the divine nature. The Spirit is the divine universalized in community, uniting and binding together many diverse persons, and binding all to God in Christ. The history of the cosmos is a history of God moving into relationship with communities of finite persons, and establishing with them a 'unity comprehending a diversity of free responsible beings' (*Principles*, p. 201).

The role of the Spirit is to bring all beings, 'everything in heaven and on earth', into the unity of the Body of Christ (Eph. 1.10). Then the community can manifest that union with the eternal Word that Jesus manifested on earth. Under the Lordship of Christ, the one who established and set the pattern of that union, the ultimate destiny of human beings is to be the 'children of God', those who enact and complete God's creative will for the cosmos, and who help to transfigure the cosmos into the divine life.

The great positive virtue of this account is that it stays close to the New Testament witness to the activities of Father, Son and Spirit, and does not stray too far into the ontological wilderness of hypostases, subsistent relations and processions. There has been a great deal of interest in the doctrine of the Trinity in recent years among theologians. Many, like John Zizioulas, Richard Swinburne and David Brown, have favoured what has been called a 'social Trinity', for which the persons are strongly distinguished as separate persons, souls, or hypostases.

The appeal of their approach has been that if God is love, love does seem to require relationship, and within a social Trinity diverse persons can give and receive love, it seems, even without the creation of any universe. The disadvantage, which I think is overwhelming, is the threat to the unity of the divine being, and the disconnection with New Testament narrative in favour of a purely speculative hypostatization of what is, truth to tell, a rather Marxist view of persons as constituted by social relationships.

Macquarrie's approach stresses that genuine self-giving love must relate the lover to what is genuinely other, relatively autonomous, and capable of accepting or rejecting love. So the statement that God is love is best construed as saying that Being essentially flows out to create other relatively autonomous persons, and embodies itself in the finite, in order to unite finite persons to God in a free community of love wherein otherness and freedom, unity and communion, can all co-exist.

Seen thus, Being has a threefold form – transcendent origin, expressive wisdom embodied in a particular finite form or forms, and unitive love, present in some fashion in all finite forms, co-operatively working to unite them to the infinite divine life. That is how the revelation of God in the person of Jesus discloses itself to us. Perhaps in the end we cannot say whether the creation of some finite universe is necessary to God, or whether God can exist in some threefold way even without creation. All we can say is that God's triune being is revealed to us in Christ. This is how we can truly conceive of God, as God is in relation to us. 'The secret things belong to the Lord our God, but the revealed things belong to us and to our children forever' (Deut. 29.29).

I have said very little in this essay that is new. That is because I think John Macquarrie basically has it right, and that his distinctive approach to the doctrine of the Trinity is the most coherent, plausible and attractive that I know. The Triune being of God remains a mystery, but it is not an absurdity. In Macquarrie's work, the doctrine of the Trinity shines with a clarity and persuasiveness that is rare in modern theology. For that all Christians owe him an enormous debt of gratitude.

Notes

1 Keith Ward, *Religion and Creation*, Oxford: Oxford University Press, 1996, ch. 13.

2 Friedrich Schleiermacher, *The Christian Faith*, New York: Harper, 1963, p. 76.

20 'Within the Constraining Framework of Modern Thought'

John Macquarrie's Post-Enlightenment Christology

NIALL COLL

When John Macquarrie published his much anticipated christological treatise, *Jesus Christ in Modern Thought* (1990), some four years after his retirement from Oxford, he stated his hope 'that the Christology in this book . . . stays within the parameters of catholic tradition and is entirely compatible with the governing intentions of Chalcedon and other classic Christian pronouncements' (p. 383). What emerges, however, is an approach to Christology firmly set within the parameters for theology inaugurated by the Enlightenment. There is, interestingly, no sense in the volume that the concerns of modernity are giving way to those of postmodernity. Indeed the term 'postmodernity' never occurs.[1] Whether or not this impression is valid, it is indisputable that Macquarrie is convinced the Enlightenment has been decisive in shaping the intellectual, social and religious outlook of contemporary Western society, and that any attempt at articulating a Christology for today that overlooks its lessons is doomed to failure. We today remain 'inevitably children of the Enlightenment',[2] he insists, and the only way we can make sense of Christ for our secular Western society is within, what he terms, 'the constraining framework of modern thought'.[3]

The Constraining Framework for Christology

For Macquarrie this constraining framework, or to put it more plainly, the modern mind since the eighteenth century, finds it difficult, if not impossible, to make contact with the classic expressions of the Church's beliefs about Jesus. The language spoken and concepts employed, for example, in the Chalcedonian definition of 451 (Jesus Christ is a divine person in whom are perfectly conjoined, without either mixture or separation, a complete divine nature, so that he is both truly God and truly man) belong to a past age. In the wake of 'the tidal wave of the Enlightenment' (*Jesus Christ*, p. 339), Macquarrie asserts that 'We cannot go back to the mythology of a former age, or to its supernaturalism, or to the spiritual authoritarianism of an infallible church or infallible Bible' (*Jesus Christ*, p. 26). If Jesus Christ is to be meaningful to modern humanity and its modern thought, he can only be so as one who shares genuinely and fully in humanity. For only such a one 'who has lived as a truly human person, has known the weaknesses and even the temptations of such a life, but has also known its possibilities for transcendence' can be a saviour (*Jesus Christ*, p. 419). The challenge to theologians is to take this fact on board and to have the courage to fashion credible replies to the question that Bonhoeffer found himself asking in prison, which has lost none of its force: 'Who really is Jesus Christ for us today?' In fact, Macquarrie employs this question as the title to the third and final section of *Jesus Christ in Modern Thought* when he brings forward his own christological constructions. His need to 'make sense of Christ for us today', to do apologetics, is driven above all by an urgent pastoral concern, though not all will hold to the appropriateness of the course he charts.

In common, then, with most contemporary scholars Macquarrie insists that Christology must begin 'from below' with an unambiguous assertion of Christ's complete humanity (*Jesus Christ*, p. 363). All docetic tendencies are to be unambiguously expunged and we are to recognize that the Christ 'who confronts us in the gospels is no mythological demigod but a genuine human being in the fullest sense' (*Jesus Christ*, p. 358). In insisting that Christology takes its departure from the human Jesus, Macquarrie argues that, one is simply going back to its original path in the earliest days of Christianity (*Jesus Christ*, p. 343). In support of this contention, he refers to Peter's preaching: 'This Jesus whom you crucified, God has made both Lord and Christ' (Acts 2.36), and asserts categorically that, for Paul, 'Jesus is beyond any question a human being who lived and taught and suffered on this planet' (*Jesus Christ*, p. 55). As we shall see below, Macquarrie finds what is termed Paul's 'Adam Christology' instructive on this point.

The Jesus who emerges within Macquarrie's framework is unambiguously human. Macquarrie finds himself in complete agreement with F.D.E. Schleiermacher's claim that Christ's divinity is a variable human attribute which has reached its maximum in Jesus of Nazareth. Macquarrie thus advocates a 'degree Christology', though he himself never uses the term. Because such Christologies more often than not fail to reach out adequately towards that other essential component of a balanced Christology, namely Christ's personal identity as the pre-existent Word or Son of God,[4] we need now to enquire as to whether Macquarrie's is any more successful.

A Limited Framework?

The doctrine of Christ's personal pre-existence teaches that Jesus of Nazareth was/is personally identical with the Son of God, who has existed from all eternity and who enters the world to be revealed in human history. Christ's personal being did not 'begin' when his visible human history began. He did not come into existence as a new person around 5 BC, the date usually held for his birth. Gerald O'Collins characterizes the doctrine as 'a necessary presupposition for any orthodox belief in the incarnation of the Word "becoming flesh"'.[5] For Macquarrie, however, it is an example of a doctrine that 'needs interpretation, simplification and modernization' (*Stubborn*, p. 134).[6] In an article written early in his academic career, he articulates an attitude towards the doctrine that has remained with him throughout:

> It seems to me . . . that the idea of pre-existence, like so many other ideas in the New Testament, does have a value that lies obscured beneath its mythological associations, and that it would be wrong to reject pre-existence in favour of a thorough-going adoptionism. Rather, we ought to look more closely at the idea of pre-existence, and see whether we can restate its essential meaning in a language that would be intelligible to our time.[7]

He claims that the classical interpretation of the doctrine threatens Jesus' true and full humanity: 'I would reject any personal pre-existence as mythological and also as undermining a genuine recognition of the humanity of Christ' (*Jesus Christ*, p. 145). Macquarrie curiously interprets the doctrine as implying the claim that the *humanity* of Christ pre-existed the incarnation; that Jesus somehow eternally pre-existed *qua Jesus*.[8] If there were any basis to this charge, it would mean that the doctrine of pre-existence would be decisively at odds with Chalcedon's teaching that Christ is consubstantial (*homoousios*) with us as to his humanity (*Denzinger-Schönmetzer* 301), since there is no suggestion that we are pre-existent in our humanity.

Looking at the scriptural witness Macquarrie contends that Paul did not hold the doctrine, and where pre-existence language is found in the New Testament, especially in John, he argues that it was never intended to be read as implying that Jesus Christ had *personally* pre-existed.[9]

Macquarrie's interpretations of these passages raise important questions about how he uses Scripture to support his theological opinions.

The Constraining Framework and the Use of Scripture

Adam Christology: Relying heavily on the controversial findings of J.D.G. Dunn,[10] Macquarrie lays great store on the significance of Paul's 'Adam Christology', which he controversially terms the 'earliest written witness to Jesus Christ'.[11] Macquarrie finds it very appealing, since it involves Dunn discerning a more conducive interpretation of those scriptural texts normally associated with the doctrine of Christ's personal pre-existence, especially Galatians 4.4; Romans 8.3; 2 Corinthians 8.9 and, 'above all', Phillippians 2.6–7 (*Jesus Christ*, p. 56). Rather than pointing to a pre-existent identity, Jesus is seen to be the new Adam or new man and is contrasted with the first Adam of Hebrew mythology, the fallen man who failed to attain his stature as a man (*Jesus Christ*, p. 249). Bearing in mind what we have already heard from Macquarrie by way of comment on the task facing modern Christology and on the need to start 'from below', it comes as no surprise that he should give a favourable assessment of this 'Adam Christology'. Thus, for example, he asserts that in it:

> we find a theology of his [Christ's] person which can serve as a model for our post-Enlightenment mentality two thousand years later. For, put at its simplest, the career of Jesus Christ is seen as a rerun of the programme that came to grief in Adam but has now achieved its purpose in Christ and with those who are joined with him in the Christ-event' (*Jesus Christ*, p. 59).

It is surprising that Macquarrie, in relying so heavily in *Jesus Christ in Modern Thought* on Dunn's exegesis, does not acknowledge the large chorus of negative reaction that has greeted the latter's theories as presented in *Christology in the Making* (published a decade earlier).[12]

While such scholars as Donald M. MacKinnon, N.T. Wright and Brendan Byrne, for example, are prepared to grant the presence of 'Adam Christology' in the Christ-hymn, they do not, *pace* Macquarrie, see that as ruling out the idea of pre-existence there as well.[13] MacKinnon asks: 'is it absurd to find a parallel inter-weaving of the notion of pre-existence and authentic Adam in Philippians 2?'[14] Byrne judges that 'finding pre-existence in the Philippians hymn in no sense excludes an allusion to Adam'.[15] C.F.D. Moule is also unconvinced by Dunn's thesis that Christ can be understood here purely in terms of Adam and by his claim that there would have been no difficulty for the first Christians in believing in the exaltation of Jesus without also believing in his pre-existence.[16] Carl R. Holladay may have succeeded in summarizing the general tone of these reviews when he characterizes Dunn's thesis as one built upon 'a fair amount of special pleading, logically and exegetically'.[17] N. T. Wright takes Macquarrie to task on his use of Dunn's exegesis and pointedly charges that he is an example of one of those 'theologians who simply choose to employ those exegetical "results" which are conditioned by the very philosophical or theological beliefs they are invoked to support.'[18] It is a matter of regret that Macquarrie does not give the criticisms of Dunn more attention.

One explanation of why Macquarrie feels able to pass over these criticisms of Dunn[19] is evident in some comments he makes on the Christologies of William Porcher DuBose and John Knox. Both of these scholars accept that Paul believed that Christ personally pre-existed. Macquarrie reveals that he sets aside their exegesis since what is at issue here is '[not] purely a question of exegesis'. His argument goes on to disclose an important insight into how he approaches his theological explorations when he notes his predilection for the principle of economy:

> If it were purely a question of exegesis, I would hesitate when two eminent New Testament scholars differ. 'Who should decide when doctors disagree?' But it seems to me that economy favours Dunn, and makes us shy away from such a dubious notion as pre-existence. If we can make sense of Paul without it, that is in itself supportive of Dunn. I remember another New Testament scholar, William Barclay, saying to me that he was an adoptionist in christology because it was the only christology he could understand! An excellent reason! (*Jesus Christ*, p. 383)

What Macquarrie is doing here, in the words of Charles C. Hefling Jr, is enunciating a dubious hermeneutical principle 'that what an ancient author could mean depends on what it is possible here and now to accept as true'.[20] The credibility of Christian doctrine is made to depend on intellectual understanding. Hefling turns to Newman for a broader vision.

Contemporary Philosophical Anthropologies

In addition to his advocacy of Dunn's reading of 'Adam Christology' Macquarrie's own christological speculations are also marked by a high level of interest in what the dynamic, philosophical anthropologies of recent decades can offer to a christological project that takes as its point of departure the humanity of Christ. What is of particular interest to him is the potential these anthropologies might afford to providing a language which allows for intelligible discourse about what he terms the 'other side of the God-man relationship' (*Jesus Christ*, p. 383), the divine side of Jesus Christ. This is all the more necessary because of his misgivings about the ontological concerns of classical Christology. In pursuing this line of thought into recent anthropologies Macquarrie goes beyond a consideration of the existentialist and process ideas that were so much a part of his early academic career[21] and includes Marxism (or neo-Marxism) and transcendental Thomism.[22] He is clearly attracted to them because of the shared emphasis they put on human transcendence. He defines transcendence as 'the idea that human nature is not a fixed essence but has an openness that seems to allow for indefinite development . . .' (*Jesus Christ*, p. 375).

Macquarrie characterizes the development of these philosophical anthropologies that stress human transcendence as 'a fact of the highest significance for christology' (*Jesus Christ*, ch.17). They involve no appeal to those special supernatural forces which are so inimical to post-Enlightenment thought. The case is rather, as Macquarrie points out:

> to call him the God-man (or whatever the preferred expression may be) is to claim that in him human transcendence has reached the point at which human life has become so closely united with the divine life that, in the traditional language, it has been 'deified'. It has not however ceased to be human – rather, for the first time, we learn what true humanity is.[23]

In this way, a Christology beginning from below, an ascending Christology, opens up to incarnational Christology. This evolutionary understanding, which ties in well with Macquarrie's christological thinking, suggests that the incarnation points to a human life in which God has become manifest. Thus he can say: 'If I were to offer a definition of "incarnation", I would say that it is the progressive presencing and self-manifestation of the Logos in the physical and historical world' (*Jesus Christ*, p. 392). It has to be acknowledged, however, that many will find this definition quite unsatisfactory: classical Christology insists that the incarnation is an entirely unique and supernatural reality.

Macquarrie's Christological Constructions within the Framework

Having outlined Macquarrie's appeal to Dunn's 'Adam Christology' and his interest in various transcendental philosophies, we shall now set out briefly where they lead him in terms of two key themes, pre-existence and post-existence.

Pre-existence in the mind and purpose of God

It should be noted that Macquarrie is prepared to accept that the Scriptures do uphold a vague notion that Jesus Christ somehow pre-existed in the mind and purpose of God, and comments: 'I doubt if one should look for any other kind of pre-existence' (*Jesus Christ*, p. 145). His argument for this 'soft view of pre-existence'[24] is twofold. First, referring to the primitive preaching recorded in Acts 2.23 which speaks of the 'definite plan and foreknowledge of God' in the event of Jesus Christ, he suggests:

> if one accepts this idea of a providential plan, of a purpose or intention of God, then one must say that from the beginning Jesus too had existed in the mind and purpose of God. This is not literal or personal pre-existence, but it may be the only pre-existence we can begin to understand and the only kind that is compatible with Jesus' true humanity. (*Jesus Christ*, pp. 390–1)

The claim for 'a very high degree of reality' in this conception of a merely intentional pre-existence of Christ seems rather unpersuasive. Surely the early Church in speaking of pre-existence meant more than the statement that Jesus Christ, in common with all men and women, existed from all eternity 'in God's thoughts', or in 'God's plan' (intentional pre-existence). Second, Macquarrie argues that the evolutionary understanding of the world that is so influential in contemporary anthropology and cosmology can be of assistance in understanding the pre-existence of Christ and that 'this earth, the human race, yes, Jesus Christ himself were already latent, already predestined, in the primaeval swirling cloud of particles' (*Jesus Christ*, pp. 391–2). Once again, this interpretation seems rather unconvincing in suggesting that there is anything special which would set Christ apart. It can be said of any human person that he or she has been 'there' in the evolving cosmos, in the whole human race's history, and in the particular history of his or her people and culture. Both notions, then, fall short of what the doctrine has traditionally been believed to uphold concerning the pre-existence of the *person* who became incarnate in Jesus the Christ.[25]

Post-existence

When Macquarrie turns to a discussion of the post-existent Christ – to the resurrection, ascension and second coming – he proposes 'an alternative scenario' in addition to the traditional 'Happy Ending'. This is called for since, 'To the modern mind, at any rate, a resurrection would be just about the last explanation to be considered' (*Jesus Christ*, p. 91). In this 'Austere Ending', the account of the career of Jesus ends with the cross so that post-Enlightenment sensibilities would not be offended by talk of 'the joyful mysteries that traditionally come after the cross'. Macquarrie finds a basis for this speculation in the Fourth Gospel, where the exaltation of Jesus is identified with his death on the cross (John 12.32–33): 'Of all the Johannine paradoxes, this one is surely the most striking. Jesus' exaltation *is* the cross! His exaltation *is* his humiliation!'[26] Macquarrie claims that this approach would not 'destroy the whole fabric of faith in Christ', since 'the two great distinctive affirmations would remain untouched – God is love, and God is revealed in Jesus Christ.[27] In allowing such a reduced ending to this utterly central Christian belief, Macquarrie is disregarding the fact that the Church down the Christian centuries has pinned its central faith on the personal passage of Christ from death to a transformed, definitive life.

Macquarrie in his *Stubborn Theological Questions* (2003) is conscious that his interpretations of pre-existence and post-existence have been read by others as offering a reductionist Christology. This has led him to repeat that, in addition to insisting on the full humanity of Christ, he also insists that Jesus 'is distinctive, though the distinction is not of such a kind as would demand supernatural powers beyond human capacity'. This approach, he acknowledges, will not please everyone, especially those critics who feel 'I have made too many concessions to the advocates of innovation and revision' (*Stubborn*, p. 134).

Such criticisms might have been lessened had Macquarrie paid more attention to exploring how we might speak about Christ's personhood and the duality of natures, both human and divine. But that is to suggest a different Christology. Instead, and entirely in keeping with his post-Enlightenment outlook, he declines to pursue such systematic reflection, asserting that the classical arguments about the two natures, the hypostatic union and whether Jesus had a human nature but not a human personality 'seem unreal to the modern reader' (*Jesus Christ*, p. 7). Hefling has perceptively commented that 'Macquarrie assumes the standpoint of Christianity's cultured despisers [and] makes comprehension from that standpoint the condition for assent . . .'[28] Yet it has to be insisted that Macquarrie himself does accept the need for an ontological Christology that enquires into the person of Christ,[29] even if he has not given it the sustained attention it deserves, because of his determination to present a Christology 'within the constraining framework of modern thought'. All in all, he appeals too readily to the Oxford Movement's 'principle of reserve', with its recognition of the limits of theological understanding and aversion to minute description in theology (*Jesus Christ*, p. 13). Thus it seems fair to say that no matter how laudable Macquarrie's intentions in framing a Christology within the framework of modern thought, the focus is too narrow for a complete Christology to emerge. Reflection on the mystery of Christ's person and work requires a broader framework because there is much more that needs to be explored and said about it than post-Enlightenment categories can bear. Also, our postmodern world with its pluralism, globalization and demand for interfaith dialogue, is bringing many different assumptions and questions, not all of them deconstructive, into the fields of religion and spirituality. Might they present opportunities for new convergences in Christology?

Notes

1 This is hardly an oversight on the part of one who has excelled as a reporter and critic of twentieth-century thought. Might it be that he sees post-modernity, with its prioritizing of irony over reason and so on, as something of a digression or interlude that will quickly fade when post-Enlightenment concerns return once again to centre stage? See the new chapter 24 in *Twentieth-Century* (2001⁵) 'Postmodernism in Religious Thought', pp. 447–76, especially p. 476: 'We must not exaggerate the importance of postmodernism, but we must not ignore it.'

2 *Jesus Christ*, p. 26. Macquarrie comments: 'Christology was in a new era, we ourselves are still in that era' (p. 339).

3 *Jesus Christ*, p. 26. Hence the *in Modern Thought* of the title.

4 See Jacques Dupuis, *Who Do You Say I Am?*, Maryknoll, New York: Orbis Books, 1994, p. 35.

5 Gerald O'Collins, *Incarnation*, London/New York: Continuum, 2002, p. 13.

6 *Stubborn Theological Questions*, 2003, p. 134. Similar sentiments are expressed by Karl-Josef Kuschel when he asserts that many today view the doctrine of the pre-existence of Christ as a quite incomprehensible myth from primeval times. He argues that 'The collapse of old theological plausibilities calls for new foundations and new credentials. We cannot just simply repeat old formulae or simplistically reject them.' See his *Born Before All Time? The Dispute over Christ's Origin*, London: SCM Press, 1992, p. 33. Kuschel's massive study of Christ's pre-existence wrestles with the Scriptures and a wide range of religious writing. Gerald O'Collins, however, has criticized it for not paying sufficient attention to what philosophers of religion have been saying about time and eternity following a 1981 article by Eleonore Stump and Norman Kretzmann, 'Eternity', *Journal of Philosophy* 78 (1981), pp. 429–58. See Gerard O'Collins and Daniel Kendall, *Focus on Jesus*, Leominster: Gracewing, 1996, p. 2.

7 'The Pre-existence of Jesus Christ', *The Expository Times* 77, 1966, pp. 199–200. Although Macquarrie never alludes to it, there are a number of Anglo-American philosophers of religion, well informed theologically, whose publications dispute the assumption that the concepts used by classical Christology, such as

pre-existence, are to be repudiated as inaccessible to contemporary human in-quiry. In their various writings, these authors struggle with many of the concepts that have been bequeathed by classical Christology and which Macquarrie argues should now be set aside. Prominent among such authors are Richard Swinburne, Stephen Davis, Thomas V. Morris, Brian Hebblethwaite and William Alston. See Coll, *Christ in Eternity and Time: Modern Anglican Perspectives*, Dublin: Four Courts Press, 2001, p. 144, n.62.

8 Another striking articulation of this viewpoint is to be found in the writings of Roger Haight when he claims that 'The problem with a notion of the pre-existence of Jesus is that it is incompatible with the doctrine of Chalcedon that Jesus is consubstantial with us'. See his *Jesus Symbol of God*, Maryknoll, New York: Orbis Books, 1999, p. 459, n.67.

9 This is his evaluation of the pre-existence language that he agrees can prob-ably be found in Hebrews, 1 Peter, Ephesians and Revelation. He believes that 'we do not need to introduce pre-existence in some of the other important New Testament witness, notably the synoptics'. *Jesus Christ*, p. 388.

10 Dunn's discussion of the question of Christ's pre-existence is to be found primarily in *Christology in the Making: An Inquiry into the Origins of the Doc-trine of the Incarnation*, London: SCM Press, 1980. Note the presence of the important 'Foreword', to the second edition, 1989, pp. xi–xxxix. Dunn also re-turns to the theme of Christ's pre-existence in *The Theology of Paul the Apostle*, Edinburgh: T. & T. Clark, 1998, pp. 266–93.

11 It is extravagant of Macquarrie to claim that Adam Christology constitutes the mainstream of Paul's Christology. There is no consensus about where it is to be found in Paul and, where it is found, what conclusions can be drawn about it. See Coll, *Christ in Eternity and Time*, p. 160, n.43.

12 Nor does Macquarrie refer to them eight years later when he speaks of Dunn's 'persuasive exegesis' in his *Christology Revisited*, p. 67.

13 Wright inverts Dunn's use of Adam here by asserting that in this Philip-pians passage 'the temptation of Christ was not to snatch at a forbidden equality with God, but to cling to his rights and thereby opt out of the task allotted to him, that he should undo the results of Adam's snatching'. See his *The Climax of the Covenant*, Edinburgh: T. & T. Clark, 1991, p. 92.

14 See MacKinnon's review of Dunn's *Christology in the Making*, *Scottish Journal of Theology* 35 (1982), p. 364.

15 B. Byrne, 'Christ's Pre-existence in Pauline Soteriology', *Theological Studies*, Vol. 58 (1997), pp. 318–19.

16 C.F.D. Moule, review of Dunn's *Christology in the Making*, *The Journal of Theological Studies* 33 (1982), p. 262.

17 C.R. Holladay, review of Dunn's *Christology in the Making*, *Journal of Biblical Literature* 101 (1982), p. 611. For an extended discussion of Macquar-rie's use of Dunn's exegesis, see Coll, *Christ in Eternity and Time*, pp. 156–62.

18 N.T. Wright, *Jesus and the Victory of God*, Minneapolis: Fortress Press, 1996, p. 8, n. 15. Elsewhere, using an agricultural analogy, Wright bemoans Macquarrie's use of Dunn's exegesis and compares it to farmers who 'select from their own farm, one or two animals that seem [sic] to be reasonably tame – and that seem to offer what they themselves want – and they import them. See his 'Jesus' Self-Understanding' in S. Davis, D. Kendall and G. O'Collins (eds), *The*

Incarnation: An Interdisciplinary Symposium on the Incarnation of the Son of God, Oxford: Oxford University Press, 2002, p. 49.

19 Something which Dunn himself also does by virtue of his restatement of his interpretation of Christ's pre-existence in his later *The Theology of Paul the Apostle*. See the following reviews: *Catholic Biblical Quarterly* 61 (1999), pp. 153–5 [B. Byrne,]; *The Tablet* 709 (30 May, 1998), [A. E. Harvey]; *Louvain Studies* 24 (1999), pp. 377–9 [V. Koperski,].

20 Hefling, Charles C., Jr, 'Reviving Adamic Adoptionism: The Example of John Macquarrie', *Theological Studies* 52 (1991), pp. 483, 491–2.

21 For a fuller discussion of Macquarrie's existential and process background see Coll, *Christ in Eternity and Time*, pp. 135–9.

22 *Jesus Christ*, p. 363. In the existentialist schools he mentions Jean-Paul Sartre and Friedrich Nietzsche (both atheists); in the (neo) Marxist one, Herbert Marcuse and Ernst Bloch; in the field of process ideas, A. N. Whitehead, Norman Pittenger and Charles Hartshorne; and in transcendental Thomism, Karl Rahner and Bernard Lonergan.

23 *Jesus Christ*, p. 363. Macquarrie refers here to 'Rahner's claim that christology is "transcendent anthropology"', and goes on to state that 'that expression would seem to imply not just a humanity that transcends itself but an anthropology that transcends itself to become theology (thus reversing Feuerbach)'.

24 As Gerald O'Collins describes it in *Incarnation*, p. 16.

25 See Macquarrie's response to these criticisms in his *Stubborn*, pp. 136–9.

26 *Jesus*, p. 413. N. T. Wright criticizes this tendency to downplay the resurrection narratives by Macquarrie and others. See his *The Resurrection and the Son of God*, Minneapolis: Fortress Press, 2003, pp. 665–6.

27 *Jesus*, p. 412. Macquarrie claims to find scriptural warrant for this approach in John 12.32–33 ('I when I am lifted up from the earth, I will draw all men to myself, He said this to show by what death he was to die'). *Jesus Christ*, p. 413.

28 Charles C. Hefling Jr, 'Revising Adamic Adoptionism', pp. 490–91.

29 Thus, for example, he acknowledges that 'we cannot reflect theologically on [New Testament] claims for Jesus Christ without getting involved in ontology'. *Jesus Christ*, p. 7. And in his latest book he notes in passing that 'although Jesus Christ is the mediator between divine and human, as the second person of the Trinity he is himself a divine person . . .' *Two Worlds*, p. 9. Owen F. Cummings *John Macquarrie: A Master of Theology*, New Jersey: Paulist Press, 2002, p. 61, defends Macquarrie from charges that he has a reductionist Christology.

21 Jesus in History and Faith: A Schleiermacherian Christology

ROBERT MORGAN

John Macquarrie's philosophical theology, like any good natural theology, speaks of God and the world, in particular God and humanity, in ways that non-Christians should find reasonable. It is written from a Christian perspective and reflects much of Christian doctrine, but is accessible to anyone willing to reflect on their humanity, whether or not they are believing, that is worshipping, Christians. They may be persuaded that reflection on human existence points to some kind of belief in God, and even leads them to some kind of religious practice, but in a pluralistic world there are many options.

Like his philosophical teachers, Macquarrie was brought up in a still largely Christian culture, and unlike many in that declining culture was brought up in a deeply Christian home where his instinctive piety was nurtured. Like a number of the most gifted Scottish students of his generation he found a vocation to the Christian ministry and studied theology, and like many intelligent ordinands he found the theology he was taught somewhat unsatisfactory. Like many clergy he left much of it behind when he entered the 'real world' and the more serious education and maturation of parish and military chaplaincy.

After about seven years he returned to academic work, combining parish and growing young family with a PhD thesis on Bultmann's use of Heidegger. This built on the German he had taught himself at school and had improved by working with prisoners-of-war, the philosophy at which he had excelled as an undergraduate, and the elementary New Testament studies of the BD ordination course. More importantly he acquired a supervisor, Ian Henderson, who understood Bultmann's philosophical theology and the positive aims of demythologizing, not merely the historical and doctrinal criticism which in post-war Britain had made Bultmann something of a bogey-man. Before even finishing his PhD, Macquarrie was appointed (ahead of more technically qualified candidates) to a university lectureship in systematic theology back at Glasgow.

Philosophy and philosophical theology are essential equipment for the systematic theologian, but despite the overlaps they are not the same. Systematic theologians need also to know well the Bible and Christian tradition, in particular the history of doctrine. There is so much that a systematic theologian (ideally) has to know that most of them are specialists in part of the Christian tradition and amateurs in the rest, knowing enough to see what they need at any point, and how to find it out. Macquarrie is not the specialist in patristic, scholastic or Reformation theology that he is in philosophy and theology from the Enlightenment to the present day, and yet he knew enough to write a monumental and long-lasting systematic theology within a few years of starting his university teaching career.

Principles of Christian Theology (1966, rev. 1977) reflects the old model of 'natural theology' being followed by 'revealed theology', but provides (Part One) a new-style natural theology which he calls 'philosophical theology' (his most original contribution), and in place of the old 'revealed theology' a systematics which he calls 'symbolic theology' leading on to 'applied theology'. In learning from Heidegger Macquarrie became a creative *philosophical* theologian with a new natural theology. His first achievement in *systematic* theology consisted in relating that new way of thinking of God and the human to the traditional language of Christian doctrine and worship. Here his most important mentors were neither Bultmann nor Heidegger, but Schleiermacher and later Rahner.

The structure of 'Part Two: Symbolic Theology' is traditional, except that The Church is deferred to 'Part Three: Applied Theology', which is surprising in view of the strongly 'symbolic' elements in its treatment, including (with due qualification) 'the Church as an "extension" of the incarnation' (p. 389): 'It is the community in which this raising of manhood to God-manhood, which we see in Christ, continues' (p. 388). In the Body of Christ 'humanity is being conformed to Christhood, a transfiguration, resurrection, ascension is going on as the believers participate in the life of Christ' (p. 388). This connects with what is said about Christology in Part Two, where the person of Jesus Christ, his work, the Holy Spirit and salvation, and the last things are set in the context of 'God's great unitary action. Creation, reconciliation, and consummation are not separate acts but only distinguishable aspects of one awe-inspiring movement of God – his love or letting-be, whereby he confers, sustains and perfects the being of the creatures' (p. 269). God's reconciling work goes on always, but the Christian gospel 'points to a new and decisive revelation of the mystery of the divine activity' in history (p. 270).

The main features of Macquarrie's christological thinking are already present here in 1966, though it is of some relevance to the argument of this essay that *Principles* has sections on 'The Historical Jesus' and 'the Christ of Faith in the Gospels' whereas in *Jesus Christ* (p. 229) he is critical of this Straussian distinction. But it was *The Myth of God Incarnate* controversy in 1977 which led him to write more on Christology. Updating his 1980 'Pilgrimage in Theology' in 1986 he anticipated completing a doctrinal trilogy by following *Humanity* (1982) and *Deity* (1984) 'with a volume on the God-man' (*Theology*, p. 9), and in retirement he wrote it: *Jesus Christ in Modern Thought* (1990). This was supplemented by *Christology Revisited* (1998) and other articles, some reprinted in *Stubborn Theological Questions* (2003).

The structure and content of the third part of *Jesus Christ* (pp. 339–422) confirm its relationship to the two earlier parts of the trilogy, but as a whole this book is a series of reflections unfolding the author's own position through (1) a historical sketch of 'the sources and the rise of the classical christology'; (2) a brilliant exposition and criticism of 'the critique of the classical christology and attempts at reconstruction' and (3) his own attempt at synthesis. Part One is thus largely a New Testament Christology – with all the historical and exegetical uncertainties this implies; Part Two picks out several major and some minor figures from Kant to Rahner and Schillebeeckx, Pannenberg and Moltmann, Ogden and Robinson; Part Three asks (echoing Bonhoeffer), 'Who really is Jesus Christ for us today?'

Influenced by his colleague at Union, John Knox, but dissenting at some points, Macquarrie finds in the New Testament both 'adoptionist' and 'incarnational' Christologies. The earlier, formulated when Jesus' ministry was still well-remembered, naturally began 'from below' with Jesus as a man (for example, Acts 2.36), but the later incarnational Christology of the Johannine prologue begins 'from above'. Macquarrie judges this 'more profound' and on reflection the necessary presupposition of the other, because 'all is from God' (1 Cor. 8.6). Although the Church opted one-sidedly for the latter, in the modern world we more naturally begin from below. However, Macquarrie sees these as complementary and preserves both, though he avoids mythological expressions of either. He understands the adoptionist type not as the 'promotion' of Jesus at his resurrection, but as speaking of the raising of a human life to the level at which it manifests God. This is possible only through the descent of God into that life. In Jesus Christ we are thus confronted with both the 'deification' of a man and the 'inhumanization' of God (*Jesus Christ*, pp. 375–6).

The word 'deification' is important in patristic theology where it refers not to Jesus but to humanity. This allows Macquarrie to connect his Chalcedonian-sounding Christology (Jesus is the one 'perfect human being' in the sense of realizing the human potential, and 'truly God', so far as God can be revealed in a human being) to his 'transcendent anthropology' and his panentheistic doctrine of God. The latter resists separating God and the world and emphasizes divine immanence without denying divine transcendence. In this scheme the *doctrine* of the incarnation (not its mythological expressions, and not its unfolding in the language of 'two natures') is central because it expresses the divine initiative, and 'that God is deeply involved in his creation', and that 'the centre of this initiative and involvement is Jesus Christ' (*Stubborn*, p. 81, from his 1977 review of *The Myth of God Incarnate*). That minimal statement, which some of the contributors to *Myth* (Wiles, Young, Houlden) would surely accept, does not say much about the aspect of the doctrine most important to Macquarrie himself, namely its coherence with a developmental view of the world (shades of Du Bose) and its relevance to the destiny of the human race as a whole (*Jesus Christ*, p. 344, and see below, note 17). He can define 'incarnation' as

> the progressive presencing and self-manifestation of the Logos in the physical and historical world. For the Christian, this process reaches its climax in Jesus Christ, but the Christ-event is not isolated from the whole series of events. That is why we can say that the difference between Christ and other *agents* of the Logos is one of degree, not of kind . . .' (*Jesus Christ*, p. 392)

Whereas most Christian theology has understood the incarnation in an exclusivist way Macquarrie notes the idea of incarnation in other religions, notably Hinduism, and calls for interpretations of it that do not stand in the way of *rapprochement* with other religions (*Stubborn*, p. 93).

The idealist cast of his thought inclines him to a more positive view of the human condition as we know it than is typical of Western theology. God and the world are potentially sufficiently similar as 'spirit' to make a 'God-man' conceivable, but only when the human potential is fully realized. In discussion with philosophical anthropologies he defends (like Rahner) a view of authentic humanity as containing within itself a principle of transcendence or affinity with God which is able to receive God. Such a spirit anthropology transcends itself and becomes theology, reversing Feuerbach's reduction of theology to anthropology (*Jesus Christ*, p. 363).

A process of growth is necessary, but it seems Macquarrie does not himself think that 'sin has so disabled the human race that it makes the emergence of a natural but unimpaired God-consciousness impossible' (*Jesus Christ*, p. 208). He expresses himself tentatively, but in removing an inconsistent residue of supernaturalism from Schleiermacher's Christology he begins to sound as semi-Pelagian as many medieval schoolmen: 'It might be the case that what we consider the "natural" resources of human nature – and these resources are, after all, given by God – are greater than we think, and, in certain circumstances, might rise above the constraints of mankind's sinful history, to achieve an unclouded God-consciousness.' (*Jesus Christ*, p. 208).

> Schleiermacher's stress on growth and development might seem to favour such a view. One need not claim that he was already perfect in the beginning of his existence in the womb (an idea which makes no sense, if we are attaching to it any moral significance) but that, in the deeds and decisions of life, he was in the language of Hebrews 'perfected', so that what is called 'sinlessness' is not a static condition but the end of a process of growing into union with God. (*Jesus Christ*, p. 208)

In his 'stress on the notions of growth, development, process' (*Jesus Christ*, p. 398) Macquarrie understands sinlessness too 'in a dynamic fashion' as the product of a history, Jesus' overcoming the distance from God which he must have recognized in the world around him, and 'his deepening union with the Father through the deeds and decisions of his life, in which he overcame sin' (p. 398). And Macquarrie 'would not hesitate to call this a progressive incarnation in the life of Jesus'(p. 398). Because sin is a negative, a distortion of true humanity, not an essential aspect of it, sinlessness is not incompatible with genuine (perfect) humanity (*Jesus Christ*, p. 204, quoting Schleiermacher *The Christian Faith*[1]).

Macquarrie can at this point appeal to Hebrews against the theology of St John's Gospel in order to make room for the real history which he insists on in a modern Christology. He criticizes Schleiermacher at this point for endangering the true humanity of Jesus. But this is immanent criticism. Schleiermacher is here failing to live up to his own best insights. The general shape of Schleiermacher's Christology is replicated by Macquarrie. The possibility argued for by a theological anthropology is actualized according to the New Testament witness in the historical person Jesus of Nazareth whom Paul understands as the second Adam (cf. *The Christian Faith*, p. 423) and whom the Church defines as truly and fully human and truly divine, the second person of the Trinity.

The reason for discussing Macquarrie's Christology against this nineteenth-century background is not to deny its originality, nor merely to clarify it by reference to the undisputed father of modern theology. The issue is larger than this, and concerns the identity and truth of Christianity which are the central concerns of any Christian theologian. Anyone who thinks that the truth of Christianity entails an essential continuity in this faith and community, a continuity which persists as its theological expression varies in different cultures, needs to say where that continuity is to be found. Macquarrie finds this 'norm' (*Christology*, p. 11) in the paradox of calling the man Jesus 'truly God' which, however late to receive conciliar definition at Nicaea and Chalcedon, he believes alone preserves the faith of the New Testament writers and subsequent generations of orthodox Christians.

Despite its flaws, Schleiermacher's Christology is the classic attempt to retain this traditional doctrinal shape of Christianity summarized in that dogmatic claim that Jesus of Nazareth, a real human being is to be called 'truly God', and to maintain that confession in an age when less orthodox theologians think of him as a human being and no more. When Macquarrie claims that without 'the absolute paradox' (Kierkegaard) or 'fundamental paradox that Jesus Christ is both human and divine . . . Christianity collapses' (*Christology*, p. 17), or that 'the paradox cannot be dissolved without the destruction of Christianity itself' (*Christology*, p. 23), he is making an assertion about the identity of Christianity, which is contested by more radical liberal Protestants today. This division is surely the most important in modern theology.

Schleiermacher made the same assertion of the divinity and perfect humanity of Jesus in the teeth of much Enlightenment and idealist philosophy and theology which (like Kant) separated the christological predicates from the historical person. In 1835, the year after Schleiermacher died, this Kantian suggestion gained ground and support through the historical criticism of D.F. Strauss's *Life of Jesus*.

It was not Strauss's own doctrinal proposal of attaching the christological idea (of the union of the human and the divine) to the human race rather than to the historical individual which had such a revolutionary effect. It was his historical criticism which undermined the credibility of the Gospels' picture of the God-man and effected a sea-change in Western thought, as Karl Marx recognized. One might disagree with Strauss's naturalism, and be prepared to believe in miracles, angels and demons as Strauss did not, but there was no denying that (like Reimarus, but far more credibly) he had not only undermined the authority of the Bible by discrediting belief in its inerrancy, but also (more importantly) had challenged the traditional picture of Jesus with an alternative construction which did not require belief in God. This alternative picture (still only a sketch in Strauss's first *Life*) was of the type produced by the dominant 'scientific' or rational methods of the day. Strauss's modern critical history was inadequate in its source criticism, but his approach could not in principle be gainsaid, whatever detailed objections might be raised. It was simply more natural, more sensible, and apparently more true to think of Jesus as a first-century human being and no more, that is, to abandon the old dogmatic claim about his divinity. This seemed to some discredited when the bad arguments (from prophecy and miracle) used in its support were discredited, as they had been already by Reimarus, but were now seen to be by a wider public.

Strauss's *Life of Jesus* (1835) made people more aware of modern gospel criticism and its corrosive effect on traditional belief. It also required a response, so led much liberal Protestant theology into one of two alternative directions. The distinction between the historical figure of Jesus and doctrinal descriptions of him was clearly inescapable in the historical study of Jesus and Christian origins. The temptation was therefore to build a modern Christology on one side or the other rather than to hold together two such different discourses. Strauss himself initially developed the Kantian alternative, building a left-wing Hegelian form of 'Christianity' on the idea of the unity of the divine and human. Most theologians rejected that because Christianity is committed to the historical figure of Jesus, but following the modern historical approach to understanding him, some found it impossible by this route to speak of his divinity. Others continued, like Schleiermacher, to combine a historical perception of humanity with a dogmatic belief in his divinity. It is this third way that Macquarrie follows. His criticisms of Schleiermacher's Christology remove its inconsistencies and weaknesses without abandoning its aims, approaches, fundamental assumption – and opponents. He firmly opposes the rejection of the doctrine of the divinity of Jesus Christ and upholds its expression in the doctrine of the incarnation. Some liberal or revisionist theologians aim to be orthodox, others do not, and a few take pleasure in being unorthodox. Macquarrie belongs with Schleiermacher and Rahner in the first group.

His Christology is perhaps less novel than his Heidegger-inspired natural theology and doctrine of God. These are, however, all connected because he draws on his own and Rahner's 'transcendental anthropology' to interpret the traditional claim that Jesus is 'truly God, truly a human being'. If his Christology is less original than the earlier work on which it draws, it is surely no less important. Christology holds the key to any understanding of Christianity. Constructed largely out of his two pillars of fundamental theological reflections on humanity and deity, but responsible to the witness of the New Testament and Christian tradition, Macquarrie's Christology becomes the coping-stone of an arch strong enough to bear the weight of a slimmed-down Christian orthodoxy.

Much of the Christian tradition had been reduced to rubble in the fires of Enlightenment criticism, and as Macquarrie like Schleiermacher sifts through it, much is discarded. But he asks 'at the end of our enquiry whether the understanding of Christ at which we arrive is continuous with the catholic tradition' (*Jesus Christ*, p. 347). In 1986 he promised to 'carry on my quest for a Christian theology truly catholic and truly critical' (*Theology*, p. 9). Twenty years on we may ask whether enough is preserved when reinterpreted for him to be expressing the 'catholic faith' held by Fathers, schoolmen, and Reformers. If he succeeds in his aim to be orthodox (and like Origen 'a man of the Church') then he joins other Anglicans such as Gore and Temple, Ramsey, Sykes and Williams, in representing orthodox Christianity in the twentieth century, and offering sound teaching for the divided Church of the twenty-first century.

If Christian orthodoxy consisted in believing everything in the *Quicunque Vult*, or so-called 'Athanasian Creed' (actually a slightly later Western composition) then John Macquarrie could not be called orthodox. But to 'hold the Catholick faith' and keep it 'whole and undefiled' is both more and less than parroting the formulae of by-gone ages, as Karl Rahner in particular taught Vatican II. Hot from that Council the young Professor Josef Ratzinger taught those of us who sat at his feet in Tübingen that conciliar definitions and other pronouncements of the magisterium should be understood in the light of the scripture that they themselves claim to be interpreting.

According to the Prayer Book version of the *Quicunque Vult*, 'the right Faith is that we believe and confess: that our Lord Jesus Christ, the Son of God, is God and Man . . . Perfect God and Perfect Man . . .'. The dots indicate that this 'creed' (or psalm) provides more detail. Macquarrie can criticize this as 'another attempt to spell out too exactly the meaning of incarnation' and 'an obscuring of the full humanity of Jesus Christ' (*Jesus Christ*, p. 375). But the small portion just quoted states what he considers definitional of authentic Christianity and the starting-point of christological reflection, rather than a formula ripe for revision. There were several strands to his hostility to *The Myth of God Incarnate*, but the most important was his conviction that to deny the divinity of Jesus Christ was to abandon the paradox which was constitutive of Christian faith.

How this may be understood is a further question and the apophatic strain in Macquarrie's mystical piety prevents him from claiming too much for any formulation. He does not 'think that theologians will ever attain to a full understanding of incarnation. Ideas like incarnation, resurrection, atonement, lie at the very frontier of understanding. God alone, seeing things from the divine side, can have a full understanding of his own acts' (*Christology*, p. 108). But theologians must try to find 'a help towards making the mystery of incarnation more intelligible' (p. 108). Macquarrie's route starts with reflection on humanity, not to 'diminish the claims made for Christ', but to 'supply a context which makes these claims more intelligible and less arbitrary' (p. 108). Humanity is made 'in the image and likeness of God', according to Genesis 1.26 and Christian belief, and if (as Paul suggests) 'Jesus Christ is the new Adam, the true man, then one must go on and conclude with Paul that he is "the image of the invisible God" (Col. 1.15)' (p. 108). Biblical specialists may feel that Paul is here being pulled out of the eschatological framework of his thought, as he was by Irenaeus and by most Christian theologians until the late nineteenth century. Whether New Testament eschatology is the only legitimate framework for understanding the New Testament theologically is a disputed question to which we shall have to return. Colossians suggests not.

Schleiermacher's pioneering attempt to make the dogma of Christ's divinity intelligible while referring it to a fully human historical figure, was criticized in his lifetime from both the conservative and the liberal or radical sides. Macquarrie's revisions and corrections yield a Schleier-macherian Christology which is one possibility for today. Whether it is for some temperaments the best, and why others prefer a different one, giving more place to eschatology and less to Jesus' presumed religious experience, will have to be considered, but the most important question is whether Schleiermacher and Macquarrie are right against Harnack and Hick, for example, that the identity and truth of Christianity are inseparable from the christological definition, truly a human being, truly (in some sense) God. Or whether a more drastic revision which appeals behind the New Testament witness (which the conciliar definition aims to protect) to a more speculative reconstruction of 'the historical Jesus' is at least viable, and perhaps even preferable. Was Harnack right about 'the essence of Christianity' or was Overbeck right to see in that construction (so clearly at odds with New Testament theology) an indication of its inessentiality?

Schleiermacher was such a good philosophical theologian that one of his earliest and most perceptive critics, F.C. Baur in 1827–8, paid *The Christian Faith* what he thought was a compliment by judging it by its Introduction as philosophical theology rather than as (a new style) dogmatics. He then criticized it for failing to unite its archetypal Christology with the historical figure of Jesus who could be understood only through a historical approach to the Gospels.[2] But Schleiermacher was describing the faith of his Protestant Church as it was, correcting it in the light of its 'essence', not making it by his reformulations into something different. And the Church speaks (rightly or wrongly – Baur and Strauss thought wrongly) of the historical figure of Jesus as 'truly God' as well as truly a human being, and indeed 'perfect' human being. It was the given faith of a 'positive religion' which he was unfolding, a system of doctrine for today based on Scripture and the Christian tradition, both interpreted in the light of contemporary knowledge and experience. He aimed to conserve as much of the traditional doctrinal language as was appropriate by interpreting and justifying it in a new way as expressions of religious self-consciousness, but he saw his task here in the *Glaubenslehre* (*The Christian Faith*) as largely descriptive. The religion he was describing was (Protestant) Christianity, which he said is 'a monotheistic faith, belonging to the teleological type of religion, and is essentially distinguished from other such faiths by the fact that in it everything is related to the redemption accomplished by Jesus of Nazareth' (§11).

His epoch-making *Speeches* (1799) had taught modern theology to start with the human phenomenon of religion, and to distinguish this from morality, and to find religion in actual religions, not in some philosophical abstraction called 'natural religion'. He had spoken there of Christianity in an echo of John 1.14 and reference to the incarnation. Unlike Kant, who had abandoned the historical reality of Jesus in favour of an ahistorical archetype, Schleiermacher remained true to Christianity as it has always existed, insisting that what Christians say about Jesus refers to the human historical figure.

Sharing modern historical sensibilities, in 1819 he became the first German professor to lecture on 'the life of Jesus'.[3] But these lectures were very different from the seventh 'fragment' that Lessing had excerpted and in 1778 published anonymously from Reimarus's manuscript.[4] They were also very different from (and became the main unidentified target of) D.F. Strauss's still unwritten *Life of Jesus* (1835).[5] And they were very different from most subsequent New Testament scholarship whose debt to Strauss increased in the twentieth century when history of traditions approaches to the Gospels became dominant.

Strauss's 1835 masterpiece cost him his university career. German theological faculties (and especially the Tübingen *Stift*) are more church-related than English ones and the church authorities were right to reject his clearly heretical opinions on Christology, expressed at the end of the book. But Strauss was right about the contradictions in the Gospels, and his view that the Fourth Gospel was historically even less reliable than the Synoptics was confirmed in 1844 and 1847 by his teacher at school and university, F.C. Baur. Schleiermacher's account of the life of Jesus had given historical precedence to the Johannine account and was out of date long before the lectures were published in 1864. In that same year Strauss had published *A Life of Jesus for the German People*, and in 1865 he wrote *The Christ of Faith and the Jesus of History*[6] to 'make even clearer several points' on which he had already 'sharply opposed Schleiermacher's views in various matters' (p. 3) in the previous year.

Strauss wrote this pamphlet not to undermine Schleiermacher's historical work (he had achieved that 30 years previously) but to attack his Christology, which he regretted was still influential among mid-nineteenth-century theologians and beginning to influence lay people. 'Nowadays' (he adds) 'one hears even ecclesiastical authorities speak from this perspective – certainly the surest proof that it has been superseded' (*Christ of Faith*, p. 4). Schleiermacher's type of theology, said Strauss, was continued by 'all those theologians who have not stiffened in dull-minded reaction, or have not moved forward to the standpoint of free science' (p. 4) – as he himself had. *The Christian Faith*, he wrote, 'has really but a single dogma, that concerning the person of Christ' (p. 4). 'In the doctrines of God and the world, and throughout the elucidation of church doctrines as well', he thought (echoing Baur), it offers 'highly worthwhile philosophical discussions' (p. 4). But its Christology 'is a last attempt to make the churchly Christ acceptable to the modern world' (p. 4). As a result of Schleiermacher's efforts, he grumbled, many people now assume 'that Christ was a man in the full sense of the word, as today's mentality desires, and at the same time, as traditional piety wishes, can be a divine redeemer, the object of our faith and of our cultus for all times' (p. 4) – admittedly with everyone defining 'that true humanity and this true divinity' as they see fit. This combination of the historical figure of Jesus with the traditional Christology, however the divinity of Christ might be redefined, was in Strauss's view a nonsense, as Baur had also argued,[7] a hybrid which was neither truly human nor truly divine.

Strauss's remark that 'everyone makes his own idea of that true humanity and this true divinity' (*Christ*, p. 4) contains the germ of an answer to his criticism. Whether we can still say with Chalcedon and traditional Christianity that Jesus is truly God may depend on what we mean by deity, and it is not simply self-evident what is meant by perfect humanity either. Schleiermacher defined the latter in terms of the constant potency of Jesus' sinless God-consciousness 'which was a veritable existence of God in him' (*Christian Faith*, p. 385), thus providing a way to understand his divinity too.

Macquarrie modifies this rather Alexandrian and Johannine picture in an Antiochene direction more like the Synoptic Gospels and the Epistle to the Hebrews to allow for Jesus' temptations and moral growth. This picture is no more demonstrable than Schleiermacher's, but it is more

credible. A picture of Jesus' sense of God does not have to be historically demonstrable in more than broad outline in order to be credible. It
seems historically very probable that Jesus 'was conscious of a vocation
from God to proclaim the kingdom' (*Jesus Christ*, p. 354), and likely
that he went to Jerusalem voluntarily, knowing the danger. Macquarrie
had argued against Bultmann for the theological necessity of a 'minimum
core of factuality' as early as *Scope* (1960), pp. 90–5. Bultmann himself
accepted such a core (*Jesus Christ*, p. 350), but he did not himself need
more than the 'mere that' and the cross. His account of the core now
looks slightly dated. By 1990 Macquarrie thinks that 'a tolerably reliable
picture can be constructed' (*Jesus Christ*, p. 353), but it contains little
about Jesus' self-consciousness. Sinlessness could in any case never be
historically demonstrated, however reliable the surviving evidence.

Macquarrie follows what Strauss called Schleiermacher's 'last attempt
to make the churchly Christ acceptable to the modern world' (*Christ
of Faith*, p. 4), only correcting the 'logical defect' of positing a 'new
implanting' of the God-consciousness in Jesus, which introduces a supernatural intervention into the incarnation which he is trying to expound
as a natural fact (*Jesus Christ*, p. 208). He also frees Schleiermacher's
construction from its association with a pre-Straussian New Testament
scholarship. Like Rahner he sees Chalcedon (and other 'classic condensa-
tions of the centuries-long work of the Church in prayer, reflection and
struggle concerning God's mysteries') as 'not the end but the beginning,
not the goal but the means, truths which open the way to the even greater
truth',[8] and the way he tries to make its definition intelligible today has
much in common with Rahner. Although he can defend its 'two natures
doctrine' against some of Schleiermacher's acute criticisms by defining
'nature' better (*Jesus Christ*, p. 385) that formulation itself (as opposed
to its 'governing intention') seems unimportant to him on account of its
dated philosophical language. But the divinity of Jesus Christ and the fact
that Jesus was 'truly and fully a human being' are the absolute paradox
and absolutely foundational, and (he believes) true to the New Testament
witness.

Strauss thought this 'paradoxical identity' (as Bultmann called it, following Kierkegaard) of history and eschatology intellectually disreput-
able, and in this he has had many successors.[9] 'Free science', that is
historical criticism of the Gospels by New Testament scholars such as
himself, had (he thought) scuppered the ancient dogmatic Christology
and neither the Pope's horses nor the King of Prussia's men could put
Humpty Dumpty together again:

The critical investigation of the life of Jesus is the test of the dogma of the person of Christ. It is well-known that this dogma in its churchly form has not survived the test well. I have maintained the same concerning the dogma in Schleiermacher's form . . . Schleiermacher's Christ is as little a real man as the Christ of the church. (*Christ of Faith*, p. 5)

Macquarrie's criticisms of Schleiermacher modify his picture of Jesus sufficiently to obviate that criticism. He thus rescues Schleiermacher's project of allowing the contrasting discourses of historical reconstruction and dogmatic definition to cohabit. Schleiermacher had not been in a position to take the historical reconstruction very far, and what he did was mostly wrong. Macquarrie does not criticize him for the state of gospel criticism in 1819, nor for disagreeing with Bretschneider's *Probabilia* (1820), which turned out to be largely right about the Fourth Gospel. Rather, he sees an inconsistency in wanting to ascribe an 'ideal' status, including an 'essential' sinlessness to this human being from Nazareth, leading to talk of a 'new implanting' of God-consciousness in him (*Jesus Christ*, pp. 207–8). Macquarrie is less of a Reformed theologian than Schleiermacher, and his more positive Greek view of our fallen human nature does not agree with *The Christian Faith* (p. 367) that our original capacity for God-consciousness was so weakened by sin that it could not be restored apart from a completely new act of creation in Jesus. He can therefore conceive of perfect humanity in a genuine human being emerging from within the evolutionary development. Finding this possibility actualized in Jesus he can benefit from over 150 years of subsequent intensive historical criticism. Not only does he avoid seeking reliable historical information about Jesus' state of mind from John; he also realizes that none of the Gospels provides that, contrary to late nineteenth-century liberal opinion.

Knowing the limitations of the Gospels as historical sources, he knows that all historical reconstructions of Jesus go beyond the evidence and are rather speculative and hypothetical. That is not an argument against them, only a caution against building a Christology on such uncertain foundations. Historians may chance their arm, using their imaginations. Systematic theologians will be persuaded by some of their assured results and be skeptical about some of their more speculative suggestions. They may even offer some speculative suggestions of their own. But to clarify the real humanity of Jesus they do not need to go far down the path of historical construction. They will want to go as far as the evidence allows while resisting damaging speculations, but they *need* only a bare outline, such as those provided by Bultmann or E.P. Sanders (*Jesus Christ*, pp. 350–8).

Like other Christians Macquarrie no doubt holds a more detailed faith-picture of Jesus than he makes explicit in his Christology. Such a faith-image may be constructed partly from secure historical information and partly from informed guesswork, partly from spiritual discernment and partly from pious imagination or childhood memories. Transposed into the more rational key of Christology some details are set aside, the imagination disciplined, and more consensual pictures achieved. Such critically sifted faith-images stem from believers' interaction with biblical texts and reflection on God and the world, but the result is a construction that looks like one historical reconstruction among others, defensible by normal critical historical argumentation. It is in reality a 'theological portrait'[10] motivated by believers' need for a credible historical picture of Jesus, but one which also corresponds to their doctrinal beliefs. To say it originates in a faith-image is to admit that it is not disinterested (and perhaps most reconstructions of the so-called 'historical Jesus' also stem either from faith-images or anti-faith images). But it has to be plausible as a historical construction in order to be credible in a modern Christology. This is possible because the evidence is so limited and ambiguous that it can be appealed to in support of a variety of historical reconstructions, all of which overlap with, and some of which correspond to, some New Testament theologians' 'theological portraits' of Jesus.

Macquarrie does not spell out in detail his own 'Jesus in history and faith' picture, perhaps because he does not want or need to be drawn far into an inconclusive historical argument. If he told us exactly how he understands the historical figure of Jesus, and in particular what he thinks Jesus meant by 'the kingdom of God', his account would be construed as a 'purely historical' reconstruction rather than as a 'New Testament theological portrait'. It would be able to defend itself as a possible historical reconstruction, perhaps even as the best possible, but the evidence allows several possible reconstructions, and what Macquarrie wants to say in Christology does not depend on this construction. His faith-image can go further than what he can prove, as do most historical portraits, but it is constructed within the constraints set by his Christian belief, as modern historians' constructions are not.

Unlike some of his successors, Schleiermacher thought it 'a divine provision, certainly of the highest significance, but not sufficiently recognized, that neither a trustworthy tradition regarding the external aspect of Christ's person, nor an authentic picture of it, has come down to us . . .' (*Christian Faith*, p. 417n.). Today that argument can be taken further in the light of twentieth-century scepticism about the historicity of the Gospels. Believers' faith-images of Jesus as a historical figure cannot be verified in detail, but neither can they easily be falsified. This is often the case with our knowledge of other persons. Macquarrie's unelaborated picture of Jesus is plainly that of a real first-century Jewish human being. It does not need much support from historians, but must be acceptable to them as one possible assessment and interpretation of the historical evidence if it is to be credible.

That is all the history that Schleiermacher needed for his Christology (cf. *Scope*, p. 99), but in those early days of gospel criticism he thought he had to win the historical argument to defend his Christology, not merely play for a stalemate which would leave room for it as one credible picture of Jesus among others. He knew that Jesus of Nazareth was a first-century Palestinian Jew, but he said less about his Jewish identity than historians and theologians do today, because he doubted that:

> Christianity in its entirety can be explained by Judaism at the stage of development which it had then reached – the stage at which it was possible for a man like Jesus to be born of it. Accordingly (in that case) Christianity was nothing but a new development of Judaism, though a development saturated with foreign philosophies then current, and Jesus was nothing but a more or less original and revolutionary reformer of the Jewish law. (*Christian Faith*, p. 380)

Schleiermacher thought with good reason that such a reductionist historical account of Jesus and Christian origins not only fails to satisfy believers, but also fails to explain the origins of Christianity. He thought there was a historical case for saying 'something more' (as Macquarrie puts it) about Jesus. This argument is still made by some today. We may agree with Schleiermacher that even historians have to reckon with what he called Jesus' 'spiritual originality' (p. 389), adding only (with Macquarrie) that this 'spiritual originality' is surely intelligible within the historical context of first-century Judaism, even if it is without parallel. It does not need a supernaturalist intervention or 'new implanting' of the God-consciousness in Jesus. But this 'spiritual originality' can only be postulated, not historically demonstrated, and demonstration is not necessary anyway.

Even non-supernaturalist accounts of Jesus and Christian origins have to say more than can be historically verified in order to explain what emerged. Subsequent biblical scholarship is full of informed guesses, and in trying to be 'purely historical' has unintentionally justified those New Testament theological portraits of Jesus that combine 'philosophical thought, critical acumen, historical insight, and religious feeling – without which no deep theology is possible'.[11] These constructions of New Testament theology, often sufficiently historical to appear as 'purely historical' reconstructions of Jesus, are forged with critical historical tools and draw on philosophical reflection, but are often guided also by Christian faith and experience, and are often intended in turn to support Christian faith. In using history to contribute to theology and support faith by constructing a credible picture of Jesus which coheres with Christian belief, Schleiermacher has had even more successors than Strauss has had in his conscientious attempt to 'destroy' by historical criticism 'all which the Scriptures declare and the Church believes of Christ' (*Life*, p. 757), or that Schweitzer had in discrediting theological portraits of Jesus 'designed by rationalism, endowed with life by liberalism, and clothed by modern theology in an historical garb' (*Quest*, p. 396).

The aim of this discussion is to defend this approach to Christology through faith-images of Jesus constructed in part by historical study, but before taking this approach further it is necessary to trace the main modern alternative to the Schleiermacher-Macquarrie model of a credible historical picture of Jesus which is compatible with traditional doctrinal definition.

This alternative, unleashed by Strauss in 1835 and still stalking the land, is signalled by Strauss in 1865 when he glosses his arguably fair comment that 'Schleiermacher's Christ is as little a real man as is the Christ of the Church' (*Christ*, p. 5) with a revealing sentence: 'By means of a truly critical treatment of the Gospels one reaches Schleiermacher's Christ as little as the church's Christ' (p. 5, omitting the translator's ambiguous 'he does'). Even if true (and it is not true of Macquarrie's Jesus), that is irrelevant. Nobody should expect to reach a satisfactory *Christology* purely by historical research. Any such demand is an *a priori* rejection of Christology. All that can and must be demanded of a Christology in this respect is that it reflects (or at least does not contradict) what can be established with some probability by historical research. Little as that is, it is enough to make clear that Christology is about (among other larger metaphysical realities) the first-century Palestinian Jew from Nazareth.

The year 1835 is a watershed in the history of modern Christology as well as in gospel criticism because Strauss's *Life of Jesus* and Baur's *Die christliche Gnosis* (which also contained strong criticism of Schleiermacher's Christology) were both published in that year, and both these Tübingen theologians, by then Hegelians, made the historian's distinction between the Jesus of history and the Christ of faith foundational for their (different) liberal Christologies. Historical critics must of course distinguish (as Reimarus had done) between traditions which they consider historically reliable and those that seem clearly to be the product of post-resurrection reflection and that seem not to reflect the historical reality of Jesus' ministry. It is also legitimate for theologians and anyone else to attempt historical reconstructions of Jesus on this basis, though with such limited reliable evidence all these attempts will be very hypothetical. It is also arguable (against Barth) that modern Christian theology has to join in this quest, at least for apologetic reasons, in order to test (hopefully to destruction) reconstructions that would subvert Christianity (such as that of Reimarus), and to look for historical constructions compatible with Christian belief. What is clearly illegitimate from the perspective of traditional Christianity, or self-evidently destructive of that, is to substitute a historical reconstruction of Jesus (which does not speak of God) for Christology (which does). Yet it seems such a natural move to make that anyone who objects must say why and where it goes wrong. To be credible this will involve saying how far historical reconstruction has a legitimate and necessary place in Christology.

Substituting a historian's reconstruction of Jesus for the christological definition is subversive of traditional Christianity because the latter calls Jesus truly God (however that is to be understood) as well as truly a human being, or even 'perfect human being' (however this is to be understood), and historical reconstructions do not speak of God or even of perfect humanity. Historical research as such says less than Christology, whether or not it is religiously motivated and whether or not its reconstructions are well-founded. Some consider disinterested historical reconstructions the only true accounts of a human being, though even they might find some truth in myths about remarkable figures. The great divide in modern theology is not between those who maintain the dogmatic formulae and those who engage in historical criticism (many do both), but between those who want their historical reconstructions to substitute for what Christology has traditionally provided (talk of God and the world), and those who, like Ritschl[12] and Kähler,[13] Macquarrie and most modern theologians, resist that dogmatically anti-dogmatic move.

That radical liberal Protestant option abandons the confession of Jesus' divinity and with it a large part (perhaps the entirety) of what (unless Nicaea and Chalcedon, and the weight of Christian experience and reflection standing behind the doctrinal definition, misunderstood the New Testament witness fundamentally) the New Testament authors intended to assert. Many of the various Jesus pictures (or 'lives' or 'quests') produced by historical research could be called 'Christs of faith', because they reflect much of what their Christian authors consider important, but they differ from orthodox Christologies in claiming to be only historical portraits and therefore in not speaking directly of God, but at best of Jesus' talk of God. To maintain an orthodox Christology and a traditional account of Christianity it is necessary to start from the traditional definition and consider what true humanity and deity might mean, as well as listening to the biblical witness and being encouraged by the historical claims it makes to engage in critical historical research and to test any conclusions reached by that route also.

One could construct a spectrum of liberal Christologies and Jesus-ologies with Schleiermacher, Rahner, Schillebeeckx, and Macquarrie on the orthodox right, maintaining the divinity of Christ as well as his humanity, and on the left those who speak of Jesus solely in human terms, and consider any doctrine of his divinity a pre-modern residue to be abandoned. Both appeal behind the witness of the New Testament authors in their (sometimes undeveloped) historical reconstructions of Jesus himself, but the latter from Reimarus to Hick pitch their total historical reconstructions against the whole New Testament witness. The former do that at particular points, but construct (or presuppose) a total picture of Jesus which coheres with the post-resurrection witness of the New Testament and subsequent Christianity. They try to make sense of the historical development of early Christianity rather than dismissing this as decline and fall, primitive superstition, or (Reimarus) worse. They accept one or another of these historical reconstructions, but insist on saying 'something more' about Jesus, and claim to represent the basic intention of pre-modern Christologies. More conservative theologians challenge their claim adequately to represent those earlier dogmatic formulations.

The various modern historical reconstructions of Jesus found right across the spectrum can be classified in terms of three (ideal) 'types', representing three main emphases: some see Jesus primarily as an Enlightenment moral teacher or a social reformer; others as an apocalyptic fanatic, expecting an imminent end to the world. These two modern reconstructions of 'the historical Jesus' emphasize either his moral teaching (Harnack and some modern American variants) or his eschatology (variously understood – sometimes politically). A third type, harder to verify and therefore less common, emphasizes Jesus' God-consciousness. This third possibility recognizes both the moral and eschatological dimensions found in Jesus' teaching and in most Jewish talk of God, but relates them to Jesus' underlying sense of God or overwhelming passion for God. This type of Jesus picture might be called 'mystical', because it focuses on Jesus' religious experience, but that term can easily mislead and requires careful qualification. Macquarrie refers to 'the numinous character of his life and ministry' (*Existentialist*, p. 185). Some call it 'theological' because it gives centrality to Jesus' experience and talk of God. Jesus' religious experience cannot be directly verified, but it can be postulated and might make the best sense both of Jesus' moral and of his eschatological teaching, and especially of how they are held together, which is always a problem for other hypotheses.

Neither Schleiermacher nor Macquarrie works this out as Heinz Schürmann has done,[14] but an argument in support of the picture of Jesus implicit in their Christologies might begin as follows: we can be quite sure that Jesus proclaimed God's rule (the kingdom of God or heaven), but even after more than 200 years of argument since Reimarus made this topic central to his account of Jesus we cannot be sure how exactly Jesus intended the phrase, or what exactly he expected. Certainly he demanded obedience to God's holy will and declared this with a sense of authority, but there is little to suggest that he expected the end of the world soon, contrary to the hypotheses of Albert Schweitzer, who built too much on Matthew 10.23 which is probably a post-resurrection saying.[15] Much first-century Jewish talk of God had both a strong futurist orientation and a strong moral component, and Jesus surely spoke of God with powerful immediacy and acted in God's name. If by proclaiming 'God's rule drawn near' (Mark 1.15) and yearned for (Matt. 6.10; Mark 14.25) and seen as already exercising its power through his healings and exorcisms (Matt. 12.28) and to be received and entered, he confronted his hearers with the near God who rules and calls for total obedience and commitment, this 'theological' interpretation of 'the kingdom of God' would include its moral and eschatological dimensions.

Such an account of Jesus' ministry challenges the one-sidedly eschatological interpretation which rode on the back of the nineteenth-century rediscovery of apocalyptic and the probably mistaken theory that Jesus thought himself the apocalyptic Son of Man figure referred to in Daniel 7.[16] Those who like Schleiermacher and Macquarrie construe the divinity of Jesus in terms of his perfect humanity are likely to find our third type of historical picture of Jesus compatible with and suggestive of that. It is constructed partly out of what seems historically very probable (that Jesus spoke of God using the phrase 'God's rule'), and partly out of what seems historically possible but cannot be proved (a suggestion about how he may have understood the phrase 'the kingdom of God'), and partly from what corresponds to the effects of Jesus' activity in the disciples' and subsequent Christians' experience.

Macquarrie is cautiously critical ('I suppose') of Schleiermacher's (and Knox's?) tying theology 'so closely to the experience of a community', and wants to reinforce what can be said on the basis of the community's experience with some rational or 'natural' theology (*Jesus Christ*, p. 210). But even if this 'argument from effects' is insufficient for Christology or soteriology it carries some historical weight and contributes more to a faith-picture than verified historical facts alone can. Most importantly, this faith-image, worked out formally in a Christology, refers to Jesus of Nazareth as well as speaking of God and the world. Whereas Strauss (and

Bousset) followed Kant in detaching the christological predicates from the historical person, and radical liberals like Schweitzer and Harnack and Troeltsch rescue Jesus from the shackles of dogma, Schleiermacher, Rahner and Macquarrie maintain the traditional shape of Christian doctrine which they believe preserves the faith of the Church, even as they offer reformulations for the Church to consider in its new intellectual milieu.

Strauss's left-wing Hegelian move which attached the christological predicates to the human race perhaps contained a grain of truth, because Christology is concerned not only with the historical figure but also with the destiny of humanity.[17] This is what led Baur to tie Christology only to the Christ of faith, not to the Jesus of history. Even Martin Kähler, contrary to his intentions, gave support to this trend by his ill-advised title (note 13 above) which echoed Strauss's 1865 pamphlet (n. 5 above). He himself opposed 'the so-called historical Jesus', and his 'historic, biblical Christ' contained as many historical elements as the Gospels themselves do, but his antithetical formulation allowed Bultmann to appeal to him in theological opposition to historical Jesus research, and in preferring instead the kerygmatic Christ. But when Kähler said that 'the real Christ is the preached Christ' he was not intending to exclude historical information about Jesus from his faith-picture.

Some kerygmatic theologians from the Bultmann school, Käsemann, Bornkamm, Fuchs and Ebeling, came to see the theological importance of historical Jesus research and connected their historical reconstructions of Jesus with early (and later) Christian faith. Unlike some more recent historical Jesus research, which can be called a 'quest' only by divesting the word of its religious connotations, this Bultmannian quest included serious christological reflection. But because it still talked of 'the historical Jesus and the Christ of faith' this 'new quest' always smacked of Nestorianism's 'two Christs' (cf. *Jesus Christ*, p. 229). The better way for Christology was that of Schleiermacher and Macquarrie, who from the outset avoided separating the historical figure of Jesus from 'the Christ of faith' in Christology (while making the distinction in their historical research), and insisted that the Church's dogmatic definition (truly human, truly God) is compatible with Jesus being a real human being, as orthodoxy had always asserted against docetism. It did not have to suggest the hybrid figure of much popular piety, or even the impersonal humanity of much ancient and not so ancient theology. The *Church Times* reviewer who warned that 'the danger of the Nestorian heresy is so ever menacing in a humanitarian age like the present that all language which seems to imply that the Lord of Glory was not only Man but a man, an individual Jew, is greatly to be deprecated'[18] echoed much orthodox Christology and Anglo-catholic piety. Macquarrie and most other theologians today would respond that any Christology which (unlike 1 Cor. 2.8) failed to understand that the Lord of Glory was this particular first-century crucified Palestinian Jew would be greatly deprecated and not taken seriously.

The genuine humanity of Jesus, not some impersonal human nature, but a real first-century circumcised human being is surely, as Macquarrie insists, the natural starting-point for Christology today. This implies that historical investigation is legitimate and even necessary, but it may not take us far and should not be expected to provide theology with much more than what any intelligent and well-informed modern reader will gain from the Gospels. Pressed for more it offers less if it claims to be more true than Christian interpretations of Jesus.

Historical research is a natural line of enquiry, at least for many modern Western intellectuals, as prior to the eighteenth century it was not. Kähler's 1892 pamphlet did not set a barrier against this study of the Gospels. He appreciated how it had restored a sense of Jesus' authentic humanity against the 'Byzantine' Christology which as a pietist he disliked. His target was rather those developments in gospel criticism and Christology since 1835 that tore apart the history and theology which the Gospels and orthodox Christianity insist belong together. In particular he objected to the liberal 'lives of Jesus' of Renan (1863) and the later Strauss (1864) and their successors, which replace Christology with purely historical portraits. The gospel sources do not give historical research much to go on, but even if they were much more detailed and historically reliable, they would not provide what Christians look for and find in them, as Macquarrie points out (*Christology*, p. 84). Christology speaks of God, not merely Jesus' belief in God. Historical Jesus research yields a variety of possible historical pictures of Jesus, which may be placed alongside the foundational christological claims, or alternatively may be embraced in preference to traditional Christianity which affirms his divinity as well as his humanity.

What 'the divinity of Jesus' might mean is (like what the resurrection might mean) not a question that historical research can answer, but it can clarify how it has been understood. It can insist that Christians have usually taken this christological predicate to refer to Jesus, who is confessed by his followers, not to his followers' state of mind. Schleiermacher and Macquarrie understand the divinity of Jesus in terms of or in close relation to his 'perfect humanity', but modern historical research still throws little light because neither 'perfect humanity' nor 'sinlessness' are categories in which historians deal. It is Christian witness based on and exemplified by Scripture that elicits faith, and faith seeking understanding by reflecting on Scripture and Christian tradition in the light of contemporary experience (and *vice versa*) that may reaffirm the traditional doctrine.

Like Schleiermacher, Macquarrie starts 'from below', seeing Jesus in his historical context as a normal human being, however extraordinary. But he does not get so side-tracked into historical research as to substitute this for Christology, nor forget his christological goal of clarifying the church's confession, as has happened in some liberal protestantism.

Associating Macquarrie's Christology so closely with Schleiermacher's suggests several lines of criticism, but the most serious of these have been corrected in this modern revision. As Schleiermacher was criticized by orthodox and radicals alike for his middle way, so has Macquarrie been criticized. Defences against both, especially the latter, have been implicit in the preceding exposition. More searching criticisms may be found in the work of some modern theologians who share his aim to be faithful to the 'governing intention' of Chalcedon and also open to all relevant modern insights. These are mostly alternative theological proposals. We may therefore ask why in the 1960s did some students prefer Hegel and Marx to Schleiermacher, Metz to Rahner, Moltmann to Bultmann or Ebeling, MacKinnon to Macquarrie? Was it merely *Zeitgeist*, or did the juniors miss something in the masters, including Macquarrie? Might this be a social and political imperative?

Most protestant theologians start from the New Testament witness rather than from the faith of the Church enshrined in Scripture and tradition as a whole. Starting with the Chalcedonian definition which guides orthodox Christian reading of scripture is compatible with beginning 'from below', reflecting on the human figure, because it knows from the outset it will reflect also on Jesus' divinity, as a more critical historical approach might not. It is a more catholic and Anglican than protestant procedure, as is the emphasis upon the Church's worship which stands behind the doctrinal development, especially Christology,[19] and it gives more weight to wider rational considerations. This orientation to the faith and worship of the catholic Church is expressed in the Prayer Book *Quicunque vult*, quoted by Macquarrie in *Jesus Christ*, p. 375, and *Christology*, pp. 75–6: 'And the Catholick Faith is this: That we worship one God in Trinity, and Trinity in Unity.' The *Quicunque* goes on to insist on believing 'rightly the Incarnation of our Lord Jesus Christ'. The creeds (which are more prominent in Anglican faith, theology, and worship than elsewhere in the Christian Church) reflect a more historical sequence in placing the main emphasis on the christological titles, mysteries and definitions, and implying the doctrine of the Trinity by the three-fold structure of the whole – it was mainly through its apprehension of the divinity of Christ that the Church came to formulate its trinitarian doctrine. The catholic tradition (including Scripture) directs us first to God in Christ and draws us into the response of worship before sending us out in the power of the Spirit to live and work to God's praise and glory.

New Testament theology, by contrast, and systematic theologies oriented to that, may make Christology central, as Gerhard Ebeling[20] and W. Thüsing do by giving unusual prominence to historical Jesus research. Or they may place greater emphasis on the atonement (Stuhlmacher), or on eschatology (Pannenberg, Moltmann). When theologians make St John their 'living centre of Scripture', as Schleiermacher and Macquarrie surely do, Christology will be central; if they make Paul central, the cross and resurrection (set in an eschatological framework) may dominate, and if the Apocalypse, then perhaps utopian politics. But much depends also on how the central texts are interpreted. If Paul and John are given an anthropological interpretation (Bultmann), the preference will be for theological anthropology.

It is perhaps his mystical temperament and philosophical temper which incline Macquarrie (like Schleiermacher) to the 'Johannine' type of theology which 'has really but a single dogma, that concerning the person of Christ' and stimulates 'highly worthwhile philosophical discussions' (Strauss, *Christ*, p. 4) of deity and humanity, and may be said to imply a 'demythologized' version of Christianity. The theological diversity of the New Testament witness licenses a certain theological pluralism in the Church, within the parameters of what all the witnesses believe (hard as it is to be certain of this). It would be unreasonable to criticize the Fourth Gospel for failing to generate much of a social ethic (beyond believers loving one another) or political engagement, because that is broadly true of the New Testament as a whole, and the implied politics of the Apocalypse are not particularly Christian, however valuable its social criticism (chapter 18 especially). But one might consider Johannine forms of Christianity deficient in this respect. Those who rightly insist on the political significance of the story of Jesus[21] place the accents differently from the biblical writers, and probably from Jesus himself (though that is contested), but this is a vital ingredient of Christian faith for some today. Whether it should be a necessary ingredient for all is less obvious.

The social and political dimensions of Christian theology have often in the twentieth century been related to eschatology and sometimes to apocalyptic, not surprisingly in view of recent European history. Despite writing eloquently about *Christian Hope* (1978) Macquarrie has been critical of the 'eschatological Christology' (*Jesus Christ*, pp. 320–7) and 'theologies of hope' (*Thinking*, pp. 221–32) of Moltmann and Pannenberg. His main objection is that they reverse Bultmann's deliteralizing of much Christian language with their insistence on the centrality of the resurrection (historical) 'event'. He is also uneasy about their 'obsession with the future' (p. 229) and their wanting to understand transcendence in this way. Like a predecessor at Christ Church he is distrustful of 'jam tomorrow and jam yesterday – never jam today' (p. 229).

Macquarrie introduced, with the help of a new natural theology, major modifications to Bultmann's doctrine of God, while defending him against those who thought he did not carry his demythologizing programme far enough. In addition to this ontological corrective, he insists on a more realistic faith-picture of Jesus than Bultmann needed, and places greater emphasis on Christian hope. These modifications make Christology central to his theology in a more traditional way than Bultmann's act of God and 'Christ-event' proposed. But in other respects Macquarrie offers a demythologizing approach to Christian doctrines rather similar to Bultmann's, and it is not surprising that conservatives find him saying less than they do (or different) on the atonement and on the resurrection even, not to mention the pre-existence of Christ, the virgin birth and his second coming. Christ's reconciling work to draw all to himself (John 12.32) is associated more with his life and perfect humanity than with his death considered as a sacrifice, and although some truth is allowed to both subjective and objective theories of atonement, the mythological ideas of a cosmic transaction are rejected, and the cross loses something of the tremendous weight that it has in some theologies. The problem of evil does not receive the attention it received from MacKinnon when it is understood with Augustine as the absence of good, or when with the Greeks the image of God in humans has not suffered Calvinistic obliteration. One Archbishop of Canterbury might say again: '*nondum consideresti* . . . You have not yet considered what a heavy weight sin is.' Or another, in the *Book of Common Prayer*, 'the burden of them is intolerable'. Neither would be called by Gregor Smith 'an existentialist without Angst'.

It is perhaps surprising that Macquarrie has not been criticized more from the conservative evangelical side. This may be due partly to his conciliatory manner, his evident piety (to the point of Anglo-catholic practices), and his sometimes ambiguous formulations. His being co-opted by Michael Green in the *Myth* controversy (1977) was ironic, since his theology is much closer to that of Wiles. It is striking that he does not choose between 'the happy ending' and 'the austere ending' in his account of the 'mysteries' of *Jesus Christ* (pp. 403–14). Christians can be more or less traditional on secondary matters, provided they are clear about God in Jesus Christ. While at this point he himself is doubtless more

Bultmannian, or (arguably) Johannine than the 'happy ending' he can say of it that 'This is the teaching of the church, and I think these ideas can make sense and be acceptable in the context of modern thought. I repeat too that the happy ending *deserves* to be true' (*Jesus Christ*, p. 412). A ringing endorsement? 'But the need to be absolutely honest compels us to look at an alternative scenario' (p. 412). 'Both conserve the essential truths of Christianity' (p. 414), that 'God is love and God is revealed in Jesus Christ' (p. 412).

Like St John, Macquarrie is more traditional than Schleiermacher at this point and re-tells the resurrection story as he preaches the Gospel. But his understanding of this mystery scarcely requires even St Paul's spiritual body because, in being 'lifted up' on the cross, Jesus is lifted up to the Father (cf. John 12.32). However, he does not quite take Bultmann to mean that 'the resurrection is primarily an event in the disciples rather than in Jesus' (*Jesus Christ*, p. 414): 'It is indeed the event of the church, which is Christ's living body, and which in its preaching and sacraments and community continues his life and work. But the meaning of resurrection is originally in Jesus himself – in the possession and mediation by him of true life, eternal life, which he brought to its highest pitch on the cross'. (p. 414). That is truly Johannine, but Macquarrie can also rightly appeal to St Paul on resurrection – against the literalism and physical resurrection (or resuscitation) of much popular piety and vulgar apologetics. His Pauline account of the 'happy ending' is not clap-happy. Does it lack the cutting-edge of more literalistic theologies? Is that the price liberals pay for holding a credible version of Christianity? If so are they prepared to die for such a faith, as they surely live by it, or does Overbeck's acid remark about the 'inessentiality' of Harnack's unorthodox neo-Protestant version of Christianity apply also to the generous orthodoxy of a liberal Anglican Catholicism? If that is *der Testfall* (von Balthasar), let nobody presume to answer for another.

Notes

1 F. Schleiermacher, *The Christian Faith*, New York: Harper, 1963, p. 385.

2 For a good discussion see Peter Hodgson, *The Formation of Historical Theology*, New York: Harper & Row, 1966, pp. 44–54.

3 These lectures from 1819 to 1832 were not published until 1864, ET *The Life of Jesus*, ed. J.C. Verheyden, Philadelphia: Fortress Press, 1975.

4 The whole manuscript was not published until 1972. The most recent English edition of the seventh 'fragment' is by C.H. Talbert, *Reimarus: Fragments*, Philadelphia: Fortress Press, 1970 and London: SCM Press, 1971.

5 ET George Eliot 1846, ed. P. C. Hodgson, Philadelphia: Fortress Press, 1972, and London: SCM Press, 1973.

6 ET ed. L. E. Keck, Philadelphia: Fortress Press, 1977.

7 See Hodgson *Formation*, pp. 47–50. Also the discussions by Brian Gerrish, Hans Frei and myself in N. Smart *et al.* (eds), *Nineteenth-Century Religious Thought in the West*, Vol. 1., Cambridge: Cambridge University Press, 1985, pp. 123–56, 215–89. In his inaugural course (1827–8) Baur claimed that 'whether the person of Jesus of Nazareth really possessed the attributes which belong to the established concept of the Redeemer is in fact a purely historical question . . .' a claim which this essay rejects.

8 Quoted from Rahner's *Theological Investigations*, Vol. 1., London: Darton, Longman & Todd, 1961, pp. 149f., in *Jesus Christ*, pp. 166, 306; *Stubborn*, pp. 141, 160.

9 Most recently, J. Hick, *The Metaphor of God Incarnate*, London: SCM Press, 2005², pp. 150–60, which contains some criticism of Macquarrie.

10 On 'theological portraiture' see E. Farley, *Ecclesial Reflection*, Philadelphia: Fortress Press, 1982, ch. 9.

11 Albert Schweitzer, *The Quest of the Historical Jesus*, London: A. & C. Black, 1910, p. 1, (2000 edn, p. 3). He evidently had some respect for the theological portraits he tried to demolish as historically inadequate.

12 *Justification and Reconciliation*, Vol. 3 (1874). ET of 3rd (1888) edn, Edinburgh: T. & T. Clark, 1900, p. 3.

13 *The so-called Historical Jesus and the Historic, Biblical Christ* (1892, 1896²) ET Philadelphia: Fortress Press, 1964.

14 For example, *Jesus – Gestalt und Geheimnis*, Paderborn: Bonifatius, 1994. My own sketch is contained in J. Barton (ed.) *The Biblical World*, Vol. 2., London: Routledge, 2002, pp. 223–57. The reference to *Existentialist*, p. 185, shows that this view of Jesus was already in place by 1955, and probably long before.

15 E.P. Sanders lays great weight on the equally fragile Matt. 19.28.

16 I argue this in 'From Reimarus to Sanders', in R. S. Barbour (ed.) *The Kingdom of God and Human Society*, Edinburgh: T. & T. Clark, 1993, pp. 80–139.

17 As Macquarrie (like Schleiermacher and DuBose) consistently emphasizes, e.g. *Jesus Christ*, p. 205. See also a 1939 remark of J.M. Creed, quoted by MacKinnon in his Preface to *The Divinity of Jesus Christ*, London: Collins Fontana, 1964², p. 10. 'Christianity now must seek to relate once more the personal figure of the Gospels to the thought of God's dealings with the race.'

18 *Church Times*, 13 Feb 1925, quoted by R.B. Slocum, *The Theology of William Porcher DuBose*, Columbia, S.C: University of South Carolina Press, 2000, p. 4.

19 So W. Bousset *Kyrios Christos* (1921² ET 1970), but as a radical liberal protestant Bousset himself rejected the development he described.

20 *Dogmatik des christlichen Glaubens*, 3 vols, Tübingen: Mohr Siebeck, 1979. Macquarrie's review of this work, and his personal contact with Ebeling, show how congenial he found 'the systematic theologian of the Bultmann school'.

21 For example, C. Rowland in Barbour, *Kingdom of God*, p. 238: 'It is impossible to abstract the story of Jesus from a political framework without irredeemably reducing its significance.'

22 The Resurrection as Myth and as Fable

The Difference After Thirty Years

CHRISTOPHER MORSE

On the bookshelf just over my shoulder from my study desk is a slender and much valued volume signed by John Macquarrie that he graciously gave me over 30 years ago when I was a doctoral student at Union preparing for a comprehensive examination with him in eschatology. Titled *The Future of Hope: Theology as Eschatology*, it contains papers from a consultation at Duke in April 1968 at which Jürgen Moltmann was first introduced to the American scene and critical responses to his thought were offered by some of the foremost theologians teaching in the United States at the time.[1] One of these respondents was Macquarrie himself, whose paper on 'Eschatology and Time' highlighted the major points then currently at issue in both the lucid and insightful manner that students and readers recognize as characterizing all his work.[2] The invitation to join with other contributors to these pages in expressing deep respect and continuing gratefulness to Professor Macquarrie provides me an opportunity to reflect upon one of the issues prominent in the discussion of eschatology then and now. It is the question of the resurrection of Jesus in the testimony of the Gospel and how it may be said to relate to present experience. What similarities and differences are to be noted on this subject after 30 years? More specifically, to keep within the specified limits I will focus upon points raised by the Duke consultation as they involved Moltmann and Macquarrie's observations in 1968 in comparison to the more recent provocation provided by Alain Badiou's *Saint Paul: The Foundation of Universalism* first published in French in 1997.[3]

The question of present-day significance was much in the minds of Moltmann's critics in 1968, and understandably so, because of the claims Moltmann had made regarding the future as the mode of God's being. In an effort to recast the gospel testimony in a manner that did not subscribe either to the objectifying cosmology to which Bultmann had earlier taken exception, or to what Moltmann viewed as the subjectifying strictures of the existential anthropology that Bultmann had alternatively proposed in his programme of demythologization, Moltmann argued for yet another way of thinking about the resurrection. He posited its reality not in any past that was presumed to be amenable to replication in present-day experience, whether that past was viewed as historically factual or mythical, but rather in a future informing the present as promise not yet realizable phenomenologically in the present's current terms. This future he designated in his early work as God's advent, an imminent coming to pass or taking place of that *novum* which has not previously been in place, in distinction from the more conventional idea of futurity as that which derives from some presently immanent potentiality that subsequently becomes actualized. Involved in this recasting of phenomenological and ontological concepts in terms of eschatological imminence rather than teleological immanence (certainly recognized in debates of the time, however evaluated, as making more than an iota's worth of difference) was also much discussion of what constitutes a historical happening and the extent to which Troeltsch's definition of historical reality as requiring a single nexus of 'unitary forces' and 'analogous occurrences', or what Troeltsch had called 'the univocity and the total interconnection of historical events', was applicable to news of the resurrection.[4] Objecting to Moltmann's contention that the resurrection of Jesus was more historical than an existential event, but yet 'without parallel' in that its only analogy lies in what is yet to come, Macquarrie countered that such 'analogy must lie within accessible experience, or it can have no value'.[5]

The title of Macquarrie's paper, 'Eschatology and Time', indicates its primary emphasis. After observing that contemporary thought in both the natural and social sciences displayed a renewed consideration of the significance of temporality, Macquarrie draws the distinction between 'clock time' or 'world time' and the temporality of human existence, which, while always occurring in such datable chronology, further relates to time internally by remembering in the present a past and anticipating a future. Christian doctrines err, in Macquarrie's judgement, when they place undue emphasis upon one of the dimensions of past, present, and future to the neglect of the others. An example cited is the doctrine of the atonement where what has already happened in the past is often stressed to the omission of anything happening now or anticipated to happen in the future. Another example is the doctrine of eschatology where the future may be so emphasized that there is a disregard of the past and of the present.

Macquarrie then refers to the main types of eschatological interpretations currently in discussion, the futuristic, the so-called realized eschatology in which the ultimate end is viewed as already having taken place, and the position he credits as more persuasive, Bultmann's demythologized eschatology which symbolizes eschatological ideas existentially as present realities. Bultmann does not escape Macquarrie's critique, however, in that objection is raised to the individualism of his position and to its lack of any future as well as cosmic dimension. While Moltmann is said to appear at first to provide for these eschatological dimensions lacking in Bultmann's account, Macquarrie registers his judgement that Bultmann, notwithstanding, is commendably 'more respectful towards the contemporary scientific and secular outlook'.[6]

It is in this context that Macquarrie raises the issue of the interpretation of Christ's resurrection. Noting that Moltmann attributes historical reality to the resurrection while Bultmann denies it, Macquarrie observes that the crucial question is what one means by 'historical event'. He opposes theological attempts to redefine history in ways inconsistent with Troeltsch's theory of analogous occurrences and a univocity of connected events, a fault he explicitly attributes in 1968 to Helmut Thielicke but suggests may be detected in Moltmann as well, and remarks, 'It would surely be a strange reversal to triumphalism if the theologian were to lay down to the historian the criteria for his research.'[7] Thus testimony to the resurrection must find some 'present analogous happening', and Macquarrie offers by way of example the possible similarities between the resurrection appearances reported in the gospel accounts and cases of visions currently being presented in psychical research.[8] The paper concludes by recommending the term 'eternal life' as most apt for incorporating philosophically the broadest range of eschatological ideas of a God confessed to be shaping the past, present, and future toward an ever new cosmic horizon. Some such speculative world-view, Macquarrie advises, while admittedly not based upon certainty, at least allows for the risk-taking that hoping within our finite existence seems to require.

What stands out most strikingly from this paper for today's reader of Badiou's *Saint Paul* is precisely the issue Macquarrie raises of the Gospels' resurrection testimony finding significance 'within accessible experience' through some 'present analogous happening'. In contrast to a position admittedly persuaded, though not uncritically, by the ontological implications for the present of an enhanced Bultmannian demythologization of the resurrection taken as myth, we are introduced in Badiou to a position admittedly persuaded, though not uncritically, by the ontological implications for the present of an enhanced neo-Marxist materialism informed by the declaration of the resurrection taken as fable. And it is solely this fabulousness (*point fabuleux*) of resurrection, the unassimil-able singularity of such unprecedented event, that must be said to resist all analogy to present experience in the sense of an assignment of its true significance to, as Badiou puts it, 'prior markings', or 'pre-constituted historical aggregates' (*Saint Paul*, pp. 4–6, 23). What Paul declares as Christ's resurrection ruptures all pre-existing classifications of reality and is 'out of place' in a manner Badiou impressively denotes as a 'nomadism of gratuitousness'. Badiou's theory proposes an account of this ontologi-cally homeless gratuitousness, based not upon an idealistic appeal to a supernatural or supra-rational transcendentalism rejective of material-ism, but congruent with what he calls an infinite 'excess' irruptive in the contingency of material situations, a 'senseless superabundance of grace' in 'what happens to us' that gives rise to a universally militant subjectiv-ity (*Saint Paul*, pp. 78–81).

The vocabularies and discursive contexts of these two construals are obviously in important respects quite foreign to each other. While traces of Kierkegaard, Heidegger, and of Pascalian wagers share in their back-grounds, the post-structuralist dismissals of ontologies of subjectivity have come more of age in confronting Badiou. Contextual caution is in order to avoid the proverbial fallacy of equating apples and oranges. That both construals explicitly address the import of the same biblical word of Christ's resurrection, however, one (in favouring a Bultman-nian perspective) by invoking the language of myth to be existentially demythologized, and the other of fable to be rediscovered in its fabulous-ness, or, so to say, ontologically re-fabulousized, permits the effort to think of them here together, at least on this point, as not simply incom-mensurate discourses.[9]

Badiou's self-described atheism assertively rejects any religious interest in Paul or in the theological contents of his writings. In this respect he considers Paul's exemplary resurrection talk a useful fiction. Rather, it is the subjectivity he finds manifest in the form of Paul's gospel declara-tion, most tellingly epitomized in the words to the Corinthians that 'Jews demand signs and Greeks desire wisdom, but we proclaim Christ cruci-fied' (1 Cor. 1.22–23 NRSV), that elicits Badiou's intensity of interest as a theorist of social militancy. The instantiation of 'things that are not' reducing to nothing, as Paul declares it, 'things that are' (1 Cor. 1.28), is seen as the singular ontological mark differentiating the falsity of total-izing schematizations of reality, as criticized in postmodernism, from the universalism of truth's eruption in conviction always as noncompli-ant event. Truth occurs when what has counted for nothing in our pro-cedures breaches what figures to be accounted for. This way that truth may be said to eventuate in situations as discounted and unclassifiable with respect to prior configurations Badiou labels, going against the anti-metaphysical grain of much contemporary thought, universal. It is this formal universality – again, not to be confused with what postmodernism rightly opposes as the overruling of difference by so-called master narratives or totalizing discourse – that Badiou finds remarkable in Paul's proclamation of the resurrection of the crucified Christ.

Deciphering Jews and Greeks in Paul's usage not as ethnic denotations – Paul was and remained proud that he was himself a Jew by birth – but as what he labels 'subjective dispositions' and 'regimes of discourse', Badiou characterizes the former as that of the prophet whose identity politics adheres to differentiating significations of the exception, while the Greek mind-set is that of the philosopher seeking correspondences in a unitary cosmos with an ordered totality of all things (*Saint Paul*, p. 41). Neither stance, in Badiou's judgement, is able to exist apart from the other or to sustain a militant subject. In the instance he typifies as Jewish prophetic exceptionality, difference is fragmentized as a denial of universality. In the instance typified by the Greek philosopher, identity is falsely universalized as a denial of difference. The illustration Badiou gives of such exclusivity and inclusivity is that of today's economic globalization with its instant communications in which capitalism configures a world of 'monetary homogenization' that paradoxically results in increasing civil controls and protesting ideological parochialisms (*Saint Paul*, p. 13).

Paul's proclamation of Christ's resurrection Badiou sees as providing a third regime of discourse that breaks with that of both Jew and Greek precisely in its refusal to conform to the subjectivity exemplified by each. In a world whose only options seem to be either encapsulation by a relativism of cultural and ideological assertions of identity, or control by an abstract homogeneity of market forces and enumerated faceless body counts, Paul declares, 'There is no longer Jew or Greek, there is no longer slave or free, there is no longer male and female; for all of you are one in Christ Jesus' (Gal. 3.28). It is this import of Paul's declared conviction regarding the significance of Christ's resurrection that Badiou, the post (not pre)-poststructuralist as atheist and non-theologian, finds to be 'a genuinely stupefying statement when one knows the rules of the ancient world' (*Saint Paul*, p. 9). That the site from which this event of resurrection occurs is said to be Christ's crucifixion carries no militant significance for Badiou, who is wary of any idealization of suffering, with the one important exception that as resurrection's 'earthen vessel' it shows this 'evental site' to be as universally contingent and engaged with materiality as is death (*Saint Paul*, p. 70). Nor does this 'materialism of grace' require an 'All-Powerful' to account for its beneficent efficacy (*Saint Paul*, p. 66).

In sum, for Badiou it is precisely that the resurrection of Christ has *no* analogy which, in Macquarrie's words, 'must lie within accessible experience' that gives it its singularly transformative and universally militant value.

A review of the debates over the eschatological significance of the resurrection from the time of the Duke consultation in 1968 with regard to Badiou's appraisals 30 years later invites consideration of where exactly the differences are. One immediately apparent contrast is that for Bultmann, whom Macquarrie most commends, it is the kerygmatic content of the gospel proclamation of the resurrection and not its mythical form that is essential for faith, while for Badiou it is the fabulous form of the Pauline gospel's declaration of the resurrection and not the content of the good news that is emphasized as the occasion for conviction.[10] Both agree on the need for deliteralization but differ as to what the proper alternative to literalization is.

Yet the disputed issue of the alternative to a literalized resurrection testimony already figured prominently in the Barth/Bultmann exchanges that influenced most of theology's renewed interest in eschatology in the twentieth century. It was Karl Barth who emphasized 'saga' as a way of differentiating the significance of eschatological testimony from both univocally historical and existentially demythologized construals. The former errs, Barth argued, in attempting to draw such significance from 'the known analogies of world history' while the latter is equally mistaken in attempting translation into ontological generalizations of what is already the case, the phenomena of 'the natural and spiritual cosmos', as he puts it.[11] Both the univocally historical and existentially demythologized accounts represent what the gospel announces as coming to pass in terms of what Paul calls 'the form (*schema*) of this world that is passing away' (1 Cor. 7:31). Barth's objection to ontological univocity in reckoning with the eschatological reality of the gospel's proclamation of 'new creation' is behind his insistence upon the *analogia fidei* (or better, *analogia gratiae*) rather than an *analogia entis*. It is generally agreed that the concept of the *analogia entis* Barth rejects is not to be found in Thomas but in distortions of analogical predication insufficiently attentive to Thomas's axiom *Deus non est in genere*.[12] But the reason for Barth's Reformed insistence that the grace of what Paul refers to as 'a new creation' creates its own analogies and is not proportional to anything prior is rooted precisely in Paul's apocalyptic sense that with the resurrection 'everything old has passed away; see, everything has become new!' (2 Cor. 6:17). This is a sense often muted or lost in the subsequent doctrines of analogy that find the Pauline declaration of the power of God's righteousness 'apocalypsed' in the gospel less 'stupefying' than does the secular Badiou (Rom. 1:17).

Readers more familiar with theological discussions of eschatology during the past 30 years than with the secular rhetorics of Continental philosophy in which Badiou engages will be quick to spot in *Saint Paul* some intriguing similarities of expression. This is all the more surprising in that Badiou has referred to his philosophical project as the attempt to think of the infinity intrinsic to social situations and their multiple possibilities 'without the theological conception'.[13] Much that one reads could pass as a transcription of statements made in the context of the 1968 Duke consultation. Christ, for example, is said by Badiou to be 'a coming [*une venue*]' (p. 48) that 'happens to us universally' (p. 60). The essence of faith is 'to publicly declare itself' (p. 88). The alternative subjectivity to the prevailing ways of being in the world is afforded by an event designated as 'grace' and most aptly characterized as the subjectivity of an 'apostle' (p. 44). Such grace is 'supernumerary' and 'incalculable' (p. 65). Most of all, resurrection is 'the opening of an epoch' that 'transforms all relations' (p. 45). It is the occasioning of 'radical novelty' (p. 53). This coming of the new does not originate from possibilities of existence as legitimated prior to its happening. Rather, as sheer gift of eventuating grace, Christ's resurrected coming constitutes a 'new creature' of collaborative militancy whose Pauline synergy is a 'working together' not under law but by grace (pp. 63–64). 'Reconciliation' is even said to be a virtual indication'- how better to denote the import of Paul's *arrabōn* (2 Cor. 1:22, 5:5) – of this new life (p. 70). And what could qualify as more orthodox to Christian ears than Badiou's Athanasian sounding claim, 'We conform to Christ insofar as he conforms to us' (p. 70)? Without exception every one of these assertions as excerpted could equally have come from the theological discussions of eschatology in the 1960s.

Yet it would be a mistake to attempt a baptism of Badiou *in absentia* against his will and not recognize that his construal of Paul's resurrection pronouncements as fable is a restatement, appropriating in more biblical expression complex ontological theory that is propounded in his other works. The theoretical matrix is his response to what he calls 'the three global tendencies in contemporary philosophy': a 'hermeneutic orientation' concerned with the uncovering by interpretation of latent or suppressed meanings obscured by discourse; an 'analytic orientation' occupied with the rules governing meaningful utterance; and a 'postmodern orientation' which aims to dismantle overriding constructs of modern thought by challenging the pretensions of their circumscriptions.[14] Without disregarding the problems addressed by each, Badiou goes against the grain of the more currently credited anti-foundationalism of his contemporaries by redirecting attention to the question of the indispensabilities of being. But he does this not by reverting to older metaphysical assumptions of pre-established harmonies or substantial uniformities, but by arguing just the opposite, that it is precisely the multiple inconsistencies and nonconformities of situations that prove to be indispensable for the breaching of repetitive series in thought and action necessary for the existence of a subject emboldened by what is happening today. How it is rationally thinkable that what counts for nothing may be said to breach repetitive series with infinite possibilities in various settings, Badiou, who in *Saint Paul* makes the case in more biblical language with respect to Christ's resurrection as fable, elsewhere demonstrates by an intricate ontological theory formulated in terms of what has come to the fore in higher mathematics since the late nineteenth century as 'set theory'.[15] The invention of 'set theory' – by which multiples are presented as belonging together not by prefigured series or, ontologically stated, in categories of like substance, but by settings of infinitely varied inconsistencies in which what is out of order provides the condition for new orderings – makes possible for the first time, so one interpreter has observed, a rational concept of infinity and its functions that does not require reference to a *Deus ex machina*.[16] It is this concept of infinity that Badiou wishes to rescue from what he considers theology and that provides his reason for claiming that 'ontology is mathematics'.[17]

This rejection of theology in matters of infinite significance Badiou finds necessary in order to hear today the radicality of Paul's proclamation. It is a truncated gospel, of course, since apocalyptic, Trinity, Christology, and incarnation are bypassed as merely the domesticating heteronomies of church theologians. The dismissive reference to the 'All-Powerful' and attempts to reascribe the creative efficacy of grace simply capitulates to the conventional Kantian prejudice of liberal modernity that human agency can only be activated by de-activating divine agency. But surely, most glaring is the abject illusion with which Badiou concludes his brilliant exposé of Paul's gospel: '. . . the Good News comes down to this: we *can* vanquish death' (*Saint Paul*, p. 45). Nothing could be so deaf to the radicality of the gift of *Christ's* resurrection victory over sin and death which Paul declares.

The eschatological debates of the 1960s and subsequently, in which John Macquarrie is a leading participant, reveal a modern theological tradition of which Badiou appears unaware. In this tradition it has not been unusual for Marxist philosophers to suggest to Christian thinkers how to attend more closely to their knitting. After all, it was Ernst Bloch's discovery of biblical apocalyptic that influenced Moltmann's theology of hope, and it was the Czech thinker Milan Machovec who during the Prague Spring of 1968 and the ensuing Marxist–Christian dialogues reminded an audience at Union that the 'grace' of which the gospel speaks could not be reduced merely to the terms of interpersonal relationships.

Something rings profoundly consonant with Christian faith in Badiou's theorizing of being as devoid of classifiable qualities yet infinitely true and beneficent, instantiating unprecedented events of truth and love. Unmistakable is a sense, as Paul expresses it, that if Christ be not raised all else is futility and in vain (1 Cor. 15:14, 17). In principle it does not sound all that different from some of Macquarrie's proposed reflections regarding 'eternal life'. With respect to the gospel language of resurrection and how most faithfully today to confess its relation to present experience, former differences over analogy will need to be recognized if there is to be further engagement with this issue. Here not only the classical and medieval disputes over analogies of being must be taken into consideration but also the other disparate uses of the term that emerged most prominently in contention primarily in Protestant eschatological discussions in and around the period of the 1960s. These include, most relevantly for Badiou's account of the significance of the resurrection, Barth's doctrine of the *analogia fidei* or *gratiae*, Troeltsch's influential insistence upon analogy in characterizing the logic of history as involving a 'univocity' of 'analogous occurrences' in a nexus of 'total interconnection', and Bultmann's claim that an existential demythologization of biblical talk of divine actions assumes an analogy with interpersonal human relationships.[18] One could find no more reliable guide to these matters than John Macquarrie.

Notes

1 Frederick Herzog (ed.), *The Future of Hope: Theology as Eschatology*, New York: Herder and Herder, 1970.

2 In Herzog, *The Future*, pp. 110–25. Parts of this paper are later reprinted in the chapter, 'Theologies of Hope: A Critical Examination', in *Thinking*, pp. 221–32. While most all of Macquarrie's other books are also on my study shelves, and he addresses eschatology in a number of them, I will here confine my remarks to issues raised in this one, yet characteristic, summary essay. For examples of his further discussion see *Principles*, pp. 351–70, *Jesus Christ*, pp. 320–7, and especially *Hope*.

3 Alain Badiou, *Saint Paul: The Foundation of Universalism*, Stanford: Stanford University Press, 2003. My brief account here is intended only as one indication of how Badiou's work provokes theological interest. For helpful guides in English to the sources and complexity of Badiou's philosophy see, in addition to the variety of comment available on internet sites, the two books of short essays by Badiou, with editors' introductions, *Infinite Thought: Truth and the Return to Philosophy*, Oliver Feltham and Justin Clemens (eds), London: Continuum,

2003, and *Manifesto For Philosophy*, Norman Madarasz (ed.), Albany: State University of New York Press, 1999; also, Jason Barker, *Alain Badiou: A Critical Introduction*, London: Pluto Press, 2002; and Peter Hallward, *Badiou: A Subject to Truth*, Minneapolis: University of Minnesota Press, 2003, with a foreword by Slavoj Žižek.

4 E. Troeltsch, [1898] 'Historical and Dogmatic Method in Theology', ET in James Luther Adams and Walter F. Bense (trs), *Religion in History*, Minneapolis: Fortress Press, 1991, pp. 13, 17, 27.

5 Herzog, *The Future*, p. 122.

6 Herzog, *The Future*, p. 120.

7 Herzog, *The Future*, p. 121. Two theological works prominently featured at the time on this subject, though not explicitly referred to in this paper by Macquarrie, were Richard R. Niebuhr, *Resurrection and Historical Reason: A Study in Theological Method*, New York: Charles Scribner's Sons, 1957, and Wolfhart Pannenberg, 1970, *Basic Questions in Theology, Vol. One*, Philadelphia: Fortress Press, and London: SCM Press, 1970, (German 1967).

8 A then just published reference cited by Macquarrie is F.H. Cleobury, *A Return to Natural Theology*, London: James Clarke, 1967.

9 For theological assessments of Badiou drawn by 'Radical Orthodoxy' from traditions of Christian thought other than the formative Protestant positions in twentieth century Christian eschatology considered here see notably John Milbank, 'Materialism and Transcendence', pp. 393–426, 2005, *Theology and the Political: The New Debate*, Creston Davis, John Milbank, and Slavoj Žižek (eds.), Durham. Duke University Press, and Catherine Pickstock, 'Postmodernism', pp. 477–485, 2004, *The Blackwell Companion to Political Theology*, Peter Scott and William T. Cavanaugh (eds.), Oxford: Blackwell. I am indebted to Trevor Eppehimer, Ph.D. candidate at Union, for directing me to these materials. See his theologically perceptive review of Badiou's *Saint Paul* in *Union Seminary Quarterly Review*, v. 9, n.3–4, (2005), pp. 187–192.

10 It is noteworthy that in their privileging of Paul's resurrection proclamation neither Bultmann nor Badiou credits Luke's and other narrative accounts of the resurrection appearances. See Rudolf Bultmann, *Theology of the New Testament*, Vol. 1, New York: Charles Scriber's Sons, 1951, and London: SCM Press, 1952, pp. 292–306, and Vol. 2, 1955, pp. 116–118; and Badiou, *Saint Paul*, pp. 33, 38–39. Insofar as 'fable' suggests a story it is not the best English translation for the non-unitary 'inconsistent multiplicity' of the fabulousness Badiou seeks to affirm.

11 Karl Barth, *Church Dogmatics*, III, 3, Edinburgh: T. & T. Clark, 1960, p. 374; CD, III,1, 1958, p. 84; CD, IV,1, 1956, pp. 335–6.

12 Thomas Aquinas, *Summa Theologiae*, 1a. 3.5

13 Badiou, 'Ontology and politics: An interview with Alain Badiou', *Infinite Thought*, p. 183

14 Badiou, *Infinite Thought*, pp. 9–57

15 See the editors' brief exposition of Badiou's use of "set theory" in *Infinite Thought*, pp. 13–34. Also, Barker, *Alain Badiou*, pp. 149–55.

16 Hallward, *Badiou*, p. 324.

17 Badiou, *Infinite Thought*, p. 184

18 Bultmann, Rudolf, *Kerygma and Myth*, London: SPCK, 1960, p. 197.

Part III

Applied Theology

23 John Macquarrie's Ecclesiology

DANIEL W. HARDY

The Place of Ecclesiology in Institutions

'The making of the theology is closely related to the making of a theologian, and eventually the actual writing of theology' (*Theologian*, p. 30). If so, the contexts of the 'making' of John Macquarrie deserve attention.

It is habitual in most theology, if not to exclude ecclesiology altogether, at least to place it in another category from doctrine as such. In Britain, that is reflected in the virtual absence of church, ministry and sacraments from most university theological syllabuses, and also in the complete absence of university positions in ecclesiology and liturgy, except in Scotland where they usually fall under 'practical theology'. Neither is necessarily true of places dedicated to the preparation of people for ordained ministry in the Church – like theological colleges in Britain or the much larger and more well-established theological seminaries found in the USA, which are more like 'theological universities' – except insofar as their syllabuses and staff are predetermined, as in Britain they often are, by validating universities. There are many reasons for the situation in Britain, of which four can be readily identified:

1. Ecclesiology *was* a latecomer in theology, emerging many centuries later in the history of church life, when people were made self-conscious – often as the result of schisms – about the legitimacy of the branch of the Church in which they were. Even then, it was more aligned with self-reflection by the Church in its context than with theology *per se*.
2. In the preoccupation with the defence of Christian faith in the face of challenges, especially in the era from the Renaissance onward, there was a tendency to fasten on issues 'on the high ground' where particular counterclaims were made – biblical, traditional, doctrinal and ethical – and not on those related to the place where these claims were made.
3. These factors came to be interwoven with the history of universities in

the nineteenth century. In due course these 'high ground' areas came to be emphasized – often with a special methodology[1] – in the configuration of universities as they were reorganized along professional lines, professionals teaching would-be professionals, and these were favoured in the construction of syllabuses and the selection of staff. Especially where the taking of holy orders was normal for all university staff, as in England until the nineteenth century, and – long after – where in practice active members of the Churches of England and Scotland predominated, familiarity with ecclesiology and liturgy was presumed rather than attended to.

4. The development of universities to embrace research gave precedence to the purely cognitive, with a corresponding de-emphasis, if not disparagement, of the realm of the 'merely practical', including matters ethical (there is still very little teaching, or staff, in ethics in the UK), ecclesiological and liturgical. To some extent this also had to do with social attitudes, where the 'thinking' and the 'practical' were disjoined, much as an educated gentility held themselves above 'tradespeople'.

This placing for ecclesiology is an interesting matter in its own right, but it is significant as the context for the formation of people like John Macquarrie.

There is one other factor we need to recognize. As noted above, theology was significantly affected by its context, including the growing need to respond to counterclaims regarding the defensibility of Christian belief; this tended to concentrate attention on the 'high ground', rather than on 'practical' matters like the Church and its life. Even among those who worked on the 'high ground', however, not all thought it necessary to *engage* with these counterclaims. In the turmoil of the 1930s, and following World War Two (Macquarrie served as a chaplain in its later stages, and the aftermath), many simply stood their ground, or many other non-Roman Catholics turned decisively to a singularly revelation-based theology, and refused to engage with what was disparagingly called 'natural theology'. Among those who made this 'turn', the two dominant figures (Barth and Bultmann) differed strongly in their placing of theology, whether in a dialectical theological encounter between the Word of God and the word of man (Barth) or in an anthropological-existential encounter in which the Word of God was known through its transformation of human beings (Bultmann). The former disallowed the value of philosophy except insofar as it stood within the encounter, the latter employed philosophy – especially the early Heidegger – in unfolding the transformation of human beings in faith.

In both cases, however, the tendency was to focus theology in the purest moment in which God acts upon human beings, and thus – again – on the 'high ground', highlighting the individual and the individual's witness to others as the place where God effected faith, with the effect that the true Church was individuals witnessing truly to each other, and to the world. Here the Church became *inter-human practice*, the practice of true witness made actual by God, with a corresponding de-emphasis of an ordered and embodied Church. In the one case, doctrine became the testing of true witness; in the other case, philosophy was employed in discerning the ways in which transformation occurred. It is significant that John Macquarrie aligned himself with the second option, and thereafter – though not always in the same way or by reference to the same people – brought theology into conversation with philosophy, in order to make theology *intelligible* in wider discussion. But several characteristics of his work – the philosophy it employed (existentialism, and later ontology), and the locating of theology in human searching – deflected explorations away from an ecclesiology of an ordered and embodied Church.

As Macquarrie went from Scotland to the USA to England, and from the Church of Scotland and the Presbyterian Church of his forefathers to the Episcopal Church in the USA and to the Church of England, we see him assuming that the Church – as in Scottish theology – is an aspect of the practical, but giving it attention only to correct distortions. When he went to New York and the (Presbyterian-founded though latterly independent) Union Theological Seminary, he found himself among a spread of professors in New Testament, Old Testament, Church history, systematics and ethics, and others concerned with practical topics in Church (though not ecclesiology as such) and ministries, an arrangement in which ecclesiology was consigned – as in Scotland – to the realm of the practical and contextual. During this period, he did come to take the Church more seriously, but still did not approach it as a directly theological topic. And when he came to Oxford, he came again into a situation where the Church was primarily a question for the Regius Professor of Moral and Pastoral Theology, for whom ecclesiology as such might or might not be important. All these institutional settings have one thing in common: they make ecclesiology a matter for practical, rarely doctrinal, concern. The same appears to be the case with Macquarrie. We need now to explore his theology to find how far this is the case.

Ecclesiology in Existential Theology

When at the invitation of J.G. Riddell, Professor of Divinity at the University of Glasgow, Macquarrie – then a Church of Scotland parish minister – returned to academic work to do a PhD, and during it was appointed to a new lectureship at Glasgow, his work was on the relationship between Rudolf Bultmann and Martin Heidegger, with the assistance of Ian Henderson, the pioneer in Bultmann studies in the UK. With the relegating of ecclesiology – as 'someone else's business' – to the sphere of practical theology that was characteristic of Scottish theology, we might expect Macquarrie to have lost sight of the topic in his work on Bultmann. Such is not the case, however.

In the book which resulted, *An Existentialist Theology* (1955), we find a striking chapter, 'Existence in the Community', in which Macquarrie takes Bultmann to task for the inadequacies of his concepts of community and the Church. As he points out, Bultmann identifies four 'ontological' kinds of community: natural, historical, cultural and religious; the issue is how each allows for *genuine selfhood*, 'the freedom and responsibility of personality'. By Macquarrie's account of Bultmann, genuine selfhood and relationships are only possible where man is 'taken out of every (more or less perverted) human community and placed before God in radical isolation' (*Existentialist*, p. 216). He must surrender both his worldly self- and world-understanding in a decision of faith. Then, but only by God's act of grace, the human being finds new relationships in Christian community; and the community of those so graced is the ἐκκλησία. (In effect, this is a notion of the invisible Church.) That 'Christian community' is to be the fulfilment of what is intended for all human community, for 'man is created to be himself, and that means to be himself in the community' (*Existentialist*, p. 218). Insofar as this is a visible community, however, institutional and doctrinal ordering is unavoidable; and this in turn causes these relationships to degenerate.

As distinct from a community of those graced for new relationships, what is *the Church* for Bultmann? The same duality appears here as before: on the one hand, 'the Church is conceived as something which does not belong to this world . . . the instrument for proclaiming God's grace, [where on the other hand] it is conceived as embodied in actual communities within the world' (*Existentialist*, p. 219). In the one case, Bultmann says, the Church happens where the Word is proclaimed; and its function is to witness 'so that men are brought to themselves and assisted to find their authentic being'. In the other case, this is interrupted by divisions bred by human belief in self-sufficiency and in the importance of worldly things.

For Macquarrie, the problem is this: where in Bultmann's argument the Church is negatively defined as a community in which worldly differences do not count, 'the body of Christ has nothing specifically Christian about it', it has nothing to make it different from others – nihilists or existentialists or Buddhists – who turn away from self-sufficiency and worldly concern (*Existentialist*, p. 220). No, proclamation of the Word must be manifest in the Christian community in 'a spirit of love and fellowship which cannot be found outside of it'. And that leads Macquarrie to a wider statement about the relation of individualism and community in Christian life which we can summarize as follows.

What is the positive place of the individual in the Church? The Church has tended to usurp it by advocating unthinking acceptance of the gospel as a tradition, transforming it into a set of dogmas to be assented to, and multiplying the rules of an organized body. It 'has taken away from the individual the real possibility of decision', the new self-understanding that comes in faith, and the freedom that belongs to the life of faith. Macquarrie concludes: '*A direct existential relationship of the believer to God in Christ is an essential and vital element in the Christian religion*' (*Existentialist*, p. 222, italics added). In Bultmann's hands, however, focusing such a relationship in hidden – not to say 'eternal' – moments of decision beyond all the worldly conditions of most human decision-making, means that their implications for socio-political practice in the public domain cannot be specified.[2]

What is the positive place of Christian fellowship and love? Here a different set of problems come into view: the very government and administration necessary for the Church to relate to other human social entities tends to assimilate it to everyday social practices, and thereby 'to fall back into the world'. 'It appears that the collective body is always more vulnerable than the individual' (*Existentialist*, p. 223). The effect is to depersonalize the life of faith, to treat the Church as a collective – 'the sum of individual Christians' – and obscure the being-with-others which 'belongs to man's being as such'. In this respect, Macquarrie concludes, neither Heidegger nor Bultmann got very far, but '*let us remember that Christian community is an unresolved problem not for [them] alone but for the Church at large, and that not only the concept but – let us confess it – the reality of κοινωνία is all too often lacking in the Church*' (*Existentialist*, p. 224, italics added). And Macquarrie goes on to consider the Word and the sacraments as vehicles of the Church's mission and organization, and as ways in which Christ is present with the worshipping Church, through which the believer may appropriate grace and continue in the full life of the Church, but he does not go far in answering the dilemma of κοινωνία to which he had pointed.

As a contribution to the ecclesiological implications of Heidegger and Bultmann, *An Existentialist Theology* is a remarkably lucid and penetrating work. It follows existentialism itself in the sense that it relocates theology in the realm of practical anthropology; this – more or less – is where the Church has been left in the British theological tradition we described earlier. And he seeks to correlate theology with Bultmann's existentialism. As seriously as he takes existentialism, however, Macquarrie also employs standards drawn from elsewhere: he quite clearly draws on elements in the New Testament and conventional Christian theology, whose source he does not trace; and it is left a puzzle how these are established in the first place. It seems that he is operating from certain practical premises which are not declared, as if to say: 'As Christians, we know there are practices in the Church which, however problematic they may be, are more than Bultmann recognizes or allows.'

All in all, at this point, Macquarrie shares much with Bultmann, but also – both directly and by implication – goes beyond him. Like Bultmann, he gives primacy to the question of the freedom and responsibility of the individual for being-in-the-world as constituted by the grace of God given in the proclamation and reception of the Word. But unlike Bultmann, he recognizes the limitations of doing so: there is a tacit acknowledgment of the huge power of the possibilities offered in the cross and resurrection for the transformation of people, and a more direct appreciation of the Church as 'speaking "in Christ's stead"' in the world (*Existentialist*, p. 227). As to what the Church *is* and *does* in the world, however, it leaves us only with a practical dilemma: 'the reality of κοινωνία is all too often lacking in the Church' (*Existentialist*, p. 224).

Such issues were the beginning of Macquarrie's searching. They opened up questions about how *God* and *God's work* in the *faithful* of the *Church* in the *world* could be made more publicly discernible and intelligible, and how they might cohere with other kinds of understanding. The next major step in these matters was *Principles of Christian Theology*, completed at Union Theological Seminary in New York. There we find a view of systematic theology – his responsibility at Union, since the chair in philosophy had (significantly) been discontinued under the influence of Barthian theology there – which emphasized a coherent and consistent thinking of Christianity as a whole, in which '[o]ne doctrine flows into another, each supports the other and strengthens the other, and the whole is a vision of incredible strength and beauty' (*Theologian*, p. 35). That was significant as a rationale for the close relating of faith and Church already begun with Macquarrie's comment on Bultmann. But Macquarrie was also affected by two other things, a move from a strictly existentialist approach to what he called an 'existential-ontological' one, which drew more directly on Heidegger[3] and Roman Catholic theologians like Karl Rahner, and fuller experience – with the encouragement of John Knox, Professor of New Testament at Union – of a Church with more catholic traditions of worship and life (he joined an Episcopal Church, and was ordained in 1965). This allowed Macquarrie to deepen his awareness of the Church as the extension of Christ, while still leaving it as the practical-theological 'home' of Christian faith.

The Ecclesial 'Home' for Experience of the Divine

The first thing to notice about his work at this stage is that Macquarrie chose to begin from human experience and man's search for a being beyond his own, and attempted to trace 'a path from our ordinary human existence to the question of ultimate Being or God' (*Theologian*, p. 36). Macquarrie's account differs from his earlier existentialism: it is not simply a matter of *encounter* with God, for that 'lacks the idea of an inward unity between human and Divine which the doctrines of incarnation and of *theopoiesis*, the inclusion of humanity in the Divine life, express'.[4] He supplements the notion of encounter, with its connotation of dualism, by a redeveloped notion of the Divine as 'the infinite ground of all being, which . . . "lets beings be and mediates itself through them"'. 'The content of revelation is "being" or "holy being" . . . given in "revelatory experiences" where man becomes aware of the presence and manifestation of holy being.'[5] This, he believes, is what is safeguarded in the Church as derivative from Jesus Christ, in whom 'the most central possibilities of humanity [are brought] to a new level of realisation' (*Jesus Christ*, p. 36). The position in which Macquarrie puts the Church is as the 'home' of revelatory experiences of holy being in Jesus Christ, in whom corporate humanity is given a new level of realization. The position he develops, while distinctive both conceptually and practically, follows the pathway for theology found in Schleiermacher. It also shares the same difficulties, those of seeing faith as an inward disclosure of – and transformation by – the mystery of the Divine being which constitutes a particular community, to which any outward expression of faith cannot be adequate.

This is probably what accounts for the persistent tendency in Macquarrie's later theology to identify a circularity of *non-verbal expressions of faith* (as 'a quality of life') from which theology grows 'in the course of involvement in the concrete situation of faith', and to which – through its exposition of ideas and symbolic expressions – it contributes. This 'circle' of 'Applied Theology' is the area to which Part Three of *Principles of Christian Theology* is dedicated. Beginning with sections on embodied existence, and the criteria and themes of applied theology, he considers Church, ministry and mission, word and sacraments, worship and prayer, and Christianity in the world. His approach moves *from* 'the understanding of the Church *already implicit* in those theological doctrines we have been studying', *to* 'its concrete, practical problems in the modern world'

(*Principles*, p. 386). Tracing the community of faith 'as far back as we can go' to the nation chosen by God, he finds:

> [t]here has always been a community of faith in the world, continuous with the Church, and its prototype; and there still is in the world a community of faith that stretches beyond the frontiers of the Church, in the narrow sense. For this reason, one cannot draw a hard and fast line between the Church and the 'world'. (*Principles*, p. 387)

The Church, however, is distinct by virtue of the fact that it 'is to be understood as the community in which this raising of manhood to God-manhood, which we see in Christ, continues'. Even if not fully attained as yet, and the Church is not to be identified with the eschatological kingdom, 'To be in Christ is to belong to a new corporate reality ... the historical embodiment of the new humanity' (*Principles*, pp. 388–9). Comparably, Macquarrie proceeds always to distinguish between, but not divide, the Church as a theological entity and as a sociological one. From sociology it can be understood as an association, but theologically it is understood as originating in creation and continuing as 'the community in which [the] raising of manhood to Godhead, which we see in Christ, continues' (*Principles*, pp. 388–9) as the anticipation of the kingdom. From that it follows, for example, that the authority for a special ordained ministry in the Church results from the conferral of a '*way of being*' in the Church.

In his concentration on the inward dynamic of existential experience as followed corporately in the Church, Macquarrie finds the 'lower' raised to the 'higher' through the conferral of being by Being, lifting all to God-manhood as exemplified in the Christ and extended in and through the Church. This is what, in the Church, people participate in. In the course of his writings, Macquarrie reflects upon each aspect of this dynamic.

Such participation in communal experience cannot be analysed 'from outside'. It rests on sharing what is formative for this faith, that is access to *primordial revelation* – whose historical factuality is 'grounded in the community of faith' – in conjunction with 'a present experience of the holy in the community of faith' (*Principles*, p. 9). 'The scriptures of a community are a major factor in maintaining stability and a sense of continuing identity in the community itself' (*Principles*, p. 10). They, together with *tradition*, provide, interpret and correct present experience, but both tradition and experience need to be *corporately* re-appropriated by discerning analysis to disentangle legitimate developments from others; this is the means of continuing the tradition in each generation. In other words, the Church provides a practical existential and experiential 'home' for faith and the attempt to explain it and its implications in theology ('to bring faith to coherent verbal expression' (*Principles*, p. 373), which in turn guides the Church.

This view of Church and theology, beginning from participation in corporate experience, continuing by thematic reflection (on aspects of the experience) pursued through symbolic and (phenomenological) philosophical analysis, and both enlarging upon and correcting experience, lies at the heart of Macquarrie's theology. What is often distinctive and enriching is the quality of Macquarrie's reflections, informed as they are by his own engagement with Heidegger, existential phenomenology and other movements of modern thought, especially those which employ this tradition. Nevertheless, it constitutes a 'loop' beginning and ending in corporate experience, with reason – a special notion of reason as phenomenological reflection – playing an intermediate role. It is presumed that this kind of reason is sufficient for the task, at least the task of analysing experience: whether it is indeed sufficient as *ecclesial reasoning* is a question not asked. This presumption begs the question of what ecclesial reasoning might be.

Does this close the gap opened – as we have seen – in most nineteenth- and twentieth-century theology, between the theological as such and practical or applied theology? To be sure, Macquarrie does bring the two together in the experiential-reflective interaction that he undertakes, but only by making both *inward*. Correspondingly, there are some aspects of Church life – those which function as 'external' constraints – about which he is always ambivalent, for example why and how there should be a reasoned polity in Church life. These are major questions for any public body about which Macquarrie equivocates.

Furthermore, as widespread as it is in theology and theological education, there is a problem with the experiential-reflective mode of theological reasoning. Reflection is always *posterior* to experience, and *prior to* further experience. It is a 'moment' after and before experience when experience is correlated with theological reflection, which (since it is often concerned with 'high ground' issues of the sort discussed earlier) is usually so generalized as to be disconnected from experience. In other words, even the best theological reflection loses touch with the particularities of experience. If this is so, after the gap between the theological and the practical has been ushered out of the front door, it returns through the back door!

One final comment. By concentrating on the experiential in his analysis, it seems to me that Macquarrie cannot proceed far with the investigation of what (after Exodus 3.14 ff.) I choose to call the *infinitely intensive identity of the Lord* and the possibility – no, the actuality – of a mysteriously intensive sociality in Israel and the Church which embraces and brings reconciliation (through both reason and love) in the *indefinite and fragmenting extensity* found in the Church and in the world today. If this is so, it decidedly limits the value of Macquarrie's theology for today's Church and its mission in the world.

Notes

1 For example, philosophy was taken as the means by which doctrinal questions were approached, and philosophy – more often than theology as such – was firmly entrenched in faculties of divinity, especially in England.

2 See Georgina Morley, *John Macquarrie's Theology: The Grace of Being*, Aldershot: Ashgate, 2003, p. 80.

3 Significantly, Macquarrie had been one of the two translators of Heidegger's *Being and Time*. It needs also to be noted that he had written a very compressed introductory history, *Twentieth Century Religious Thought* (1963) tracing the interaction of philosophy, *including social philosophy*, and theology. This displayed the options available, but did not attempt an overall, or master, argument. Nonetheless, the preparation of the book made him aware of contemporary Roman Catholic thought (like Hans Urs von Balthasar and Karl Rahner) which – in Rahner's case – resembled the position he was developing.

4 Keith Ward, *Religion and Revelation*, Oxford: Clarendon Press, 1994, p. 228.

5 *Religion and Revelation*, p. 228, quoting *Principles*, pp. 95, 90.

24 Theology of, by, and for the People of God

PAUL WIGNALL

Of the People, by the People, for the People

In *The Faith of the People of God* (1972), significantly subtitled *A Lay Theology*, John Macquarrie proposes a 'theology of the people of God, by the people of God, for the people of God' (*People*, p. 6). As the finished form of work first presented as the McMath Lectures in the Diocese of Michigan and the Prideaux Lectures at the University of Exeter, *People* explores what it might mean to speak of a 'lay theology' and ends by envisioning:

> a radically new type of community so drastically transformed, so discontinuous with the communities we now know and so transcendent of current utopias, that it could fairly be called eschatological; and yet, as a community recognisably human, personal and fulfilling, it would be in another sense continuous with the communities we now know and are already prefigured in that community we call the people of God ... (*People*, 1972, p. 108)

Writing in the decade following the Second Vatican Council, Macquarrie's commitment to a 'lay theology' is supported on a flood tide of thinking within the churches in which studies of the *laos* – the whole people of God – opened up new options in ecclesiology and sacramental theology, as well as in issues of church order and discipline.[1] This, of course, reflects a cultural moment in which colonialism was giving way to hopeful autonomy, supported by the ideals of the United Nations and the increasingly normative use of rights language in moral and political theory and practice – notwithstanding other more pessimistic assessments at the height of the Cold War. It also reflects the impact of nearly universal education in Europe and America especially, and with it the desire of many articulate 'lay' people to share in church government, in ministry, and in theological explorations *from the perspective of those who wish to remain outside the professionalized clergy.*

The 1980s saw the collapse of many of the ideals and hopes for a new polity which would bring about the abolition of the laity[2] as a distinct category and foster an ecclesial reordering of a single people of God internally differentiated by function rather than by any special status conferred at priestly ordination or episcopal consecration. But Vatican II took the cork out of the bottle and released a new energy into churches whose polity had been essentially catholic, episcopal and hierarchical. And a part of this energy is without doubt the development of what Macquarrie looked for: theology 'of the people ... by the people ... for the people'. Just as the subsequent development of contextual Bible study and base ecclesial communities in South Africa and Latin America (for example) recontextualized the forum for theological study, so in the 1990s in the United Kingdom the growth of 'local theology' (John Reader) and 'ordinary theology' (Jeff Astley)[3] offered the possibilities of a new language and new settings for theology with direct impact back into ecclesial theory, polity and practice.

Reframing Ecclesiology

Traditional ecclesiology assumes stable, status-filled communities in which boundaries are secure and secured by tight definitions of belonging and in which conflict is transitory and ended either by repentance or ejection. This is often, again, seen to mirror the nature of God as changelessly trinitarian. In this polity Christology is predicated on obedience – the obedience of the Son to the Father, even to death, rewarded by resurrection; the obedience to Christ of his people, rewarded by eternal life. And the work of the Holy Spirit as guide into all truth is about ensuring that (through obedience to a priesthood and episcopate specially endowed with the Spirit) we do and believe what we need to do and believe to stay in an obedient relationship to God through Christ.

A caricature? Maybe, but perhaps not far away from ecclesial ideology[4] as experienced, and defended, by many in Catholic and Anglican traditions – and indeed in non-episcopal polities, where professionalization of ministry has had similar effects. Stable communities inside secure boundaries are crucial to this ideology. However, there is an increasing recognition that such assumed stabilities and securities are illusory.

Cognitive geographers argue that we perceive our environment through a complex process of creating, storing and using our acquired spatial knowledge.[5] But this knowledge is not static: it depends upon our awareness of how we move through spaces and how we interact with others as they move through the same spaces. Cognitive mapping is therefore a dynamic process in which our world is constantly being reassessed as we adjust the paths we take through the places and spaces on which we lay the footprints of our daily lives.

For ecologists and environmental scientists, community is also better defined as a set of diverse populations inhabiting a space.[6] While some communities are closed – their boundaries tightly defined by geographical or climatic conditions – most are open, with porous boundaries. Both within and between open communities we can identify flows of energy, migrations for example, often closely linked with the food chain. Such flows operate between and through nodes – places where different forms of energy are present: copulation, ingestation, sleep, for example. To define a community, then, it is necessary to define the energy flows and the nodal points of which it consists. Community as a set of diverse populations interacting as they flow through nodes may have the appearance of stability, but it is a stability born of energy and movement.

Almost all human societies are open communities in this sense: movements of trade, work, learning, leisure or spiritual activities passing through nodes which absorb and retain or recycle energy. Nodes may include private homes, pubs, schools, medical centres, churches or chapels. Because contemporary communities are open the energy flows pass beyond obvious geographical boundaries of administrative convenience (Welcome to Truro) and into other spaces: we are likely to travel to work, to school, even to church in the morning, and return to our homes in the evening. We may go out to the 'local' for a drink, or travel out again for recreation. But energy finds its own flows and individuals tend to create routes between nodes that will enhance and recycle energy rather than block it. Flows always find the short cuts, whether, for example, they are rat runs to avoid traffic jams and conserve physical energy or, rather differently, passing through the so-called 'thin places' where the transcendent seems to be experienced ('I always walk through the churchyard on the way to the post office') and spiritual energy is recycled.

If communities are essentially dynamic, energy-filled systems made up of sets of a range of populations, then any ecclesiology (but especially one which attempts to do justice to a local community) must itself be capable of expressing a dynamism in the way it both receives and recycles (or blocks) energy flows from the surrounding environment, recognizing that it both gains and loses some of its dynamism from those flows. Which is just a somewhat systems-theory way of saying 'Pray for the welfare of the city, for on its welfare will your welfare depend' (Jer. 29.7).

Actual energy flows within communities are unmediated. Leaving Euston railway station, walking towards Euston Square, the wide concrete path arrives at a small flight of steps, and at the bottom bears right towards the pedestrian crossing. At the top of the steps, and down the bank, a pathway has been made across the grass where countless commuters have taken a short cut – of no more than ten metres. The flow of energy has by-passed the steps and found an alternative. Jeremiah 29–31 bear witness to just such a creative alternative, and one, says the prophet, endorsed by the Lord. That alternative has three elements, each of which endorses the principle of personal responsibility.[7]

Jeremiah calls on the exiles in Babylon to take wives from the people they are living among, to build houses and live in them, to pray for the welfare of the city to which they have been exiled, and to refuse to listen to the 'prophets and the diviners' who are deceiving them with an easy future (Jer. 29.5–9). They are, in other words, to take responsibility for their life and their welfare in exile and to accept that it is pleasing to the Lord (29.11). Second, the people are called to take personal responsibility for their shortcomings – 'all shall die for their own sins' (31.30) – the outcome of which is a blessing by the Lord and a time of carnival and plenty (31.13). And finally this carnival celebration of the new covenant, written on each and every heart (31.33–34) will take place in an enlarged Jerusalem (31.38–40), extended for all who 'know the Lord' – an open community, with boundaries able to encompass all who have returned from exile.

As David Rhymer points out, this vision of Jeremiah is in stark contrast to the control over those who have returned from exile we find in Nehemiah 8:5–8 where Ezra 'standing above the people' on a specially made wooden platform, reads the book of the law and a named list of authorized people 'helped the people to understand the law . . . [and] gave the sense' (8.7b, 8b). For Jeremiah, direct unmediated access to Torah is not only desirable it is also possible; for Ezra/Nehemiah there is only officially mediated and interpreted Torah.

The outcome of unmediated reading for Jeremiah is both a widening and relaxing of boundaries and also an atmosphere of carnival – it is characterized by new flows and new nodes of energy; it also implies a radically non-hierarchical understanding of religious community.

Similar issues are raised in the late New Testament document known as 1 Peter. Bruce Winter argues that Jeremiah 29 lies behind the earlier sections, at least, of this social ethic for third generation Christians.[8] For Winter this social ethic stands alongside 'a living eschatological hope [t]hat enabled the Christian to place personal concerns second to the needs of others in the city' (p. 19). This puts 1 Peter in a similar stable to the somewhat later Letter to Diognetus in which Christians are said to 'take part in everything as citizens' but rather more precisely as 'resident

THEOLOGY OF, BY, AND FOR THE PEOPLE OF GOD

aliens' whose home is elsewhere. What is lacking, of course, from this early Christian social ethic is any sense of Jeremiah's reciprocity. The exiles in Babylon would gain their welfare from the welfare of the city; the diaspora Christians are characterized rather as being no threat to the city (indeed at best public benefactors). All that Christians will gain from these Graeco-Roman interactions significantly goes unremarked.

Top Down / Bottom Up

Theology 'of the people of God, by the people of God, for the people of God', suggests Macquarrie. Does this imply (or could it imply) the sort of unmediated reading and practice at which Jeremiah hints? Macquarrie's phrase is deliberately redolent of the ending of the speech delivered by Abraham Lincoln at the dedication of the Gettysburg military cemetery on 19 November 1863: 'this nation, under God, shall have a new birth of freedom – and . . . government of the people, by the people, for the people, shall not perish from the earth.' The same speech begins by looking back to United States Declaration of Independence on 4 July 1776 with its vision of democratic government and equality under God. Of course, for the founding fathers, equality and democracy excluded women, children and slaves. But, as Lincoln eloquently reminded his hearers, that vision lays down the possibility of a widening of boundaries of mutuality and equality and democracy; a widening that would later take in the protests of Rosa Parks and Martin Luther King and lay down a precedent for human rights theory and practice. In using Lincoln's phrase, Macquarrie invokes essentially republican ideals as he sets an agenda for lay theology.

Vatican II envisaged a crucial witnessing role which properly belonged to the whole people of God, out of which ministries emerge. But there is no incipient republicanism here: what is given with one hand is quickly taken away with the other. In *Lumen Gentium* II.10 we read:

> Though they differ from one another in essence and not only in degree, the common priesthood of the faithful and the ministerial or hierarchical priesthood are nonetheless interrelated: each of them in its own special way is a participation in the one priesthood of Christ. The ministerial priest, by the sacred power he enjoys, teaches and rules the priestly people; acting in the person of Christ, he makes present the eucharistic sacrifice, and offers it to God in the name of all the people. But the faithful, in virtue of their royal priesthood, join in the offering of the Eucharist. They likewise exercise that priesthood in receiving the

sacraments, in prayer and thanksgiving, in the witness of a holy life, and by self-denial and active charity.

This is a fundamentally assymetrical relationship. The priesthood of the faithful is in every significant sense passive: they are the seedbed for the 'ministerial or hierarchical priesthood', they receive teaching and the sacraments, they deny self. Not only passive, but subsidiary to the witness of the bishop. The decree *Ad Gentes* sees the order of bishops, as the successors of the apostles, as the key witnesses, missionaries and martyrs 'with the prayers and help of the whole Church' (I.6).

This ecclesiology sits in stark contrast to that embraced by the World Council of Churches in the declaration at Lima in 1982.[9] In the section on Christian Ministry, the Lima document begins from a position not far from that of Jeremiah 31: 'Christ established a new access to the Father' (M4). In just the same way, it is the community that receives 'diverse and complementary gifts' and all members are called to discover 'with the help of the community' the gifts they have received and then to use them (M5). Similarly:

> ministry in its broadest sense denotes service to which the whole people of God is called, whether as individuals, as a local community, or as the universal Church. Ministry or ministries can also denote the particular institutional forms which this service may take . . . The term ordained ministry refers to persons who have received a charism and whom the church appoints for service by ordination through the invocation of the Spirit and the laying on of hands. (M7 b–c)

Ministry here is 'of the people, by the people and for . . .' everyone. The boundaries are made wider to encompass the world. Ministry is not, in the Lima document, a covert form of evangelization, but simply service to the world made by God, which includes service within the Church itself. It is still derived from the apostles but their witness is 'unique and unrepeatable' (M10). The ordained ministry exercises a special witness and role as 'heralds . . . leaders and teachers . . . pastors.' (M11). In other words, to support the people of God in their varied ministries and callings in the world – which is the primary ministry, practically as well as ecclesially and theologically.

Practice in Anglicanism (and, as the reductions in the number of ordinations to the priesthood takes effect, in European and American Roman Catholicism too) has undoubtedly embraced the Lima model rather than that of Vatican II. Most English Anglican dioceses now have options for authorized lay ministries in pastoral care, evangelism and the leading of worship over and above the traditional lay roles of Reader and churchwarden.[10] The resources too of those who are ordained but remain in secular employment, though often underestimated and even ignored by stipendiary clergy and those responsible for diocesan planning and strategy, grow in value year by year. But there remains a great deal of ambivalence: are those who hold such ministries, lay and ordained, often alongside full time jobs and therefore with much needed insights and skills, seen as much more than spare pairs of hands to be delegated tasks others cannot do? The Church of England, as the report on the proposed new patterns of training for lay and ordained cannot hide, still finds it hard to understand, accept, resource or use truly collaborative models of ministry.[11]

Anglican ecclesiology has not yet taken seriously either the insights of contemporary cognitive geography with its awareness of interacting energy flows, or what we might call Jeremiah's ecclesiology, in which the many overlapping populations in a community are blessings to one another. We remain disturbingly in the world of Ezra/Nehemiah, the pulpit and the mediated reading of Scripture.

Perhaps 'Nehemiah, who was the governor, and Ezra the priest and scribe, and the Levites who taught the people' (Neh. 8.9a) were concerned that wrong interpretation would lead the people astray, but it feels more like an exercise in political and social realism – fear of the loss of control, and potential chaos, of Jeremiah's stress on personal responsibility and the power of the people to interpret Torah for themselves through the covenant written on their hearts. The outcome, to be sure, is great rejoicing (Neh. 8.10–12) but it is followed by a day of mourning (9.1) and then the great separation in which 'those of Israelite descent separated themselves from all foreigners' (9.2), a process which ends with the revisioning of the covenant 'written on their hearts' (Jer. 31.33) into a contract 'a sealed agreement in writing' signed by 'our officials, our Levites, and our priests' (Neh. 9.38). The fear of chaos lurks not too far behind the assertion of order alongside law.

In the end the issue is one of language. The literary critic and philosopher of language, Mikhail Bakhtin, argues that language is fundamentally dialogic in character and that any one language is really a set of different language uses (dialects), each with its own world view.[12] He writes:

> At any given moment of its evolution, language is stratified . . . into languages that are socio-ideological: languages of social groups, 'professional' and 'generic' languages, languages of generations and so forth . . . heteroglot languages . . . [T]his is . . . what insures [sic] its dynamics: stratification and heteroglossia widen and deepen as long as language is alive and developing . . . .[13]

As well as this centrifugal tendency of language, says Bakhtin, there is also a centripetal energy which works to make it *monoglossic*, unifying the range of dialects. For Bakhtin, this monoglossic tendency includes the languages of discipline, regulation and dogma. Language also creates ways of thinking: dialects constrain the imagination unless they can be brought into dynamic interaction with one another. In Bakhtin's terms, language needs the polyglossic and heteroglossic options – spaces where dialects can contest with one another: 'Only polyglossia fully frees consciousness from the tyranny of its own language and its own myth of language.'[14] Polyglossia operates across languages while heteroglossia operates between dialects within a language.

In our terms, the interacting energy-flows within a community each have their own linguistic dialect, with all that implies about world-view and consciousness. But these flows need spaces (nodes) where contestation is possible. For Jeremiah, the physical, moral, and even erotic ('marry their daughters') spaces created by the Babylonian exile were just such nodes in which a new, richer understanding of the Lord and the covenant could be found. But polyglossic and heteroglossic possibilities are the enemies of the monoglossic forces – or any group who would seek to impose their world-view and understanding on the wider community – squeezing the centripetal opportunities of language and the enrichment of world-view through the interaction of diverse populations into a single channel of so-called blessing.

The language of 'the people of God' is a struggle between the heteroglossic and the monoglossic. Ironically, a crucial boost of energy to diversify the language with which to describe, and therefore live out, the Christian faith in late twentieth-century Britain has probably come from the study of religions other than Christianity. A space has been created for the polyglossic option and so to enable us to look from other angles at Christian linguistic practices. This has been reinforced by extending the 'religious studies' option into the heart of the religious education syllabus, and in the growth in the study of theology by adult lay-people. Indeed one counter-argument to the development of so-called 'faith schools' must be the long-term impoverishment of religious language (and therefore religious experience) which such a monoglossic drift would entail.

Don't Stop the Carnival

Jeremiah looks to a time of carnival; so too does Bakhtin.[15] For him, carnival is that social moment when languages enter the world of joyful parody, a time of cultural subversion which reveals the ideological tendencies of any one language by putting into playful contests with others. Carnival is the crucial node in which linguistic energy flows come together to be re-energized, widened, reborn. Carnival is, of course, also a time of risk, when language and its allied social energies may spin out of control. But perhaps an ecclesiology 'of the people of God, by the people of God and for the people of God' needs to be willing to take just those risks and make a space for carnival so that Christian language and practice can be re-energized and enriched by other languages and other experiences. 'Pray for the welfare of the city, on its welfare will your welfare depend.'

Notes

1 Relevant documents from Vatican II include the Constitutions *Lumen Gentium* and *Guadium et Spes* and the decree *Ad Gentes*. For an informal, lightly fictionalized, account see Malachi Martin, *Vatican*, London: HarperCollins, 1986. Readers of this novel will see something of the power of reaction against the use of the phrase, and concept, *the People of God*, both at the Council and in its aftermath.

2 The phrase is from R. Paul Stevens, *The Abolition of the Laity*, Carlisle: Paternoster Press, 1999.

3 J. Reader, *Local Theology: Church and Community in Dialogue*, London: SPCK, 1994; J. Astley, *Ordinary Theology: Looking, Listening and Learning in Theology*, Aldershot: Ashgate, 2002.

4 I am using *ideology* here as a close relative of Marx's theory of commodity fetishism. A meaning which, in Terry Eagleton's words, 'retains an emphasis on false or deceptive beliefs but regards such beliefs as arising not from the interests of a dominant class but from the material structure of society as a whole': T. Eagleton, *Ideology*, London: Verso, 1991, p. 30.

5 For an introduction to the disciplines of cognitive geography and cognitive mapping see B. Bartley *et al.*, *Space, Theory and Contemporary Human Geography*, London: Continuum, 2002; R. Kitchin and M. Blades, *The Cognition of Geographic Space*, London: I.B. Tauris, 2001.

6 The classic text on community ecology is E.P. Odum, *Fundamentals of Ecology*, Philadelphia and London: W.B. Saunders Co., 1959.

7 I am indebted to my colleague David Rhymer for his insights into this passage, and for conversations with him in which its implications for contemporary church polity and practice have been explored. See D. Rhymer, 'Jeremiah 31:31–34' in *Interpretation* 59/3, July 2005, pp. 294–6

8 Bruce W. Winter, *Seek the Welfare of the City*, Carlisle: Paternoster Press, 1994, esp. pp. 11–23.

9 World Council of Churches Faith and Order Paper 111, 1982, sections M2–M11.

10 Important texts here include: *All Are Called: Towards a Theology of the*

Laity, London: CIO Publishing, 1985; A. Bowden and M. West, *Dynamic Local Ministry*, London: Continuum, 2000; A. Bowden, *Ministry in the Countryside: A Model for the Future*, London: Continuum, 2003.

11 *Shaping the Future: Formation for Ministry within a Learning Church*, London: Church House Publishing, 2005.

12 A valuable resource and introduction to Bakhtin's work can be found in M Holquist, (ed.), *The Dialogic Imagination: Four* Essays, University of Texas Press, 1982.

13 M. Bakhtin, 'Discourse in the Novel', in P. Rice and P. Waugh (eds), *Modern Literary Theory: A Reader*, London: Hodder Arnold, 2001, p. 199.

14 In Holquist, *Dialogic Imagination*, p. 61.

15 See especially, M. Bakhtin, *Rabelais and His World*, Indiana University Press, 1984.

25 Body Language:
John Macquarrie on the Eucharist

PETER GROVES

Anglican Catholicism, at least since the mid-nineteenth century, has among its panoply of distinguished scholars produced relatively few 'theologians', if by that unsatisfactory term we do not mean those whose expertise is principally in biblical and historical studies. Tractarianism lost its greatest theologian when John Henry Newman underwent the most significant of the many Victorian conversions to Roman Catholicism and was received into the Roman Catholic church at Littlemore in 1845. The controversialists who remained and fought the Tractarian corner, and their successors in the ritualist and liturgical disputes which followed, tended to focus their arguments on the interpretation of historical texts and formularies, rather than any attempt to produce philosophically original doctrinal theology. Well into the twentieth century one can identify giants of patristic scholarship, biblical studies, liturgical history, all of whom would have been happy to think of themselves as catholic Anglicans, but systematic and philosophical theology did not fare so well before the writings of Austin Farrer, Eric Mascall and the subject of this volume, John Macquarrie.

At first sight, there would seem to be little to connect Macquarrie with one of his celebrated predecessors as a Canon Professor at Christ Church, Edward Bouverie Pusey. Pusey was an orientalist, a linguist and a historian of terrifying erudition but overwhelming biblical conservatism, and certainly no philosopher. Macquarrie, by contrast, has been an ambassador for existentialism, and a mainstay of bibliographies in philosophy as well as theology departments, and has never shown the slightest fear of developments in biblical criticism and New Testament history. Despite the distance between them, I should like to suggest in what follows that Macquarrie's writings on eucharistic theology, and on the doctrine of the eucharistic presence in particular, are very strikingly Tractarian in style and content, and not simply in the fact that they defend catholic eucharistic theology from within the Anglican tradition. Tractarian eucharistic theologies, such as those of William Palmer, Isaac Williams, and Pusey himself, so scandalous in their own time and place (Pusey was suspended from preaching in 1843 as a result of an otherwise innocuous sermon which defended, in passing, an objective eucharistic presence), now look moderate and inclusive and might be applauded by many more recent critics of transubstantiation. Macquarrie's work reflects such a moderate account. However, he makes an interesting departure from the Tractarians at least, if not from their ritualistic descendants, in his championing of the practice of eucharistic devotion outside the liturgical context of the celebration itself, specifically in his defence of Benediction of the Blessed Sacrament. Whether this defence can sit altogether happily with his otherwise inclusive account of eucharistic theology I shall try to explore.

Macquarrie insists that authentic Christian theology comes from within a context of prayer and worship. His work *A Guide to the Sacraments* (1997) is a testimony to his own maxim, not least because it is clear and accessible to many Christian worshippers who have had little academic engagement with theology or Christian history. Philosophically the work is grounded in a robust understanding of the 'sacramental principle', whereby the divine initiative in creation provides us with a universe made up of objects which are never simply things, inert and unable to bear meaning or enter into relationship. In this 'sacramental universe', a term borrowed from William Temple, *Nature and Man* (1934), the matter of creation becomes 'transparent' in so far as it is able to point beyond itself and engage us in a network of interaction and relationship through its symbolic character. In Jesus Christ humanity has become completely transparent in its revelation of the divine, and thus, with Edward Schillebeeckx, Macquarrie insists that Christ is the 'primordial sacrament' (*Sacraments*, ch. 4).

In *A Guide to the Sacraments*, discussion of the Eucharist begins with the ordinary and the everyday, Macquarrie is keen first and foremost to emphasize that the Eucharist is a meal, that bread and wine are food, that developments such as the decline of grace before meals are consonant with a loss of a sense of a meal as something sacred, a loss which reflects what elsewhere he calls 'the lack of any feeling for the holy, the failure to recognise that anything is sacred' (*Sacraments*, p. 81).

This work echoes the earlier *Principles of Christian Theology*, in rejecting Aquinas's teaching on transubstantiation. Two specific reasons are given in *Principles* for this rejection, and one of these is philosophical. It is also unsurprising. The terms 'substance' and 'accidents' are unacceptable because, in Macquarrie's system, 'the world is seen not as an aggregate of substances but as a structure of meaning' (*Principles*, p. 479), and substantial language must be replaced with existential-ontological vocabulary. In the Eucharist we have to do with the presence and manifestation of Being, focused in a particular act. We are drawn into this act by the initiative of the divine (Being-itself), and participate in it (just as we participate in Being) as living members of the Body of Christ.

We might wonder whether Macquarrie is not having his philosophical cake and eating it here. Unlike those critics who unthinkingly call Aquinas's teaching on transubstantiation 'Aristotelian' – P. J. Fitzpatrick remarks nicely that the terms are Aristotelian only in the same sense as forged 'money' is money[1] – Macquarrie appreciates Aquinas's concern to rule out more than he rules in. He calls the account 'one of the strongest possible safeguards against . . . magical views' (*Principles*, p. 479). However, the shortage of space he gives to the topic prevents an acknowledgement of all the rigorous denials Aquinas goes on to make, denials that leave one wondering to what extent this talk of 'substance' has any connection with the schematic metaphysics of substance that Macquarrie rejects: after discussing transubstantiation itself, Aquinas goes on to deny that Christ is present in the Eucharist as in a place, or that his presence can be seen, or that the Body of Christ is moved when the host is moved, that one is nearer to it at the altar than one is to distant objects.[2] His philosophical understanding of substance has been quite exploded by the doctrine of transubstantiation, and he is at best able to offer a way of talking which – while it might not clearly make sense – is at least not manifestly self-contradictory. Macquarrie, by contrast, finds room for the presence-and-manifestation (sic) of Being in the sacrament of the Eucharist with very little philosophical sleight of hand.

In the later *Guide to the Sacraments*, the sympathetic reading of Aquinas returns, and added to it is a sketch of a more recent idea, transignification, an idea Macquarrie introduces not because he thinks it can offer a thoroughgoing philosophical explanation, but because ' it throws some light on the eucharistic mystery without involving us in any materialism or magic' (*Sacraments*, p. 134). Traditional accounts of transubstantiation are often criticized for seeming to treat the question of the eucharistic presence in isolation from the ritual action which is the celebration itself. Macquarrie notes that eucharistic language is 'performative'. There is a connection to be made, it seems, between his caution concerning 'substance' (which risks describing something like a static physical object) and the essentially performative nature of the church's eucharistic action, an action that involves something always being given.

This performative nature brings us to the subject of 'body language'. The phrase which gives this essay its title is Macquarrie's own term for an important 'test' in eucharistic theology (*Sacraments*, p. 125), a test that can illuminate not just our talk of the real presence, but also of the Eucharist as a meal, and its sacrificial character. The 'body language' concerned is almost always devotional. It involves liturgical practice, physical setting, the vocabulary of worship, individual acts of piety, all of which tell us something about what it is we are doing when we celebrate the Eucharist. In this the translator of Heidegger finds a parallel in the translator of Wittgenstein. In her remarkable paper 'On Transubstantiation', Elizabeth Anscombe began with the extraordinary words, 'It is easiest to tell what transubstantiation is by saying this: little children should be taught about it as early as possible.'[3] She goes on to demonstrate how this might be done: not by using the word 'transubstantiation', but to focus the child's attention on the action of the priest, by encouraging the child to pray the Eucharist itself, in words and in actions, acknowledging the presence of Christ as Lord, bowing one's head as if to a monarch, and so on. Wittgenstein himself used the example of the real presence[4] to emphasize, against the empiricism of G. E. Moore and others, the importance of the context in which our claims to knowledge and belief are made. The interwoven forms of life that allow us to make doctrinal statements are essential to understanding those statements: remove doctrine from practice and its statements become empty.

Body language is important, but it is not alone decisive. Eucharistic teaching can be better or worse teaching, as the brief critique of Aquinas makes clear. It is in his survey and analysis of differing eucharistic theologies that Macquarrie is at his most Tractarian, something we can see as much in his choice of subject as his conclusions. First of all, he is concerned to adopt as inclusive an interpretation of the word 'transubstantiation' as can reasonably be offered. It was a commonplace of Tractarian apologetics that Anglicans ought to believe in the real objective presence of Christ in the Eucharist, but that they ought also to reject the doctrine of transubstantiation. This doctrine they clearly understood as something 'carnal', a word which appears repeatedly in Pusey's polemic against Roman Catholicism.[5] Such an understanding is, of course, unfair to Catholic theology as represented by Aquinas for example, but even a fairer interpretation of transubstantiation needs, in Macquarrie's view, to be widened, so that the term denotes not simply a particular philosophical approach to the problem of establishing a vocabulary to describe the eucharistic change and the real presence, but any account which emphasizes the fact of that presence, rather than the 'how' of its mechanism. Thus, to return to Tractarian claims, the general term 'real presence' receives a tick while the particular philosophical use of 'transubstantiation' does not.

More noticeable, however, to anyone familiar with the endless back-and-forth arguments of Tractarians and their various opponents (most obviously, Roman Catholics on the one hand, and Protestant Anglicans on the other) is Macquarrie's concern to support his position by recourse to the classic documents of these aged debates. So in *A Guide to the Sacraments* we find approving discussion of The First Prayer Book of King Edward VI, 1549, and its formula of administration: 'The body of our Lord Jesus Christ which was given for thee, preserve thy body and soul unto everlasting life.' That document is naturally contrasted with its successor (since the 1552 Prayer Book has communion given with the words: 'Take and eat this in remembrance that Christ died for thee, and feed on him in thy heart by faith with thanksgiving'). Mention is made several times of Cranmer, with the stress coming always upon the liturgical text produced rather than the theological writings of the individual compiler. Also appearing are the Articles of Religion, and in particular Article XXVIII with its observation that the sacrament of the Eucharist 'was not by Christ's ordinance reserved, carried about, lifted up, or worshipped'. In all of this discussion, Macquarrie seems to do what he admits to when considering eucharistic sacrifice: 'as far as Anglicanism is concerned' to 'follow Cardinal Newman's policy and read its classic documents in the most catholic sense they will bear' (*Sacraments*, p. 142).

The point of interest here is not so much whether Macquarrie's defence of the Catholicism of the historic Anglican formularies holds water (though the Tractarian reading of the sixteenth- and seventeenth-century Church of England could hardly be said to be fashionable among contemporary historians). Rather, what is remarkable is seeing one of the giants of recent philosophical theology rehearsing the debates of the nineteenth century, debates never settled within Anglicanism. This historical approach to doctrinal questions is precisely that adopted by adherents to the Oxford Movement from William Palmer onwards, and Pusey's voluminous writings on the subject of the Eucharist consist almost entirely of the tireless adducing of authorities from the early Church, as well as from the seventeenth-century Church of England, in opposition to what he thinks is Roman Catholic teaching.

Pusey's views on the subject did develop. He acknowledges that the 'carnal' understanding which he finds repugnant is not taught by Trent. His later insistence that Roman transubstantiation entailed a doctrine of physical change, in spite of Robert Wilberforce's protestations to the contrary, might be interpreted as a piece of self-defence, in that maintaining the integrity of his own position in opposition to transubstantiation would prove extremely difficult if 'transubstantiation' required not a corporeal or carnal, but a spiritual or sacramental, change as he himself

insisted. By the time of the *Eirenicon* (a work whose title belies its controversialism) he admitted that what the Articles deny in one sense (physical
change), Trent affirms in another (metaphysical change).[6] Macquarrie
too allows that it is a 'corrupt' form of the doctrine of transubstantiation
that is found to be problematic: 'we must conclude that by the fifteenth
century the austere doctrine of transubstantiation had degenerated into
the semi-magical teaching which the reformers attacked' (*Sacraments*,
p. 129).

However, the difficulties which Pusey and Macquarrie have in common
are not solved if we simply remove the physicalist interpretation which
they reject. There is, it seems, something that is in principle inappropriate
about the theological discourse of transubstantiation. *A Guide to the
Sacraments* reflects a theological style we might call devotional. The same
word can aptly describe the approach to theologies of the eucharistic
presence that one finds in Pusey and his followers. There is a sense, in
this style, that danger lurks in over-intellectualizing something so miraculous as Christ's condescension in the Church's offering of the Eucharist.
When Pusey, in his *Letter to the Bishop of Oxford*, writes 'with good Bp.
Andrewes I leave it a mystery' both aspects of the Tractarian eucharistic
style are evident: Pusey is stating a firm opinion, and citing an early modern authority, while not venturing too far in speculation or philosophical
analysis.

In a paper delivered as part of the anniversary celebrations of the
Oxford Movement which took place in 1983, Macquarrie says that
'Pusey explicitly rejected the doctrine of transubstantiation because . . .
it offended against the Tractarian principle of reserve'.[7] Pusey also felt
that the 'carnal' understanding of transubstantiation which was his target was something contrary to Scripture, but Macquarrie's invocation of
'reserve' is telling. Here, caution is noted as being a principle of eucharistic theology in particular, a principle that characterizes the 'devotional'
approach to the subject we have identified. I commented earlier that in
the *Principles* two reasons are given for rejecting Aquinas's account.
One is philosophical, but the other devotional: it is 'perhaps an attempt
to reach too precise an interpretation of what must remain mysterious'
(*Principles*, p. 480).

Much is said about the wide applications of the Tractarian principle of
'reserve'. The treatise of Isaac Williams (printed in two parts, as Tracts 80
and 87) is, among other things, an exercise in theological conservatism,
which might provide a methodological defence against almost any form
of theological modernism. When considering the practical applications of
'reserve', Williams's work exemplifies the provocative controversialism
of the 1830s:

Whenever, also, there is a secret doubt of an opinion which we wish to entertain, there is a disposition to dispute and persuade, in order that by obtaining the persuasions of others, we may establish our own convictions. This may be seen in the origin of the doctrine of Transubstantiation: it arose in a dereliction and forgetfulness of the discipline of reserve on that subject; in a want of the high and ancient reverence; in a desire to establish and prove to the world a great secret of GOD.[8]

The 'low and carnal conceit which Transubstantiation introduced' has left humanity trying 'to look into the ark of God, to pry into those secret things which the Almighty has reserved unto himself' (p. 101). Strong stuff, but force of polemic aside, the point is the same: the eucharistic presence is not appropriate for human theorizing. As we have seen, an element of such an attitude runs through Macquarrie's work, both early and more recent. In one particular context, however, we find the principle of 'reserve' taken to something of an extreme, despite the fact that that context – the practice of Benediction – is an example of the very innovatory tendency which Williams, Pusey and the other Tractarians were so quick to criticize.

Benediction is a popular service, that is to say, a people's service. The clever and the sophisticated do not come much to Benediction, but the simple, the poor, those who acknowledge an emptiness in their lives that only God can fill. Even those who might not come to Holy Communion will sometimes come to Benediction where God reaches out to them though they think they are only on the fringes. I think of some of those with whom I have knelt at Benediction: harassed citydwellers in New York, working-class people from the back streets of Dublin, soldiers serving in the deserts of North Africa, Indian Christians living as a tiny minority . . . They have all had the grace of humility.[9]

Benediction, we learn, is fundamentally something for the simple. Scholastic enquiry, it seems, will prevent us from knowing our need of God. The choice of Beatitude is noteworthy: Macquarrie is careful not to imply that attendance at Benediction constitutes 'seeing God'. Here, in the defence of eucharistic adoration, body language again becomes important. Attendance at Benediction is an act of worship, a devotional act in which the one who seeks God comes to offer himself or herself in the presence of Christ. The Tractarians were, of course, distinctly uneasy about the ritualistic fervour that followed so quickly upon their theological disputation. His devotion to Benediction takes Macquarrie some distance away from Palmer, Pusey and Williams. In stark contrast to Macquarrie's attractive approach of simplicity, Williams's tract on 'reserve' lists this very practice as an indulgence which shows not reverence but desire for effect rather than truth:

> The want of reserve and reverence which attends the elevation of the Host, and the public processions connected with it, is very great indeed: . . . it is popular impression, and not a sense of GOD's presence, which is considered: for here there can be no true veneration . . .[10]

Difference of context goes a long way to explain difference of opinion in this case. More interesting, however, is whether this extreme of eucharistic practice can be consonant with Macquarrie's reserved and inclusive approach to the theology of the eucharistic presence. Is Benediction itself not an example of the lack of austerity which he criticizes so firmly in the corrupt form of 'transubstantiation'?

In trying to answer this question, we must skirt all too briefly over another great topic of Anglican controversy, the sacrificial character of the Eucharist. What is needed, and what I suggest can be gleaned from elsewhere in Macquarrie's output, is a eucharistic understanding of redemptive sacrifice, and of such sacrifice as focused upon, but not entirely contained within, Christ's self-offering on the cross. However greatly they stress the notion of victory, soteriologies might fairly be called 'classic' which connect sacrifice and kenosis – here understood not as a theory of incarnation, but as an insight into the self-offering of the Trinitarian persons – with the Athanasian notion that the incarnation is transformative of humanity. John Milbank provides a recent example.[11] Macquarrie is not as explicitly Trinitarian in his sacrificial doctrine, but nevertheless is clear that 'the self-giving of Christ, understood as the new sacrifice in which priest and victim are one and the same, brings God's constant self-giving for his creation right into the creation' (*Principles*, p. 320).

The self-giving of God in the incarnation reflects the life of God himself, the eternal self-giving which Christians call the Trinity. The life, death, resurrection and ascension of Christ are the living out of this divine life as a human being. Another giant of Anglo-catholicism, Richard Meux Benson, once noted that much misunderstanding of eucharistic theology flows from an inadequate doctrine of the ascension of Christ.[12] If we assert the presence of the body of Christ then presumably, unless we share the confusions of Cranmer's 1552 black rubric (in which the body of Christ is 'in heaven and not here'), we assert something about the glorified humanity of Christ. The grammar of the ascension (Macquarrie, *Principles*, p. 290, sees it as no literal, physical event – as Benson implies, in what could such an event physically consist?) completes a notion that Christ's humanity is itself redemptive, that what God has done in becoming incarnate is to have drawn real and complete humanity up into the life of eternal self-giving which is the life of Father, Son and Spirit. The sacrifice of Christ, his perfect self-offering to the father, is a type of this triune self-offering, and the sacrificial character of the Eucharist then consists in our being drawn, by the divine initiative, into this perfect offering by our participation in the sacramental offering which we celebrate.

Central to this offering is the notion of intercession. Macquarrie repeatedly points to the double indwelling (we in him and he in us) which the classic Anglican formularies retain (*Sacraments*, pp. 119, 144). What is present to us in the eucharistic elements is a personal presence, and it is the personal presence of the one who is always and perfectly interceding for all of humanity. The eucharistic sacrifice consists in our presenting to God our unworthy offering in order that it be taken by Christ and transformed into his perfect offering before being given back to the worshipper as the food by which the life of the Church, the Body of Christ, is sustained. In extra-eucharistic liturgy, that principal dramatic action of taking, offering, and feeding is not played out, but the presence of Christ, if it is real and 'objective', is the presence of that dynamic context of giving and receiving. The body language of Benediction must be a language of offering and self-giving, both the physical body language of the kneeling participant and the theological body language of humanity redeemed by identification with the self-giving of the Trinity. Macquarrie attributes to the worshippers 'the grace of humility' because participation in Benediction must be an act of worship, of self-offering, to that which is itself the perfect exemplar of self-offering, of self-sacrifice.

A final and etymological trick will help us. Sacrifice is used too frequently simply to mean 'give something up', and the sense of 'make something holy' is forgotten. The self-giving of God the Son in the incarnation is the sacrifice of humanity, the making holy, setting apart, of the created human race in order that it be offered – in Christ, in the Eucharist – to the Father. The Eucharist is sacrificial because by it Christ makes holy not just bread and wine, but every member of his body, by drawing them into the life of God, the life of perfect offering, the presence which is always being given – to the Father in perfect love, to humanity in the initiative of grace. The extremities of Benediction, perhaps, respond to what is fundamentally a simple acknowledgement: the Holy One tabernacles with his people.

Notes

1 P. J. Fitzpatrick, *In Breaking of Bread*, Cambridge: Cambridge University Press, 1993, p. 11.

2 *Summa Theologiae* IIIa. 76.

3 G.E.M. Anscombe, 'On Transubstantiation', in *Ethics, Religion and Politics*, Oxford: Oxford University Press, 1981, p. 107

4 'Catholics believe as well that in certain circumstances a wafer completely changes its nature, and that at the same time all evidence proves the contrary. And so if Moore said "I know this is wine and not blood", Catholics would contradict him.' Ludwig Wittgenstein, *On Certainty*, Oxford: Blackwell, 1969, p. 239.

5 In, for example, the treatises he addressed as letters to individual authorities: the *Letter to the Bishop of Oxford*, 1839, the *Letter to the Revd R.W. Jelf*, 1841, and the *Letter to the Bishop of London*, 1851.

6 E.B. Pusey, *Letter to the Bishop of Oxford*, 1841, and *Eirenicon*, 1865, part I, p. 229.

7 'The Oxford Movement and Theology' in *Stubborn*, pp. 164–74. Here p. 174.

8 Isaac Williams, 'On Reserve in Communicating Religious Knowledge', *Tracts for the Times*, 87, 1838, Part VI.5.

9 John Macquarrie, *Benediction*, London: The Church Union, 1975, p. 1.

10 Isaac Williams, 'On Reserve', VI.5.

11 John Milbank, *Being Reconciled: Ontology and Pardon*, London: Routledge, 2003, ch. 6.

12 Darwall Stone, *A History of the Doctrine of the Holy Eucharist*, London: Longmans Green, 1909, p. 588, quoting from a letter of Benson's published in *The Cowley Evangelist*, July 1907.

26 Subjectivity and Objectivity in Theology and Worship

GEOFFREY WAINWRIGHT

My title reproduces that of a chapter in John Macquarrie's *Paths in Spirituality* (1972). The reflections which follow will focus on that chapter, which despite its brevity is quite representative of its author's thought at its most influential, both in its speculative and in its practical dimensions. 'Subjectivity and objectivity', 'theology and worship': those are typical of such pairings that characteristically occur throughout Macquarrie's writings. Quite close to the first pair (which generally belongs on the more philosophical side of things), one may find in the opening pages of his *Principles of Christian Theology* (1966; revised edition 1977) 'stability and flexibility', 'tradition and novelty', 'the vagaries of individual experiences [and] a continuing identity in the community'. Regarding the pairing of 'theology and worship', we are told in the chapter from which our title comes that 'genuine theology is shaped by living knowledge of God in prayer and worship' and thus 'transcends the subjective-objective disjunction, and draws its contributions from both sides of the divide'. Immediately, however, we are reminded that worship 'must in turn be subjected to the reflective criticism which theological thought engenders'. This 'reciprocity' of relationship is a regular feature of Macquarrie's handling of 'pairs'. The relationship may sometimes be more 'dialectical'; there may be 'tension' between the poles, especially when these are located at extremes. In other cases, the correlation is viewed more as complementarity; 'balance' is a favourite word of our author.

My purpose here is to suggest how 'doctrine' – a term and notion that occurs surprisingly seldom in Macquarrie's writings (it is not an item in the index of *Principles*) – may help in the regulation of 'subjectivity and objectivity' first in 'worship', then in the relation between 'worship and theology', and finally in 'theology', which is Macquarrie's chief area of professional expertise. By doctrine I mean both the substance and the act of teaching in their ecclesial reference. We shall inevitably have occasion to speak of 'authority', another relatively rare expression in Macquarrie's usage.

Basic Epistemology

We may appropriately begin with epistemology, since that is rightly a constant concern of Macquarrie's. In the chapter principally under consideration, like all theologians he recognizes that knowledge of God is 'a unique kind of knowledge' (*Spirituality*, p. 53). As the transcendent creator of both the world and ourselves, God 'comes before every object and every subject': 'It is he who makes it possible for there to be objects or subjects at all, and so he himself cannot be included either in what we know as object or in what we know subjectively' (p. 54). We can know God 'only by letting him grasp us' (p. 55), and this is a knowledge that 'transcends both subjective and objective, and encompasses both' (p. 55), since God is, in the language of Karl Jaspers, 'the encompassing' (*das Umgreifende*). This 'unique kind of knowledge is perhaps at its highest and most intense pitch of awareness in silent adoration before the presence of God' (and Macquarrie quotes Joseph Addison's hymn, where 'Transported with the view, I'm lost in wonder, love and praise'); and yet, 'because we are rational and social beings, we must speak of our experiences in order to communicate them, explore them and criticize them' (p. 55). The job of theology is to 'put into words the knowledge that God has given of himself'; its problem is to find:

a language properly balanced or dialectical in which to speak of God – a language in which our subjective and objective ways of speaking must be combined and held in tension with each other, so that we are pointed to the unique Being who comes before all subjects and objects and cannot be reduced either to the one or the other. (pp. 55–6)

I would add that language is a constitutive feature of worship: wonder precisely calls forth praise, and grace evokes the expression of gratitude. We not only speak *of* God, we also speak (and sing) *to* God. The theologian will be positively accountable to authentic liturgy.

Subjectivity and Objectivity in Worship

First, now, let us look at the question of subjectivity and objectivity in worship. Macquarrie considers it 'a basic weakness of Protestantism' always to 'think of God's presence and approach to man almost exclusively in terms of the word of preaching':

The stress has been on preaching, instruction, hearing, understanding, that is to say, on what goes on in our minds. There is a kind of docetism in all this, as if we were almost disembodied spiritual beings, so that everything of which the Gospel speaks, finally God himself, has to be drawn into our minds. This intellectualism (perhaps better called conceptualism) leads toward subjectivism. (p. 58)

The opposite fault was found in medieval Catholicism: 'In the Middle Ages, the objectivity of the Sacraments was overstressed. They became so separated from the Word and from the appropriation of the believer that distortion took place' (p. 59).

Now Macquarrie finds the solution to lie in the Eucharist, since 'in a remarkable way, it holds together Word and Sacrament in a unity'; and so, 'to give to the Eucharist a central place is to choose a basis which already militates against a damaging onesidedness' (p. 59). Under the stimulus of the Liturgical Movement, progress towards a full-orbed celebration of the Lord's Supper as the principal service of the Lord's people on the Lord's day is indeed a considerable ecumenical achievement of the past two or three generations. So much is registered in the Lima text of WCC Faith and Order, *Baptism, Eucharist and Ministry* (*BEM*) (1982).

Nevertheless, it may be wondered whether Macquarrie's account quite does justice – historically or systematically – to the interplay between objective and subjective in *both* word and sacrament. Certainly it seems odd to find Karl Barth among those who – albeit unwittingly by his dismissal of 'religion' – encouraged subjectivism. Classical Protestantism's championship of the Word read and proclaimed has surely served the priority of grace. The Reformation confessions rely on the promise of Jesus made to those whom he sent out on mission: 'Whoever hears you hears me' (Luke 10.16). The Second Helvetic Confession formulated the principle '*Praedicatio verbi divini est verbum divinum*'. The proclamation aims, of course, at a response of faith and love. Doubtless, there is a certain ephemerality about any particular sermon (mercifully, one is sometimes tempted to think; but even – or perhaps precisely – the best preaching is addressed to the moment). The sermon's objectivity will derive from its proper grounding in the Scriptures as the *permanent* testimony to the historically unsurpassable self-communication of God in the Word incarnate, Jesus Christ. The Second Vatican Council listed this among the modes of Christ's presence: 'It is he himself who speaks when the holy Scriptures are read in the Church' (Constitution on the Sacred Liturgy, *Sacrosanctum Concilium*, 7). The same document depicts not only 'the table of the Lord's Body' (48) but also 'the table of God's Word' as nourishing the faithful (51; cf. the Constitution on Divine Revelation, *Dei Verbum*, 21).

Correspondingly, the subjective side of the Eucharist needs proper recognition as well as the sacramental objectivity on which Macquarrie insists. Macquarrie hints at this other side when speaks of 'appropriation' by 'the believer', but he does not much develop the point here (apart from a final reference to 'preparing for and receiving of the Sacrament', p. 61). The Lima text met with no contradiction when it stated that 'while Christ's real presence in the eucharist does not depend on the faith of the individual, all agree that to discern the body and blood of Christ, faith is required' (BEM: Eucharist, 13). Since the same text later declared that 'it is Christ who invites to the meal and who presides at it' (29), it could perhaps be taken for granted that an intentionally *receptive assembly* is nevertheless a positive presupposition of any eucharistic celebration.

That brings me now, in a first pass, to my point about doctrine. In its substantive sense, doctrine is indispensable to the Eucharist. It sets the semantic context of the action. That is why all communities with ecclesial claims seek at least some measure of agreement concerning what the Eucharist is, before engaging in 'communion' with one another. An 'objective' content, linguistically formulated, needs to be met by 'subjective' acceptance. The Lima text registered at least a 'convergence' in doctrine among ecumenically engaged churches. An almost unanimous welcome was given to the statement that 'the Church confesses Christ's real, living and active presence in the eucharist' (13), but many official responses did not see the text as sufficient to 'accommodate' the 'differences' between the 'churches' over the relation between Christ's presence and the bread and wine.

As the act of teaching, doctrine also has both an objective and a subjective side in connection with worship. Doctrine brings into each assembly a body of material from outside: it will consist at least of the Scriptures, and indeed these as carried across the generations by a historic community in some form. Some attendant practices – for example, the manner of celebrating the sacraments or saying prayers – will almost certainly come, too. Whether it comes in written form or by oral and practical tradition, this material is to be assimilated; teaching is addressed to learners, who indeed gather in order to learn, all to the glory of God. While Protestantism may sometimes be faulted for an overly didactic style, Catholicism has recovered the liturgy – thanks, say, to Dom Lambert Beauduin – as the 'school' of Christian faith and life. Both Catholic and Protestant bodies have lately rediscovered the value of a 'catechumenate', whether initial or remedial or even life-long formation.

Doctrine, as both substance and act, clearly involves questions of authority. Where did the teaching originate? If in a definitive self-communication of God in Jesus Christ, how is the testimony of its recipients borne and received across time? By what means does the Holy Spirit raise up, preserve and increase a faithful community? How is the office of teaching shaped and performed? Who specifies and provides the instruments to be used, not least in worship (rituals, prayer books, hymnals, song sheets, catechisms)? We shall return to the topic of ecclesiology. Macquarrie himself judged it necessary to add a final section on 'authority' to the chapter 'The Church' in the second edition of *Principles* (pp. 416–19).

The Relation between Worship and Theology

'When we try to give theological expression to the knowledge of God,' writes Macquarrie, 'we must keep in closest touch with the ways in which he makes himself known to the worshipping community, and this will be found to constitute our great safeguard against a false subjectivism. The dictum *Lex orandi lex credendi* contains a profound truth,' for (as we have already heard Macquarrie say) 'a genuine theology is shaped by the living knowledge of God in prayer and worship' (p. 58). Then, however, Macquarrie immediately leaps to the reverse movement requiring that worship 'in turn be subjected to the reflective criticism which theological thought engenders' (*Spirituality*, p. 58).

Three qualifying remarks are, I think, called for. First, it would be advisable to make a distinction between what some have called *theologia prima* and *theologia secunda*. A kind of primordial theology occurs already in the words, acts and gestures of the worship event itself; here is intelligible speech from God, about God, and to God. Certainly, the distinction between first-order and second-order theology should not be drawn too sharply. According to Macquarrie's definition in the introduction to *Principles*, 'theology' happens only 'when faith has been subjected to thought'. From where else, then, but theological reflection would have emerged the acclamations of Christ's mediating role in creation that figure in the 'hymns' embedded in the New Testament epistles? Again, 'reflective theology' – which has 'taken a step back', as Macquarrie says, 'from the immediate experiences of faith' – has probably already played a part, by virtue of what Macquarrie terms its 'architectonic' function, in the shaping (say) of an anaphora or eucharistic prayer. In those two cases, theology has passed, in perhaps varying degrees, into normative doctrine. And preaching is properly informed by theological reflection while remaining within what is judged to be a sound doctrinal framework; first and second order theology meet in that liturgical act (the homily, says Vatican II, is *'pars ipsius liturgiae'*; *Sacrosanctum Concilium*, 52, cf. 35).

This pesky matter of 'doctrine' arises again in connection, second, with what Macquarrie calls the 'dictum' of '*lex orandi lex credendi*'. The phrase derives from an argument over doctrine. A fifth-century theologian was seeking to establish it as the teaching of the Church that the very beginnings of faith, let alone its growth and perseverance, depend on divine grace. The apostolic injunction to *pray* for the whole human race (1 Tim. 2.1–4) – which the Church obeys in its regular intercessions – establishes the obligation to *believe* that faith is from start to finish a work of grace. Such a move was not a novelty: Irenaeus and Tertullian had pointed to the sacramental use of water, bread and wine in order to refute Gnostic teaching that depreciated the material creation; and Athanasius and the Cappadocians had invoked the threefold baptismal profession of faith, grounded in Matt. 28.16–20, in order to establish the doctrine of the Trinity over against various forms of 'Arianism'. Now the use of liturgy – with scriptural (apostolic and even dominical) and traditional backing – as a 'source' of doctrine implies a corresponding responsibility on the part of authoritative teachers, whoever they may be, to keep an eye on the worship practices of the communities in their charge. Thus Pope Pius XII, in his encyclical *Mediator Dei* (1947), affirmed the 'dictum' also in the reverse direction: '*lex credendi legem statuat supplicandi*'; strongly put, the liturgy is 'subject to the Church's supreme teaching authority'.

This is the moment, third, at which to bring in Macquarrie's point about worship's need to be 'subjected to the reflective criticism which theological thought engenders'. Certainly, the sixteenth-century Reformation would never have taken place without the 'reflective criticism' of theologians upon the liturgy and associated practices. In the light of Scripture, the Reformers sought to re-establish the sole mediatorship of Christ ('*solus Christus*' over against the meritorious intercession of the saints) and the objective primacy of grace as received in the dependent subjectivity of faith ('*sola gratia*' and '*sola fide*' over against the '*facere quod in se est*'). The shift to the vernacular in Bible and prayers served the two-way communication between God and the worshippers. The 'theologians' who made these criticisms and then provided the textual means for the reform of worship did so in the face of constituted ecclesiastical authority ('Rome') and relied on 'godly princes' for their implementation. The principal appeal of the Reformers was to Scripture, although this was read with the aid of the ancient creeds and conciliar decisions that were taken to be in conformity with it. In turn, the Reformers set out 'true doctrine' in confessional statements that were usually crafted in conciliar fashion; and these were intended to govern the worship practices of the churches. Hence the ecumenical significance, almost 500 years later, of the 'Joint Declaration' between the Lutherans and the Roman Catholic Church on precisely 'the *Doctrine* of Justification' (1999), which is expected to 'influence the life and teachings of our churches' in such areas as 'the relationship between the word of God and church doctrine', 'ecclesiology, ecclesial authority, church unity, ministry, the sacraments', and 'social ethics'.

Clearly, attention is needed to the relationship between the roles of constructive and critical 'theologians', on the one hand, and the magisterial government of the various communities claiming ecclesial status. And again, 'doctrine' will have to find a place as we consider the relation between subjectivity and objectivity in 'theology'.

Subjectivity and Objectivity in Theology

John Macquarrie's initial definition of 'theology' in *Principles* (to which our attention now shifts for the sake of fuller exposition) is as 'the study which, through participation in and reflection upon a religious faith, seeks to express the content of this faith in the clearest and most coherent language available' (*Principles*, p. 1). This faith must always be that of 'an historic community' in which the theologian 'participates'. In delivering the fruit of his 'reflection', 'every theologian must write from his own perspective' (p. vi). While 'theologians have their individual styles and to some extent grapple with the problems that they themselves have found especially challenging,' yet 'if they remain theologians, they are not expressing a private faith, but have become spokesmen for their community, charged with a special responsibility within it' (p. 2). On those terms, it is of constitutive importance how a theologian identifies the religious community (in the Christian case, the ecclesial community) to which he or she belongs – and how in turn that community views the particular theologian.

It appears that theologians are 'given' in an objective way 'the faith which is believed' (often distinguished as the *fides quae creditur*); on this '*datum*' (Macquarrie's word) they then 'reflect' from within their own subjective faith (*fides quâ creditur*), though 'stepping back' a little from it; their intention, at least initially, must be to understand the faith of their community and then, assuming they remain believers, serve their community and its faith by such procedures as interpreting and explicating, perhaps even developing or (where needed) criticizing, the 'given' that is to be proclaimed and transmitted. This is a high calling that needs to be set in relation to established 'authorities', both in the substantive sense (usually called 'sources') and in the sense of those persons within the community who are appointed to oversight in a more comprehensive pastoral or governmental office.

Christianity affirms its own historicity. The 'classic' revelation has taken place in the past. Scripture, in Macquarrie's understanding, is a means 'by which the community of faith keeps open its access to that primordial revelation on which the community has been founded': 'The scriptures do not indeed automatically lay this revelation before us but, in conjunction with a present experience of the holy in the community of faith, the scriptures come alive, so to speak, and renew for us the disclosure of the holy which was the content of the primordial revelation' (*Principles*, p. 9). Since Scripture 'is not a frozen or petrified record' (as Macquarrie polemically puts it over against 'biblicism' though perhaps with some threat to Scripture's 'objectivity') but 'comes alive only in the ongoing life of the community which first gave birth to scripture and has since proclaimed and interpreted the teaching of scripture' (p. 11), it is a fact that 'tradition always has had its place in helping to determine the doctrine and practice of the Christian community' (p. 11). Scripture 'needs the complement of tradition in order to guard against private interpretations of scripture', and 'some control has to be exercised by the mind of the Church as expressed in received interpretations' (p. 12). As far as the individual theologian is concerned:

A Christian theology can no more fly in the face of the mainstream of tradition than it can in the face of scripture. To deny fundamental doctrines, like that of the Trinity; to reject the creeds; to set aside the beliefs of the early councils of the still undivided Church – these may be actions to which individuals are impelled by their own thinking on these matters, but they cannot take place in Christian theology, for they amount to a rejection of the history and therefore of the continuing identity within which Christian theologizing takes place. (*Principles*, p. 12)

Scripture and inherited tradition, then, constitute the most objective sources of theology. But tradition 'can become dead and mechanical, so that all growth and healthy development are inhibited' (p. 13). Theology has its part to play in keeping tradition alive, especially in its function of 'interpretation' or, as Macquarrie perhaps more often says, '*reinterpretation*'. Here active subjectivity sets to work; and here, too, 'culture' – one of Macquarrie's 'formative factors' in theology – becomes more prominent, for the theologian is both influenced in his or her own thinking by the contemporary intellectual and social environment and also seeks to render the faith intelligible in that context (*Principles*, pp. 13–15). Writing in the 1960s and 1970s, John Macquarrie was critical of the 'subjectivism and individualism' that characterized much 'modern' theology. It may be that such a warning is even more necessary in the face of 'postmodern' culture and 'postmodernist' thought, where 'facts' have dissolved and 'values' are asserted *ad libitum*. Certainly the ideological pluralism that denies truth as an objective category was targeted by the Roman Congregation for the Doctrine of the Faith as it put bishops, theologians, and all the faithful on their guard in the declaration of 2000, *Dominus Iesus*; and Cardinal Joseph Ratzinger, on the eve of his election as Pope Benedict XVI, decried the philosophically and practically regnant 'dictatorship of relativism'.

With that, we approach a question that may be gently put to John Macquarrie's theology: where does it locate 'the Church'?

The Question of Ecclesiology

Macquarrie's mid-career masterpiece, *Principles of Christian Theology*, bears a tripartite structure: (1) 'philosophical theology' (or 'new-style natural theology', which 'lays bare the fundamental concepts of theology and investigates the conditions that make any theology possible', *Principles*, p. 39); (2) 'symbolical theology' (meaning 'the unfolding and interpretation of the great symbols or images in which the revealed truths of the faith are set forth – the triune God, creation, the fall of man, incarnation, atonement, eschatology, and whatever else belongs to the specific faith of the Christian Church', p. 40); and (3) 'applied theology' (dealing with 'the expression of faith in concrete existence' and providing the 'theological principles' for the more 'practical' disciplines as they move into 'the institutional, cultic, and ethical aspects of the life of faith', p. 40). Curiously, the author does not include ecclesiology in the 'core' of his work, even though he recognizes that 'dogmatic' theology (a term he avoids on account of the adjective's 'pejorative connotation in ordinary usage', while the noun 'dogma' may still be convenient for 'some restricted technical uses', p. 40) traditionally dealt (past tense!) with 'the Church, the sacraments, and other matters' that in this book figure only in a third and distinct part (p. 40). These matters, according to our author, 'do not have the same centrality as, let us say, the doctrines of creation or of the work of Christ' (p. 378). Nevertheless, they constitute 'the most controversial area of theology' (p. 378). Most significantly for our question: here lie the points at which Christians are tangibly, institutionally divided.

Now if an 'historic community' is the locus and bearer of the faith, one would expect the Church to be concretely identified. For Macquarrie, 'the Church has indefinite edges' (p. 402) as, in an eschatological perspective, an 'ever-widening fellowship which cannot stop short of all creation' (p. 408). Nevertheless, he must risk a tangible, institutional definition. As he surveys the field of claimants to ecclesiality, he categorizes them according to where they place the weight of authority: among classical Protestants, the stress has fallen on supremacy of the Bible; the Roman Catholic Church has chiefly stressed tradition (and attributed to its supreme magisterium an infallibility which Macquarrie denies to the earthly Church, except as a 'directedness toward the truth'); among 'liberal Protestant groups', 'authority belongs to reason and conscience'. Macquarrie seeks to 'hold a balance among the various criteria'; and he finds in Richard Hooker (1564–1600) 'the great historical exemplar of a multiform authority':

> On the one hand he opposed the claims of papal authority, but on the other hand he was equally resistant to the Puritan demand that everything should be based on a more or less literalistic interpretation of scripture. In Hooker's synthesis, scripture, tradition, and reason all had their place. (*Principles*, p. 381)

Biographically, as a self-avowed 'man of moderation', John Macquarrie found his ecclesial home in 'the Christian communion' that 'has for long been celebrated for the *via media Anglicana*' (*Principles*, preface).

Having its treasure in earthen vessels, 'the Church exhibits "more or less" the unity, holiness, catholicity and apostolicity which will fully belong to it only when it gives itself up in order to become the kingdom of God' (p. 411). To its four characteristic 'notes' correspond the Scriptures (as 'the most obvious visible sign of the Church's unity', p. 404), the sacraments (as 'the visible embodiment of the Church's holiness', p. 406), the 'catholic creeds' (as giving 'considered expression to the mind of the universal Church', p. 407), and 'the historic episcopate' (as 'the overt institutional vehicle for ensuring the continuity of that heritage of faith and practice which was transmitted by the apostles', p. 410). Handily, those features match the four points put forward in the Chicago-Lambeth Quadrilateral as 'the *sine qua non* for a reunion of the Church' (p. 412). Meanwhile, 'the unity represented by a body like the Anglican communion, provided it is a genuine union of concern and mutual responsibility' is a 'far more effective witness to unity in Christ' than any 'national "merger" of denominations' (p. 404) or a particular see with an undifferentiated universal jurisdiction and an 'infallible' magisterium.

Since John Macquarrie wrote along those lines in the 1960s and 1970s, the doctrinal flexibility and diffused authority of Anglicanism have been severely tested for their adequacy to hold the Communion itself together.

27 Deconstructing the Blessed Virgin

ALISTAIR KEE

When I was a theology student in Glasgow it was a great privilege and pleasure to have John Macquarrie as one of my teachers. Lectures in the Faculty of Divinity took place on two sites and JM was a slightly mysterious figure to us as he walked purposefully between them carrying a small leather suitcase. Today he might have been stopped and questioned, but it would have been discovered that he carried nothing more dangerous than a teaching gown and lecture notes. JM lectured on Christian doctrine in the east quad of the Gilbert Scott building; Willie Barclay lectured on New Testament in the Venetian towered Trinity College. Thus we had heresy defined at 9 and exemplified at 11. In the urban mythology of students JM had the reputation of being very radical, a devotee of this Bultmann chappy. Little did we know: he had little sympathy for Bultmann, but was one of the leading experts in the world on Heidegger. I believe that JM completed Heidegger's ontology and certainly made it comprehensible. Another urban myth was that Germans read his translation of *Sein und Zeit* to understand it properly. However, all of this was obscured for us by the fact that JM never lectured to us on the subject. As the junior member of the Department he introduced us to psychology of religion and to world religions. As William Temple observed, there is nothing like teaching to complete your own education.

I was fortunate to have JM also as my director of studies, before I knew what that was. As it implied also some pastoral oversight, a small group of us would be invited from time to time to the family home. Students are always entertained to observe academic giants reduced to mortal stature by their children. JM had a small but well appointed study at home in which at that time he was reading voraciously for what was to become *Twentieth-Century Religious Thought*. Since he had followed the Scottish academic tradition of graduating in philosophy before going on to theology, 'religious thought' was predominantly philosophy of religion or philosophical theology. What struck me most about the work, in addition to its extraordinary range, was JM's characteristic way of proceeding. He would first of all provide a very fair, informed exposition of the main features of a writer. This was followed by a positive assessment of his contribution. And then, but only then, would there be an evaluation, some critical observations, points which opened up the discussion in a constructive way but entirely lacking in the rancour and partisanship which has marred so much theology.

By the time *Principles of Christian Theology* was published I had enrolled as a post-graduate student at Union Theological Seminary, New York and JM had been appointed to the Faculty there. It was a larger stage and JM soon became a world figure in theology and a leading intellectual in the Anglican Communion. Two things struck me about this major work. Like Tillich before him, he was able to bring a new ontology to bear on Christian doctrine. This gave his work a freshness and flexibility both for the exposition and for the defence of the faith. The second feature of the work was its conservatism. Since this term might suggest the opposite of 'freshness and flexibility', perhaps I should describe it rather as his appreciation of and commitment to the catholic tradition. This was exhibited in a subtle change in the procedure that was so much a feature of his earlier work. Now he began with an exposition of a doctrine, carefully expounding the classical developments along the way. This was followed by a judicious evaluation of the work of the main contributors. But now this was followed by an attempt, through the new ontology, to find a fresh and flexible way to recover and maintain the old beliefs and practices. My attention was first drawn to this feature of *Principles of Christian Theology* by the section on 'the holy angels'. A true Bultmannian would have demythologized them in short order, but JM, as noted earlier, had no sympathy for this approach. There was also a section on the Blessed Virgin Mary, and it is to this subject that I now turn in more detail.

If having to teach a subject completes one's education, for JM's generation even more formative was military service. Among the more positive elements in that experience as an army chaplain was the time he spent in Palestine. I recall that he mentioned having lectured to German prisoners of war on Heidegger, an act which I suspect was in contravention of the Geneva Conventions on the treatment of prisoners. But he also took the opportunity to visit the Church of the Annunciation. The occasion made a considerable impression on this young man in his twenties: his appreciation of the spirituality of Marian devotion predated his theological reflection on Marian doctrine. We shall see later that this order of things was significant. On his return to the UK from Union, to take up his appointment as a canon of Christ Church, Oxford and Lady Margaret Professor he became a member of the Ecumenical Society of the

Blessed Virgin Mary, a body founded in Brussels in 1966. He has been an active participant in the association and in 1990 published *Mary for All Christians*. Most of the chapters had begun as talks or lectures given to the association.

The expansion of the universities in the 1960s and again in the 1980s led to the proliferation of departments of theology and religious studies. It also led to the secularization of the subject. Theology was permitted in the modern university on condition that it functioned just like any other arts subject. Theology's dialogue partner became the university and not the Church. *Twentieth-Century Religious Thought* fits in well with that ethos; *Principles of Christian Theology* less so; *Mary for All Christians* not at all. In the book JM brings much of his considerable scholarship to bear on the subject, but from the outset the premise is that the Marian cult is entirely justified and must be defended and maintained. The now familiar approach means that the book provides an account of the historical development of the cult. In his characteristic desire to be fair and open, JM not only deals with familiar objections, but goes out of his way to make sure that readers are aware of further objections that might not have occurred to them. There is no concession to secularization, just as there was no concession to demythologizing. Inevitably the Marian cult reflects its premodern origins. All that remains is for JM to suggest how Mary is still relevant to Christians in the modern (and presumably postmodern) world.

He assumes that the main opponents of Marian devotion are Protestants whose objections stem from the motto *sola gratia*. In this brief article, written from a Reformed perspective, I wish to draw attention to three quite different issues.

1. *Biblical material*. The New Testament is a very slim collection of texts for a world religion and within it the teaching of Jesus is very slight indeed. It is therefore surprising that it is not given a more decisive position in the life of some churches. For example, Jesus taught his disciples that, in the context of religious institutions, they should 'call no man your father on earth . . .', yet this is the constant title assumed by priests. The practice of adults calling another adult (sometimes younger) 'father' leads to the infantalization of the laity, the patriarchalization of the Church and the legitimation of clerical power. But the words of Jesus are set aside. This should alert us to the fact that there are powerful forces at work within Christianity which simply overrule the original catholic tradition. A second example of the setting aside of the explicit teaching of Jesus concerns his views on his mother and his family. At several points in the Gospels he makes a clear division between his natural family and

his spiritual family. Jesus makes it quite explicit that his family have no faith in him and no understanding of his teaching. Yet in the Marian cult this is simply set aside. The devotees of the Blessed Virgin know better than Jesus and simply assert that Mary was supportive of Jesus throughout his life. Once again we are alerted to the fact that there are powerful forces at work within Christianity which simply overrule the original catholic tradition. A third example of the setting aside of the teaching of Jesus occurs in relation to the Bodily Assumption. JM, in defending the dogma says that 'it seems impossible that she who conceived Christ, bore him, fed him with her milk, held him in her arms and pressed him to her bosom, should after this earthly life be separated from him in either body or soul.' Yet Jesus rejected the suggestion that this natural relationship between him and his mother had any spiritual significance whatsoever. JM expresses the sentiments of the woman in Luke who cries out, 'Blessed is the womb that bore you and the breasts that you sucked!' It is a sentiment repeated in Marian art which pictures the Virgin directing a flow of milk from her breast to the mouth of the devotee. And yet Jesus specifically closed the door to any association between his mother and spiritual efficacy. 'Blessed *rather* are those who hear the word of God and keep it!' By implication, Mary did not hear the word of God in Jesus, and her nurturing relationship gave her no special place compared to those who heard Jesus and believed. For a third time we should be alert to the fact that that there are powerful forces at work within Christianity which simply overrule the original catholic tradition. If we wish to be true to that catholic tradition, the tradition of Jesus himself, then what we need is *not a Marian reading of the Bible but a biblical reading of Mary.*

2. *Exaltation. Principles of Christian Theology* is dedicated to John Knox, a colleague at Union who had also become an Episcopalian. It seemed clear to me that in his New Testament scholarship Knox was deeply influenced by his time in Chicago, although he denied it. I recall John Knox speaking about Christology as a process. Whenever a question was raised the church always chose the higher alternative. Was Jesus acknowledged by God first at the resurrection? No, he must already have been the chosen one. Was that adoption at the baptism? No, his conception must have been already arranged before his birth. Was it only at his conception? No, it was 'in the beginning'. We can see something of the same process with regard to the growth of the Marian cult. She begins as a mother who has no faith in her son and no spiritual understanding of him. But in order to give Jesus status for those who had certain religious assumptions, she is made into a virgin mother. This is pursued back into the legends about her parents, Joachim and Anna. It is developed for-

wards as she comes to occupy positions of privilege and power in the Church, culminating (one assumes, but who knows) in the dogmas of the Immaculate Conception and the Bodily Assumption. The dynamic begins by attributing higher status to Jesus, but as it continues it achieves another goal. JM sees the Marian cult as always directed to the glory of Christ. If only that were the case. The evolution of the Marian cult is guided by religious assumptions that are contrary to the original catholic tradition. It comes to have a dynamic of its own, apart from and over against the glory of God as revealed in Jesus. Consider the following examples. One of the greatest works of European art is the altarpiece in the church of the Frari in Venice. Even from the main door of the church the sight of Titian's masterpiece in gold and red makes a tremendous visual impact: it is truly breathtaking. The subject is not Jesus Christ, but the scene of the Assumption of the Blessed Virgin: it is the Basilica of Santa Maria Gloriosa. No hint of the presence of Jesus Christ detracts from the glory of the Virgin. The Marian cult has a life of its own, independent of the original exaltation of Christ. Or again, JM can refer to the shrine of the Virgin of Guadalupe, but it is widely acknowledged within Latin America that the religion of that subcontinent is Marian rather than Christian. In conversation, one of the first generation of liberation theologians recommended that men should pray to Christ and women should pray to the Blessed Virgin. In practice, all pray to the Blessed Virgin. Or again, at time of writing, a six-month exhibition has just ended in Madrid. The *Inmaculada* was staged in the Cathedral of the Almudena. It was a considerable organizational feat to bring together so many paintings and pieces of sculpture and to present them so dramatically. No one who walked through the darkened rooms could fail to have a powerful aesthetic experience. There was also a cumulative religious experience. This was not devotion to a woman who once lived in Palestine. Here was a cult of virginity. JM acknowledges that the Blessed Virgin Mary is a constructed figure. After pondering on the *Inmaculada* we must wonder what are the religious values and interests that lay behind the construction of this subject. As masters of suspicion we should be alert to the fact that there are powerful forces at work within Christianity which simply overrule the original catholic tradition. What then are these religious values?

3. *Religious values.* Virginity will always be with us: it is a physiological fact of evolutionary value. In some societies, in the context of betrothal, it is a cultural fact of traditional value. In the context of marriage it can also be an economic fact: virgins have an exchange value. In some religions it can be a significant fact, where purity is a value. Of course we

are not speaking here of moral purity, which has nothing to do with virginity. Rather it is a distinction found in some religions between what is pure and what is polluted, what is clean and what is unclean. It is found in Islam and of course in Judaism. It is entirely absent from Christianity, specifically rejected by Jesus himself both in his teaching and in his conduct. This may be one of Christianity's greatest gifts to the world. It quickly appears in the earliest catholic traditions, both of Peter and Paul. It was Peter who declared that for Christians there is no longer clean or unclean. This was a reference to food, but it was extended to apply to Jews and gentiles. Paul was to incorporate it into his list of 'neithers' in Galatians 3. Virginity for Christians has no religious value at all. For those who are 'in Christ' there is neither virgin nor non-virgin. It is surprising therefore that JM does not discuss the *theological* value of virginity. It had no value in the catholic tradition of Jesus, Peter and Paul. Once again we should be alert to the fact that that there are powerful forces at work within Christianity which simply overrule the original catholic tradition. If it had a value in the religiously eclectic Hellenistic culture of the fourth century, it must have come from non-Christian sources. There is no shortage of materials from which to construct a Christian cult of virginity. Near Aswan, just above the first cataract of the Nile is to be found the little island of Philae on which stand the ruins of an ancient temple. Beyond the hypostile hall, in the third room of the innermost sanctuary there is a relief cut into the stone wall. It is of the goddess Isis, Queen of Heaven, with the moon and the stars in the mantle of her hair. Her name, Isis, means 'throne' and standing on her thighs is the boy king, the Lord Horus who rules the world from his mother's lap. Ephesus was a centre of the cult of the Virgin Queen of Heaven.

JM in several of his writings suggests that the Blessed Virgin Mary is an affirmation of women. But is this not to mistake the disease for the cure? The Blessed Virgin is a stereotype constructed by those who find a religious value in virginity. The implication is that virginity is a higher or more complete religious state: in Christianity it should not be thought of as a religious state at all. The status of married women is lower in cultures that are Marian. (Ask the women, not the priests who rush forward to speak for them.) JM speaks in general about the Church discriminating against women. This needs to be more nuanced. JM was first ordained in the Church of Scotland, which last year had as its Moderator Alison Elliot. Dr Elliot was an excellent moderator. She is an intelligent, well-educated professional woman, a laywoman, married with two fine children. She is also Session Clerk, the most senior elder, in the congregation of Greyfriars, one of the historic churches of the Reformation in Scotland. Why should we have a 'Mary for All Christians'? Why not an Alison, so to speak? John Paul II reaffirmed the rule of celibacy for Roman Catholic priests. Why? I believe the reason is the cult of the Blessed Virgin. To end the rule of celibacy would acknowledge that virginity has no theological value. It has had the most catastrophic effects on the lives of many young men and many children, but that apparently it is a small price to pay for the continuation of the cult.

This brief article is written as a response to *Mary for All Christians*. In it I suggest that the Marian cult runs counter to the catholic tradition of Jesus, Peter and Paul. However, I do not think that such arguments will have any influence whatsoever on the devotees of the cult. Why should this be so? I have repeated several times the warning that there are powerful forces at work within Christianity which simply overrule the original catholic tradition. The dynamics of the construction of the Marian cult can be illustrated by applying Judith Butler's theory of performativity with its familiar reversal. It is not the Blessed Virgin Mary who inspires the cult of Marian devotion, it is a predisposition to affirm certain values, religious and psychological, which constructs the Blessed Virgin.

Bibliography

(compiled by Georgina Morley)

Primary Literature by John Macquarrie

'Feeling and Understanding', *Theology* 58, 1955
An Existentialist Theology, London: SCM Press, 1955
Helmut Thielicke, 'Reflections on Bultmann's Hermeneutic' (tr.), *The Expository Times* 67, 1956
'Demonology and the Classic Idea of the Atonement', *The Expository Times* 68, 1956
'A New Kind of Demythologizing?', *Theology* 59, 1956
'Bultmann's Existential Approach to Theology', *Union Seminary Quarterly Review* 13, 1957
'Changing Attitudes to Religion in Contemporary English Philosophy', *The Expository Times* 68, 1957
'The Service of Theology', *The Reformed & Presbyterian World* 25, 1958
'Demythologizing and the Gospel', *The Chaplain* 16, 1959
'Modern Issues in Biblical Studies: Christian Existentialism', *The Expository Times* 71, 1960
The Scope of Demythologizing, London: SCM Press, 1960
'The Natural Theology of Teilhard de Chardin', *The Expository Times* 72, 1961
'Existentialism and the Christian Vocabulary', *The London Quarterly and Holborn Review* 186, 1961
'History and the Christ of Faith', *The Listener* 67, 1962
With Edward Robinson (tr.), M. Heidegger, *Being and Time*, London: SCM Press, 1962
'How is Theology Possible?', *Union Seminary Quarterly Review* 18, 1963
'True Life in Death', *The Journal of Bible and Religion* 21, 1963
'Beelzebub' and other entries, in *Hastings' Dictionary of the Bible*, ed. F. C. Grant and H.H. Rowley, Edinburgh: T & T Clark, 1963[2]
Twentieth-Century Religious Thought, London: SCM Press, 1963, 2001[5]
'Theologians of our Time: Karl Rahner', *The Expository Times* 74, 1963
'Second Thoughts: The Philosophical School of Logical Analysis', *The Expository Times* 75, 1963
'The Problem of Natural Theology', *Pittsburgh Perspective* 5, 1964
'Christianity and Other Faiths', *Union Seminary Quarterly Review* 19, 1964

'Christianity and Other Faiths [A Rejoinder]', *Union Seminary Quarterly Review* 20, 1965

'How Can We Think of God?', *Theology Today* 22, 1965

'A Dilemma in Christology', *The Expository Times* 76, 1965

'Rudolf Bultmann', in Martin E. Marty and Dean G. Peerman (eds), *A Handbook of Christian Theologians*, Nashville: Abingdon 1965

'Benediction of the Blessed Sacrament', *Ave* 34, 1965

Studies in Christian Existentialism, London: SCM Press, 1966 (Montreal, 1965)

Principles of Christian Theology, London: SCM Press, 1966, 1977, 2003

'God and Secularity', *Holy Cross Magazine* 77, 1966

'Mother of the Church', *Holy Cross Magazine* 77, 1966

'Philosophy and Theology in Bultmann's Thought', in Charles W. Kegley (ed.), *The Theology of Rudolf Bultmann*, London: SCM Press, 1966

'The Pre-existence of Jesus Christ', *The Expository Times* 77, 1966

'The Tri-unity of God', *Union Seminary Quarterly Review* 21, 1966

'Some Thoughts on Heresy', *Christianity and Crisis* 26, 1966

'Stations of the Cross', *Ave* 36, 1967

'Maurice Blondel' and other entries, in Paul Edwards (ed.), *The Encyclopaedia of Philosophy*, New York: Macmillan and Free Press, 1967

'I Recommend You to Read: Some Recent Books on Theology', *The Expository Times* 78, 1967

'Faith, Worship, Life', *Holy Cross Magazine* 78, 1967

Realistic Reflections on Church Union (ed.), Albany: Argus-Greenwood, 1967

'Heidegger's Earlier and Later Work Compared', *Anglican Theological Review* 49, 1967

God-Talk, London: SCM Press, 1967, 1994

'Will and Existence', in James Lapsley (ed.), *The Concept of Willing*, Nashville: Abingdon Press, 1967

'New Ways in Moral Theology', *The Nashotah Quarterly Review* 7, 1967

'Divine Omnipotence', *Proceedings of the Seventh Inter-American Congress of Philosophy*, Quebec: Laval University Press, 1967

'The New Man and the Christian Ethic', *St Luke's Journal* 11, 1967

A Dictionary of Christian Ethics (ed.), London: SCM Press, 1967, 1984

A New Look at the New Theology, Cincinnati: Forward Movement Publications, 1967

God and Secularity, London: SCM Press, 1968

Martin Heidegger, London: Lutterworth Press, 1968

'Existentialism and Christian Thought', in P. LeFevre (ed.), *Philosophical Resources for Christian Thought*, Nashville: Abingdon Press, 1968

'God and Secularity', in William Hordern (ed.), *New Directions in Theology Today*, London: Lutterworth Press, 1968

Contemporary Religious Thinkers (ed.), London: SCM Press, 1968

'Bultmann's Understanding of God', *The Expository Times* 79, 1968

'The Doctrine of Creation and Human Responsibility', in Walter J. Ong (ed.), *Knowledge and the Future of Man*, New York: Holt, Rinehart & Winston, 1968

'Subjectivity and Objectivity in Theology and Worship', *Theology* 72, 1969

'Karl Barth' and other entries, in Alan Richardson (ed.), *A Dictionary of Christian Theology*, London: SCM Press, 1969

'Some Comments on the Trial Liturgy', *American Church Quarterly* 6, 1969

'Priesthood and the Trial Liturgy', in D.L. Garfield (ed.), *Towards a Living Liturgy*, New York: Church of St Mary the Virgin, 1969

'What's Next in Theology', *The Tower*, Union Seminary Alumni Magazine, Spring 1969

'The Nature of Theological Language', in A.M. Ramsey (ed.), *Lambeth Essays on Faith*, London: SPCK, 1969

'Schleiermacher Reconsidered', *The Expository Times* 80, 1969

'Religious Language and Recent Analytical Philosophy', *Concilium*, 1969

'Secular Ecumenism', *The American Ecclesiastical Review* 161, 1969)

'Self-Transcending Man', *Commonweal* 91, 1969)

'The Ministry and the Proposed New Anglican-Methodist Ordinal', *The Anglican* 25, 1969

Prayer is Thinking, New York: Sentinel Press, 1969

'What Still Separates Us from the Catholic Church? An Anglican Reply', *Concilium*, 1970

Three Issues in Ethics, London: SCM Press, 1970

'What is the Gospel?', *The Expository Times* 81, 1970

'Word and Idea', *International Journal for the Philosophy of Religion* 1, 1970

'Eschatology and Time', in Frederick Herzog (ed.), *The Future of Hope*, New York: Herder and Herder, 1970

'On Gods and Gardeners', in H.E. Keifer and M.K. Munitz (eds), *Perspectives on Education, Religion and the Arts*, Albany: State University of New York, 1970

'Eucharistic Presence', in D.L. Garfield (ed.), *Worship in Spirit and Truth*, New York: Church of St Mary the Virgin, 1970

'Is Organic Union Desirable?', *Theology* 73, 1970

'The Humanity of Christ', *Theology* 74, 1971

'Theologies of Hope: a Critical Examination', *The Expository Times* 82, 1971

'A Modern Scottish Theologian: Ian Henderson, 1910–69', *The Expository Times* 82, 1971

Martin Heidegger 'From the Last Marburg Lecture Course' (tr.), in James Robinson *The Future of Our Religious Past* (ed.), London: SCM Press, 1971

'Martin Heidegger', in G.L. Hunt, *Twelve Makers of Protestant Thought*, New York: Association Press, 1971

'Creation and Environment', *The Expository Times* 83, 1971

'John McLeod Campbell 1800–72', *The Expository Times* 83, 1971

Paths in Spirituality, London: SCM Press, 1972, 1992 (enlarged edition)

'Pluralism in Religion', *Veritas* 3, 1972

Existentialism, London: Hutchinson, 1972, London: Penguin, 1973²

'Anglican-Methodist Dialogue on the Unification of Ministries', *Concilium*, 1972

'Anglicanism and Ecumenism', in F.T. Kingston (ed.), *Anglicanism and Principles of Christian Unity*, Windsor: Canterbury College, 1972

'Liberal and Radical Theologians: an historical comparison', *The Modern Churchman* 15, 1972

The Faith of the People of God, London: SCM Press, 1972

'The Real God and Real Prayer', in D.L. Edwards (ed.), *The British Churches Turn to the* Future, London: SCM Press, 1972

'What Place has Individual Conscience in Christianity?', in *Asking Them Questions*, New Series Part I, Oxford: Oxford University Press, 1972

'God and the World: One Reality or Two?', *Theology* 75, 1972

The Problem of God Today, London: Christian Evidence Society, 1972

Mystery and Truth, Milwaukee: Marquette University, 1973

'The Struggle of Conscience for Authentic Selfhood', in C.E. Nelson (ed.), *Conscience; Theological and Psychological Perspectives*, New York: Newman Press 1973

'A theology of alienation', in Frank Johnson, *Alienation: Concept, Term and Meanings*, New York: Seminar Press 1973

The Concept of Peace, London: SCM Press, 1973, 1990

'Women and Ordination: A Mediating View', in H.K. Lutge, *Sexuality, Theology, Priesthood*, San Gabriel: Concerned Fellow Episcopalians, 1973

'What Kind of Unity?', *Faith and Unity* 18, 1974

'Kenoticism Reconsidered', *Theology* 77, 1974

'Ethical Standards in World Religions: Christianity', *The Expository Times* 85, 1974

'Some Reflections on Freedom', in *The University Forum*, Charlotte: University of North Carolina, 1974

'The Hundredth Archbishop of Canterbury', *New Divinity* 4, 1974

'Whither Theology?', in C. Martin (ed.), *Great Christian Centuries to Come*, Oxford: Mowbray, 1974

'What a Theologian Expects from a Philosopher', in George F. Mclean (ed.), *The Impact of Belief*, Lancaster: Concorde Publishing 1974

'Some Problems of Modern Christology', *The Indian Journal of Theology* 23, 1974

'Burns: Poet, Prophet, Philosopher', *The Expository Times* 86, 1975

Thinking about God, London: SCM Press, 1975

Christian Unity and Christian Diversity, London: SCM Press, 1975

'God and the Feminine', *The Way* Supplement 25, 1975

'The Uses of Diversity', *The Tablet*, 19 July 1975

'The Meeting of Religions in the Modern World: Opportunities and Dangers', *The Journal of Dharma* 1, 1975

'The Idea of a Theology of Nature', *Union Seminary Quarterly Review* 30, 1975

'The Importance of Belief', *New Fire* 3, 1975

'New Thoughts on Benediction', *Ave* 44, 1975

'On the Idea of Transcendence', *Encounter and Exchange* Bulletin 14, 1975

'The Church and Ministry', *The Expository Times* 87, 1975

'Priestly Character', in R.E. Terwilliger and U.T. Holmes (eds.), *To Be A Priest*, New York: Seabury Press, 1975

'Authority in Anglicanism', *Agnus Dei* 2, 1976

'Recent Thinking on Christian Beliefs: Christology', *The Expository Times* 88, 1976

'Unity', in Ruth Coffman (ed.), *The Upper Room Disciplines*, Nashville: The Upper Room, 1976

'Rest and Restlessness in Christian Spirituality', in W.B. Green and Madeleine L'Engle (eds), *Spirit and Light*, New York: Seabury Press, 1976

'Why Believe?', *Hillingdon Papers* I, 1976

'A Magnificent Achievement of the Christian Intellect', *Christian Media Today* I, 1976

'Recent Thinking on Christian Beliefs: Christology', *The Expository Times* 88, 1976

'Christianity Without Incarnation? Some Critical Comments', in Michael Green (ed.), *The Truth of God Incarnate*, London: Hodder and Stoughton, 1977

'Pride in the Church', *Communio* 4, 1977

'Philosophy and Religion in the Nineteenth and Twentieth Centuries: Continuities and Discontinuities', *Monist* 60, 1977

'Death and Eternal Life', *The Expository Times* 89, 1977

'The Bishop and Theologians', in John Howe (ed.), *Today's Church and Today's World*, London: CIO Publishing, 1977

The Humility of God, London: SCM Press, 1978

The Significance of Jesus Christ Today, Toronto: Anglican Book Centre, 1978

'Christian Reflections on Death', *St Francis Burial Society Quarterly* 2, 1978

'Faith in Jesus Christ', *Christian World* 1, 1978

'Religious Experience', *Humanities* 12, 1978

'The One and the Many: Complementarity of Religions', in Thomas Aykara (ed.), *Meeting of Religions*, Bangalore: Dharmaram Publications, 1978

'The Recognition of Ministries', *Christian World* 1, 1978

Christian Hope, London: SCM Press, 1978

'The Purposes of Reservation', *The Server* 11, 1978

'On the Ordination of Women to the Priesthood', in Michael Perry (ed.), *Report of the Lambeth Conference 1978*, London: CIO Publishing, 1978

Immaculate Conception, London: Ecumenical Society of the Blessed Virgin Mary 1978

'Existentialism and Theological Method', *Communio* 6, 1979

'Foundation Documents of the Faith: The Chalcedonian Definition', *The Expository Times* 91, 1979

Benediction, London: Church Literature Association, 1979

'The aims of Christianity', *USA Today* 108, 1979

'The Humility of God', in D.R. McDonald (ed.), *The Myth/Truth of God Incarnate*, Wilton: Morehouse-Barlow, 1979

'Commitment and Openness: Christianity's Relation to Other Faiths', *Theology Digest* 27, 1979

'Transcendent Belief', in R.E. Patterson (ed.), *Science, Faith and Revelation*, Nashville: Broadman Press, 1979

'Today's Word for Today: Jürgen Moltmann', *The Expository Times* 92, 1980

'God in Experience and Argument', in Eugene T. Long (ed.), *Experience, Reason and God*, Washington: Catholic University Press of America, 1980

'Religion' and other entries, in *Academic American Encyclopaedia*, Princeton: Arete Publishing Company, 1980

'Why Theology?', in E. Hulmes and B. Watson (eds), *Religious Studies and Public Examinations*, Oxford: Farmington Institute, 1980

'Systematic Theology and Biblical Studies', *Kairos* 2, 1980

Glorious Assumption, Walsingham Parish Church, 1980

'Tradition, Truth and Christology', *Heythrop Journal* 21, 1980

'A Generation of Demythologizing', in J. van Noppen (ed.), Theolinguistics, Brussels: Free University, 1981

'Truth in Christology' and 'The Concept of a Christ Event', in A.E. Harvey (ed.), *God Incarnate: Story and Belief*, London: SPCK 1981

'Existentialist Christology', in R.E. Berkey and S.A. Edwards (eds), *Christological Perspectives*, New York: Pilgrim Press, 1982

'The End of Empiricism?', *Union Seminary Quarterly Review* 27, 1972

'Being and Giving', in F. Sontag and M.D. Bryant (eds.), *God: the Contemporary Discussion*, New York: Rose of Sharon Press, 1982

'Aspects of the Human Being', *The Virginia Seminary Journal* 34, 1982

'Structures for Unity', in M. Santer (ed.), *Their Lord and Ours*, London: SPCK, 1982

In Search of Humanity, London: SCM Press, 1982

'The Need for a Lay Ministry', *The Times Higher Education Supplement* 529, 1982

'The Future of Anglo-Catholicism', *The Church Times*, 20 May 1983

'William Temple: Philosopher, Theologian, Churchman', in F.K. Hare (ed.), *The Experiment of Life*, Toronto: The University Press 1983

'God' and other entries, in *Funk & Wagnall's New Encyclopaedia*, New York: Funk & Wagnall, 1983

'Celtic Spirituality' and other entries, in Gordon Wakefield (ed.), *A Dictionary of Christian Spirituality*, London: SCM Press, 1983

'Being' and other entries, in Alan Richardson and John Bowden (eds), *A New Dictionary of Christian Theology*, London: SCM Press, 1983

'Theological Implications of the Oxford Movement', in J. Wright (ed.), *Lift High the Cross*, Cincinatti: Forward Movement Publications, 1983

In Search of Deity, London: SCM Press, 1984, 1993

'Wycliff on Dominion', *Wycliff College Insight* 17, 1984

'The Anthropological Approach to Theology', *Heythrop Journal* 25, 1984

The Church and the Ministry, Birmingham: Additional Curates Society, 1985

'Pilgrimage in Theology', in Alistair Kee and Eugene Thomas Long (eds), *Being and Truth*, London: SCM Press, 1986

'Prayer and Theological Reflection', in Cheslyn Jones (ed.), *The Study of Spirituality*, London: SPCK, 1986

Theology, Church and Ministry, London: SCM Press, 1986

'Enlightened about Enlightenment', *The Expository Times* 97, 1986

With James F. Childress (eds), *A New Dictionary of Christian Ethics*, London: SCM Press, 1986, 1995

'The Idea of a People of God', in Val McInnes (ed.), *Renewing the Jewish-Christian Wellsprings*, New York: Crossroad, 1987

'A Theology of Personal Being', in Arthur Peacocke and Grant Gillett (eds), *Persons and Personality*, Oxford: Blackwell, 1987

'Individual and Social Values: Love and Peace', in Elaine Kaye (ed.), *Peace Studies: the Hard Questions*, London: Rex Collings, 1987

'W.P. Dubose and Modern Thought', *St Luke's Journal of Theology* 31, 1987

'Baptism, Confirmation, Eucharist', in E. Russell and J. Greenhalgh (eds), *Signs of Faith, Hope and Love*, London: St Mary's Bourne Street, 1987

The Reconciliation of a Penitent, London: General Synod of the Church of England 1987

'Convergence of Religious Traditions on One Experience', *Scottish Journal of Religious Studies* 10, 1989

'Believing in God Today', *Colloquium* 21, 1989

'The Papacy in a Unified Church', *Pacifica* 2, 1989

'The Anglican Communion Today', *The Episcopalian* 155, 1990

Jesus Christ in Modern Thought, London: SCM Press, 1990, 2003

Arthur Michael Ramsey: Life and Times, New York: All Saints Church, 1990

'Truth', in *The Blackwell Encyclopaedia of Modern Thought*, Oxford: Blackwell 1990

Mary for all Christians, London: Collins 1991

'Antropologie filosofiche e teologiche', in G. Ferretti (ed.), *Filosofia e teologia nel futuro dell' Europa*, Genoa: Maretti, 1992

'Updatings on the Trinity', *The Expository Times* 103, 1992

'The Logic of Religious and Theological Language', *Journal of Dharma* 17, 1992

'Heidegger's Philosophy of Religion', in Val McInness (ed.), *New* Visions, New York: Crossroad, 1993

'Incarnation', 'Natural Theology', in A.E. McGrath (ed.), *The Blackwell Encyclopaedia of Modern Christian Thought*, Oxford: Blackwell, 1993

'Development of Doctrine: Searching for Criteria', in S. Coakley and D. Pailin (eds), *The Making and Remaking of Christian Doctrine*, Oxford: Oxford University Press, 1993

'If it's metaphor, handle with care', *Church Times*, 29 October 1993

'The Annunciation', *The Marian Library Newsletter* 28, 1994

Heidegger and Christianity, London: SCM Press, 1994

Starting from Scratch, Oxford: H. Copeman, 1994, reprinted as *Invitation to Faith*, London: SCM Press, 1995

The Mediators, London: SCM Press, 1995

'Theological Reflections on Disability', in Marilyn E. Bishop (ed.), *Religion and Disability*, Kansas: Sheed & Ward, 1995

Thinghood and Sacramentality, Colchester: Centre for the Study of Theology in the University of Essex, 1995

'The Figure of Jesus Christ in Contemporary Christianity', in P. Byrne and L. Houlden (eds), *Companion Encyclopaedia of Theology*, London: Routledge, 1995

'Incarnation as the Root of the Sacramental Principle', in David Brown and Ann Loades (eds), *Christ: the Sacramental Word*, London: SPCK, 1996

'Peace', in P.B. Clarke and A. Linzey (eds), *Dictionary of Ethics, Theology and Society*, London: Routledge, 1996

'I Saw Signs of Growth in the Chinese Church', *Church of England Newspaper* 4 April, 1996

'This Bread and This Cup', *Church Times* 4 April, 1996

'Ebb and Flow of Hope: Christian Theology at the End of the Second Millennium', *The Expository Times* 107, 1996

Judgement, Heaven and Hell, Oxford: Friends of St Andrew's Church, 1996
'The legacy of Bultmann', *Heythrop Journal* 37, 1996
A Guide to the Sacraments, London: SCM Press, 1997
'Dialogue Among the World Religions', *The Expository Times* 108, 1997
'And it Came to Pass in Those Days', *Church Times* 19 December, 1997
'Current Trends in Anglican Christology', *Anglican Theological Review* 79, 1997
Christology Revisited, London: SCM Press, 1998, 2003
'Mascall, E.L.', in A.E. McGrath (ed.), *Handbook of Anglican Theologians*, London: SPCK, 1998
'Mascall and Thomism', *Tufton Review* 2, 1998
'Train Them, then Allow Them to Think', *Church Times*, 23 October 1998
On Being a Theologian, London: SCM Press, 1999
'The Shape of Christology', *The Expository Times* 110, 1999
'Jesus Symbol of God', *The Expository Times* 111, 1999
'That All May Be One', *The Expository Times* 111, 2000
'Tradition and Imagination: Revelation and Change', *Journal of Theological Studies* 52, 2001
'Discipleship and Imagination: Christian Tradition and Truth', *Journal of Theological Studies* 52, 2001
'Postmodernism in Philosophy of Religion and Theology', *International Journal for Philosophy of Religion* 50, 2001
'A Sketch of David Brown', *Anglican Theological Review* 84, 2002
Stubborn Theological Questions, London: SCM Press, 2003
'God and the Future: Wolfhart Pannenberg's Eschatological Doctrine of God', *Journal of Theological Studies* 55, 2004
Two Worlds Are Ours, London: SCM Press, 2004
'Heidegger's Language and the Problems of Translation', *Studia Phenomenologica* 5, 2005
'The Theological Legacy of Maurice Wiles', *Anglican Theological Review* 88, 2006

Secondary literature

Tim Bradshaw, 'John Macquarrie', in Alister E. McGrath (ed.), *The SPCK Handbook of Anglican Theologians*, London: SPCK, 1998
B.R. Brinkman, 'On Christ and the Church: Macquarrie, Schillebeeckx and Moltmann', *Heythrop Journal* 32, 1991
Niall Coll, *Some Anglican Interpretations of Christ's Pre-existence*, Rome: Pontifica Universitas Gregoriana, 1995
Owen Cummings, *John Macquarrie: a Master of Theology*, New Jersey: Paulist Press, 2002
Jeannine Graham, *Representation and Substitution in the Atonement Theologies of Dorothee Soelle, John Macquarrie and Karl Barth*, New York: Peter Lang, 2005
William B. Green, 'Profile: John Macquarrie', *Epworth Review* 24/4, 1997
Daniel W Hardy, 'Theology through Philosophy', in David F. Ford (ed.), *The Modern Theologians*, Oxford: Blackwell, 1997[2]

Charles C. Hefling, 'Reviving Adamic Adoptionism: The Example of John Macquarrie', *Theological Studies* 52, 1991

Marion Lars Hendrickson, *Behold The Man! An Anthropological Comparison of the Christologies of John Macquarrie and Wolfhart Pannenberg,* Lanham: University Press of America, 1998

David Jenkins, *The Scope and Limits of John Macquarrie's Existential Theology,* Uppsala: University Press, 1987

Alistair Kee and Eugene T. Long (eds), *Being and Truth,* London: SCM Press, 1986

B. Krigler, 'Macquarrie on Reality and Meaning: Comment', *Ultimate Reality and Meaning* 6, 1983

Eugene T. Long, 'Macquarrie on Language, Being and God', *Review of Metaphysics* 30, 1976

Eugene T. Long, 'Macquarrie on God Exists', *International Journal for Philosophy of Religion* 10, 1979

Eugene T. Long, 'John Macquarrie on God', *Perspectives in Religious Studies* 8, 1980

Eugene T. Long, 'John Macquarrie on Ultimate Reality and Meaning', *Ultimate Reality and Meaning: Interdisciplinary Studies in the Philosophy of Understanding* 6, 1983

Eugene T. Long, *Existence, Being and God,* New York: Paragon House, 1985

John McIntyre, *The Shape of Christology,* 2nd edn, London: SPCK, 1998

Georgina Morley, 'Connectivity and Agency in John Macquarrie's Theology', in ed. Susan F. Parsons (ed.), *Challenging Women's Orthodoxies in the Context of Faith,* Aldershot: Ashgate, 2000

Georgina Morley, 'The Social Trinity and the Triune God', in Robley Edward Whitson (ed.), *Faculty Essays for Ministry Professionals,* Indiana: Wyndham Hall Press, 2000

Georgina Morley, *John Macquarrie's Natural Theology: the Grace of Being,* Aldershot: Ashgate 2003

Christopher Myers, 'The Paradoxical Character of Revelation: a sympathetic essay on dialectical Theism', *Colloquium: The Australian and New Zealand Theological Society* 23, 1990

Stephen W. Need, 'Macquarrie, John (b. 1919)', in Leslie Houlden (ed.), *Jesus: The Complete Guide,* 2nd edn, London and New York: Continuum, 2005, pp. 569–71

P.S. Newey, 'Revelation and Dialectical Theism: Beyond John Macquarrie', *Colloquium: the Australian and New Zealand Theological Society* 22, 1989

Douglas G. Pratt, 'Existential-Ontological Theism and the question of the relatedness of God: Macquarrie revisited', *Colloquium: The Australian and New Zealand Theological Society* 17, 1984

Douglas G. Pratt, 'The imago Dei in the thought of John Macquarrie: a reflection on John 10.10', *Asian Journal of Theology* 3, 1989

Douglas G. Pratt, *Relational Deity: Hartshorne and Macquarrie on God,* New York: University Press of America, 2002